HEALING THE UNIMAGINABLE

HEALING THE UNIMAGINABLE
Treating Ritual Abuse and Mind Control

Alison Miller

KARNAC

First published in 2012 by
Karnac Books Ltd
118 Finchley Road, London NW3 5HT

Reprinted in 2015 with a revised index and minor corrections

British Library Cataloguing in Publication Data

A C.I.P. for this book is available from the British Library

ISBN: 978 1 85575 882 7

Edited, designed and produced by The Studio Publishing Services Ltd
www.publishingservicesuk.co.uk
e-mail: studio@publishingservicesuk.co.uk

Printed in Great Britain

www.karnacbooks.com

CONTENTS

*This book is dedicated to the many courageous therapists who have
taken on the challenge of facing the unimaginable with their clients.*

Only the small secrets need to be protected. The big ones are kept secret by public incredulity.
Marshall McCluhan

The most authentic thing about us is our capacity to create, to overcome, to endure,
to transform, to love and to be greater than our suffering.
Ben Okri, Nigerian Poet & Novelist

Our sorrows and wounds are healed only when we touch them with compassion.
Mohandas Gandhi

ACKNOWLEDGEMENTS

First of all, I want to thank all the clients who, over the past twenty years, have shared with me their painful stories of ritual abuse and mind control. They have been my most important teachers, and without them I would not have been able to even conceive of writing such a book. Some of them will recognize themselves in these pages, and I know it will be important to them to know they have contributed to the knowledge and skills of many therapists.

Beyond that, words cannot express how grateful I am to those courageous survivors who contributed to this book: Old Lady, Adriana Green, Trish Fotheringham, Jeannie Riseman, Stella Katz, LisaBri, Robin Morgan, Carol Rutz, and Jen Callow. Their bravery in facing their experiences, their hard-won internal cooperation and maturity, and their willingness to speak up constitute a unique contribution to our understanding both of these abuses and to their healing process.

I want to express my appreciation to my local friend, Adrienne Carter, who uses her vacations to work with trauma survivors in disaster areas all over the planet. She has been my support for many years in facing my clients' difficult memories and recovery issues.

Over the years of my learning, many online friends and colleagues have been an ongoing support system, as we all struggle together to understand and deal with these monstrosities. I particularly appreciate the contributions of Eroca Shaler and Jeannie Riseman in reading some early chapters of this book and giving me feedback, as well as all the "critters" with whom I have had dialogue over the years. (They will know what that message means, and who they are.)

There is one person without whom this book would never have come to fruition: my online friend, author and therapist E. Sue Blume, whom I have never met in person. She has supported me, insisted on the importance of my book, criticized my writing, found synonyms, sorted out my paragraphs, told me what is missing, and been the most creative and practical editor anyone can imagine, all before my publisher, Karnac Books, became involved. Thank you so much, E. Sue.

Disclaimer

This book is designed to give information to licensed and credentialed psychotherapists for the purpose of understanding and helping clients or patients who report memories of ritual abuse or mind control.

It is not designed for individuals who believe they may have had these experiences themselves, and want to explore what that entails.

This area is one about which understanding is developing slowly, as the practices of organized child abusing perpetrator groups are generally hidden from view, and often intentionally disguised by the perpetrators. Therefore, some of the information in here may be either incomplete or inaccurate.

The author and Karnac Books shall have neither liability nor responsibility to any person or entity with respect to any loss or damage caused, or alleged to have been caused, directly or indirectly, by the information contained in this book.

If you do not wish to be bound by the above, you may return this book to the publisher for a full refund.

ABOUT THE AUTHOR

Alison Miller is a clinical psychologist in private practice in Victoria, British Columbia, Canada. She worked for many years in child and youth mental health services, treating children and families. She is the original developer of the Living in Families Effectively (LIFE) Seminars (www.lifeseminars.com), and has co-authored two books on parenting with Dr Allison Rees. Since 1991, Dr Miller has been treating and learning from persons with dissociative disorders, in particular survivors of ritual abuse and mind control, and has developed a protocol for effective treatment.

"In a time of universal deceit, telling the truth becomes a revolutionary act"

(George Orwell)

From the beginning, ritual abuse and other forms of child abuse aimed at creating mind control have presented unique challenges to treatment professionals. After all, when we therapists first heard about these crimes in our offices, we were only in the infancy of understanding child-hood sexual trauma. Available texts on incest could be counted on the fingers of one hand. In the late 1980s, when I was preparing my own book, *Secret Survivors: Uncovering Incest and its Aftereffects in Women*, I knew nothing of ritual abuse. I had to negotiate with my first publisher, John Wiley, to allow me to add a brief mention of it just before the book went to press.

Ritual abuse was a complex and intimidating phenomenon for which we were totally unprepared, both professionally and personally. Therapists in the USA, Canada, the UK, and elsewhere around the world found themselves listening to horrifying, shocking, and sometimes unbelievable disclosures by terrorized clients. Survivors reported being accessed and abused while in treatment. They also conveyed threats that were made against us, some of which were carried out. Clients—and often therapists—became convinced that they were being tracked by an invisible network of omnipresent and omnipotent abusers, with no escape. These abuses continued even when survivors appeared to follow all the recommended rules of self-protec-tion. Desperate staffs turned hospital-based inpatient treatment protocols on their ears to protect patients from a force no one totally understood, but some patients reported being abused while in hospitals.

The treatment process itself would also prove endlessly complicated, even dangerous. Survivors often began therapy with determination and resolve, only to drop out because their memories flooded them, or because self-destructive behaviors took them over. The training and skills we brought to these clients often seemed to make things worse. The normal rules just did not apply. On a desperate journey to meet our clients' needs, we reached out for guidance from some pioneering professionals and brave survivors (the real experts). What they had to offer was invaluable, but we still could not figure out what the new rules needed to be.

Some healed. Many did not. They tried. We tried. Treating ritual abuse felt frightening, overwhelming, confusing, and, frankly, sometimes impossible.

And now we found ourselves facing a new challenge. In the USA, although its tentacles spread to other places, a curious group of people launched a campaign to discredit and destroy all of those involved with helping survivors of hidden (dissociated) trauma, in particular ritual abuse, and its survivors. The media colluded with the agenda of this movement, and society welcomed it.

Someone once said that there is no taboo against incest, just a taboo against talking about it. That was certainly what we saw now regarding ritual abuse and mind control. Anyone attempting to recognize this still new and alien occurrence was blacklisted. The conspiracy of silence about child abuse had now become a conspiracy of censorship, even within the profession charged with its treatment. As a result, the truth about ritual abuse could no longer find a forum. Research and education ground to a halt.

Yet, somehow, in this oppressive climate, without support from any professional organizations or literature—or, in many cases, their peers—many therapists quietly continued to do their jobs.

Fortunately, one of those people was Alison Miller. Now, in *Treating the Unimaginable*, Dr Miller spells out the step-by-step protocol she developed over decades of working with, and learning from, survivors. This straightforward and sensible guide provides the tools you need to break "mind control" programming and recovery into practical explanations and orderly tasks.

Treating the Unimaginable reveals that abusers have relied on lies and tricks to control their victims' thinking from infancy onward. It provides the explanations and guidelines necessary to make the challenging task of treating survivors both possible and manageable. After discussing the clear differences between spontaneously developed dissociative disorders and those intentionally structured and implanted by such abusers, Dr Miller offers information that is precise, indispensable, and long overdue: in example after example, she describes exactly how abusers execute mind control that ensures ongoing contact and control, the psychological and cognitive impact it is designed to have on developing children, and the tasks necessary for clients to break free of the programs their abusers have devised.

Treating the Unimaginable is a reasonable, understandable, non-threatening book. It is calm in the face of confusion: exactly what this issue has needed from the beginning. And it is revolutionary. Because she tells the truth about ritual abuse. And that continues to be as important as ever, because—whether we want to acknowledge it or not—ritual abuse and other forms of mind control do happen, and there are survivors who need you. Now, with Dr Miller's wise and experienced guidance, those of you who choose to accept the formidable honor of treating those survivors will find encouragement here.

E. Sue Blume, LCSW, Diplomate in Clinical Social Work

Those of us who work in the field of trauma and abuse, whether psychologists, psychoanalysts, social workers, doctors, counselors, or psychotherapists, have been provided with beautiful tools for understanding the impact of trauma. We become adept at understanding the dynamic of why the messenger is always shot and broadcast the Bionic insight of why the visionary is not bearable to the group.

However, when it comes to military mind control, abuse within religious belief groups or cults, and deliberately created dissociative identity disorder, we enter the least resourced field of all. This makes a new book on the subject have a far greater impact. While some new books fail to justify a historical, theoretical, or clinical place, this is a book that will provide immediate psychological aid to the practitioner who takes on mind control work. Or, as more usually happens, this will aid the clinician of integrity who never knew about such work, never intended to work in this field, but has slowly uncovered the traumatic reasons for why a mind has become splintered.

This book is necessary because, for many professionals who are not survivor-professionals, as well as for some who are, all psychic tools can temporarily disappear in the face of this work. We succumb to a variety of defenses, become numbed, dissociative, overwhelmed, over-zealous, over-skeptical, over-theoretical, over-academic, or speechless.

How do we find words for describing levels of betrayal and emotional, physical, sexual, and spiritual torture that fragment and destroy a child or adult and cast traumatic shadows over the whole of their adult life? We might, as a society, slowly find it possible to accept that one in four citizens are likely to have experienced some form of emotional, physical, sexual, or spiritual abuse (McQueen, Itzin, Kennedy, Sinason, & Maxted, 2008), in itself a figure unimaginable and hidden twenty years ago. However, accepting the way a hurt and hurting parent or stranger re-enacts their disturbance with a vulnerable child or children remains far easier to digest than to consider the intellectually planned, scientific, methodical procedures of organized child-abusing perpetrators—in other words, torture.

While we might hold to the sentiment that *humani nihil a me alienum puto* (nothing human is alien to me), it needs to be faced that there are areas of torture we have not imagined, that, indeed, are unimaginable to us. Bearing witness and sitting alongside such trauma can also be unimaginable and lead to secondary traumatization.

When I first encountered organized ritual abuse and mind control (Badouk-Epstein, Schwartz, & Wingfield, 2011; Sachs & Galton, 2008; Sinason, 1994), I was reminded only too well of Nietzsche's comment "Beware. When you look into the abyss, the abyss looks into you". Although a consultant psychotherapist at a leading clinical training and treatment center in the UK (the Tavistock Clinic), like Alison Miller, nothing in my training initially prepared me for this work except for the psychological strengthening that came from my own psychoanalytic treatment. I will always be grateful to my former psychoanalyst, the late Dr Mervin Glasser, for his support and to Dr Robert Hale, former Director of the Portman Clinic, who shared the pain of our ritual abuse project.

The abyss is the unimaginable, the place worse than nightmares. When it looks into us, to find a home, to find a mirror, to find someone, somewhere who can face the "daymare" that some people's lives consist of, we indeed face the worst that humans are capable of.

What does it mean to work with those whose days are worse than the worst nightmare we could imagine having? Who inhabits Orwell's Room 101? Whose truth means facing the reality not just of what the hurt and hurting loner is capable of, but what highly functioning middle class groups might do?

Dr Alison Miller waited twenty years for someone to write this book and finally decided to write it herself. Although a licensed psychologist in Canada, her thoughts and work are well known internationally, despite the initial low profile that often comes with this work. However, there is an important transition to be made when a key thinker moves from verbal communications in talks to writing a book for Karnac, a major psychodynamic publishing house that is based in the UK and respected worldwide.

This is the book that I and many other colleagues in the UK and the rest of Europe have also waited for and not written.

If you do not have a patient who has gone through these experiences, this is initially a deeply frightening book as well as a crucial book. It is not a book that soft-soaps the reader along the grades of obscene hierarchy between "mild" trauma and major. It goes straight to the jugular of the worst realities that exist, and is not trying to apologize for, or justify, their existence. Enough research has been carried out; enough survivors have come forward with their unique constellations of physical and mental pain. Alison Miller is writing for those who know what exists and want and need help in understanding it further.

In addition to her own insights, honed from years of practice, gained from her survivor-teachers, the book is also strengthened by the direct contributions of experts through terrible lived experience. Some are already known to UK specialists through their published work or websites (Jeannie Riseman, Carol Rutz, LisaBri) or through speaking at the Conferences held by the Clinic for Dissociative Studies, Bowlby Centre (Badouk-Epstein, Schwartz, & Wingfield, 2011) and Paracelsus Trust (Trish Fotheringham), and some are new, bringing different pearls from their painful paths (LisaBri, Jen Callow, Adrianna Green, Stella Katz, "Old Lady", and Robin Morgan).

Although there is such a strong advisory survivor presence, Alison Miller is clear that she is writing for the professionals who work with this subject and warns survivors of the dangers of accessing this book.

Within the UK, the newly formed Campaign for the Understanding and Inclusion of DID held a historic meeting at the London Voluntary Resource Centre on March 12th 2011, at which all fifteen keynote plenary talks and exhibitions were given by survivors. Mind Control was a key theme. This was followed by a smaller presentation at Church House, Westminster with the aim of educating MPs and Peers as well as Health Service commissioners on the way children and adults who have gone through these experiences face a further trauma due to the national lack of training in this subject.

Karnac Books is to be thanked for aiding the new generations of trauma workers to understand the problems in work with mind control patients. Dr Alison Miller and her Survivor Teachers are to be thanked for this painful, clear, knowledgeable, and yet also unwelcome gift for those who have yet to face this work.

For those who *are* facing this work, whatever their theoretical orientation, this is a book which helps the novice and experienced clinician alike understand the meaning of mind control and how to deal with it, step by step. Instead of feeling overwhelmed and referring on, the new clinician armed with this book will feel they have a guide with them.

The details of cult programming desribed here are largely Western based. It needs to be understood that such cruelty is not restricted to the West and that all around the world there are equivalent programs that come from a different military, ritual, religious, and social history.

Cultural relativism aside, this book takes care to remind the reader and clinician that all DID systems are different. There is no short-cut to learning the meaning and experience of the universe that is each person. However, aided by a book like this, the initially unprepared professional can deal more wisely with the paradigm shift that follows.

Mind control is built on lies and manipulation of attachment needs. This book breaks down the lies, the structures and the tasks ahead into manageable pieces. It provides hope that is not delusional. It makes it possible to consider undertaking this work, whether in private practice or in the public Health Service. It also reminds all of us that we are citizens of a global culture and we, as citizens, are also responsible for the kind of culture our children grow up in.

Valerie Sinason

Introduction

I waited twenty years for someone else to write this book. Every day I became more aware of how much a book such as this was needed. Finally, I decided to write it myself.

My first awareness that I was working with ritually abused and mind controlled clients came in 1991. They were the most challenging clients I had ever encountered. Not only had they endured the worst abuses I had ever heard of, they had been forced to participate in the torture, rape, and murder of others. Just listening to them was traumatizing.

Since the 1980s, therapists have reported encountering clients or patients who had experienced extreme abuses featuring physical, sexual, emotional, spiritual, and cognitive aspects, along with a premeditated structure of torture-enforced lessons. The phenomena was first labeled "ritual abuse," and, later, as our understanding developed, "mind control." A few pioneers came forward who specialized in ritual abuse treatment, but, as much as they understood and as many effective interventions as they were able to develop, they were muddling along just like I was. Many others found themselves working with one, or a few, identified survivors of these abuses, and they were really struggling. This population can overwhelm an unprepared therapist, and without proper knowledge the therapist cannot protect the client from numerous pitfalls inherent in recovery from these experiences.

Then, suddenly, the work became dangerous, not only for clients but for therapists as well. A well-funded, highly organized opposition appeared, seemingly out of nowhere, in the early 1990s. Its goal was to discredit the existence of ritual abuse, and one of its tactics was to actively undermine any effort to discover what had been done to these clients and anyone who attempted to help them recover. This movement capitalized on every mistake those pioneers made. When one of my early teachers, for instance, recognized that many ritually abused clients were still being abused while in treatment, she insisted that they could not be treated on an outpatient basis, but should be hospitalized and kept from their families. She was targeted with a series of court cases involving false accusations that she had allegedly abused clients in hospital. The experience was devastating to her.

And she was not alone. Many others faced persistent attempts to discredit their professional expertise, or legal assaults that robbed them of time, energy, and even the courage to continue to treat clients, write, or teach. Therapy professionals in both direct services and policy making, members of the criminal and civil justice systems, and the general public were systematically indoctrinated via the media. Many now share the view that people who disclose ritual abuse or mind control content suffer from "false memories" induced by "over-zealous therapists," and that dissociative disorders are iatrogenic (or else they do not exist at all).

Although the issue disappeared from the media, and, therefore, became invisible to society (which, to many, means it no longer exists), a recent survey (Rutz et al., 2008) that looked at the experiences of over 1400 survivors of extreme abuse in thirty-one countries found that almost four out of five reported either ritual abuse, or mind control, or both.

I have spent the past twenty years looking for help, and what I found was very limited. I looked for a manual to tell me what was going on in these people, and to give me some clear guidelines for treating them, but I found none. I immersed myself in learning the fundamentals of dissociative disorders, the psychiatric diagnosis most commonly associated with this population, disorders which themselves were just beginning to be understood. This knowledge was basic to my work, but it was not enough to fully address the needs of these clients. Since those early years, much has been written about dissociation, and many professional workshops, courses, and conferences have taken place. However, an understanding of the relationship between dissociative disorders and ritual abuse and mind control survivors (and, therefore, the specific needs) has yet to reach the mainstream of professionals in that field, or any other.

A number of books were published, mostly edited collections of articles, that discussed ritual abuse and mind control, but, unfortunately, most of the articles addressed either "the existence problem" (giving continuing and undue credibility to the claim of that political movement), the horrific and sometimes sensationalized specifics of the abuses perpetrated, or the characteristics of survivors. Yet, still, no one told us how to treat them. Many websites also appeared in the past two decades, many by survivors and professionals who have studied them. They can provide a great deal of useful information, but there is much disinformation out there as well.

At first, it felt as if nothing in my training as a psychologist or my (then) fifteen years' experience had prepared me for the particular demands of treating this population. I knew there was a long road ahead. Fortunately, however, everything I had studied and worked with so far had prepared me to undertake the journey. I had considerable experience in child development, family systems, and attachment issues. I had developed educational seminars for parents who had suffered from abuse and neglect in their own childhoods, and I was beginning to understand the effect of childhood trauma in creating what I clearly understood to be "mental injuries" (not mental illnesses) that can last a lifetime. And I had the ability to respect and be open to the wisdom and expertise of my clients, the persons who had experienced these atrocities, who could, I knew, be my greatest teachers.

Soon, I understood what made this population, and therefore this treatment, different from anything we had ever encountered before: not only the total separation between the "inner children" found in certain dissociative disorders, but the deliberately splitting of children's psyches by these "organized perpetrator groups" to create and control alternate personalities. Not only the inner systems that exist in persons with "DID" (dissociative identity disorder, formerly MPD) and "DDNOS" (a similar disorder, labeled "Dissociative disorder not otherwise specified") but complex personality systems, intentionally structured into multi-layered hierarchies. Not only the hideous abuses that children can be subjected to, often by their most trusted caregivers, out of hedonism or sadism, but the elaborate, premeditated, and incredibly inhumane lengths that human beings will go to to harm children in the service of ideologies, for profit and power.

And so I learnt as I went. My first years of doing this unique work were like trying to find my way around a new country. I had to make a lot of quick decisions that had major consequences for my clients. I was drained by the complexity of the work. It was unnerving and exhausting. I suffered vicarious traumatization from the horror of my clients' life experiences, which included, as my beleaguered colleague and others had previously recognized, their continuing abduction and torture by perpetrator groups even as I worked with them. These were clients who faced a constant risk of self-harm and suicide. There was a minefield of things I did not yet understand.

However, over the course of the twenty years I spent working with these clients, dialoguing with survivors who were in all stages of healing, and studying everything I could find, I am no longer overwhelmed. I understand what needs to be done for successful treatment of survivors of ritual abuse and mind control, and I have developed a protocol that makes it manageable. I offer it now to you.

Healing the Unimaginable is the book I wish I had had in 1991. My goal is to provide you with a practical, down-to-earth treatment manual, an updated road map that corrects the errors of those that preceded it. It cannot provide you with any treatment shortcut that bypasses the time-consuming tasks ahead. However, it will, I hope, get you there faster than the previous maps, because it will not lead you astray.

That is not to say you should take every word I say as gospel. You will still need to honor your own journey, and your clients'. You should never allow anyone to dictate how you think. This is the lesson your clients will be learning, but it is also something you should be aware of.

In the spring of 2009 I had an experience that highlighted all these truths for me, which I would like to share with you.

I was on my way to be a plenary speaker on the topic of mind control at a conference in the UK. The organizers had sent me a map on which a road called the A6 ran east across the country from near Manchester airport to the main British motorway, the M1. It appeared to be a direct route. However, when I attempted to drive from the airport to the conference center, I could not find it. Several times, I stopped to ask for help, but the hand-drawn maps and conflicting directions I got were not helpful. Repeatedly, I would follow a supposed route, only to have it peter out into a maze of ordinary streets.

Finally, someone explained to me that the A6 was not a highway at all, but a historical route that was no longer identified by signage, but goes along many different roads with different names. Rather than cutting across the middle of the country on the A6, I would have to go back to the main ring road, follow it north, take one motorway east, and yet another south. This was a big disappointment. The conference's map had seemed so clear and direct. But it offered me a route that did not exist.

As I tried to get back to the Manchester ring road, I found myself in the middle of a huge traffic jam. I drove around lost for about three hours. I was not only jetlagged, but dazed. I needed food and a bathroom break, yet there was something strangely comforting about this traffic jam. After all, how could I go wrong when the path I was on was being traveled by so many others?

I kept having to remind myself that even if that path did lead somewhere worthwhile, it very probably did not lead to my destination.

It took considerable willpower, but I left this stream of cars behind and forged off on my own. Once again, I was wandering blindly. Finally, I saw a sign that directed me back to the ring road. And, after following a series of highways north, east, and then south, I arrived at the conference center, just as the first meeting was starting.

As late, stressed, and exhausted as I was, I understood the symbolic value of my ordeal. It paralleled my experience of learning to work with survivors of ritual abuse and mind control. In my early work with these clients, I had kept trying to follow road maps developed by others, only to find them inadequate, or just plain wrong. The therapeutic approaches in vogue at the time were largely irrelevant to this population, and consultations based on these approaches got me nowhere. Without accurate direction, it would be possible to waste years of my clients' lives while they continued to suffer and to be traumatized. With no accurate professional text or training program to be found, I had no choice but to take the big risk of going "off the beaten track" to help these people. Fortunately, I was willing to honor the guidance my clients provided. I might not have known where I was going, but they had had the experience, they knew how my interventions were affecting them, and they knew what worked for their recovery. And so it is even today: experience has taught me that although not everything every survivor says is accurate, people who have done their recovery work are still our most fruitful sources of knowledge about ritual abuse and mind control, as those subjects cannot be studied directly when they occur.

For that reason, I have asked some of my survivor teachers to be contributors to this book. I value their involvement enormously. Their contributions illustrate the nature of the abuse, the problems encountered in the healing process, and the creative ways survivors have found to make their way to recovery. Nine courageous survivors made contributions to this book, and others have granted me permission to quote their writings. They have been so generous in sharing their priceless wisdom, creativity, and knowledge, all with brutal honesty, no matter how painful. I owe a debt of gratitude to them, and believe the field of psychotherapy—and society—do as well.

That is not to say that one should assume that every client who talks about such things is necessarily a survivor of these experiences, or that everything such a survivor discloses is accurate or even literally true. My book will address that, and help you to know how to correctly assess what your clients present to you. This point corresponds to the other lesson that I learnt that day as I traveled across England. The humbling experience of getting lost before my first venture into the big world of being a plenary conference speaker taught me that the road map I was giving to the conference participants that day could not be assumed to be 100% accurate. I would not have wanted my audience to trust me so deeply that I would lead them astray. Likewise, although I do believe that in many or most cases you will discover this map, derived in part from the disclosures of survivors, to be correct, I must also warn you that parts might not always be so. It will need to change over time as the roads to recovery change. As I tell my clients, do not trust me so much that you turn your thought process over to me. Trust has to be earned. Experiment with this map, make corrections, improve it. And, please, let others know where it is wrong. Just as I have invited some of the most knowledgeable contributors I know to participate in this treatment manual, the more people who bring their evolving knowledge and experience to this difficult issue, the more we can all remain current and effective in what we are trying to do for our clients.

What you will find here

Healing the Unimaginable is grounded in the assumption that ritual abuse and mind control abuses do exist. It does not indulge the debate about the existence of these phenomena. (For those interested in these questions, I recommend the books and articles listed in Appendix 1.)

The first section focuses on understanding the phenomena of ritual abuse and mind control: how they work, and their results in the people who have undergone experiences which begin in childhood but might continue in a variety of ways into adulthood as well. It addresses how working with survivors of such horrendous abuse affects the therapist. It humanizes this experience through five first-person contributions by survivors. In one, a survivor who served as a programmer in a ritually abusive cult training center shares a unique insider's view of the methods and thought process employed by these groups. I evaluate checklists that have been developed over the years to help therapists recognize those who might be survivors of these abuses, and provide a checklist that I developed, through which the internal, structural characteristics of the personality systems installed by abusers can be used by therapists to recognize mind control or ritual abuse survivors among their clients or patients. The original purpose of the implantation of such designs is also addressed. Finally, a chapter looks at the indoctrination or "programming" that characterizes these abuses.

The second section of the book provides a step-by-step guide to treatment. It includes: understanding the experience of having a dissociative disorder and the basics of treatment, developing a secure therapeutic relationship, working with structured personality systems and clients' inner worlds, the critical and often misunderstood issues of external and internal safety, and how to counter the lies and tricks on which mind control is based. Special attention is given to sexuality, and also guilt and shame over forced perpetration. "Deprogramming" and attempted removal of "spiritual attachments" or "demons" are discussed and evaluated. Managing and working through traumatic memories is addressed in this section, as is the widespread question of belief and disbelief. The final chapter looks at successful resolution, either through integration of the personality or through cooperative co-consciousness. Here, the reader will find stories of successful recovery.

Working with survivors of ritual abuse and mind control can be the biggest challenge of your professional career. As you read this book, and the references I provide, your intellect and your courage might well to be challenged to their limits. But you will have learnt, as I have in my own journey, an enormous amount about how human beings work, and how to help those who, when they were the most vulnerable, were the most damaged.

A word to survivors

Most therapists do not yet have specific training in working with persons who are or may be survivors of ritual abuse and/or mind control, and *Healing the Unimaginable* is written specifically to help them. I do *not* recommend that you read it.

If you are wondering whether or not you are a survivor of ritual abuse or mind control, *Healing the Unimaginable* is not for you. If you know you are such a survivor and have done considerable recovery work already, *Healing the Unimaginable* is not for you.

Here's why:

1. You do not want your memories to be contaminated by reading the details contained on these pages about what ritual abusers and mind controllers do. Genuine survivors have difficulty in any case believing their memories, and it is easier to believe what comes up from within you if you do not have other people's information to confuse you.
2. There are some graphic details of abuses here, and they can trigger flashbacks or trained behaviors in people who are actually survivors of such abuses. This can be unpleasant and destabilizing for you.

If you want to benefit from this book, recommend it to your therapist. What she or he learns will "trickle down," and you will benefit through your recovery. Certain sections were written by survivors who have stated that their work may be shared with other survivors. Your therapist is urged to share these with you if they are right for you. Feel free to discuss this with your therapist.

So here is what this means: if you are a survivor, and determined to read this book, you do so at your own risk. Please do not let your "detective" parts have the final say, but evaluate carefully whether or not reading this information yourself will be beneficial to you. Remember that your safety—not only physical, but emotional—and your successful recovery are what is most important.

CHAPTER ONE

A therapist's first experience with ritual abuse and mind control

Working with ritual abuse and mind control survivors is probably the biggest challenge you will ever have in your professional life. For many therapists, one of the most demanding, upsetting and exciting periods occurs at the very beginning of such work. It is a kind of "hit the ground running" time. They must deal with disclosures that force them to face unimaginable realities for the first time, which will almost immediately demand new skills and knowledge. And sometimes, they must also contend with whether or not the other healthcare systems involved in their clients' care will be willing and able to help them appropriately.

My initiation into this work came through a group of four ritually abused clients, one of whom was "Lorraine."

In memoriam Lorraine

A few weeks before it happened, she asked me earnestly, "Is it a mortal sin if you kill yourself?" And I said no. I knew I was giving her permission, in a sense. I *had* told the parts of her that wanted to die that if they killed the parts that did not want to die it would be murder. They kept taking an internal vote, and each time more of them wanted to go. I never told them not to.

Lorraine was one of my first few clients with what was then called MPD, multiple personality disorder. She was crippled with severe osteoarthritis, and had to use a wheelchair. When she was Lorraine, she was a sweet-natured, gentle, considerate, laughing, roly-poly woman who loved to read and to sew. When she was Big Susie, she was a playful five-year-old who had a collection of giant dolls and a huge stuffed gorilla. Lorraine sewed clothes for the dolls. When she was Little Susie, she was a terrified, mute three-year-old. I was also acquainted with Morgue, pronounced Mor-Gew, who called for the suicide votes.

I got to know Lorraine because she was the best friend of another client who also suffered from what we now call DID, dissociative identity disorder. (The name change reflected the revised view that someone with the disorder was one fragmented person rather than a lot of different people sharing one body. But most who have the disorder feel more as if it is MPD.) My other client, whom I will call Teresa, thought Lorraine had MPD and hoped I could help her. Almost no one recognized this condition in those days.

Lorraine was forty years old and had been in and out of psychiatric hospitals since she was thirteen. She had had various diagnoses, mainly severe depression, and she had made quite a few serious suicide attempts before I even met her. She had been given many courses of electric shock therapy, which would confuse her so much that she could not get together a coherent suicide plan for quite a while.

Lorraine's psychiatrist was initially opposed to my seeing her, as her friend Teresa had been stigmatized with the "borderline personality disorder" diagnosis when in hospital, so was seen as a bad influence on her. But after Lorraine spent a couple of months in hospital calling herself Susie and acting consistently like a child, he was humble enough to acknowledge that perhaps he could learn some new things, and someone else's help might be a good idea.

It had taken me a while to recognize MPD in any of my clients. Teresa was the first. She kept talking about her "inner child." And I did not realize how real this child was until one day she stole a wheelchair from the hospital to which my clinic was attached, and took it for a joyride around the grounds. When confronted by hospital staff, she told them she was my employee. I began to pay attention to this "inner child," named Stuffy, from having been stuffed in a closet.

As soon as realized that I was treating MPD clients, I read the few existing books on the condition, attended a workshop at the Justice Institute, and used some sexual abuse prevention money to organize a workshop where therapists could exchange information and educate each other about dissociation. There, I learnt something that I found really shocking. Many people suffering from MPD had been severely abused throughout their childhood years by organized groups, including Satanic and other "dark-side" religious cults. Moreover, quite a few of them were still involved in those groups, although they were not aware of their involvement, because it was other "personalities"—dissociated parts of them—who went off to the groups' rituals. I was skeptical, to say the least.

Shortly after I began work with Teresa, I acquired another MPD client, a supposedly schizophrenic young man I will call Tony. He called in to the clinic on a day I was on telephone duty, saying he was having flashbacks of "ritual abuse." I did not yet know what that was. Tony became my client. He could be quite entertaining. I have a vivid memory of him as a three-year-old, "Tiny Tony," standing on his head on my office couch, and running down the hall to try unsuccessfully to make it to the bathroom. He had in his head the entire rock band of Guns'n'Roses, and I got to know Axl, the band leader, quite well. I remember the time Tony was in hospital and I went to visit him; Axl popped out and said, "Remember, we're schizophrenic in here!"

The last of my first four was a teenage girl whom I will call Jennifer, who had been removed from her home because she had disclosed sexually abusing her younger brother. Although she was in foster care, Jennifer told me that she kept seeing her mother, with whom she was supposed to have no contact, outside her foster home or at the bus stop she used. I did not know what this meant. Then one day Tony told me that he'd "woken up" at midnight standing on the corner at the gas station near where he lived, apparently waiting for a ride.

One day, I gave Teresa a ride home from treatment. Her ancient grandmother was at her apartment helping her pack her things for a move. By this time Teresa had disclosed sexual abuse by her father as well as both her parents being alcoholics. I took this opportunity for a confrontation, as people did in those days. I said to the grandmother triumphantly, "Teresa has told me all about what happened to her!" "Oh?" the old woman said in a creaky voice. "And just what has she told you?" "Alcoholism and sexual abuse!" I proclaimed triumphantly. The grandmother breathed what appeared to be a sigh of relief, and said, "Oh, I'm just an old woman, I wouldn't know about those things." It was a very strange response.

Then another strange thing happened. Teresa was the single parent of a very young child, and had been seeing me about her parenting difficulties. Her child was in and out of foster care. One day, she called both me and the child protection worker and said she could not handle the little girl any longer and had to give her up for adoption. She was determined to sign the papers and give her up, but I was mystified by it, because Teresa's parenting had improved considerably and I knew she really loved her daughter. I would not be able to make sense of these mysteries until I had learnt all about the lives of the rest of my "first four."

Gradually, the story came out. Teresa mentioned that she had known Tony in junior high school. It turned out that she still knew him—he was part of the cult group she still attended, along with her family. So was Jennifer (and her family). And Lorraine, whom at that point I had only been seeing for a short time. Tony's mother was the cult's high priestess, his stepfather was a kind of regional manager. All four of these clients not only had been abused by the same people, mostly their family members, but they were still being abused and forced to take part in abusive rituals. So, of course, was Teresa's little daughter, until Teresa gave her up permanently. It was not until Teresa gave up the child for adoption that she began to disclose her own ritual abuse.

My initial excitement at working with this newly understood diagnosis was rapidly diminishing. At the same time I was developing compassion for these people who lived part of their lives in a living hell, and this motivated me to embrace the challenges they presented. I worked hard with them, and I soon discovered that other people—the cult—were working with them, too. They lurked outside my office waiting to kidnap my clients and take them somewhere to re-abuse them as a punishment for talking to me. They set off "programs," the conditioned responses which my clients' child parts had been trained to perform, such as falling asleep in session, calling them and reporting what we'd talked about, being unable to understand English, cutting themselves, or trying to hurt me. They made various threats to terrified child parts of my clients, that they would harm or kill them or me or other people they cared for if they did not stop coming to therapy and stop talking about what had happened and was happening to them. (I did not believe they would be stupid enough to kill me, since I knew their names and had given them to the police.)

Also, I discovered that the cult had a regular pick-up system for their members outside the mental hospital at dinnertime, so any members who were currently hospitalized would go out there for a "smoke", and be picked up and returned before hospital staff could check on them. I shared this information with Lorraine's psychiatrist. He began putting her in the general hospital rather than the psychiatric hospital when she needed respite. She did much better there, though she told me that cult members had come by at night and threatened her. Lorraine had been living in a group home for the mentally ill, but now she had the new MPD diagnosis, the managers refused to house her. She was given an apartment on the top floor of a seniors' building. From there she would venture out in her wheelchair to go to the library or shopping. I soon discovered that she was not safe, that cult people would ambush her whenever she was out and took great sport in harming her. They obtained a key to her apartment and could get in whenever they wanted. They would get her to invite Teresa over, then show up and hurt both of them. It was a nightmare.

I could not cancel everything else in my life because I was seeing these people. In the summer I took a month-long vacation with my family, traveling around Europe; it was something I had to do before my eldest child left home. When I returned, Lorraine was in the psychiatric emergency ward, where she had apparently been almost the entire time. The hospital had scheduled a meeting regarding her for the day I returned, a Wednesday. She was to be discharged the next day.

I visited Lorraine in hospital just before the meeting. She told me that she had been picked up on the street by some cult people, who had told her that if she did not kill herself properly this time, they would kill me, her psychiatrist, her sister in a neighboring city, and her sister's children. Most parts of Lorraine were children, and they believed this threat. She had been tortured enough to know these people were indeed capable of murder. On leaving, I wrote a note in the ward's book, which was only for hospital staff, saying, "Do not discharge her until I've had a chance to see her again. If you do, she will kill herself." I described the threat. Then I went to the meeting at the hospital. There, I learned that the powers-that-be had decided Lorraine was too much trouble, so she was to be transferred to housing in another city, where I could not see her any longer.

The psychiatrist called me that night. He had read my note and believed me. He said that he would not be able to keep Lorraine in hospital until I could see her the next week, and asked whether it would make a difference if he discharged her on Thursday or Sunday. I said no, she was not safe either way. I had a full schedule for the first two weeks, since a lot of people had been waiting to see me. I could not see her until Monday at the earliest. He discharged her on Thursday. Early on Saturday morning, he called to tell me that Lorraine had fallen, or jumped, out of the window of her apartment to her death. There was no investigation. She had been suicidal for many years, so it was assumed to be suicide, not murder.

But to me, it was very suspicious. The bathroom window Lorraine had gone out of was a tiny one, and almost impossible to open, let alone to squeeze through, as it was quite high up from the floor. Lorraine was fat and had no muscle tone; I could not imagine her doing it alone. Her apartment door was locked.

Lorraine had no relatives in town who cared about her. She had grown up in a group home, where her original cult abuse had happened, as the group home parents were cult-involved and used the children they looked after in the cult rituals and other evil activities.

Lorraine's younger sister came to town to dispose of her possessions, and there was a brief memorial service at the funeral chapel. I was one of the people who spoke about Lorraine and Susie to those who attended, including several suspicious-looking people. I was sad, but not as sad as I had been when Lorraine was alive and constantly being re-abused and tortured by people who were not acknowledged to exist. At least she was no longer subject to this lack of safety. It was over. She could not go through that any longer. I made it clear to the cult at the memorial service that on this subject at least I agreed with them.

Teresa, overcome with grief, was hospitalized shortly after Lorraine's death. I was aware that she and Lorraine had made a suicide pact years earlier that if one of them died the other would follow. When I tried to visit her in the hospital, I was met at the door by the psychiatrist in charge of the ward, whose job was specifically to exclude me. He gave me a story about how therapists who were not on the hospital staff could not do therapy in the hospital as it could subject the hospital to liability if anything then happened to their patients. Oh, yes. That was their main concern, liability. Of course, if the psychiatric hospital system had only taken the threats and disclosures seriously and kept Lorraine safe, none of this would have happened. If some outside therapist had exposed their failure to care for the most vulnerable of their patients, what would have happened?

They did not invite her psychiatrist or me to her obligatory "death review." They were probably glad to be rid of her.

Teresa did not kill herself, despite ongoing abuse. Both she and Jennifer survived murder attempts disguised as suicide, but this time there was no question: people broke into their apartments and stuffed all their pills down their throats. Teresa was sufficiently recovered to make contacts in another city far away. She moved there, and is now doing well.

I managed to get Tony's father, who lived on the other side of the continent, to take custody of him and try to get him help there, but Tony disappeared the next summer and reappeared in our city with his mother, once more diagnosed "schizophrenic." I completed therapy with Jennifer, and she moved to another country, where she is also doing well. So, two out of the four made it to safety and relative health. Two were lost.

I remember Lorraine's freckled face, her sweet smile, and her gentle nature. I still have her stuffed bear, which other clients hold when they need comfort. I wish I had been able to keep her safe. I wish the mental health system had recognized the evil that they were abetting when they misdiagnosed her and kept her subject to so many more years of abuse. I applaud the psychiatrist who had the courage to look at a new diagnosis and break rank to attempt to work with me. I sincerely hope Lorraine's next life, or her afterlife (if she has one), is the opposite of what this one was.

As some of you already know, the first experience of a therapist working with ritual abuse or mind control survivors involves shock, disbelief, and confusion. I remember that with Teresa, I became first shocked, then disbelieving, as she disclosed sexual abuse by one person after another before the ritual abuse became evident. I thought, "How could one person be abused by so many people?" It did not occur to me initially that these abusers were all connected to the cult or to her parents. I could not conceive the true nature of the abuse that would unfold.

I was also very confused about Teresa's multiplicity, and discounted her "inner child" as part of the latest self-help fad. I did not really realize that it was possible for a person to have different self-states separated by walls of amnesia, so total that one state would not remember what another state had done. Teresa had a habit of confabulating to cover when she did not remember what happened, and she had acquired quite a reputation among service providers because of what they called "lying." In actual fact, she just did not remember, so she made something up. My first task with her and my other dissociative clients was to learn about dissociative disorders. If you do not know about dissociative disorders, stop right here. You will need to read some of the books recommended in Appendix I before you proceed. The deliberate creation of dissociative disorders is basic to ritual abuse and mind control, and unless you understand how dissociative disorders work, you will be very confused by these clients and will not be able to help them.

The second reaction of most therapists working with these clients is a combination of horror and fear. First of all, there is the sheer horror of the memories they are disclosing. Sadistic torture, murder of fetuses, painful electroshock to infants and children, gang rapes, necrophilia, bestiality, drowning, near-death experiences . . . you name it, you will hear about it. Your clients need you to be able to hear these memories with calm compassion. You need to be strong enough to hear these things and not have the color drain from your face. Your client will see such involuntary reactions as indicators that you cannot handle what they are disclosing, and you will hear no more.

We are all traumatized, especially by the first few clients with these kinds of experiences that we encounter. We have to pay attention to our own vicarious traumatization (see Pearlman & Saakvitne, 1995), and make sure we take care of ourselves so that we are not constantly living in a state of trauma. Any of our own past trauma, too, can be activated by what our clients disclose. So it is important to have competent supervision or consultation and, if necessary, our own therapy. It is important that the supervision and consultation be with someone who is experienced with dissociative disorders and ideally with ritual abuse and mind control, too, although at this point not many experienced therapists have such a background.

And we must address the risk to the clients. Many of our ritually abused or mind-controlled clients engage in self-harming behavior, which is actually the behavior of parts who have been trained to do this as punishment for disclosures. Most therapists do not realize this, and spend a lot of time and energy on trying to convince clients not to "act out." The clients commonly attempt suicide, also a trained behavior, induced by parts of the mind who either think they must kill themselves before the perpetrators kill them in a gruesome manner, think someone they love will be killed if they do not (like Lorraine), or believe they will not die but will be rewarded when the body dies.

This is very stressful for therapists. We spend a lot of time and energy worrying about our clients' safety, and feeling helpless in the face of these behaviors. These behaviors can also get our clients involved in the psychiatric hospital system, which can, in some cases, be helpful, but in other cases can be problematic, bringing on peer pressure to treat the clients with medication and confinement and give them other diagnoses than the correct one of dissociative disorder.

But this is only the beginning of the feeling of risk. When we discover that in many, though not all cases, the clients are still being abused and are being forced to take part in abuse of others, our protective instincts go on constant alert. If the clients have children, we realize that these children are at risk and we have to make decisions about reporting something that will probably not be believed. We become anxious about every cult or family holiday time, along with our client, and we imagine the horrors they might be going through.

Acknowledging that our clients are often in "current contact" with their abusers is frustrating and, often, frightening. As therapy progresses with "current contact" clients, and the clients stop going back to the group when they are supposed to, the risk to the clients does increase.

The teenager, Jennifer, came to one session late with her arms badly slashed. She told me that she had not done it; a cult person had waylaid her on the way to the office and done it in the hope of getting her admitted to hospital where they could have more access to her. I chose to believe her, since she had never lied to me. Remember that both she and Teresa experienced attempted murder disguised as suicide attempts, and Lorraine's death was either murder or forced suicide. I felt as if I were living in a horror movie.

Then there is the fear for ourselves and our families. The first generation of therapists doing this work were told by their clients that the one massive cult was everywhere, knew everything, had access to state-of-the-art technology, and was willing to kill both clients and therapists to stop the information from getting out. When I worked with my first ritually abused clients, I was constantly hearing threats to my life. Teresa, in particular, would come for an appointment and relate in great detail how the cult high priest (whose identity I knew) was going to lie in wait in the hallway of my office building and how he would kill me. The worst threat was when I found out from one of these first four clients that the cult leaders had taken them all in a van to the driveway of my home, had them abused while drugged by a woman impersonating me, and then told them my address and instructed them to go there and set fire to my house while my children and I were asleep. This event was corroborated about a year later by another one of these clients. I took precautions, leaving copies of my records with a lawyer, and the abusers' names in a sealed envelope with the police. I calculated (correctly) that killing me would be a greater security risk to the group than leaving me alive and trying to discredit me in professional circles. But still, I was afraid. It is difficult not to keep on imagining these horrors when you hear them in such detail.

The reality is that even before stories of ritual abuse and mind control began coming out to therapists, the groups had agreed on what kind of disinformation to spread, so that clients would be afraid to tell their therapists what had happened to them, and therapists would be afraid to work with these clients. It is true that keeping the secrets is crucial to all groups who use mind control. But this is also a reason why they are highly unlikely to kill therapists—they do not want any formal investigations. The issue of safety for clients and therapists will be explored in detail in Chapter Eleven, "'Stabilization' takes on a new meaning".

The last major stressor on the therapist working with these clients is isolation and peer pressure. It was particularly bad during the "memory wars" of the 1990s. The diagnosis of dissociative disorder was not widely accepted, and an organized political group, the False Memory Syndrome Foundation, along with other similar groups, took up the task of informing the media that unethical therapists were suggesting to helpless clients that they had been sexually abused, or worse, by family members. A leading journal, *Treating Abuse Today*, was forced out of business by picketers representing supposedly innocent accused parents. Leading therapists in the dissociative disorders field, such as Bennett Braun and Judith Peterson, were targeted for lawsuits and, in Peterson's case, even criminal charges. Insurance companies chose to settle most lawsuits out of court, giving the impression that the therapists were guilty.

While some therapists were doubtless foolish and unethical, many were not, but almost all were unprepared for this well-organized political attack. Since many of the lawsuits were about cases where ritual abuse was alleged, the remaining leaders in the field of dissociative disorders pulled back and took a skeptical position regarding the existence of ritual abuse. This left the therapists such as myself, whose clients were reporting this, in a position of isolation. We were attacked by skeptics when we mentioned ritual abuse in online discussion forums. We had no local colleagues who understood what we were dealing with. There were no textbooks to guide us. We saw those from whom we had learnt being publicly ridiculed and humiliated. So, most of us learnt to do our work in private, developing our own techniques, without reporting them publicly.

The situation is somewhat better now. Because the problem of ritual abuse and mind control has not gone away—the survivors are still there—many more therapists have learnt about it. Survivors have spoken out and written their stories, and therapists have learnt a great deal from those brave survivors who have discovered what was done to them. There is a large special interest group on Ritual Abuse and Mind Control within the International Society for the Study of Dissociation. Those therapists who have learnt in isolation or in small private online forums are once again sharing their knowledge widely, and books such as this one are beginning to be published again. The work is still very difficult and challenging, but we now know so much more than we did. We know that there is not one massive Satanic cult, but many different interrelated groups, including religious, military/political, and organized crime, using mind control on children and adult survivors. We know that there are effective treatments. We know that many of the paralyzing beliefs our clients lived by are the result of lies and tricks perpetrated by their abusers. And we know that, as therapists, we can combat this evil with wise and compassionate therapy.

CHAPTER TWO

Ritual abuse and mind control: the definition evolves

The story of our evolving understanding of ritual abuse is one of many unrelated people discovering different parts of the body of a new species in a darkened room and trying to understand what the whole animal looks like. According to Child Abuse Wiki, the term "ritual abuse" was first coined in 1980 in the popular book *Michelle Remembers*, by Canadian psychiatrist Larry Pazder, and Michelle Smith (1989), his long-time patient. Under Pazder's care, Michelle had remembered childhood abuse in the context of a Satanic cult. He defined the phenomenon as "repeated physical, emotional, mental, and spiritual assaults combined with a systematic use of symbols, ceremonies, and machinations designed and orchestrated to attain malevolent effects" (Pazder, cited in Kahaner (1988), p. 201).

Subsequent definitions came primarily from professionals addressing alleged ritual abuse in childcare settings. Child Abuse Wiki states that Finkelhor, Williams, Burns, and Kalinowski elaborated on Pazder's definition, defining ritual abuse as "abuse that occurs in a context linked to some symbols or group activity that have a religious, magical or supernatural connotation, and where the invocations of these symbols or activities are repeated over time and used to frighten and intimidate the children" (1988, p. 52). and that Kelley referred to ritual abuse as the "repetitive and systematic sexual, physical, and psychological abuse of children by adults as part of cult or Satanic worship" (1988, p. 228).

Because Satanic cult abuse was the first to surface, these early definitions of ritual abuse focused on its religious (specifically Satanic) aspects. For a long time the phenomena were referred to as "Satanic ritual abuse" (SRA). Over time, however, more than Satanism emerged. In the religious form of the abuse, other deities than Satan were worshipped, notably Lucifer, and a Gnostic form of the Christian god who kept good and evil in balance. Various ancient gods were represented.

Most of these survivors appeared to be from intergenerational cult groups, where many generations of a family would be involved. Others were abused as young children in daycare settings, even though their parents were not part of the abuse. In fact, these parents were often dedicated advocates on their children's behalf, often at great personal and emotional expense.

As therapists continued to work with clients who described experiences of this kind of abuse, it became evident that the phenomenon was much broader than what was initially seen. Survivors began to disclose a similar manifestation, which occurred in secretive military/political and organized criminal groups. This abuse seems to be more pragmatic than spiritual or creed-based in nature. Some cases include Satanist scenarios, but these seem to be staged more for the purpose of controlling and frightening the children or for use in pornography. Different scenarios, such as experiments or military training, predominate.

As you can see, the term "ritual abuse" is a complicated thing, whose definition evolves as more survivors reveal and come to understand their experiences. Like dissociation, it appears on a spectrum, according to some. For instance, the FAQs on the website of Survivorship, a group devoted to survivors of ritual abuse, offer both broad and narrow definitions of ritual abuse. The broad definition states that

> Ritual abuse is the abuse of a child, weaker adult, or animal in a ritual setting or manner. In a broad sense, many of our overtly or covertly socially sanctioned actions can be seen as ritual abuse, such as military basic training, hazing, racism, spanking children, and partner-battering. Some abuse is private (Jeffrey Dahmer, for example), some public. Public ritual abuse may be either open or secret.

Once again we see a definition that uses the term "ritual", but separates it from religion and applies it to any repetitive abusive activity. The website also provides this narrower definition of ritual abuse: "Repeated, extreme, sadistic abuse, especially of children, within a group setting. The group's ideology is used to justify the abuse, and abuse is used to teach the group's ideology. The activities are kept secret from society at large, as they violate norms and laws." This definition could apply to abuse by an intelligence agency, as well as that by a religious group.

When therapists first discovered ritual abuse, the focus was on the horrors the child victims endured. The mind control that is created by these groups was seen as secondary, and was not well understood. Over time, we grew to understand that this mind control is primary, and is actually the goal of all such abuse. The term "ritual abuse" then came to be used to apply to both the classic religiously based abuse specifically, and generically to the universal aspect of mind control.

Although there is a large body of knowledge, including a number of websites, devoted to mind control, the term has yet to appear in the *Oxford English Dictionary*. The commonly accepted definition can be found in Wikipedia, which describes mind control as involving

> a broad range of psychological tactics able to subvert an individual's control of his or her own thinking, behavior, emotions, or decisions . . . The goal is to have those individuals carry out actions which ordinarily would go counter to human nature. This training involves physical, sexual and emotional torture, the use of drugs, and, in some cases, the use of technologies which directly affect brain function.

In an online article entitled "Simplifying complex programming," Jeannie Riseman, a leading light in Survivorship, talks about methods of influencing or controlling thought as being on a continuum. She points out that conditioning is the way we transmit our culture to our children, through repetition and reinforcement. Some conditioning is good; other conditioning, such as that for racial prejudice, is not. The use of force and violence, however, reduces a child to a survival level in which she enters an altered state of consciousness. At this point, Riseman begins using the term "programming."

At the far end of the conditioning-programming spectrum, according to Riseman, is deliberate mind control, which is extremely complicated and malevolent. "When such violence is unexpected or unpredictable, when it is a common occurrence, when it is bizarre, and when it is done in secret or denied, it has a larger effect on the child. All these things are the case for children raised in dangerous cults."

In 1991, the report of the Los Angeles County Commission for Women's Ritual Abuse Task Force reflected their early understanding of the issue. It stated,

> Mind control is the cornerstone of ritual abuse, the key element in the subjugation and silencing of its victims. Victims of ritual abuse are subjected to a rigorously applied system of mind control designed to rob them of their sense of free will and to impose upon them the will of the cult and its leaders. Most often these ritually abusive cults are motivated by a Satanic belief system. The mind control is achieved through an elaborate system of brainwashing, programming, indoctrination, hypnosis, and the use of various mind-altering drugs. The purpose of the mind control is to compel ritual abuse victims to keep the secret of their abuse, to conform to the beliefs and behaviors of the cult, and to become functioning members who serve the cult by carrying out the directives of its leaders without being detected within society at large.

Child Abuse Wiki reaffirms this, defining ritual abuse as:

> a brutal form of abuse of children, adolescents, and adults, consisting of physical, sexual, and psychological abuse, and involving the use of rituals. Ritual does not necessarily mean Satanic. However, most survivors state that they were ritually abused as part of Satanic worship for the purpose of indoctrinating them into Satanic beliefs and practices. Ritual abuse rarely consists of a single episode. It usually involves repeated abuse over an extended period of time. The physical abuse is severe, sometimes including torture and killing. The sexual abuse is usually painful, sadistic, and humiliating, intended as means of gaining dominance over the victim. The psychological abuse is devastating and involves the use of ritual/indoctrination, which includes mind control techniques and mind altering drugs, and ritual/intimidation which conveys to the victim a profound terror of the cult members and of the evil spirits they believe cult members can command. Both during and after the abuse, most victims are in a state of terror, mind control, and dissociation in which disclosure is exceedingly difficult.

Note the inclusion of the concept of dissociation in this definition.

Even when the term "mind control" is not used, many applications or definitions of the term "ritual abuse" allude to it. Authors Randy Noblitt and Pamela Perskin Noblitt (2008), authors and editors of two important books on ritual abuse, define it as "abuse that occurs in a ceremonial or circumscribed manner for the purpose of creating or manipulating already created alter mental states." You will notice that the religious aspect of the abuse has almost disappeared from this definition, and Satanism is not mentioned at all. The Noblitts believe that this is a simple and clear definition that can generate testable hypotheses.

On the other hand, some others prefer a more detailed description of what is entailed in the abusive situation or a description of alleged perpetrators or perpetrating groups. Ellen Lacter, in her extensive website devoted to the issue of ritual abuse, gives this definition:

Ritual abuse consists of conditioning and torture carried out in a ceremonial or calculated manner for the purpose of effecting control over a victim's mind and behavior. It is international in scope, with similarities and variations across cultures.

Ritual abuse often involves the following:

- Extreme, sadistic, repetitious, physical abuse/torture, often to near-death
- Exploitation of the mind's capacity to dissociate trauma, to manipulate behavior, create amnesia, and to prevent disclosure
- Mind control and brainwashing techniques for the purpose of indoctrination and control
- Drugs to induce immobility, pain, confusion, hallucinations, unconscious states, depersonalization and derealization
- Systematic abuse and rituals to coerce and indoctrinate victims into the abusers' beliefs and world view
- Force, threats, and manipulation to coerce victims to harm others
- Sexual abuse of children and adults including rape, prostitution, pornography, snuff films, and bestiality
- Trafficking and slavery of children and adults
- Abuse beginning in infancy and childhood, with the goal of life-long control
- Deprivation of basic needs and human contact, including confinement and isolation
- Human and animal sacrifice to appease and empower humans and their deities
- Unconsenting medical and psychological experimentation to increase the ability to control a victim's mind and behavior
- Attempts to control or dominate the "soul", "spirit", or their equivalents cross-culturally.

Programming and mind control in visible and hidden cults

The term "cult" is often used to describe certain visible religious or ideological groups that attempt to practice mind control. Conway and Siegelman's 1978 book "Snapping" details effects of brainwashing, or mind control, attempts in visible cults. Ritually abusive cults, which are generally hidden, are usually not recognized by these descriptions, although they should be. The Advanced Bonewits Cult Danger Evaluation Frame developed by Isaac Bonewits, an influential neopagan leader and author, lists eighteen different criteria by which to evaluate the dangerousness of a cult. These include Internal Control, External Control, Wisdom/Knowledge Claimed by Leaders, Wisdom/Knowledge Credited to Leaders by Members, Dogma, Recruiting, Front Groups, Wealth, Sexual Manipulation, Sexual Favoritism, Censorship, Isolation, Dropout Control, Violence, Paranoia, Grimness, Surrender of Will, and Hypocrisy.

If Bonewits' criteria were applied to the average Satanic or Luciferian cult, or the typical military or organized crime group described by mind-controlled clients in therapy offices, we would see extremely high scores on almost all items. The tactics of these groups, however, are quite different from, and more extreme than, those found in visible cults. They are much more violent, for one thing. Their methods are more sophisticated and the consequences of those tactics more complex. Their invisibility makes them particularly dangerous, and makes treating their victims/survivors more complicated. In order to keep their existence secret, members have to maintain "normal" lives while continuing to be involved with these groups.

Additionally, unlike members of the visible cults, members of ritually abusive cults are either born into cult families or recruited as very young children through caregivers outside the family. According to survivor accounts, all these invisible cults, as well as military and organized crime groups, begin their "brainwashing" with children.

The mind control of which we speak in this book achieves its power over its victims through "programming." Survivor Robin Morgan (see Chapter Ten) defines programming as follows: "Programming is the act of installing internal, pre-established reactions to external stimuli so that a person will automatically react in a predetermined manner to things like an auditory, visual or tactile signal or perform a specific set of actions according to a date and/or time."

Popular media representations of mind control involves trained spies or assassins working for the CIA or other military/political groups or even companies without their conscious knowledge, because they have other "personalities" who engage in these activities. Think of Jason Bourne, or the hero of *Conspiracy Theory*, or Echo in television's *Dollhouse*, as well as other American television shows and films. The stories concocted about these mind-controlled special agents suggest that they are recruited in adulthood, even making a conscious choice to participate. Once they have been recruited, their previous memories are erased and new "personalities" created with special skills and manufactured memories.

The awful reality, however, is that there is only one way to create persons who can engage in activities such as spying, sex slavery, assassination, or ritual murder without *any* conscious awareness of this. The way is through abuse and torture of small children, separating parts of their minds that are then indoctrinated and trained individually as the abusers see fit. There is no adult who volunteers his loyalty to such a group because of thought-out belief in its goals; there are only small children who are trained by these groups through torture, and, as a consequence, grow up with major dissociative disorders. Worse, in most cases these children's own parents are involved in their torture and the training of their parts. Amnesia related to the traumatic events is much more likely if caregivers are involved in the abuse, and if it has to be kept secret, as Jennifer Freyd points out in *Betrayal Trauma* (1996).[1]

Systematic child abuse and its consequences

The consensus among professionals who have treated and studied people with dissociative disorders is that the vast majority have suffered severe, and often secretive, childhood trauma—usually, but not always, child abuse. This abuse often involves both betrayal and secrecy. Many people who appear in psychotherapy offices alleging histories of ritual abuse and/or mind control are found to suffer from a major dissociative disorder such as dissociative identity disorder (DID), or a close variant, "dissociative disorder not otherwise specified" (DDNOS). The traumatic dissociation that creates such disorders is usually deliberately designed by these abusers.

Mind control, including ritual abuse, is usually deliberately designed to produce traumatic dissociation particularly as found in DDNOS, in which many parts with distinct identities switch behind an apparently normal presenting personality. These disorders are very similar, in that they both involve separate ego states that switch behind an apparently normal presenting personality, who is seen by outsiders as the "real" person. However, DID is distinguished by the fact that inside parts periodically take over and act in the outside world, leaving the main personality with amnesia about what happened during these time periods. Both dissociative disorders prevent the secrets of abuser groups from being discovered. It appears that DDNOS is the intentional goal of these abusers, but DID sometimes results from a failure of programming.

What we are discussing in these pages is not new. Organized groups have always abused children for their own purposes. "Possession" is known in many cultures. It is likely that the kind of systematized abuse that created dissociative disorders was originally confined to religious groups which wanted to produce "possession" states. Eventually—in the mid to late twentieth century—the abuse appears to have become more scientific, designed to split the children's psyches in such ways that they could be used for the purposes of the abusing group. Although abusers continued to tell children they were inserting "demons" or "spirits" into them, these groups became aware that what they were really doing was creating dissociative disorders.

Dissociative disorders

Appropriate treatment for dissociative disorders requires additional knowledge, skills, and training beyond the basics required for general psychotherapy. There are several excellent books on dissociation diagnosis and treatment, and online courses offered by the International Society for the Study of Trauma and Dissociation (www.isstd.org) that contain a great deal of practical guidance. Conferences and study groups on DID and related disorders take place in various locations around the world. If you are new to the field, it is important to find a supervisor or consultant experienced in the dissociative disorders field, ideally one with RA/MC treatment experience. In the meantime, here are some basics, as they relate to the subjects of this book.

An essential component of mind control programming is the creation of a number of separate identity states, which may also be referred to as ego states or alternate identities ("alters"). Most trained "alter personalities" are created and trained in childhood. Abusers purposely create complex dissociative disorders in which additional personalities can be added at later dates in victims who have been properly prepared.

Different training is given to each state or group of similar states. Each is assigned and trained to do a specific "jobs" or to have a different function. The more complex the abuse and mind control training the child has experienced, the more complex the personality system. In this way, the perpetrator group can create the ideal sex slave, drug courier, or cult priest, who does not know he or she has been victimized by, or committed, a crime, and, thus, will genuinely and convincingly claim innocence if caught. This structuring of the personality system allows perpetrator groups to continue abusing and training children without those children breaking the secret. Child victims will, in their everyday lives, be unaware that any of this has happened.

Typically, some of these identity states will interact with the "normal" world, and others will perform functions only for the perpetrator group as a result of being cued. Some of those can take over executive function of the body. Identity states will have no access to, or memory of, the thoughts and activities of the other states. Only those who know how to activate a particular trained identity state will be able to talk to the person in that identity state. This is one thing that differentiates such structured systems from the more "organic" form of multiplicity that comes from non-mind control-based, albeit severe, child abuse. (With military/political mind control, some identity states can only be accessed through certain other specific identity states.)

Many of the states, even in adults, will continue to experience themselves as young children. Some of the parts believe their only choice is to remain loyal to the group in order for themselves, or others, to stay alive. This is essential to understand if one is to treat this population with empathy.

Typically, emotions "leak through" from the hidden states to the main everyday personality, and this leakage of anxiety or sadness or anger is what brings the person to therapy. In these cases, cognitive behavioral treatments are unsuccessful because the hidden states will continue to exist, along with the extreme emotions created by their abuse.

Trainees discarded by the perpetrator groups because they are rebellious or security risks are often programmed to self-destruct with drugs and alcohol and risky behaviors. Successfully programmed survivors are reported to be highly functional in the identity states that perform cult rituals or other tasks required by their group.

Mind control methods are constantly evolving. Jeannie Riseman of Survivorship summarizes the process succinctly:

> what we are referring to when we talk of mind-control experimentation is the deliberate and skillful manipulation of parts of a person's mind so that it becomes, and remains, under the control of another. The experimenters, trainers, and handlers have a particular goal in mind and they select the techniques that will enable them to achieve that goal. They are familiar with many different techniques and when they aren't satisfied with the results, they modify their plan. They are thorough and systematic. They know what they are doing. The technology they have at their command is much more complicated and sophisticated than what is available to the average abusive group. It's cutting edge and can be pretty expensive. This technology includes electroshock, implants, equipment to deliver information to different parts of the brain, as in split brain techniques, and many other things.

Systematic child abuse, government experimentation, and networking

Mind control abuses designed and perpetrated by US intelligence agencies and those of other countries are now widely understood to have occurred. These activities were assigned such names as MKULTRA, BLUEBIRD, and PAPERCLIP, which involved Nazi doctors and scientists who had been given asylum in the USA. The Cold War was used as justification for mind control abuses intended to create spies or assassins who lacked conscious awareness of their involvement.

Described in CIA documents that became available through the American Freedom of Information Act in the latter part of the twentieth century, these activities have been the subject of senate hearings in the USA and much media attention. Colin Ross documented them in his 2000 book, *Bluebird*. It is definitively documented that some mind control abuses that we identify as emanating from the government were designed, promoted, and executed by the most respected psychiatrists and psychologists of the day, in the most revered learning and behavioral health institutions. Some perpetrators have been exposed for practicing such techniques on persons who came to them for help. For example, Canada's Dr Donald Ewen Cameron was a leading Montreal psychiatrist who, in the 1950s and 1960s, with the support of CIA funding, engaged in unethical experiments on people who sought help for run-of-the-mill emotional difficulties, destroying memories of their entire previous lives (see the Wikipedia entry regarding Cameron).

We know that the dissociation created by childhood mind control can yield a perfectly invisible spy or political assassin. What is not generally known is that some of these projects involved experimentation on children. It is suspected that most documents regarding this were destroyed. In her 2001 book, *A Nation Betrayed: The Chilling True Story of Secret Cold War Experiments Performed on Our Children and Other Innocent People*, survivor Carol Rutz (see Chapter Twelve of this book) describes the years of government mind control experiments to which she was subjected. Her memories of sexual abuse, hypnosis, drugs, ESP, and other experiences are specific and meticulous, but she wanted more. In 1999, at the age of fifty-two, after submitting a FOIA request, she received the validation she had been waiting for. It came in the form of three CD ROMs:

> On December 17, 1999 I turned 52 years old. On that day I received three CD ROMs from the CIA in response to my FOIA request. Forty-eight years after I was first experimented on, I found solid proof of my memories—proof that was in the government vaults of the nearly 18,000 pages of declassified documents from the Bluebird/Artichoke and MKULTRA programs. One of the documents specifically stated that experimental studies of the postulated abilities of a few specially gifted subjects would be conducted. [Subproject 136 of MKULTRA CIA Mori ID#17395 ESP Research, 1961 and 1962, declassified documents from CIA]. The document states 'that in working with individual subjects, special attention will be given to dissociative states which tend to accompany spontaneous ESP experiences. Such states can be induced and controlled to some extent with hypnosis and drugs ... The data used in the study will be obtained from special groups such as psychotics, children and mediums ...'

> The document continues,

> 'Learning studies will be instituted in which the subject will be rewarded or punished for his overall performance and reinforced in various ways by being told whether he was right, by being told what the target was, with electric shock etc.'

> The proposal then goes on to say,

> 'In other cases drugs and psychological tricks will be used to modify his attitudes. The experimenters will be particularly interested in dissociative states, from the abaissement de niveau mental, to multiple personality in so-called mediums; and an attempt will be made to induce a number of states of this kind, using hypnosis.' The government had finally handed me the validation I had been searching for. To say my heart stopped that day is almost true.

Some of these government documents show that experiments were done on children as well as adults. One of the declassified documents from MKULTRA describes two experiments on two girls in 1951, in which children, after being taught to respond to code words which would function as post-hypnotic suggestions, were successfully trained to place an incendiary device or steal a person's belongings while in a trance state, and then be amnesic about doing it.

Survivor accounts such as that of Carol Rutz are corroborated by others who indicate that governmental groups wanting to create mind-controlled spies used not only hypnosis, but electroshock, torture, and complex technology. We know that a large number of these documents have been destroyed, and it does not defy the imagination to imagine that the perpetrators would not want the public to know they had tortured children in the name of national defense.

Perpetrator groups and connections

The CIA is not the only political group to have engaged in mind control on children. It appears that other government agencies in the USA and the intelligence agencies of other countries, as well as neo-Nazi groups, have also engaged in similar practices, with similar goals. We know that the Nazis experimented on children in ruthless ways. There is evidence that some Nazi doctors were imported to the United States (Bower, 1987), where they continued their research for a different employer (and covertly for the neo-Nazis, if they believed their original ideology). Many ritual abuse survivors report "doctors" at their cult training centers who assisted with their training.

Where did these groups access the children on whom they experimented and whom they trained? According to survivors, during the second half of the twentieth century there appears to have been some collaboration between the secretive military and political organizations and the occult religious groups who were already engaging in deliberate systematized child abuse. Many survivors report being abused by religious groups, more than one military or political group (for example, CIA and neo-Nazis and Ku Klux Klan), and also organized criminal groups. These groups apparently share children, strategies, and even trainers. Groups who use children in child pornography often borrow them from multi-generational incestuous families, such as are found in organized cults. Military mind control trainers also find cult children readily trainable as potential spies and killers because a dissociative foundation has already been created in them. Whether criminal, religious, or political/military, abusers on an international scale are aware that dissociation is the lynchpin of power and secrecy. What better source of already dissociative children than the parents who were abusing them in ritualistic cults?

All these groups employ the same torture, interrogation, and training techniques used on adults by military and police all over the world. Evidence is that many of the techniques of ritual abuse and mind control are used for child pornography, the training of child soldiers (notably in Africa) and the human trafficking of sex trade workers (*Guardian*, 2009). The behavior of at least some suicide bombers and terrorists is consistent with that found in programmed survivors who present for therapy.

Organized crime has also been involved, using children (often the same ones) for child prostitution and pornographic filming, and wanting ways to control those children and make sure of their secrecy. We can speculate that these enterprises are an important income source for both ritualistic cults and intelligence agencies.

When working with this population, it is extremely important to remember that you are dealing with survivors of powerful and violent organized abusive groups who have a high stake in keeping what they are doing hidden from the general public. It does not matter whether the perpetrators are parents, occult religious groups, military and intelligence operations, or traditional organized crime. They are well organized to prevent disclosures and to stop disclosures from continuing if they have been made.

> When you have eliminated the impossible, whatever remains, however improbable, must be the truth. (Sir Arthur Conan Doyle)

> Men occasionally stumble over the truth, but most of them pick themselves up and hurry off as if nothing ever happened. (Winston Churchill)

> I have sworn . . . eternal hostility against every form of tyranny over the mind of man. (Thomas Jefferson)

Note

1. Adults without pre-existing dissociative disorders can apparently be coerced into a form of dissociation which Robert Jay Lifton, in his book, *The Nazi Doctors*, calls "doubling," in which they behave very differently at home from the way they behave in daily coercive life-threatening situations, but they do have some awareness of what they are doing and have to find ways to justify it. For example, he states that "By not quite seeing it, doctors could distance themselves from the very killing they were actively supervising" (1986, p. 199). They developed what Lifton calls an "Auschwitz self," different from the pre-war and the post-war self, who justified what they were doing by racial and religious ideologies.

CHAPTER THREE

The basics of therapy

H ere are some basic points regarding treatment of persons with dissociative disorders, and mind control histories. This initial material will not be new for some of you, although others may need help to understand the internal experience of a person who is multiple, or some of the fundamentals of how to approach such clients.

Developing empathy for people with dissociative disorders

Mind control programming builds on the natural, reactive dissociative fragmenting caused by childhood trauma. The trauma-based developing of many selves that begins in early childhood and results from extreme (often life-threatening) trauma is not merely psychological. It is also a biological process in the brain. It is not something that the person chooses, and it cannot begin in adulthood. Most survivors of organized mind control and/or ritual abuse are "polyfragmented"—that is, they have a large number of alter personalities. In order to properly help them, we need to understand what it is like to be them.

Recognizing and respecting differences

People tend to assume that other people are similar to them, unless those people are in some way visibly different. It is easy for us to accept that someone who has a different skin color may be different in their background and way of thinking, but more difficult when people look and sound the same as us. Sometimes, someone may appear just like you physically, but their accent may reveal an alien background and culture. They look the same, but they are different. These differences we can also recognize.

We therapists often make inaccurate assumptions about people living with DID and DDNOS. They often appear to be "just like us," so we often assume their experience of life reflects our own. But this is profoundly untrue. It results in a communication gap, and, as a consequence, treatment errors. Because the dominant culture is one of persons with a single sense of self, most with multiple "selves" have learned to hide their multiplicity and imitate those who are singletons (that is, have a single, non-fragmented personality). Therapists who do not understand this sometimes describe their clients' alters without acknowledging their dissociation, saying only that they have different "moods." In overlooking dissociation, this description fails to recognize the essential truth of such disorders, and of the alters.

It was difficult for me to comprehend what life was like for my first few dissociative clients. I had experienced mood states in my own life, especially during my teens, but through introspection, I could eventually identify the needs they represented and make sure I met those needs. I had also experienced the usual teenage identity confusion of struggling to figure out what kind of a self could encompass all aspects of me, but, still, I had always had a strong adult self. I had never "lost time," never heard voices, and never experienced myself as being more than one person. I knew what I was doing at all times and had a relatively consistent set of skills and behaviors. In short, my daily experience of life was light years away from that of my dissociative clients.

Fortunately, my clients could teach me about their culture of multiplicity.

Those who are aware of their condition and experience themselves as "multiple" might refer to themselves as "we" rather than "I." I shall use the term "multiple" at times, in respect for their internal experience. It is important to point out, however, that I recognize that someone who is multiple is actually a single fragmented person rather than many people. On the outside, a multiple is probably not visibly different from anyone else. But that image is only an imitation: people who are multiple cannot think like the rest of us, and we cannot think like them. (In fact, since it is difficult for the multiple to understand how singletons think, some of them might think it is *you* who are strange.)

Just as a singleton cannot become a multiple at will, a multiple cannot become a singleton, until and unless the barriers between the parts of the self are removed. Those barriers were put up to enable the child to tolerate, and so survive, unavoidable abuse.

In addition to pursuing educational resources, ask the person you are working with to be your teacher about being multiple. Those who are aware of their condition are usually glad to be asked. It can be very lonely to not be understood by other people. Once you start meeting the insiders, you might find that the child personalities in adult bodies feel nobody else "gets" them or recognizes their existence. It is also important for you to know that they generally prefer to be talked to as the age they feel they are rather than the age the body is. However, you must be careful with recognizing and addressing them, because, like all of us, child alters are all different: some are shy and some are outgoing; some like attention and others hate it. And some inner systems are very afraid of being known.

Be careful not to treat the person you are working with as a curiosity. Perhaps you do not have a point of reference for this, but I remember how embarrassed I felt on my first night as a student in India, when, as I changed for bed in a university residence, a crowd gathered to stare at me and see whether I was the same color all over. I did not like having to perform (for me, it was singing English popular songs) for other students in India while they all giggled and talked about how cute I was. Multiples do not like having to "perform" (for example, let child alters come out) for the entertainment of singletons. Their human dignity is no less important than anyone else's.

When being multiple is someone's normal state of mind, it may be seen as normal for everyone else, too. I have met several multiples who just assume that everyone else "loses" periods of time (when another alter personality is in charge of the body), finds themselves in places without knowing how they got there, and/or hears voices inside their head. These are typical experiences for them.

Multiplicity is called a "disorder", but has served the person as a valuable, creative asset. It is not an inferior way of being. We who are singletons are well adapted for living in safety, being conscious of everything that happens to us. Being multiple is well-adapted for living with ongoing trauma. I once heard a prison psychologist say he would not treat multiples, because prison is so traumatic that you needed to be multiple to survive well.

Even in "normal" life, there are sometimes advantages to being multiple, because in some cases it permits heightened abilities. I knew a multiple whose alter, "Brain," memorized all her textbooks and was able to remember everything on exams word for word. I knew another who had alters with all kinds of special savant abilities. Without the distractions of emotions, everyday life, and other thoughts, an alter with a singular focus can sometimes do amazing things.

Here is a final point to remember: just as you should not assume that someone from another culture should want to join your culture and give up his or her own, do not assume that every multiple wants to become a singleton. Some do, some do not. Many well-adapted multiples, whose alter personalities are extremely cooperative, prefer to stay as a community of coordinated selves rather than seeking to achieve the therapeutic goal of "integration".

As you can see, understanding your clients who are multiple demands a cultural sensitivity not different from that which many of you might have employed when working with clients from other ethnic groups.

The "apparently normal personality"—the alter you view as "the client"

You should not assume that the adult who functions in the world, or who presents to you, week after week, is the "real" person, and the other personalities are less real. The client who comes to therapy is not "the" person; there are other personalities to meet and work with.

When DID was still officially called MPD, the "person" who lived life on the outside was known as the "host" personality, and the *other* parts known as alters. These terms, unfortunately, implied that all the parts other than the host were guests, and therefore of less importance than the host. They were somehow secondary. The currently favored theory of structural dissociation (Nijenhuis & Den Boer, 2009; van der Hart, Nijenhuis, & Steele, 2006), which more accurately describes the way personality systems operate, instead distinguishes between two kinds of states: the apparently normal personality, or *ANP*, and the emotional personality, or *EP*, both of which could include a number of parts. As Barlow and Freyd (2009) describe the distinction,

> EPs hold traumatic memory, often being stuck in the sensory experience of the memory and unaware of the passage of time. ANPs, in contrast, manage the tasks of daily life, such as working,

and the functions of attachment and caretaking. They may be emotionally unconnected to, or amnesic for, past traumatic events. [p. 101]

A child who is being abused on an ongoing basis needs to be able to function despite the trauma that dominates his or her daily life. That becomes the job of at least one ANP, whom the child creates to be unaware of the abuse and also of the multiplicity, and to "pass as normal" in the real world. The ANP is just an alter specialized for handling the adult world—in other words, the "front person" for the system.

Even therapists who are experienced at working with multiples often struggle with this, making statements such as, "Is this Jane, or one of the alters?" This is very irritating to dissociative systems who are aware of their multiplicity, and confusing to those who are not, especially if it happens not to be Jane who is "out."

Because of their countertransference with the ANP as the client, many therapists are also resistant to the fact that working to strengthen the main presenting personality might help, but is not primary, and generally will achieve only superficial improvements. Inside is where the work occurs.

ANPs, themselves, often have a great deal of difficulty accepting that they are multiple. The words "personalities" or "alters" may frighten them. In the old view of "hosts" and "alternates", "the client" has this difficulty. In reality, whether the person acknowledges that he or she is multiple at any given time depends on who is "out," or in conscious control of the body, and on how much contact the ANP has with the "inside world."

It is common that in early stages of therapy or of recovery, the ANP knows very little about the other alters. This is one reason to be careful to avoid another common mistake, one which I have made: being too blunt early in therapy with the ANP about his or her role. Having worked with many multiples who are well aware of their condition, I forget what a shock it is to receive the initial diagnosis. "What do you mean, I'm only an alter?" I rush to reassure them that they are a very specialized and important alter, perhaps the only one who can handle the adult world successfully. But that does not erase the shock.

In fact, rather than being "more" than the others, the ANP is generally one that is very limited, with little power in the system, little memory of what happened, and limited energy or emotions. Many ANPs are what used to be called "depleted hosts," alters who have very little energy or strength and are chronically depressed. Although the job of handling everyday adult life is important, some alters who attempt this are too porous to be effective in the world. Two of my long-term dissociative clients chose to replace their outside personalities with other alters who were less permeable to the emotional states of the other parts. (Yes, that is a choice that multiples can make.) In both cases the change made them much more functional.

It is unlikely that one ANP will serve as a constant throughout the person's life. Your client is, therefore, likely to have others besides the one you know, or several who you might think of as "the host". Adults with dissociative disorders often have several ANPs from earlier stages of life inside. They usually have the same name but are of different ages. Sometimes, there are several current ANPs, each of whom assumes she or he is the "real" person and is amnesic of the existence of the others. Their current knowledge and experience may overlap, while their other characteristics differ somewhat. This makes them glide easily from one to the other, and the therapist can easily miss the switch.

One client of mine has four ANPs by the same name who alternate with one another and with some teenage parts at the workplace. One of them is severely depressed and suicidal, another is just a functionary who does her job, another loves music and art and nature, and another is an investigator who wants to know what has gone on in her life to create her symptoms. What they all have in common is their ignorance about the abuse the client suffered and their ability to function somewhat in the adult world. They are not unemotional, although they do not necessarily know the sources of those emotions or recall what they relate to. Emotions from the inside parts leak into the suicidal one more than into the others.

The ANP is almost never the original person, especially in those with extensive abuse histories. You might say that the "original" is an untraumatized child, infant, or even fetus from whom the first split was made. (Two of my clients who integrated fully, and another integrated DID, found such an infant and incorporated all the life experiences of the other alters into that infant, who gradually grew older.) Or you could say that all parts are parts of the original person: some people believe that infants and babies do not have an integrated self, but are a collection of emotional and bodily states whose selfhood is knitted together by the attachment to, and reflection of, a loving caregiver. Many multiples never have this experience, so remain disintegrated.

In one of my clients, the primary ANP had integrated with other parts, and the whole multiplex system went by the body's name, but no alter had that name. In my experience, the only multiples in whom there is one strong ANP are those who were abused or traumatized for only a brief period of time, usually outside the home. Their long period of safety allows them to build a strong "outside world" personality. However, they still have hidden split-off parts who come out only occasionally, or never come out but influence the person's behavior and feelings from time to time. My client who has only three alter personalities besides the ANP was unaware of her multiplicity until she encountered a work-related trauma at age sixty. She became symptomatic as the hidden parts emerged to deal with the recent trauma. Her ANP was very strong until that trauma awakened the emotional states from the original child abuse. At that point, these emotions leaked into the ANP from the other alters. The youngest alter is probably the original person from whom the others were split. Three of her four parts were originally ANPs during her childhood and teens.

In DDNOS, ANPs are merely shells through which the other alters are manifested without overt switching. This makes the multiplicity of your client much less obvious, and supports the fact that you need to be capable of assessing and diagnosing the dissociative disorder properly. I recently consulted to a therapist who felt he had accomplished something by getting his dissociative client to remain in her ANP throughout her sessions with him. His view reflects the fundamental mistake that untrained therapists tend to make with DID and DDNOS. Although his client was properly diagnosed, he assumed that the ANP should be encouraged to take charge of the other parts at all times. He also expected her to speak for them—in other words, to do their therapy. This denied the other parts the opportunity to reveal their secrets, heal their pain, or correct their childhood-based beliefs about the world.

If you were doing family therapy, would it be a good idea to only meet with the father, especially if he had not talked with his children or his spouse in years? Would the other family members feel as if their experiences and feelings mattered? Would they be able to improve their relationships? You must work with the parts who are *inside* of the system. Directly.

What daily life is like for "a multiple"

Imagine that you have periods of "lost time." You may find writings or drawings which you must have done, but do not remember producing. Perhaps you find child-sized clothing or toys in your home but have no children. You might also hear voices or babies crying in your head. Imagine that you can never predict when you will be able to have certain knowledge or social skills, and your emotions and your energy level seem to change at the drop of a hat, and for no apparent reason. You cannot understand why you feel what you feel, and, if you are in therapy, you cannot explore those feelings when asked. Your life feels disjointed and often confusing. It is a frightening experience. It feels out of control, and you probably think you are going crazy. That is what it is like to be multiple, and all of it is experienced by the ANPs.

A multiple may also experience very concrete problems, even life-threatening ones. My client whose multiplicity emerged at the age of sixty came home from a meeting to find that an alter had begun to cook something and then left the pot on the stove, almost burning her house down. ANPs and EPs alike may struggle with the serious consequences of this complication.

Your client will probably not know what is responsible for these experiences, and might well have sought help from many therapists who did not know, either.

The following is a categorization of what an ANP might experience.

Amnesia

Amnesia is a major distinguishing characteristic of multiples who are DID, but not of those who are DDNOS. Most people with DID experience periods of amnesia, although they may not know it. Some alters are able to watch all of current life, so are aware of what happens; others, including most ANPs, are very unaware of what has happened while they are not "out" in the body. Some basic indicators of amnesia for persons with ritual abuse and mind control histories include discovering that you have a cut, burn, or bruises with no memory of how it happened.

When one client's brother visited, and talked incessantly in foul language, her oldest "insider" decided to tell him off. The next morning he told his little sister, "You give as good as you get; I didn't know you had it in you." She had no idea what she had said to him. I had to get the story from the alter and tell her. This protector alter was able to observe while the main person was interacting with the brother, but the main person was not able to observe when the other alter was out. It is common that other alters generally observe, although the ANP is unaware of it.

Some dissociative people dissimulate to cover for their periods of amnesia. Imagine what it must be like to experience your own life as if it were a television series, only you do not appear in many of the episodes, and you have no idea what happens in them. (Imagine never being able to recall what happened from one therapy session to the next.)

Sometimes, things happen which the ANP would never have done. One forty-year-old married woman I worked with years ago discovered her multiplicity when a teenage alter developed an online romance with a young man in another part of the continent. Believing herself to be a teenager, she made arrangements to fly to his city to meet him. Another client was caught on a store video pocketing an item without paying for it, an act that was entirely out of character for her. (In her case, it appeared to be a brief stress-related dissociative episode rather than an ongoing dissociative disorder.)

Voices and visions

Hearing voices is another of the most important parts of the experience for most multiples. The voices, of course, are usually the other alters. Those multiples who do not understand their condition frequently seek out help from churches, who perform exorcisms, or from mental health facilities, who diagnose psychosis, medicating heavily and inappropriately. Many therapists believe that these voices are distinguished from the voices of schizophrenia by the fact that they are experienced as coming from inside the head. But this is not always the case. One of my first DID clients, diagnosed with schizophrenia, heard the alters' voices coming out of his television set. I asked one of the main alters why this happened. "If we talk inside his head, he thinks we're demons and doesn't listen to us. But he believes everything he hears or sees on TV." Lesson to learn: there are as many ways to be multiple as there are multiples.

The voices may sound to the ANP like background noise in a crowded place, or they may stand out individually. In some cases, they are just experienced as thoughts rather than heard as voices, but they still feel alien to the person experiencing them, and contribute to the person feeling he or she is going crazy. They may be strong thoughts that come "out of nowhere" and do not really seem to belong to the person. "Thought-snatching," having one's thoughts disappear as inside parts take them away, is also common.

Some voices may cry or give orders or call the ANP names. They may be helpful or reassuring, coming from inner self-helpers. However, their reassurance might or might not be based on facts. Often the voices are critical. Everyone has an "inner critic," of course, but the inner critics of multiples are generally very unpleasant, and are internally audible to the person who is trying to accomplish things or carry on a conversation. No matter what one of my clients does, he hears some inside complainers complaining about it, usually in foul language. He used to speak to them out loud, and nastily. He appeared psychotic. He has now learnt to think to them, and, since he realizes they are small child alters, to reassure them and tell them he loves them. As a result, they are more cooperative, but they still complain in the only kind of language they know, the language they heard at home while attempting to grow up. You will notice that some voices often tell the person to shut up or be quiet, call him or her a liar, and say that certain events never happened. Others may suggest self-harm or suicide. These are all persecutor/ protector alters, which we shall discuss in detail later. They are common in mind-controlled personality systems, where they are supposed to say these things to make sure the secrets of the abuse do not leak out. They often engage in more severe reprisals if they are not heeded.

It is common for multiples to hear the sound of infants or small children crying. Abusers often punish children severely for crying (suffocation is the treatment of choice for many cult children being trained not to cry), so the crying goes "inside." An alter who never comes out into the world holds the tears and the crying sound.

Many multiples not only hear, but also see their alters. They might be afraid of alters who resemble their perpetrators, or demons or monsters or animals. They might be afraid to go near alters who appear hurt or dirty or in the conditions in which they were abused. (They also might see their alters' faces in mirrors, which is part of why they often avoid mirrors.)

Sometimes, the voices being heard are not the other alters, but parts of traumatic memories being played back, for example, the voice of an abuser telling the child not to talk about what had happened on pain of death. This is particularly true with mind-control survivors.

Above all, remember that these voices are *communicating*. Some of your clients understand their condition and have developed effective inner communication. It is important to allow periods of silence in your conversations with them, so that they may consult internally when they hear something or when there is a problem. When they communicate in a way the ANP cannot understand, it is your job to facilitate.

There are some multiples who do not hear voices at all, even when they try to. That is the experience of my client with only three alters. It is difficult for the ANP to communicate with the alters, because they are unable to hear one another, and have to write in a book or talk via me.

Depersonalization and derealization

Depersonalization and derealization are dissociative problems that can exist independently or be part of a more major dissociative disorder. They can make the person feel as if he or she is no longer himself or herself, or feel that familiar places are strange. When alters first appear, the person may have the experience of watching themselves doing things they have no control over, such as harming the body. Another alter is actually "out" and is doing it, and the usual "host" is relegated to a "back seat." This situation can make the world feel unreal to the person who isn't fully present. It can be quite frightening. Imagine how out of control it must feel, as well.

Intrusions of traumatic material

Dissociation protects against overwhelming trauma. When the dissociation is reduced, the post-traumatic intrusive symptoms—flashbacks and nightmares of trauma—can be expected to increase. These may be visual, auditory, or tactile (including physical or emotional pain). Small things in the present environment could trigger flashbacks and feelings of overwhelm and an inability to cope. Intrusions are more common than we generally realize: depression, anxiety, panic attacks, obsessions and compulsions are often emotional intrusions from past traumatic memories that are not recognized as such.

In mind-controlled multiples, these flashbacks should not automatically be treated as spontaneous eruptions of dissociated material, however; they might also be deliberately administered by trained alters in response to behaviors disobedient to the perpetrators, especially telling about the abuse.

Different alters, different awarenesses

While the ANP generally has continuity of memory for most of his or her current life, and hears only some of the alters as voices or thoughts, the other parts often have much more awareness of the personality system. In the first place, unlike the ANP, they are likely to recognize that they are part of a "personality system". They may use the first person plural ("we") when referring to that system.

When someone who is multiple has been in treatment for the dissociative disorder for some time, the ANP may gain some degree of similar awareness, and may then be able to talk with insiders. In many or most cases, however, the ANP does not naturally "go inside" to interact with other parts, but simply "blanks out" while another alter takes over, while the wall of dissociation is maintained between them. It is essential for the therapist to teach the ANP to communicate with the other alters, if the ANP lacks this skill or habit. A lifelong habit of looking outward, and not speaking with the voices, is difficult to overcome. I find it helpful to frequently ask the ANPs of my multiple clients to "ask inside" when they want to know something about, for example, the source of a symptom they are experiencing.

The ANP is generally oriented to time and place, but many of the other alters might not be. They generally believe it is still the year and place where their abuse happened, and they interpret all current events in terms of the experience of that time and place.

Although all the selves of a multiple are really wounded parts of one person, in most cases they experience themselves and one another as separate people. They are just as real to themselves as people on the outside. They might actually see the other selves in locations in the inner world. It is when they are aware of the existence of other selves that they feel multiple. In addition, when mind control has been involved, some of the selves might believe things about their identities and purposes which were deliberately taught to them by their abusers.

However, all the alters are very limited, not just the ANP. The parts or selves feel themselves to be complete persons, but each tends to have a specific function and an unambiguous emotional state. And they are all specialists in only their own particular emotional positions. In those ways, most of them are one-dimensional. Alters have separate and different memories, feelings, and approaches to life, and a sense of separate identity and agency. They do not necessarily know what the other alters do or think. Many alters feel hollow, depersonalized, or uncertain of their identity, precisely because they *are* just part of a whole. It is together that they form a complete person.

Switching

Imagine there are a number of identical brothers or sisters who impersonate one another. You do not know when they change places, perhaps because they can do this so fast that you can not detect it, and you may talk to many different ones within one conversation. However, if you know them as individuals, you learn to recognize them not by their physical appearance but by their characteristic moods, tones of voice, facial expressions, and other body language. It is the same with alter personalities of multiples. They generally look the same, but they might act differently. You might also see physical evidence of them changing places, in overt behaviors such as eye movements, body tremors, losing track of conversation, or in other, more subtle signs, such as shifts in mood. This is what you see when you see a person with overt dissociative identity disorder.

Most multiples, however, do not show dramatic physical symptoms of switching. The larger the number of alters, the less detectable will be the switches. My client with only three alter personalities switches very visibly: she becomes sleepy, her eyes roll, and then after a few seconds one of the younger parts comes "out" into the body. There is a similar visual switching process when the part goes back inside. The ANP emerges with no memory of what just happened, but with some physical symptoms attributable to the alter, such as a dry mouth or a sore throat (belonging to an alter who had chronic tonsillitis in childhood).

Since alters in a DID system change places often, you should not assume that the person you are talking to remembers what the body has seen, heard, done, or said, even five minutes ago. Switching can be problematic even for those with DDNOS. The shell alter bridges the transitions smoothly so that the individual does not appear multiple at all. When an ANP is a shell, his or her awareness or behavior varies according to which other alters are conscious at any given time. One long-term client of mine, who had a shell ANP, used to switch constantly just behind the surface. A conversation with him was about ten conversations at the same time. He would switch in mid-sentence, and raise a completely different topic, then resume the original topic when the alter who began that topic re-emerged. It took him a long time to gain control over the switching and train his alters to take their turns, and he was unable to accomplish this until his personality system chose a different alter to be "out front" than the one who was originally there, one who had more ego strength and was less permeable to the others inside.

Multiples and responsibility

Remember not to assume that the ANP is able to control the behavior of the alters if she or he only "takes responsibility". If the ANP of a multiple tells you that someone inside wants to kill her, for example, she is telling you that she does not have control over it, and instructing her to take control will not help. You will need to work with the alters involved.

Alter personalities hold memories only of the parts of the person's life that they, as alters, have actually *lived*. Sometimes, to repeat a point, when an inappropriate behavior happens, the ANP just does not know about it, and is only aware of lost time, or is aware but unable to control it. An alter cannot be held responsible for events they truly do not remember or had no control over at the time. I once treated a ten-year-old girl who had just one alter personality in addition to the host, a three-year-old with the same name as her. When she got bored in school, the ten-year-old would "go inside" her head, and the three-year-old would come out into the body and behave like a three-year-old, which was inappropriate for the classroom. The ten-year-old would then find herself in the school office in trouble with the principal, without any idea of what had happened. While the whole person could be said to be responsible for the behavior, the ten-year-old was not, and the three-year-old was too young to realize what was wrong with her behavior.

In order to deal with issues of responsibility, find and talk with the alter who is actually responsible—either the one who performed the behavior, or another alter who made him or her do it. Remember to be gentle even with the alter who is responsible. Generally, multiples have been abused emotionally as well as physically and sexually, and are very sensitive to blame. The whole story of alters' lives in the outside world is of being held responsible for things they do not remember doing. They get accused of lying and of manipulating. They might, at times, lie and manipulate, especially when parts are out who are very young or who do not have access to certain parts of the brain; for example, they cannot feel pain or cannot feel guilt. But much of the time they just do not know what happened. The alters have learnt to do this because of living with severe punishment. It takes experience in a safe world to learn more direct and honest strategies for having one's needs met.

Identifying ritual abuse and mind control survivors

Once you recognize that you have a client with a major dissociative disorder, you need to determine whether he or she also has a history of ritual abuse or mind control. This may be a controversial perspective, but there is considerable evidence to support it. Here are some statistics provided by Dr Catherine Gould in 1995:

> Among 2,709 members of the American Psychological Association who responded to a poll, 2,292 cases of ritual abuse were reported (Bottoms, Shaver, & Goodman, 1993). In 1992 alone, Childhelp USA logged 1,741 calls pertaining to ritual abuse, Monarch Resources of Los Angeles logged approximately 5,000, Real Active Survivors tallied nearly 3,600, Justus Unlimited of Colorado received almost 7,000, and Looking Up of Maine handled around 6,000. Even allowing for some of these calls to have been made by people who assist survivors but are not themselves survivors, and for some survivors to have called more than one helpline or made multiple calls to the same helpline, these numbers suggest that at a minimum there must be tens of thousands of survivors of ritual abuse in the United States.

Unfortunately, no similar research has been conducted since the "memory wars" of the 1990s. However, the online Extreme Abuse Survey (Rutz, Becker, Overkamp, & Karriker, 2008), with 1471 respondents reporting extreme child abuse, found the majority had endured either ritual abuse or mind control or both. Californian psychologist Randy Noblitt, who specializes in ritual abuse, believes that there are no people with dissociative disorders who have not experienced ritual abuse or mind control. I would not go that far. On the other hand, I am suspicious when a therapist states that he or she has seen many dissociative clients and has never encountered a survivor of these atrocities.

It is possible for a therapist to work right through a dissociative client's non-mind-control memories without touching the parts of the personality system who have experienced ritual abuse or mind control. Jane Wakefield, a psychologist who has worked extensively with survivors of military/political mind control, is convinced that many ritual abuse survivors have also experienced these other kinds of mind control, but their therapists do not access the parts of their personality systems who have these memories. In the Extreme Abuse Survey, of 987 self-identified survivors of extreme child abuse, 19% stated they experienced ritual abuse, 7% stated they experienced mind control, and 52% stated they experienced both ritual abuse and mind control. Twenty-two percent stated they had experienced neither. The definition of mind control used there was: "MC refers to all mind control procedures designed to make a victim follow directives of the programmer without conscious awareness including, but not limited to, government-sponsored mind control experiments."

Ritually abusive cults deliberately divide the personality system down the middle of the head, making sure that there is no communication between the two sides. (This may not be a literal physiological fact, since alters are contained in brain circuitry rather than specific sites in the brain, but it is a belief system common to ritual abusers and their victims, and has real treatment ramifications.) "Left side" alters might be instructed to speak to no one other than the perpetrators. Although emotions may leak out from these alters, the person could go through years of therapy without the therapist ever suspecting that they exist. In ritually abused personality systems, there is often also mind control of other types, and the alters belonging to these events may be segregated in some way. One client of mine has Ku Klux Klan alters hidden "beneath the ground" in her inner world.

If you do not diagnose and treat ritual abuse and/or mind control when it is present, your survivor client will remain unhealed.

Indicator lists

There are standardized assessment tools and guidelines for diagnosing DID. However, there is nothing comparable as yet for diagnosing ritual abuse (RA) and mind control (MC). Since the beginning of the current therapeutic focus on incest recovery, therapists and survivors have been developing checklists of characteristics of such a history, one purpose of which has been to assist in assessing for such trauma. In part, these have arisen from the fact that incest frequently results in a hidden, or, as Denise Galinas has called it, a disguised presentation. (Blume's "Incest survivors aftereffects checklist" (ISAC), found in her book, *Secret Survivors: Uncovering Incest and its Aftereffects in Women*, is one of the most well known of such lists.) Similar checklists have been developed regarding the sub-group of survivors who have experienced RA/MC.

One early handout by Californian psychologist Pamela Reagor includes the following indicators for a child/adolescent history of ritualistic abuse, without apparent cult contact in adulthood: diagnosis of MPD or DDNOS; poor or problematic response to competent treatment for MPD/DDNOS; drawings characterized by ritual-like features, for example, lots of red and black, knives, fire, cages, robes, body parts, blood, etc.; notable preoccupation with, or avoidance of, newscasts, magazine articles, conversation, etc. about ritual abuse; involvement with, or manipulation by, other ritual abuse survivors, or reports by other survivors that that person "responds to triggers," and a pattern of decompensation and/or hospitalization during, for example, Satanic ritual holiday periods.

Ellen Lacter provides a current, and comprehensive, list of indicators on her website, (www.endritualabuse.org). Lacter's list for adult survivors of ritual abuse has forty-three items. Some that resonate with my experience of ritual abuse survivors include:

- history of significant self-mutilation, particularly cuts in patterns, shapes, or letters, and genital self-harm or introduction of sharp objects into genitalia;
- fears, phobias, and nightmares associated with religion; health care; bodily fluids and excretions; weapons; birthdays and weddings; police, jails, and cages; baths and drowning; insects, snakes, spiders, and rats; cameras and being photographed; specific colors or shapes; sexual perversion, intrusive thoughts or impulses, especially sado-masochism, pedophilia, zoophilia.

Critics associated with the "false memory syndrome" movement of the 1990s have attempted to discredit such indicator lists. The criticisms levied against Blume's checklist are typical. For one thing, it is said that individual items on the Incest Survivors Aftereffects Checklist (ISAC) can be explained by a variety of experiences that are not the subject of the list. When we apply this to Reagor's indicators, we can see easily that not all people diagnosed with DID or DDNOS have experienced ritual trauma, even if they have a poor response to competent treatment. Drawings with ritual-like features might indicate an obsession with rock bands. Preoccupation with media portrayals of ritual abuse could indicate a "wannabe," and avoidance could indicate a sensitive soul. Decompensation around birthdays or holidays might indicate a family history of alcoholism, with drunken violence at those times. However, what might account for someone responding to mind control triggers? Or patterned self-mutilation (from Lacter's list), or a combination of all the phobias listed by Lacter?

Further, critics suggest that list originators, or therapists, conclude that if someone has one or just a few of the indicators on the lists, they must be survivors of the alleged abuse. This argument, too, is invalid, and misrepresents such lists. The ISAC, for instance, states in several places that incest should only be suspected when one has the majority of items on the list. Items in these checklists, like those on symptom lists for cancer or other diseases diagnosed by physicians, are not intended as individual indicators. Once again referencing the above example of Reagor's list, in medicine the same symptom might be indicative of a number of different conditions, some serious and some benign. It is the configuration and pattern of the symptoms that makes a difference. We see that when all the items of Reagor's list are taken together, they accurately present a profile that can alert the clinician to the possibility of a ritual abuse history. Lacter states at the start of her list, "Remember, indicator lists only provide common associated signs. Most survivors will have many indicators. The presence of indicators does not prove the existence of ritual trauma. The absence does not mean a person has no such trauma."

Dr Catherine Gould issued a comprehensive four-page long, single-spaced, small type "Signs and symptoms of ritual abuse in children" in 1988. It included problems associated with such ordinary activities as toileting and the bathroom, certain colors, eating, family relationships, play and peer relations, the doctor's office, religion and the supernatural, and sexual behavior and beliefs, as well as emotional problems including speech, sleep, and learning problems. Although these particular items could arise from many causes, Gould's list also included a number that are very specific, some of which are very suspicious for sexual abuse, and others for abuse that is specifically associated with rituals. Examples include:

- child sings odd, ritualistic songs or chants, sometimes in a language incomprehensible to the parent; sings songs with a sexual, bizarre, or "you better not tell" theme;
- child shuts pets or other children in closets, or otherwise attempts to entrap or confine them;
- child expresses fears of being tied (usually by one leg) and hung upside down;
- child states that (s)he is "practicing" to be dead, or is dead;
- child is excessively fearful of blood tests; asks if (s)he will die from blood tests or whether someone will drink the blood;.
- child refuses to ingest foods or drinks because they are red or brown (e.g., red drinks, meat); becomes agitated at meal times;

- child talks about "my other mommy", "my other daddy", or "my other family" (in the cult);
- child expresses fears that a sibling or pet will be killed, kidnapped, molested;
- child acts out death, mutilation, cannibalism, and burial themes by pretending to kill play figures, taking out eyes, pulling off heads and limbs, pretending to eat the figures or drink their blood, and burying them;
- child fears the police will come and put him/her in jail, or states that a "bad policeman" hurt or threatened him/her;
- child believes or fears there is something foreign inside her chest or stomach, for example, Satan's heart, a demon or monster, a bomb, etc.

The beliefs and behaviors in Dr Gould's list are sufficiently odd to require an explanation other than a child's imagination.

Most of the items in all the lists discussed so far are more likely to indicate cult abuse than other forms of mind control. Lacter also has a list of indicators of trauma-based mind control programming. Many of the indicators on this list can apply to ritual abuse as well as to other forms of mind control: for example, severe flinching or spasms (as if being electroshocked) when approaching trauma material. Electroshock appears to be a punishment of choice by all kinds of mind-controlling groups, as it leaves few visible marks.

One item that is not on these lists concerns spinning. If the client frequently feels vertigo or a sensation of spinning (often along with nausea), and/or if the client draws spiral shapes, that can be an indicator of abuse that involves spinning, something that is common in both ritual abuse and other kinds of mind control. (See Chapter Four, "Markers of mind control and ritual abuse".)

Like the extensive list of indicators of borderline personality disorder in the *DSM*, these behavioral and emotional checklists draw attention to symptoms, without stating that a particular abuse or syndrome *necessarily* exists in a client who merely demonstrates some of those indicators. They are designed to raise our index of suspicion for conditions or histories that we might otherwise overlook, while assuming that we know that one of the cardinal rules of good therapy is never to suggest (rather than ask, as part of a required history taking) to a client what might or might not have happened to him or her. They can be very helpful with ritual abuse and mind control survivors, especially; as hidden as an incest history might be because of inherent psychological and literal threats to survivors, mind control and ritual abuse are hidden by design.

The important thing for you as a therapist is to have your eyes open to the possibility that your client has had such experiences. At one time, a friend of mine who works for a government agency dealing with youth sent me a young woman with DID. She had worked extensively with this client, who had aged-out from her service. She stated specifically that the client had never experienced any ritual abuse. Then she sent me the client's artwork. It was filled with words like "Satan" and "Kill," as well as drawings of sacrifices, red drops of blood, and so forth. Sure enough, when I inquired of the client, she disclosed that this abuse had indeed occurred. The previous therapist had somehow missed the obvious clues. What you do not look for, you will not see.

This is not to say that everything that looks like a clue should be accepted at face value. For instance, with artwork, images may be symbolic. But when images such as these are drawn by child alters, it is my opinion that they are more likely to be literal. Children do not engage in symbolic imagery as much as adults; they are concrete thinkers. At one time, I had two clients who reported "seeing" a little girl alone in a room, covered with blood. The one client knew it was a memory; the other stated that it was symbolic. The one who believed it to be symbolic later discovered that it was literal, when the rest of the memory emerged.

So what do you do if a client is exhibiting signs of a ritual abuse or mind control history, but has not disclosed such events? You take your time. You inquire gently about the artwork or the other symptoms, and wait for alters to emerge who will tell you more. You do not make suggestions about what might have happened. This is important even if you believe the client is obviously a survivor of these things. Remain calm. It is important to convey to the client that you can handle whatever they disclose, without suggesting what they might disclose.

The key in every case is getting to know the alters and developing a trusting relationship with them. The alters are the key to finding out about the trauma, to finding out about present safety, and to healing.

What do you do if a new client starts exhibiting some out-of-control or therapy-sabotaging behaviors before you have had a chance to establish a relationship with anyone inside? Set boundaries gently but firmly about the therapeutic relationship, and bring in any other resources that might be needed. Then, slow down. Do not make inquiries about the traumatic history until the person is sufficiently stabilized and trust has been regained.

Kinds of alter personalities generally found in ritually abused and mind-controlled persons

Shell ANPs

In her online book, *Svali First Series: How the Illuminati Programs People*, former Illuminati programmer Svali calls the deliberate creation of shell ANPs "shell programming," which is designed to hide the person's multiplicity from the outside world. She describes how it works:

> It is important to realize that what the system is actually doing is co-presenting, although not co-consciously. For a shell program to work, the shell alters have been taught to allow co-presentation with the other alters in the systems. Other alters in the back may not always be aware that this is what is happening, and the front shell especially will not know that they are being "gone through" for co-presentation . . . Allowing both the shell alters and the other alters to recognize that this is how they have been presenting, and why, will be an important step. Back alters may then begin presenting without going through the shell, *and the person may look "more multiple" than they ever have for a period, with accents or young ones coming through. What is actually happening is that the back is presenting without masking who they are through the shell.* [my italics]

One ritual mind control survivor multiple with a shell ANP described herself to me as having someone like a plastic lens in the front, with four chairs just behind it, and different people occupying those chairs at different times. She described the experience of "seeing" one of her alters get up and walk out of the room during a meeting. Trish Fotheringham's account of her system in Chapter Six exemplifies this structure; she was designed to have four alters "onstage" at any given time.

Child alters

In systems created by mind-controlling child abusers, many, usually a majority, of alters feel themselves to be children or teenagers. There may be some who are too young to talk or to understand language, or who can only speak a language that has not been spoken since childhood. I believe that the child parts of any multiple split off during childhood, not later, remain developmentally children. (This may be difficult for you as the therapist to remember when many of them speak in an adult way and sound like your adult client.) They are not "normal" children, however. They are alters with a job to do. In general, one may say that there are "happy" ones who tend to deny negative reality and get themselves into abusive situations, as well as "unhappy" ones who hold strong emotions such as fear and anger.

Child alters believe themselves still to be children. They are often concrete and literal in their thought processes and awkward with their bodies. One of my clients, an adult woman, sat on the floor and put out her feet for me to tie her shoes, assuming she was in preschool. I have been in session with an adult man when he stood on his head on his couch, because the child that he "was" at that moment preferred that position. I have met with adults whose "out" personalities knew no English, but spoke languages the host had learnt in early childhood and then forgotten. And one client fell down my office stairs because a baby alter who did not know how to walk came out at the top of the stairs.

These alters might hold superstitious childish beliefs, communicated to them by abusers during the person's actual childhood. They believe things they were told under extremely traumatic conditions, and cannot readily grasp present-day reality. They will often echo the words of their adult abusers, and since the ANP (and you) cannot actually see them, will appear older than they are.

I frequently have to remind my client with the foul-mouthed critical alters to ask them their ages. There is a pause while he asks internally, then, "Oh." The one who believes her to be his abusive mother (i.e., his father's sexual partner) is four. She understands things like a four-year-old, but she swears like an old pro.

Some therapists who work with dissociative disorders believe that child alters are actually adults' conceptions of what children are like, rather than actual children. I do not believe this. I do believe that a part who says he or she is older than the body is not really older, but rather is a child's, or a young adult's, conception of an older person. And an opposite-sex alter (a male in a female body, for instance) is more like a young girl's idea of what a boy is like than like a "real" boy. Boys in women's bodies usually represent the part of the person who has traits that are traditionally considered masculine, such as bravery or anger; girls in men's bodies often have supposedly "feminine" traits such as fearfulness.

Alters who see themselves as different from the body

In addition to gender and age differences, alters may see themselves in many ways that are not "real". Some are "copy" alters (introjects) who believe they are someone else entirely, for example, a relative or an abuser. Some experience themselves as blind or deaf or mute, often as a result of a literal response to their abusers ("Don't talk about this," or "You didn't see anything.") I take particular delight in letting them know that they can recover their sight or hearing or ability to speak once we have worked through the memories that made them become handicapped. Some alters might report that certain other alters are dead. This usually indicates that those alters either have been hidden from the rest of the system, or they are caught in a memory of a trauma in which they felt they were being killed. Since the person's brain is still alive, they are not really dead. Their feelings still leak through to other alters. They can be revived.

Often a child who has been shamed, verbally abused, and told they are evil, or made to do evil things by an abuser, can believe itself to be a demon. Some perpetrator groups actually tell child alters they are demons or devils or ghosts. Trying to exorcise "demon" parts of a person will only hinder their progress. (This will be addressed in more detail in Chapter Nine.) They need to be cared for like any child, and the responsibility for their abuse given back to the abusers rather than to any part of the child.

In any case, it is not worth arguing with alters about whether or not they really are what they believe they are. It is more important to treat the whole person with respect, in whatever aspect she presents herself, and to develop real empathy for the life experiences and world view of each part. Do not deny the experience of any alter. They genuinely believe they are the person's mother, or a person of the opposite sex, or a dog. Your client had very important reasons for making alters the way they are. For example, an alter may be a boy because boys do not have vaginas so he cannot be vaginally raped, as your female client was. Or a "mother" alter in a male survivor client might be the one who was forced to have sex with the boy's father.

As you will see later in this book, alters arising from these abuses were often deliberately deceived into believing they are something they are not. In some cases, it is a relief to them to discover that they are human. I like showing a "Beast" alter that he has hands, and wondering why he may have seen furry paws when he first came out, and whether anyone else inside knows why he saw paws instead of the hands he now has. But it may also be frightening to others to recognize, for example, that they do belong to the body that was tortured or that they were instructed to kill. Timing is very important in attempting to remove alters' illusions.

Alters who have alters inside

Particularly with ritual abuse and mind control survivors, you can expect that some alters will themselves be multiple. Alters are hidden within alters. So, for example, one of my clients had several "tough guy" alters, each of whom concealed a hurt child part. Another had an in-charge "Satan" alter, whose inside parts included one who held sadness and another who held fear, emotions which Satans were not allowed to have. Jennifer had internal copies of her mother and brothers, each of which had within it copies of the alters which were in her actual mother and brothers. So, when you speak with an alter who appears to be a certain way, bear in mind that it may have internal parts who hold very different emotions.

How categories of alters relate to their origins

Because it is so overwhelming, clear conscious memory of childhood sexual and betrayal trauma does not develop, at least in an ANP. This process is both psychological and organic.

From the organic perspective, the different aspects of the traumatizing experience are stored in separated brain circuits. When the trauma is extreme and complex, begins in early childhood (under the age of six), and involves pain, betrayal, and threats to life, the various aspects of the overwhelming traumatic memories and their responses are divided between different alter personalities. One alter may be aware of the first part of the story, another alter of the next part, and so on. Or one alter may hold the pictures, another the "sound track," another the feeling of sadness, another the anger, another the physical pain, and another the sexual arousal. If there are repeated traumas of a particular kind, these aspects of experience go into the same brain circuits that held them previously, and these specialized circuits become alter personalities. Mind controllers, aware of this process, utilize it to control their victims.

Regardless of how they view themselves, you are likely to see the following categories of alter personalities in dissociative people with ritual abuse and mind control histories:

1. *Parts from before the trauma*: Relatively untraumatized child parts who hold positive memories. They stop growing and are put away when they experience trauma or serious deprivation.
2. Parts created during the trauma:
    (a) *Hurt children* who have unfulfilled needs and/or hold traumatic pain or emotions.
    (b) *Protectors* (including internalized perpetrators). These parts generally live in the past and think the trauma is still happening. (In some cases it might be.)
    (c) *Observers*, recorders, watchers, parts in the sky, etc.
3. *Parts from after the trauma*: Survivors, usually the body's chronological age. They have to deal with everyday life, so must not be affected by the trauma, which they often do not remember. They may be high-functioning; or may be "depleted hosts" or have PTSD. ANPs belong in this category.

It helps to think of the needs and purposes of each of these categories as you engage in therapy with multiples. Frightening or angry parts are often protectors. Observer parts can be helpful for putting memories in order and knowing what really happened (*vs.* what illusion the abusers created). Parts from after the trauma need to be protected from much of the trauma until it has been worked through with those parts who actually went through it.

Making and sharing the dissociative disorder diagnosis

It takes a good deal of childhood trauma to create a dissociative disorder, and it takes a long time to establish trust in the therapeutic relationship, help the client attain stability, and work through the traumatic memories sufficiently to achieve either co-consciousness or integration of the parts. These tasks are particularly difficult if the client has been subjected to ritual abuse and/or mind control. In this general overview of DID/DDNOS treatment, we address how treatment must be altered for ritually abused and mind-controlled persons.

The ANP's experiences—amnesia, hearing voices, depersonalization and derealization, and post-traumatic intrusions—might well be what drives him or her to therapy, although the outside person will generally be unaware of there being other alters inside. In that case, you should administer certain assessment tools for dissociative disorders. The Dissociative Experiences Scale (DES) is a quick and easy device. Another instrument, Dell's Multidimensional Instrument of Dissociation (MID, 2006), includes more items. New assessment tools are constantly being developed, and the ISSTD website (www.isst-d.org/) gives information about these.

Confusing or disjointed presentations are an indication of switching that may not be otherwise visible to the outsider. If the alter who was "out" when something happened has "gone inside", the ANP—your presenting client—will not remember what happened. Multiples learn to cover up for loss of time. Someone who does not yet know she (or he) is multiple, and does not realize she loses time, will deny doing things she has been seen doing. This will lead to a reputation as a liar. If she realizes that another alter may have done it, she will often pretend to remember the incident to hide the time loss, or may make up excuses or explanations such as alcoholic blackouts. This is particularly common in child multiples, who are not as adept at covering their tracks as adults are.

In DDNOS, the ANP is always present, even when another part is in control of the behavior and feelings. People with DDNOS (having shell ANPs) can be just as complex internally as people with DID, and in many ways the distinction is a relatively unimportant technicality. Treatment is essentially the same. Many things are easier for DDNOS than for DID multiples, because they do not lose time or find they have eaten six breakfasts. However, it is easier for them than for DIDs to mistakenly assume that their negative feelings are caused by present situations rather than old traumas that have been triggered by something in the present. And it is harder for a therapist to detect their multiplicity.

As happens with ritual abuse, most people, including therapists, do not see multiplicity because they do not look for it. We write off changes in demeanor as just different emotional states, and in many cases they are. But if you are attuned to multiplicity, you can detect switches, and can sense the other parts lurking behind the presenting alter. As one of my DID clients' young alters says of our work together, it is because I "look inside" that I was able to detect her multiplicity. Most people, however, do not look inside. When my client did a practicum in a mental hospital as a community mental health worker, she recognized that some of the patients also looked inside. But none of the staff did.

Once you have determined that your client has DID or DDNOS, you will need to gently introduce them to the notion of dissociation, explaining that it is a psychological and physiological response to childhood trauma. Explain it as a normal reaction to an abnormal situation. Make it clear that having a dissociative disorder like this is not the same as being crazy.

Be careful, by the way, about using the word "alter" with your client. Many multiples, especially ritual abuse survivors, have a negative reaction to that word, usually because of its resemblance to the word "altar," a central feature in both church and occult rituals. I have used the word "alter" in this book because it is less ambiguous than "parts" and less confusing (and more accurate) than "personalities" or "inside people." Respect for your client, however, demands that you call the parts whatever term is most comfortable for your client. I use different terms with different clients.

I like to tell such clients that a dissociative disorder is mental injury rather than mental illness, and, therefore, requires a different treatment. For a broken leg you would put the bone parts back together and keep them connected so they could heal, even though it might be painful. Similarly, with a broken mind, you bring the parts back together by introducing them to one another, and you clean the wound by helping the person resolve what happened to make the parts split from one another. You might recommend books such as Steinberg's *The Stranger in the Mirror* (2000) to help the client understand their experience, or a newsletter by and for multiples such as "Many Voices" (contact www.manyvoicespress.com/newsletter.html).

Communicating with the personality system

The following guidelines will help you to communicate with the personality system of some-one who is multiple.

Talking through the presenting alter

Once you apply your solid understanding of dissociation, in many ways talking with the parts of a multiple client is no different from talking to a singleton client about his or her problems.

Although only one alter at a time can control the multiple's voice and actually talk with you, many—especially the important ones—can hear you and can send messages to you. Someone else may choose to "take the phone" and speak with you, or someone can be sent to get them. Always assume that some others inside can hear you. This applies even when the presenting alter is deaf, catatonic, or a baby. (Note that misunderstandings may happen with other parts even when the one outside understands perfectly, and you need to check for this.) You can talk through the presenting alter to others in the system. Not everyone can hear you, but many, especially the important ones, can. Remember that, especially with a ritually abused multiple, the important alter personalities are always listening in order to guard the person's safety in the outside world.

Exploring passive influences

You should also be aware of what is known as "passive influence." Alters often make them-selves known by exerting influence on the "outside" or presenting part. Passive influence is very common, and can be detected simply by asking about it. When the alter who is out reports a feeling that she or he does not understand, someone inside may really be experiencing the feeling which is "leaking through" to the alter who is out. Once some internal communication has been established, you can follow the feelings to find who inside is their source. If it is voices, talk to the voices. If it is pictures, find out which alters they are coming from. Remember that the real source of the feelings is the part that needs and will benefit from your attention.

Techniques for meeting alters

In the early days of therapists' awareness of DID, there was a focus on techniques for meeting the alter personalities, as though this process needed some special (usually hypnotic) methods in order to be successful. These techniques are not necessary for that purpose, in my view, although they can be helpful in working with systems. The "Middleman technique," for instance, which simply means speaking to one part through another presenting part, can be very useful. I use it in diagnosis, while administering the Dissociative Experiences Scale. If the person says yes to the question about hearing voices, I ask if one is speaking to them right now. If yes (it is usually yes), I ask what it is saying. Then I engage it in dialogue via the presenting part, whom I instruct to "think to it and listen for the answer." Eventually the voice may agree to speak with me directly. There is nothing magical or highly technical about this: it is simply a natural result of understanding how multiples work.

Fraser's Dissociative Table Technique (1991), in which you use guided imagery to create a boardroom or table or equivalent, can be helpful with "regular" or "reactive" multiples, as can other guided fantasies such as walking to a cottage and asking people to come out. But these techniques are unlikely to access the important parts of a deliberately constructed personality system.

It shows how much we are "foreigners" to multiples when thinking we must resort to techniques to communicate with them. For the most part, we simply have to understand how multiplicity works, and communication will come naturally. It is true that, in some cases, alters have been forbidden to talk to outsiders, so it may take considerable time to build up enough trust for them to actually speak with you. In this case, it is important to "talk through" to them via the ANP. I often make it explicit, once the ANP has acknowledged that others exist inside, saying such things as "Now I'm talking to them, not you." Be aware that when people have shell ANPs, you will not see much difference as the alters come to speak through the shell.

Speaking directly with alters

One of my clients who is a mind control survivor had a therapist who believed that talking to the parts reified them (made them more real). She would only communicate with the parts through the outside adult. Unfortunately, the parts had been trained to never speak to the outside adult, in order to keep the abuse hidden from the adult part. Once I began to speak with the parts, they made fast progress.

Speaking to the alters directly is the general rule for work with this population. It is the most expedient and effective way to do this work. Once you talk to the right "person," often a simple explanation of reality can lead to big changes. I recently consulted for another therapist whose client had an inside child who kept picking at her foot until it bled. The therapist was very disturbed about this, and made all kinds of unsuccessful plans with the main personality to get it to stop. Finally, I saw the client myself, and asked to speak to the little girl alter. She came out at once. She had never come out with the original therapist simply because the therapist had not asked. I asked why she picked at the foot, and she explained it was to keep the adult from going to sleep at night, because the foster father came in and abused her at night. I told her that it hurt the adult, which the child did not know; she did not want to hurt the adult. I explained to her that the foster father was dead and could not come. When I explained to the adult what the child had told me, she arranged to sleep in a different bedroom with a lock on the door, to make the little girl feel safer.

It is not always that easy, but, again, in every case the key is communicating with the alters responsible. This is the key even with survivors of extreme organized abuse. You and the rest of the personality system have the opportunity to introduce these parts to the safe present (assuming the person has gotten away from her abusers; these issues will be discussed in Chapter Eleven). They get to see what it is like to be with a safe and caring person. They can tell you the false beliefs the abusers put into their heads, and you can explain the truth, or show them the trickery involved. Cognitive work with the alter personalities pays great dividends. As soon as one part is convinced to work together with you for healing, another will appear who is supposed to stop this process, *but secretly wants you to help them too.* You may have to work your way through many layers, but you will get there.

Helping newly discovered alters meet the present-day world

How do you speak with alters about the fact that they are all parts of one person, and inhabit the same body, at least in this "real" world? Some therapists minimize their separateness. For example, Spiegel (1993) stated that "these patients . . . have the bizarre delusion that their body is inhabited by more than one independent personality" (p. 87), and Putnam (1989, p. 103) wrote, "Whatever an alter personality is, it is not a separate person. It is a serious therapeutic error to relate to the alter personalities as if they were separate people. Although many alters will emphatically insist that they are separate people, the therapist must not buy into this delusion of separateness."

Sadly, the term "delusion of separateness," which became widely used in DID treatment circles, resulted in such countertherapeutic approaches as refusing to speak with all alters except the ANP, and trying to get the ANP to take responsibility for the behavior of all alters.

In a sense, the separateness is not really a delusion. Although the parts are all in one body, they represent different brain circuitry that appears to have been separated by some biological process that we do not sufficiently understand. Brain imaging studies show different brain pathways activated with different alters, and other studies show physiological differences between different personality states (Birnbaum & Thomann, 1996; Hughes, Kuhlman, Fichtner, & Gruenfeld, 1990; Miller, 1989; Miller & Triggiano, 1992; Miller, Blackburn, Scholes, White, & Mamalis, 1991; Putnam, Zahn, & Post, 1990).

Richard Kluft (personal e-mail communication, 2010), a pioneer in dissociation treatment, does not like the term, believing it to be "too strong a description, because often the awareness of the truth of commonality co-exists with the subjective truth of the genuineness and completeness of separateness, perhaps an expression of trance logic." Instead, "Taking a hint from European phenomenologists, who called an hallucination a pseudo-hallucination if the person knew it was a hallucination," he developed the term "pseudo-illusion of separateness," because it "made more sense" to him.

It takes work to help alters adjust to the fact that they live in an older body who looks like the ANP, not the way they believe they personally look. In many cases, the alters "see" one another in the inner world, and state that they experience one another as real people. An alter who emerges into the real world does not see him or herself, and assumes s/he has the body in which s/he lives in the inner world and which s/he inhabited the last time s/he was "out."

Most of the alters in mind-controlled personality systems have not come directly out into the world since childhood, so they know nothing of the present. Many of them are not supposed to emerge directly into the world unless called out by a perpetrator, so they will be very afraid or hostile when they emerge. I encourage newly discovered parts to look around

THE BASICS OF THERAPY

my office and see that it is daylight and we have our clothes on and there are no weapons. If the alter does not know much about me and has never met me before, I ask the others inside to fill that part in on our history together and why they think I am safe. Often alters do not know that the body has grown up. I find it helpful to have a newspaper or magazine with a recent date to show them the year. I also have a mirror so they can see what their body looks like now, but I use it sparingly, especially with survivors of ritual abuse or mind control, since mirrors are used a lot in programming to deceive alters about their nature. It is more useful with multiples who have not experienced mind control. For example, I used it to show one alter that her tonsils, which had always been very painfully infected, were now gone.

Particularly with alters in a mind-controlled system, do not ask too many questions; it may feel like interrogation, and many of these people have been interrogated as part of their abuse. Just be open and sympathetic, until they are ready to talk. It can be helpful to ask the client to map the system if she is willing. However, do not insist on this, or on knowing internal names, as some parts might feel this gives you or hostile parts power over them. This is particularly true for ritual abuse survivors, where the abusers call the parts out by name.

It is important to match your communication to the kind of part who is presenting, just as you would for a singleton client. Be especially sensitive to nonverbal communication of emotions. Some parts need hugs, but others will take them as a sexual approach. Some parts cannot stand direct eye contact. Some use strong, challenging language, and will respond to dares and challenges and humor. Other parts are terrified and just need listening. Some cannot speak and may need to communicate through writing, through drawing, or through another part.

Be careful with your language, especially with mind control and ritual abuse survivors. Innocuous words have often been given sinister meanings by the perpetrator groups. If you notice your client flinching or showing other signs of distress when you use words like "love" or "safe" or "feel," you can ask the client what the word in question means to him or her, and you can train yourself to substitute another word when you speak with that particular client. With one client, I have to substitute "believe" for "think," and "sense in your body" for "feel," since the original words were used by the perpetrators as part of torture.

Remember that it is very important to treat all parts with equal kindness; do not pick favorites. Every alter is there for a purpose, and is an important part of the system. So, for instance, do not be afraid of hostile alters. It has been said that every persecutor is a misguided protector. Most hostile alters are using anger to protect vulnerable parts inside, usually younger children. If they seem dangerous, talk with them at first through another alter. But if you act scared, you will create a self-fulfilling prophecy.

Similarly, untraumatized child parts can be distracting, adorable, entertaining, and uplifting—but spending too much time with them can distract you from the task of dealing with the trauma. Watch out for good kid–bad kid dichotomies. You need to appreciate them all, just as they all need to accept each other. In the end, remember they are all parts of one person, and that *person* needs to know you accept all of the selves, just as he or she eventually will, including the parts she does not want or like.

Internal conflict, internal communication

Do not expect the client with untreated DID or DDNOS to be consistent or to have internal harmony.

A DID personality system is like a family. It contains polarities, boundaries, etc. For instance, if one polarity exists, the other polarity probably does as well. A knowledge of family systems therapy, particularly its application to multiples (Goulding & Schwartz, 1995) can be helpful.

At the start of therapy, most multiples have internal battles for control. The ANP usually has little or no control over switching. The alters may fight to be out, or may push others out in order to stay inside. It is important to assist your multiple client in improving internal communication, negotiation, and cooperation. Democratic decision-making is not usually learnt in the childhood of a multiple and can be incredibly difficult. "Eww, Jane got us dressed this morning," or "I don't like her having sex with *my* body" are typical comments that one alter will make about another. One of my first DID clients would repeatedly throw out everything given him by his abusive mother and then retrieve it from the garbage disposal when he switched to another alter. Alters will often express anger and even hatred for one another. It is hard for them to realize that they all represent legitimate parts of one person, and to respect how each part helped the person survive the extreme situation in which they grew up. Each can only see things *their* way.

Consider inviting other alters to speak to the one who is out and talking. I respect the ones who come out spontaneously to talk with me, but I also ask to speak to others, and if they will not (or are not permitted to) speak to me directly, then I ask that messages be relayed back and forth to them. When I know the client well, I usually target my conversations at the alters I deem to be important at any given moment, regardless of which ones are initially talking to me. It is common that alters will be put "out" to entertain the therapist so that no real work will be done in therapy.

You can help the alters to speak with one another. Although talking internally might seem to make the person "more" multiple, the long-term result will be that they will become better organized and work more like an integrated person. You are seeking to help them achieve "co-consciousness," with whichever alter is out in the body being aware of the needs and viewpoints of all the other alters, and shared understanding among all those inside, so that effective decisions can be made by the whole person rather than by just one part at a time.

Spontaneously created personality systems are more likely to be quite chaotic when the alters first begin to communicate with one another. Systems structured by perpetrator groups, on the other hand, tend to be better organized, but in a military-style hierarchy. It is wise not to interfere with this hierarchical organization at first, and over time to help the leaders change the governmental system to a more democratic one. Chapters Four and Nine are devoted to the unique characteristics of mind-controlled personality systems, and more advanced strategies for working with them.

Learning from multiplicity

It is an exciting adventure to get to know someone who is multiple. They have a lot to teach us, not only about the way the human mind can work, but also about the way the human race works. I sometimes think of the human race as one gigantic dissociative person, with myself as only one part of it. There are other parts who are very different from me, whom I do not understand. Some of them scare me, and some of them arouse my anger. But only as I—we all—learn to understand and cooperate with the other parts of the "body" of humanity, can humankind learn to stop all the dangerous and damaging things we do to one another. In this way, I feel it is a privilege to know my clients and other multiples, human beings who are learning to live as communities rather than as isolated individuals.

Working with dissociation in folks with ritual abuse or mind control histories requires specialized knowledge, built on a solid, up-to-date understanding of dissociative disorders and their treatment. This, itself, is built on the therapist's respect for all parts of your client, the willingness to listen, and sensitivity to their needs. Survivor LisaBri's simple and sincere plea to therapists (see her contributions in Chapters Nine, Twelve, and Thirteen) sums it up as well as anything I have seen:

> Please learn all you can about Dissociative Identity Disorder and ritual assault. The chances that you will have a client with one of these is great. You need to be ready to help them in a safe and healthy way. Most importantly, if you are attempting something new with your client, and she says it doesn't feel right—listen to her. She knows her system in a way no one else could ever imagine.

CHAPTER FOUR

Markers of mind control and ritual abuse

T he personality systems of ritual abuse and mind control survivors are different from those of dissociative individuals whose abuse has been less systematic, such as in severe physical or sexual abuse by a family member. Even a person who was abused in a back-woods family cult, in a doomsday cult, or by teenage Satanic dabblers would not manifest the degree of internal organization seen when a person has been trained by an organized group for the purpose of achieving mind control. Such personality systems do have certain identifiable characteristics.

In Chapter Two, I discussed indicator lists for organized, group perpetrated, ritual abuse and mind control that have been developed over the years by others. These lists are based on the consequences and external manifestations of these abuses. I would like to share with you now a list of functional indicators that I developed based on my clinical work with survivors. This is a different kind of list, in that it describes internal dynamics that result from program-ming. These indicators will reveal themselves only after therapy with a dissociative client has proceeded long enough that the therapist can become aware of them. They are not the kind of characteristics that might be observed by the typical outsider. They are all "red flags" for organized abuse because they describe the intended (mind-controlling) consequences of such abuse.

As with other such lists, remember that other than a few "red flags", an individual item does not mean the syndrome exists. For example, introjects (internal copies) of abusers are common in dissociative disorders; occasionally a client will have alters arranged in a hierarchy as a result of abuse in a family, for example, by a militaristic father; someone raised in a strict fundamentalist religion might have "demon" alters. But these persons will not have all the other indicators on this list.

Common characteristics of the personality systems of mind-control survivors:

1. An internal structure or a complex inner world in which the dissociated identities ("alters" for short) are placed.
2. Trained alters with "jobs";
3. A "dump" for alters who have proved uncooperative and so are of no use to the perpetrators.
4. A hierarchy of alters.
5. Observer and recorder/reporter alters who know and can report everything that has happened to the person.
6. A security system including punishments for disobedience.
7. Gatekeeper alters.
8. Internal filing systems for memories, especially of training sessions.
9. Alters who believe they are animals or demons or aliens.
10. Deliberately created introjects (internal copies) of the perpetrators (i.e., there are memories of their deliberate creation).
11. Internal calendars with "jobs" to be done on certain dates.
12. Spinner alters who send out feelings or impulses to the rest of the system.
13. Deliberately placed "triggers" for learned behaviors or symptoms ("programs").
14. "Booby traps" of despair or suicidality triggered by talking about the abuse.
15. Recycling of memories and reappearance of trained behaviors.
16. Reported use of tricks and technologies in training.

Most of these things will not just be spontaneously created by children who are abused in random ways. If you have a client who has most or all of these characteristics, you may suspect he or she has been abused by an organized criminal group. You will see many of these indicators in the following two chapters, and will obtain more depth of understanding in Chapter Seven, which examines the creation of these characteristics from a programming perspective. Following is a discussion of all items listed above.

1.   An internal structure (or structures) and/or a complex dissociated inner world

If a client is talking about an internal geometric structure, this can be seen as a "red flag" for organized perpetrator group abuse (including that done by both ritual abusers and mind control by political/military groups). The alters are mentally located in an internal structure with a particular shape. A typical RA/MC structure may be shaped like a pyramid, or a prism, or a tetrahedron, or a spider web. Many MC survivors have an internal world which contains several or many structures or "worlds."

These structures are neither random nor merely created for the purpose of organization. They are used by perpetrating groups to locate specific alters, and to call out specific combinations of alters for certain tasks. Often, there are codes for each space in the structure or matrix, as we will see in Jeannie Riseman's example. The adults who deliberately create these structures or inner worlds do so at a stage of the child's development when the child is able to internalize things s/he sees in the outside world. They stage settings in the real world that they want replicated in the inner world of the child's mind. Often, there is both a structure and an inner world.

In Chapter Seven, you will see how very young children are taught to create their inner world or structure, as described by Stella Katz. The child builds an actual, real-life, physical structure, while the child's trainer explains that this structure is to be replicated inside the child's mind as a place for the alters to live. The building materials vary according to what is available at the time of building; Jeannie Riseman's system, discussed in Chapter Six, created in the 1940s, might well have been built with Tinker Toys. Others use Lego or blocks. In Stella's example, a builder alter is trained to build a structure with building blocks of varying colors, and to place dolls of the same colors representing the alters in their proper places in the structure. They are instructed that everyone must be kept in their places.

The structure is gradually developed and elaborated over the years. Walls between the alters or alter groups prevent their communication. Taking down the walls will cause alters to integrate. Often the builder alter is supposed to take down certain walls when the survivor gets to a certain age; for example, some survivors are programmed for their everyday life alters to integrate with the cult-loyal ones, leaving out the pain holders. When this happens, the everyday life alters come to know that they have been involved in the cult or group, but since the pain is being held by hidden alters, the person does not realize how gruesomely they have suffered.

Knowing the nature of the structure will help the therapist discover how many alters there are and which ones are most important to work with. However, this is unlikely to be revealed until well into therapy. It does not matter much what kind of structure or structures exists; the therapeutic approach to dealing with them is still the same. Explore each part of the structure and its purpose and which alters "live" there.

Many survivors have been encouraged to create, either instead of or in addition to a structure, a complex inner world in which the alters live. It is often based on fairy tales, stories, or movies that have been shown to the child. It may have frightening places in it, some copied from the outside world (e.g., a "pit" or a "torture chamber") and some created by suggestion. Internal disasters can be triggered to happen in this inner world. The trainer gives the child suggestions about the appearance of the internal world, through showing the child a picture of a tree, or a pyramid, or a house or a box, and playing games of "Let's pretend (whatever alter is out at the time) lives in the roots of a tree." Trish Fotheringham's account in Chapter Six describes the way in which she was taught to construct her inner world. In her case, an actual theatre with a stage was used, enabling the abusers to create the "stage of life." When Trish was first involved in therapy, she believed that her alters and her own imagination had created the inner world in which the alters lived. She engaged actively with this world, going "inside" to see how each of the alters was doing and adding things to the inner world to make it more comfortable for the alters, such as a healing hot tub for those who were in pain. It was only after many years of therapy that she came to recognize that most of the features of the inner world had been deliberately installed by the abusers.

If the internal world is frightening, the therapist can help the client use his or her own imagination later to redesign it and put the alters in safer places. But first it is necessary to overcome the effects of the training that dictates that everyone inside must stay in his or her place.

A survivor of childhood trauma whose alters were not deliberately created by an organized group may also have an inside structure, but it is usually only a place for the alters to "live" inside, such as a house. One of my ritually abused clients has cult-trained alters housed in an upside-down pyramid, and abused-at-home alters living in an internal house.

Sometimes, places or structures that have been installed inside are copies of outside places, including places where abuse happened. This is true for both structured and reactive multiples, but many whose abuse was not perpetrated by an organized group have no inner world at all, and alters, when not "out", simply disappear into blackness or exercise an effect on the person's emotions without being internally visible.

In "Simplifying complex programming" on the Survivorship website, Jeannie Riseman states,

> Often the alters are arranged in complex patterns—sometimes geometric patterns (as in Cabala-based or matrix programs), sometimes patterns based on things or communities. Some people have systems that replicate an organizational structure, with a CEO, advisory boards, etc. Sometimes the pattern is more like a video game, with castles and dragons and all sorts of tricks and booby traps for the unwary.

2.   Trained alters with "jobs"

All alters in a deliberately created system have jobs to do, and doing one's job is the most important expectation after compliance and silence. The "blocks" of alters described by Katz, and the "color paths" to which Fotheringham's alters belonged, exemplify the kinds of jobs.

The first alters of this kind of which a therapist is likely to become aware are the ones who punish others for disclosures. If a client appears to be experiencing pain or flashbacks right in my office, I like to casually ask whether it is someone's job to punish the person for what they have told me. If they say yes, this is a red flag for probable mind control.

Many other dissociative clients have experienced some degree of mind control and they may have internal punishers who replicate the behavior (for example, of abusive parents) even in the absence of organized group abuse, but these alters are less likely to refer to what they do as a "job."

3.   A dump containing discarded alters

Stella Katz, in Chapter Seven, points out the importance of "garbage kids," alters that were discarded because they either would not comply in training, or could not learn quickly enough. Often, garbage kids are hidden pain-holders, and continue to participate in some memories. If they have been "killed," they are stuck in the memory of being unconscious, and have not actually been destroyed. I believe that it is important to find these alters, and process their part of any traumatic memories which need to be worked with. Often they have the most resistance to the perpetrators, and can become helpful allies. However, they have usually been severely traumatized. One of my mind-controlled clients refers to her dump of discarded alters as "the blue pile." When I asked why the pile of alters was blue, it turned out to be because they were black and blue with bruises. As long as the garbage kids remain hidden, the trauma cannot be worked through thoroughly; the training of the other alters will still have some power in the survivor's life, even if s/he is working hard to resist the pull of the abusers' instructions.

4.   A hierarchy of alters

Most deliberately created systems are hierarchically organized. There are levels or layers, and each level has a boss, who reports to someone on the next higher level. There are often several alters with the same name but different functions, usually on different levels. The ones in charge usually have titles representing their authority. In military or political systems there are captains, leaders, and soldiers; in ritual systems there are demons, Satans, Lucifers, high priests or priestesses, as well as representations of family members who have authority in the person's life. Each layer in a Satanic system usually includes a Satan, a few demons, a high priest or priestess, a copy of the primary trainer, and various guards. Authoritative alters have the job of disciplining others under them for disobedience (such as talking about the abuse). If the disciplinarian on one level fails to do its job, the discipline moves up to a higher level.

There are usually also fail-safe alters outside the "layers" whose job it is to deal with the problem if the ones in charge prove disloyal. These have been told they are such entities as ghosts, chameleons (who can impersonate other alters), deceivers, and spiritual guides.

Not all systems are equally complicated. Some complicated systems might have several different groups of alters, each with its own layers, trained by different perpetrators or for different purposes. A "criss-cross" security system might have alters from one group disciplining those from the other groups. The alters in charge of the system are usually aware of what goes on in the outside world, but rarely intervene directly at first. As they can with any dissociative client, therapists can "talk through" the system to them, as they are usually listening.

In doing therapy with a survivor of organized abuse, a primary objective is to get through to the alters in charge of the hierarchy and convince them that they have been deceived. They often believe they know everything about what has happened to the person (which is invariably not true), and believe they have never been hurt—in fact, they might believe that they do not belong to the body at all.

By gently exposing their false beliefs, as you work up the hierarchy and talk to alters that have increasing authority, you will gradually build trust and help clients see what has really happened to them. *It is necessary to understand that you cannot succeed in therapy with a survivor of organized abuse unless the alters in charge of the hierarchy allow you to proceed at first, and later actively cooperate with you.*

Although these alters have observed the "real" world, they have rarely been out in it, and have very limited experience of anything in life other than group events and training. Their rewards have been sex, drugs, and power; they know nothing of love or caring or pets or snow or anything else positive in life. Other alters can share these positive experiences with them to help them see what they have been missing. We shall discuss ways to approach these alters in more detail in Chapter Nine.

5.   Observer and recorder/reporter alters

When dissociative disorders were first studied in the 1980s and 1990s, much was made of "inner self-helper" alters or ISHes. It is likely that many of these were deliberately created observer or watcher alters. Survivors of organized abuse generally have observers or watchers who are trained to be aware of, and remember everything that happens. These alters tend to be told that they can see everything but cannot and must not act in the outside world. They might have been taught (through trickery) to believe they are non-human, for example, aliens or whales or spirits. These alters can be very helpful in accessing memories for processing.

The observers and recorders are often the reporters who have the job of telling the person's handler what the person has said or done. We shall learn more about their jobs in Chapter Eleven, "'Stabilization' takes on a new meaning", as getting them to cooperate is essential to maintaining the client's safety while therapy proceeds.

Also, look for "floating alters." These are not deliberately created parts of the system, but alters that were accidentally split off at the same time as others. They are able to float around the system, learning everything they can, often unnoticed by the other alters. Since the perpetrating group is unaware of them, they do not get hurt unless they get in the way accidentally or they choose to take someone's pain. They can be an incredible source of information about the system and about what has happened and of great assistance to the therapist, as they have not been instructed by the abusers. Organized perpetrator groups try to find the floaters and assign them to the dump, but if the floaters are able to hide effectively, they can be the key to undoing the programming. One of my ritually abused clients has one such alter who calls himself "The Observer"; he detected many of the tricks which deceived the trained alters, and when we process their memories he chimes in with his observations about what was really going on.

6.   A security system including punishments for disobedience

The structured personality system of a mind-control survivor is always protected by a security system. The observers and reporters watch any alters who are "out" in the body, and sometimes those who speak to one another internally. They report to others in the hierarchy, who then order punishments to be administered by those alters who are trained to punish. Punishments include such things as flashbacks, flooding of unbearable emotions, painful body memories, flooding of memories in which the survivor perpetrated against others, self-harm, and suicide attempts. These will be discussed in Chapter Eleven, "'Stabilization' takes on a new meaning". Each alter who punishes has his or her place in the hierarchy, and if s/he fails to do the assigned job, a backup will do it while the disloyal punisher himself experiences punishment or is banished.

7.   Gatekeeper alters

According to Stella Katz, most ritually abused systems include Gatekeeper alters, who are special kinds of guards. They are told they are in control of the mind and all emotions. They work in combination with those in charge of the pain. A Gatekeeper is never hurt himself after his initial creation or "birth", holds feelings and memories back, and observes everything that happens. I have encountered Gatekeepers who hold in memories, and Gatekeepers or Controllers who hold in alters, only permitting certain ones to come out into the body or to influence those out in the body.

8.   Internal filing systems for memories, especially of training sessions

Many survivors of organized abuse have internal filing systems, usually with a "control room," files, a file manager or controller, and labels on the files which refer to such things as the type of training, age, and place where it was done. For more, see Trish Fotheringham's and Jeannie Riseman's descriptions of their filing systems in Chapter Six. When you come to working with the memories, it is very important to work with the file manager alters. In some cases, there are "program codes" which, when said in the right order, will make certain programs or pieces of training cease to work.

Usually a type of training session, or "program," is repeated at different ages, so that by the time the person reaches adulthood the training is well established and the conditioned response automatic. All the times this particular training was given will be noted in the internal files, as well as which alters were involved. These files make it easier to access the memories with mind-controlled survivors than with "ordinary" dissociative clients, once you have got past the security systems and gained the cooperation of the alters in charge of the system.

9.   Alters who believe they are animals, demons, or aliens

Organized abusers often want alters to believe they are anything other than parts of an abused child. One simple way of creating non-human alters is to split off an alter by inflicting pain while the child is exposed to circumstances that lead her to believe she is not human. For example, the child is given a hallucinogenic drug while suggestions are made about demons, and the other people are wearing demon costumes. When the new alter appears, she is shown a "mirror" with a picture of a demon on it and told this is her. Or the child is put in a cage with a fierce dog, and only fed dog food when she begs for it like a dog. Or the child is given a paralyzing drug so that she cannot move, shown movies about aliens, and told she is an alien who can observe this world but cannot act in it. To add to the effect, the child may be costumed while drugged to unconsciousness. Katz gives more detail on the purposes of demon and animal alters. Demon alters are led to believe they are entirely evil and are therefore not loveable by anyone except Satan. They also believe they are very ugly, so that anyone from outside will be afraid of them.

Because alters who believe they are aliens, ghosts, or spirits typically believe they do not belong to the body, if they are created while the child is under the influence of a strong analgesic drug, they will not feel the body's pain. This makes them very useful to the perpetrator group when the person requires punishment such as self-harm or suicide attempts. They may have been taught that they will live on if the body dies, since they think their "internal bodies" are the real ones, or that they do not have bodies at all.

10.   Deliberately created introjects of the perpetrators

Many perpetrators put their own stamp on to a personality system by putting "themselves" inside it. This is often done by splitting off alters during a rape, and instructing those alters that they are the perpetrator, or "born from his seed", and have to do what he does if the person is disloyal. In less cruel groups, a cardboard cut-out of the perpetrator is placed in the model of the internal world or structure, so that the alters inside will always "see" the perpetrator. This is not an alter personality, just a trick to scare the young child parts. Introjects of perpetrators are also common in personality systems that are not created by organized abuse. The internal punitive "mother" or "father" warns the child not to perform behaviors which will get the child punished by the real external mother or father, often by giving a reminder of the pain of the real parent's punishment. Organized abuser groups have capitalized on this phenomenon by deliberately creating (and therefore controlling) these introjects.

11.   Internal calendars with jobs to be done on certain dates

If the group has a long-term agenda—and most ritual and political groups do—there are alters who hold a "calendar" which lays out the "jobs" to be done on certain dates. Regular ritual dates are part of the calendar for any ritual abuse survivor, and are learnt in a normal every-day way, just as we learn the dates of our birthday and Christmas. Some survivors also have alters who hold significant future dates, such as the anticipated return of Satan (in 2012), or the date of the political group's alleged battle to take over the world.

In addition, some groups implant personal dates which are years in which survivors are to return to the group, integrate real-life alters with cult-loyal alters, commit suicide, or become ill. Young adult members of ritually abusive groups are frequently let go in their twenties to create an identity in the world, then recalled to the group at a certain age. During this "growing up" period, the main identity usually is unaware of the mind control or of the other internal identities. There are often internal punishments, such as a very annoying sound, spinning, or a sensation of being shocked, if the person does not return to the group when they are supposed to.

12.   Spinner alters who send out feelings or impulses to the rest of the personality system

Cults and mind control agencies often use physical spinning of the child. Katz describes in detail the purpose and nature of spinning. I do not know the neurological explanation of why spinning can have the effect of spreading post traumatic effects throughout the personality system. I only know that it does. "Spin programming," a term commonly used, is a misnomer. Spinning is not a program. It is a means to that end. It is used very generally, in many kinds of training, just as torture and rape and disgusting creatures are. Some survivors report having been spun on a huge Catherine Wheel, sometimes going in and out of water. This is also known to have been used in political torture, and has shown up in movies.

Spinner alters have the job of sending out feelings or impulses to all the other alters, the host, or a group of selected alters. Many of the "booby traps" or "fail-safe" programs involve spinning. Often, when a certain training is in operation, the survivor feels dizzy, as though something or someone is "spinning" inside her head. If this is happening, the therapist can ask to speak to the spinning alter and ask her to stop spinning. If she is unable to do so, the therapist can talk to whoever is making her spin. This strategy, of working up through the chain of command, applies to mind control treatment in general. Another tactic a therapist can use is to ask the spinner to spin in the opposite direction, which will often put away whatever is being spun. If permitted by those alters in charge, a spinner can also replace whatever lesson she is spinning with something positive, such as a feeling of calmness, taken from a positive memory.

For a complicated target behavior that must not be set off by accident, some military/political mind control groups use sequential alters rather than a group who are spun together. For example, alters are trained to sing the songs on a record in the head to get out one alter after another in a sequence until the final one performs an assassination.

13.   Deliberately placed triggers for learned behaviors or symptoms (programs)

Although all abuse and trauma survivors may be "triggered" into intrusive flashbacks by present-day experiences which remind them of the trauma, the triggers deliberately installed by mind controllers are different, in that they are cues for conditioned behaviors, only some of which are traumatic intrusions.

The basic training (compliance, loyalty and silence) is given to all alters, and cannot be turned off. However, many other specific trained behaviors, such as self-harm or disrupting therapy, have "on" and "off" triggers or switches. This training of alters functions like post-hypnotic suggestions. Triggers are installed using drugs and punishment, repeated over and over while the child is in a semi-conscious state. Classical conditioning (often aversive conditioning) is also used, as well as hypnosis. The child learns to respond to certain touches or sounds or words with a behavior that is so well learnt that it is automatic. The result is that a survivor might open the door when she hears a certain pattern of knocks, or she might fall asleep when a certain word is spoken. The MKUltra experiment described in Chapter Two gives an example of this, and Katz's chapter describes the installation of touch triggers in infancy. Carol Rutz says that whenever someone said "Knock, Knock," she would switch to a vacant, mindless person by the name of "Nobody's Home." You can see how easy it is for perpetrators to access and use their targets.

Some personality systems are set up with an inner world full of wires or strings that connect switches to their effects. These might facilitate a series of actions by a series of alters. For example, one alter watches the person function in the outside world, and presses a button if she sees the person disobeying instructions. The button is connected to a wire, which rings a bell in the ear of another alter. This alter then engages in his or her trained behavior, opening a door to release the pain of a rape, or cutting the person's arm in a certain pattern, or pushing out a child alter. So the watcher has no idea of who the other alter is or what s/he does. These events can be quite complicated.

Triggered behaviors can sometimes be temporarily stopped if the therapist can speak with the alters responsible and get them to agree to turn off the programs which have been triggered. In some systems it is possible to explore the whole chain of planned events from an outside perspective, so that all alters can be shown how the situation was set up. Once the alters see how they were tricked, and come to know that their perpetrators are no longer in their lives (if this is true), they can agree to stop their trained behaviors.

On and off triggers include sights or sounds or touches. For example, one client of mine had a habit of pushing on the fingers of her left hand with her thumb. This turned out to be the introject (inside copy) of an abuser warning her not to talk. Although many triggers are idiosyncratic, like that one, others are used widely. One common trigger looks like a reassuring rub on the crown of the head, to silence a child. The husband of one client discovered that this calmed the client down when she was upset. He had no idea he was using a pre-installed trigger. The Satanic "horned hand" (so often used by heavy metal musicians, as well as John Lennon, who was studying Alistair Crowley at the time) is a common sight trigger to identify survivors to cult members. Beeping sounds on the telephone convey particular messages, such as "go outside."

One of my early clients compiled a catalogue of "touch triggers" and what they meant. I have discovered that many of them are familiar to other clients, including unrelated people from very different geographical locations.

14.   Booby traps

"Booby traps" or "fail-safes" are dangerous internal events that are triggered to happen if the client (with or without a therapist) investigates too much of his or her own training, and/or becomes aware of memories she is not supposed to know. The effects of booby traps include such things as suicide attempts, serious self-harm, or falling into terrible depression. Both Katz and Fotheringham describe these traps in detail.

A booby trap can be set off without the knowledge of the main outside personality. The person might leave a therapy session feeling just fine, then go and jump off a building. Because of such traps, *it is very important to go very slowly in therapy with survivors of this kind of abuse.* Even though alters are involved in setting off the booby traps, they might not know the effects of what they are doing (pushing buttons, turning switches, and so forth), and it may be difficult to anticipate what will happen.

15.   Recycling of memories and reappearance of trained behaviors

A recycler (or reactivator) alter is one who has been trained to keep a small piece of each training memory, so that the survivor will be unable to recover the entire memory and thereby undo the training. The recycler may be given a name like Piece Keeper or Puzzle Maker or Collector or Juggler or Key Holder, and will be instructed to do something with the pieces, which are not kept in the files with the rest of the memories. When the therapist and client are ready to go through the training memories and undo the effects of the training, it is essential to find any recycler alters and ask them to put in their pieces as well. Otherwise, the memories that have been processed will be redissociated and the training will begin to work again.

Here is an example of a Recycle Program: In an extended programming session, Piece Keepers, Runners, a Grower, and a Collector of program pieces are created (through pain), and they are all given jobs. The result is that damaged programs (e.g., programs which have been largely undone through therapy) are "grown" from the pieces that were kept separately. When each program is made, a small part of it (some words said at the end, or a little piece of pain) are separated from the rest of the program and given to a particular group of alters, the Piece Keepers, who give them to the Collector of the pieces. If the survivor works through the memory with the main alters involved, the collector gives the saved pieces of that program to the Runners, who run and take them to the Growers, who somehow grow the program back into its original shape. (Note that this example also demonstrates the alter chains that are often involved in the installation and execution of programs.)

No doubt the development of Recycling programs was based on the observation that an incompletely worked through traumatic memory creates flashbacks more than a completely dissociated traumatic memory. Because these recycling alters exist, it is important to enlist their cooperation before you start working through the traumatic memories, especially those of training or programming events. That way the recycling pieces can be put in with the memories the first time you work on them, and the programs will not reappear.

16.   Tricks and technologies used for deception and training

Stage magic is used extensively to create non-human alters and simulate various false scenarios such as murders or alien abductions. (All of this will be explored in Chapter Eight, "The programming: indoctrination, lies and tricks", where numerous other examples will be provided.) Costumes are used for demons and animals. Bags of blood are stabbed on top of bodies to make a child think s/he has murdered someone. Dentists numb children's tongues and then tell the alters in the chair that their tongues have been cut out.

I remember one of my first ritually abused clients confessing to me that for a long time she had remembered being abducted by aliens, but had not told me because she did not want me to disbelieve her other memories because of it. We worked through the "alien abduction" memory and discovered that the "spaceship" was parked in the courtyard of the cult training center. In my client who had confessed her "alien abduction" experience, an alter had been instructed that if she began to remember the ritual abuse she was to remember the alien abduction, so that nobody would believe her account of the ritual abuse. This program did not work with us, but you can imagine the larger consequences of such a ruse.

Besides stage magic props and settings, ritually abusing groups use technology, such as that described by Katz and Fotheringham. Military/political groups have the most sophisticated technologies, and much training or programming is now done with virtual reality equipment. Movies and holograms are used to deceive a child into believing in things that are unreal.

When a client says to you "I don't know if it's real; how can it be real?" remember that there are several options, not just two: (1) It happened just as s/he remembers; (2) it did not happen at all; (3) something happened, but due to technology and/or trickery it was not what s/he thinks it was; (4) the thought that the memory must be unreal is itself a program, as described in Chapter Twelve, "Maybe I made it up."

Now, let's see how these characteristics manifest in, and are created by, real people.

CHAPTER FIVE

Ritual abuse: religious and creed-based abuses

The stories in the following chapters will be difficult to read, but they can help to prepare you for what you are likely to hear from your clients. Be warned that graphic details of sexual abuse and physical torture are included, so you as a therapist can understand more fully what your clients may have experienced and be better prepared when you hear it for the first few times. It is also my hope that these testimonies will help readers to see the humanity behind what has for so long been sensationalized, misunderstood, or dismissed.

As a therapist, you will be called upon to "bear witness" to the atrocities your clients have endured. The term "unimaginable" in the title of this book does not only apply to their sexual, physical, or even emotional aspects. In this chapter, we look at examples of traditional "ritual" abuse, abuse which centers around occult religion.

One of the worst features of ritual abuse is spiritual abuse. It consists of: (1) simulation of religious figures in perverted ways; (2) forced teaching of occult beliefs; (3) forced perpetration, especially real or simulated sacrifice of animals, babies, and/or adults, followed by teaching the child that s/he is evil.

Military/political mind controllers also simulate deities and teach children to violate their own natural moral codes. However, the spiritual abuse involved is not primarily religious. Rather, hypnosis and military training of alter personalities leads victims to violate their own moral codes, much as soldiers do in war. Many survivors have experienced both religious and military/political abuse. It should be pointed out, also, that filming of such events is common in both groups, leading us to suspect that financial motives also predominate even when it appears that the motive of the abusers is religious or patriotic.

One survivor, "Old Lady" (a name given by her young alter personalities) had a particularly complex series of spiritual trainings as part of mind control by supposedly different groups.[1] It will be instructive to look at what she experienced, as any or all of these things may be the experience of your ritually abused or mind-controlled client. Her writing sometimes comes from the adult, and sometimes from the young child alters. I have corrected the grammar and spelling of the child alters' writing somewhat to make the story more comprehensible. For instance, she says, "We say 'I' cos I didn't know that there were and are brother and sister parts; the other parts today are sharing what they know and speaking through old lady's fingers." These stories are the "Christian" ritual part of Old Lady's spiritual training. (Yes, there is "Christian" ritual abuse.)

The special child's spiritual training: Old Lady

Age 3, special birthday

When I was a baby, a priest put a cross on my forehead with his finger and blessed me. The cross symbol scares our system because we were taught and tricked by the same group of abusers, but under different group names ("Freemasons" and "Luciferians"), to fear, obey and be loyal to God and hate evil/darkness or to fear, obey and be loyal to Lucifer and hate God, the light.

The actual spiritual training begins when I turn three. There is a special ceremony for me. It is my birthday so I am the special, holy child who gets to be sacrificed to God. I am dressed in a white frilly dress, white leotards and black shiny shoes for my birthday and I am excited because it is a special day for me.

My mom and dad take me to a church basement. The basement is dark; only lit with candles and dimmed lights. The brightest part of the church basement is where the priest is standing. With a black and gold robe and sword hanging from his right shoulder to his left waist, he stands at the front of the church on a raised stage-like platform. The altar is a few steps below the platform. Everyone is already inside the church waiting for us to come in; they are singing "How Great Thou Art." Mom, dad and I take off our coats and hang them up in the closet. Then my parents leave and two men dressed in black hooded robes take each one of my arms and walk me down the aisle towards the altar.

The two men put me down on my back on the altar, with my arms and legs spread apart like the position you are in when making angels in the snow. The altar is made of wood so it feels hard and cold on my back. I don't like it, but kids aren't allowed to talk: 'Children are seen and not heard'. The priest prays to God in a funny language. I have never heard it before—it sounds like rambling sounds, not real words. These are the words that they will teach me to say over and over and over again until I learn them. Then the priest says that "God is Good; God is Light", and to "fear God because He knows everything and is everywhere". And we fear the light 'cos the doctors used the light (a real light) to burn the bottoms of our feet and blind us when we were in the hospital in Montreal. The priest says "It is important to obey God and me, for I am the one who speaks to God on your behalf. Children are lambs of God; Children are special; Come unto me little children; Children are sacrificed to God because they are pure and innocent".

The priest rambles his prayer again to God with his hands raised; the congregation stands up and starts walking over towards me. They are holding candles, and rambling words/sounds in a monotone that I don't understand. Two men take my clothes off and lay me back down on the altar and tape my ankles and wrists to the table so I can't move. It is so dark and I can feel the cool air on my body; I am cold and scared. I don't know what is going on. I can't see mom and dad and start crying for them.

Remember, children aren't supposed to talk. A woman in a hooded robe puts her finger up to her mouth and looks down at me to be quiet. I am scared and so I try to stop making crying sounds, but it is hard. Then I remember what the doctors did to me in the Montreal hospital—there was a priest there too but he was just standing in the left back corner of the hospital room when the men dressed in doctor uniforms did abusive things to me. These people scare me like the people in the hospital so I stop crying and just lie there.

I am told by the priest that this day is special because it is my birthday and I get to be sacrificed to God. The congregation keep circling me and saying their prayers in a low droning sound, which makes me sleepy. I am also getting dizzy watching the congregation keep circling me in a counter clock-wise motion. I go into a trance with listening to their droning noise and watching them circling me. I fall asleep and wake up with people who look like my mom and my dad on top of me naked, doing sex stuff, and a big light is shining down on us. The rest of the place looks dark—someone is filming us doing sex stuff. I pee myself. The adults don't like this. It makes them wet so they get off of me.

I don't feel special now. I feel dirty, confused and scared. I want my mom, but I don't want her because I think she will do sex stuff to me. She has never done sex stuff to me before. My dad has and so I don't really like him or want him to save me. I want my mom and then, I get mad (the beasty in me gets mad) because I am scared of her too. I have no one to save me that day.

Everyone leaves me on the altar. I am still naked, cold, frightened and wet. The priest comes over to me and says I am dirty. I need to be forgiven and cleansed for my sins. I have to go with him in a private and dark place, behind a curtain somewhere. It is very dark. I can't see, but the priest's big hand strokes the left side of my face and then the back of my head. He pulls me into him and his right hand undoes his pants. The priest pushes the back of my head into his penis. I have to put it in my mouth and not bite it—the priest will get mad if I do, just like my dad and uncle do. You have to be nice to the priest and do what he wants because you need to be forgiven and made clean again.

It is my birthday and I am special. I want to throw up when the priest has his thing in my mouth because it's too big, and slimy stuff comes into my mouth, but I'm not supposed to get sick. I have to keep doing stuff to the priest with my fingers on his wrinkly parts, and keep my mouth open for him.

After the priest pulls out of me and does his pants up, he takes me by the hand to two men in black hooded robes. They use towels on me and put my dress on but they don't know how to do the leotards very good. I have to help them by putting my hand on their shoulders and they grab each ankle and stick my feet in the leotards then put my shoes on. Then they take me to the place where our coats are on hooks and mom and dad take me home. I don't speak; I just sit in the back seat of the car and want to sleep. I feel sick, and mom and dad are quiet. Mom gives me a bath when we get home and I go to bed.

The upstairs church

Before I become four, me, mom, dad, and my sisters go to the top part of the church and listen to the priest and the Freemasons' council speak about God being Holy; God is the Light who Shines Away Darkness and Evil. Fear God when he gets mad; don't make him mad. Be good and obey your parents and the elders of the church. There is power in the blood; be a good soldier. God tests us to make sure we are good and obey him, the priest and the men elders. We can't tell our friends or people who don't go to our church that we are soldiers of God who keep secrets. We can't tell them about our special ceremonies like the sex stuff and giving baby and children's hearts to the priest and drinking blood from the special Christ cup.

When we pray together with the adults, I always feel funny, sleepy and not me. I'm a boy soldier. You say a prayer from the pew then follow people on your left or right row by row to be blessed by the priest. He makes a cross symbol with his fingers on your forehead with his ointment and takes the bread which is Christ's body broken for us. Then we say more of the same prayer and get up again to get the cross put on our forehead with the priest's finger and to drink Christ's blood—He bled for us on the cross and died to take away our sins. Blessed is he who is pure in heart, body, mind and soul, for he will go to heaven with God and live with God for eternity. There is no evil or darkness or Lucifer or Satan or Beelzebub in heaven. Heaven is good, a place of peace and tranquility, but you have to be forgiven of your sins first before you can go there. The priest speaks to God for you and tells him whether you can go to heaven or not. If you don't go to heaven, you go to hell, the place of fire, darkness and turmoil/agony for the soul.

We sing "Stand up, stand up for Jesus, ye soldiers of the cross", "There's power in the blood", "Onward Christian soldiers." The priest says we are a special group, that not everyone will understand us and will try to destroy us and break up the group, so we don't share what goes on here in our church, the family of God. We learn that God fights evil. Lucifer is the head of evil/darkness. There is no place for darkness in God's family; we have to be lanterns for God, because we aren't bright and powerful and righteous bright lights like God is. He is the only bright, righteous and just light.

Initiation

Children are taken by congregation members and tested to see if they will tell secrets or get scared and go to the devil. But first you have to be initiated into the Freemasons' group.

When I am four, Bob takes me down into the cellar of his house. This is where he keeps his home-made wine and stores stuff; this is where dead bodies are. It is stinky, musty, damp and not much light, just one light bulb. The cellar is narrow and gets dark near the end of the long bench I have to sit on. I just sit there and wait. Bob comes to get me and takes me upstairs into the living room. Men are there sitting in a circle with hooded black robes. Bob brings me into the center of the circle and has me lie down on my back with my hands and feet spread apart like when I was three, but this time I can keep my clothes on. I lie on my back and Bob is behind my head and looks down at me; I have to only look into his eyes and nowhere else. My ankles and wrists are held down by the hands of men; they say stuff that I can't understand and someone gets ointment and pins. I have to stay still, not move.

It is a test to see if I am a good and loyal soldier of God. I know that I have to obey because they are God's family, God's men, and you have to obey them or you will go to hell. So I lie there and they put pins into my hand, five of them in a circle. My fingers want to fold up and I want to close my hand. I try but the weight of the man on my left wrist keeps my hand and fingers from closing. After the second one I know what to expect and the stings make my hand go numb. My hand won't close; it is numb, like it isn't my hand. I feel like my whole body is going numb. I can't look at my hand, only into Bob's big brown ugly eyes. He is evil. I know God doesn't like him.

Meeting Beelzebub and Satan

Another time when we were four, we/I had to go to church with my uncle Bob and aunt Emily. They leave me with some men in hooded robes and I'm getting really scared because I know bad things are going to happen again, but I don't say anything to let them know I'm scared.

The priest in a white robe and a gold scarf round his shoulders comes out from the dark place and from among the other men in robes and he comes to me. He says, 'Today is a special day. You learn about good and evil and to trust your family here and to keep their secrets."

I say 'You teach me to be like you.' He says 'No, to be a follower of God. Do you love God?" I say yes. He says 'How much?' I say lots. I say 'I'm good, I don't tell lies, I behave and fear God's light. Cause God knows everything and is everywhere and hates the devil and the dark. That's why you wear white, right, cos you're special. God speaks through you and tell me to be good or else I go to hell. Right?' He says, 'Very good. You have been listening and learning about God and his rules and his power. You're a holy child and will be a good follower of God, I am sure.' This makes me feel good cos I please the priest and think maybe he won't hurt me or do things like sex stuff to me maybe, but he does it anyway. He always does sex stuff to me.

The priest leaves and the place is dark. It's only lit by candles and no chairs for pews. I think I am in the middle of the church basement but I'm not sure cos it's so dark. A black robe with no hood is put on me by a man in a hooded robe and I'm supposed to follow a flashlight or spotlight that moves somewhere. I don't know where it's going to go but it seems scary to me. I hope I please the elders and priest and God so nothing bad happens. I don't want to go to the bad place, hell, that the priest speaks about.

Then this ugly animal-looking beasty monster appears. He's really scary cause he has horns and an animal face with a long nose and tusks like an elephant. He's wearing a red robe too, so I'm not sure if he's a man playing costume games or a real monster. I just stand there and am afraid. It's not Halloween so I'm not sure what we're doing. Maybe we have to pose again for more pictures and films but there are no bright lights, just the light where I'm standing and where the beasty is standing. He says 'Come unto me, child. I am your father. The father of darkness.' I say 'You don't sound like my dad. The priest says I'm a follower of light, God's light, and you sound like some man, not my dad, and you say darkness. So I don't think it's right.' He says really loud and angrily to me, 'Don't think, child. Just do what I say and come unto me. I am your father, the father of darkness.' I'm scared now cos he's big and he may eat me with his big tusks and I'm afraid of going to hell with the devil, so I say 'No' and then 'Stop' cause the priest told me to obey the elders and obey the priest and God. But this don't look like an elder so I'm confused and then I say 'No' with a strong voice cause I'm getting angry, and Beasty inside don't like this beast monster. So I say no to the beast monster and he says 'I am Beelzebub, one of the fathers of darkness, and your father of the darkness within you. Now come here or I will destroy you.' I say 'No, I'm not going with you cause the priest says to obey the light and obey God and you're not my dad and you're of darkness.'

I say no, then suddenly the light gets brighter and I hear from somewhere, 'Good child. You passed the first test this day.'

It goes dark again and there's only a spotlight or flashlight again on the floor. The floor has red carpet. I follow the flashlight path and it takes me somewhere in the church basement again and then it stops and I stand still. Then suddenly Satan appears. He's dressed in a red robe and has black hair and a thin mustache and horns like devil horns that you see in movies. He's really scary cause he looks mad and powerful. I think I am in hell maybe, cos I see him, and I want to see the priest again cos he is of the light of God and will save me from hell, cos the priest just said I was good and will be a follower of God. I'm really scared and hope that Satan doesn't take me to hell. I've seen hell on TV and it was scary, with fire and lots of people who are dead and crying and moaning.

I'm really scared but just stand there and wait for God maybe or the priest to speak to me. He doesn't.

Satan says he's my father and the father of evil and darkness. That he is all powerful and knows everything about me and everyone. Satan's father is Lucifer and he is the ultimate father of evil and darkness, and I must be loyal to Satan, Beelzebub and Lucifer. I say 'Who are Beelzebub and Lucifer?' Satan says it is not for me to ask questions and to speak without being spoken to. Now come with me, and come now or you will be destroyed. I remember the light and God and the priest, and something inside me says no. I say no, cos before it was a test and I passed it and the priest came out and I felt better when I saw him. He is of the light and of God and will protect me from darkness and this Satan, who is really scary cos he looks like Satan on TV. He must be the real Satan cause he's in the TV and now here. He must be of the spirit world and of hell. And this makes me really scared. I say 'No I'm not going with you cause I'm a follower of God, the light and the priest, and you're not my dad or nice.' Satan then vanishes in smoke and I'm left there alone and it is really quiet. I'm really scared now and think I'm going to hell.

Easter

One time I went to church and we (me and my parts) had to give a heart to the priest. The priest says we are a Holy Child of God (*Ha ma nada*) and have to obey him cause he is God. We show God our loyalty to him by giving the priest of the Freemasons the baby's heart. When we hold the baby's heart in our hands, we have the power of life and death in our hands. This is the power that God has over us, and he can take our life away whenever he wants to so it is good and honorable to obey him, for he created life and can take life.

It was Easter time and I was not four yet. Me, mom and dad go to the church. We go to the basement of the church and hang up our coats again. Mom and dad leave. They go into the church while two men in black hooded robes again take me and put my black gown on. Then they take me into the church that is lit again with candles and low lights. Everyone except the priest is dressed in black hooded robes. The priest is dressed in a white robe and a gold scarf draped around his neck and straight down his chest to his feet; this time he is wearing a white hat with spikes and gold ball things on top of each spike.

The congregation is singing praise songs. The two men sit me down with them near the front of the church and the altar. I don't move or squirm cos you have to sit very still and not sneeze or say anything or else you get your hand squeezed tight and it hurts. I'm afraid of the men and women dressed in black hooded robes. It's creepy like Halloween. The priest teaches us about how Christ was sacrificed on the cross. He died for our sins, we are sinful people, bad people put him up there, but he went willingly cos he loves us and was obeying God, his father. It is important to obey God cos he has the power over life and death. You don't want to make him mad cos he can hurt you, like when he caused the flood and famines and stuff like that.

The two men in black hooded robes take me up to the altar after the singing and preaching. It is quiet and I know something bad is going to happen again, cos I see the altar with a baby in the basket on it. The altar is covered with a white cloth and two red ribbons draped on either side of it. There is a silver knife on the edge of the altar near the steps of the church's platform where the priest stands behind a podium. There is a gold (brass) cup and two white candles in gold (brass) candle holders on the altar. The baby is in the basket with white cloths in it, like Moses when his mother put him in the water so the bad people wouldn't get him. But this is not the same cos the people here scare us but we don't say nothing cause they're bigger and smarter than us.

The baby has a diaper on but he's not crying or anything. His eyes are closed. His tummy is not moving. He is white not blue so I'm not sure if he's dead or not. Sometimes people make us sleepy with a smelly cloth so we don't know, but we don't like it cos it's scary. The two men go back to their pews and I stand on one side of the altar and the priest comes down and stands at the other side. He faces the congregation, not me. He takes a silver knife from the altar and cuts the baby's tummy from the chest to above the belly button. Then the priest cuts across the baby's chest. Blood comes out but not spraying like other times. The baby doesn't cry. I'm looking, and am scared, I pee myself and hope no one sees it. I don't want the priest to do it to me. The priest looks at me and I want to cry and my tummy feels sick. Two of the men from the congregation get up and come over to me. The congregation starts chanting in a different language; it doesn't make sense; I don't know what they're saying. They keep chanting while the priest puts on his white gloves and pulls the skin back on the baby's tummy. I'm watching and am scared. I almost get sick. I gag but the man beside me puts his left hand on my shoulder and presses down on it and my body stops like a scared rabbit.

Then the man moves me to stand beside the priest. The priest cuts round the red organ thing under the shoulder bones and in the middle of the body. The knife goes right through big veins and the priest has to use a cloth to soak the blood up cause it squirts and he doesn't want to get his robe dirty. The congregation is still chanting. It's scary cause they get loud and then soft, loud then soft. The priest goes back to his podium and motions me to move closer to the baby. I don't know what he means or wants but I don't say anything. The man in the black robe comes round to me and tells me to move closer to the baby, where the priest cuts round the heart. The priest says to me 'Reach in, little one, into the baby's chest and take out his heart with your hands, feel the blood and warm fluid, feel the heart in your fingers. Don't squeeze it too hard or drop it because you will contaminate it and make it useless for God.'

I don't want to do it but I have to and the man is next to me and another across from me. They have swords across them like the priest had before when it was my birthday. I don't want them to kill me or hurt me. My legs are wobbly and I try to look around for my mom and dad but can't see them. It's too dark, only candles and low lights again are in the church. I put my fingers in and take them out cos it's warm and sticky and I don't wanna do it but the man moves closer to me and the priest says 'It's God's wish for you to obey. Hurry up and take the heart out and put it in the cup then bring it to me'. I pee myself again and do what the priest says while trying to not look at the baby. Instead I just think of it as a doll and we're playing doctor/operation. This helps me to do it and I give the heart to the priest. I'm careful not to spill the cup and I don't want to trip over my gown so I go slow and give it to the priest. He strokes the left side of my face and motions a cross on my forehead and says I'm a special child, holy child, and this is good that I obey God. 'You now know what it's like to have the power of life and death in your hands. Blessed are the children for they belong to God. You will not go to hell now for you obeyed God. You are good. Now go back to the men behind you.'

I go back down where the men are at the altar and they take me out to get my coat on and wait for mom and dad to come and get me and take me home. I'm tired and feel sick and the pee has dried on my legs. I need a bath cause I'm dirty and stinky.

Christmas

It's Christmas time, not Christmas day, and I am still not four yet, and mom and dad take me to church. We go to the church, go downstairs, and hang up our coats. Christmas decorations are up, green stuff with red cherries. Mom and dad go with other people into the church. They're wearing black hooded robes like the people of the church do. Two men in red and black robes (red sash) take me into the church. I have a white robe on (no hood) this time. This time we have to give the priest baby Jesus's heart to cleanse our sins and make us pure. We know we're not going to like it cos we did it before, but we had to cos we're special and the priest says we have to obey God. So we do it but it's a little easier this time. It's a black baby, not like the other baby that was white. Black babies are evil. They have to go to God to be made into light. We see his tummy not move and his eyes are shut so we're not sure if he's dead or not. He's in a baby diaper too and a basket like other one. The table's the same as before, with some green stuff on it to make it look Christmassy.

We praise Jesus and God, sing songs and take the sacrament before we cut the baby up and give his heart to the priest. Blood in a cup, blood of Christ and bread, his bones broken for us, his flesh pure as gold. It's his birthday this day but we're not sure why we're not singing 'Happy Birthday Jesus.' Instead we sing 'Power in the Blood' and some other songs. The church is little bit brighter with Christmas lights, candles and dim lights and brighter ones where the priest and the altar is. Everything is the same as before but we're not as scared.

We're getting used to it, but still don't like seeing the priest cut the heart out. I get to help this time. I stand where the priest stands with the priest's arms on each side of me, and hold his hand as he takes the knife and cuts from the chest to the top of the belly button. 'The skin is dark meat,' dad says too, 'because he's a black nigger.' Niggers have black skin but when we cut the skin it goes pink and white. I think maybe blood makes the skin pink, but it's white too, that's funny, why white? He must be bad like bananas that go bad when they're left in the sun too long. Blood oozes out and runs like before and the priest cleans it with a cloth. The cloth goes red and soggy but we keep going and take a knife and cut across the top like before and pull the skin back. Ucky. We don't like doing that, cause it's a baby, but we have to do what the priest's hand does, and they pull the skin back to get to the heart. We cut through veins and have to saw sometimes, but we do it and we pull the heart out carefully cause we don't want to damage it.

So then the priest leaves me and wipes his hands and goes to the podium, and the men at the altar in black and red robes tell me to put the heart in the cup and wait for the priest to tell me to bring it him. So I do, and then I have to see the priest after, to be cleansed from the blood and wish Jesus happy birthday and kiss his dick. We don't like it cos he always makes us put our mouth round it and it makes our mouth ache and choke like we're gonna get sick but can't cos we get in trouble, so we obey and be good and then get cleaned up by two men before we see mom and dad again.

*   *   *

Old Lady also had Luciferian training for a different set of alter personalities, with similar events. It is common that mind control survivors have several belief systems, held in different sets of alters. Just because you have unearthed one particular group of trained alters does not mean there are not others.

Here she describes the teachings of the respective different spiritual groups.

"Freemasons"[2] teachings:

- God is all knowing, all powerful and to be feared.
- God is good, eternal, light and Satan is evil, bad, darkness.
- Children are sacred, innocent and need to be sacrificed to God, as Abraham sacrificed Isaac. You hold the baby's heart in your hand and give it to the priest; there is power in the blood.

- Once I have killed babies or anyone or even animals, I am bad and need God's forgiveness through a sex act or I will go to hell.
- The priest's sperm makes you one with the priest.
- I am a holy child of God (*ha ma nada*) through the sex act with the priest.
- To kill myself is honorable, and is what God wants me to do if I tell you about God's group or the Freemasons' secrets.
- Killing myself is also the ultimate thing to do if I leave the group or share information about the group with anyone outside the group.
- If I kill myself I will be with God in heaven for eternity and this is the greatest place to be.
- On my birthday, I became the 'bride' of the priest. I was 'killed' (or made unconscious), then raised from the dead, raised on a cross in a ceremony with the congregation/group surrounding me.

Luciferians' teachings

- Lucifer (the same priest in a different costume) is the God of darkness; Satan is second in command, and Beelzebub is third.
- Lucifer is a spiritual being who is all knowing, all powerful, and to be feared.
- Lucifer, Satan and Beelzebub are good and God is bad.
- Darkness and evil is 'good', and light and God is 'bad'.
- The priest is human, a man and not of the same spiritual level or status as Lucifer (even though he is the same person, as we discovered in therapy).
- Light is bad (I was burned with physical light to make their point and enforce the word and imagery of light as being bad/hurtful/wrong.)
- Sacrificing animals, babies and other humans and eating them is good, it gives power ("power in the blood"). People becoming beasts who tear the bodies apart, feed on the blood and eating flesh is good.
- Lucifer's sperm makes you one with him.
- It is honorable, and righteous to kill myself. I will be with Lucifer. His sperm in me makes me spiritually powerful (not as powerful as him); I will be with Lucifer in hell if I kill myself. This is the ultimate goal.
- I am to kill myself if I share the group's information with anyone outside the group or if I escape or leave the group.
- Hell is used as a reward, and is seen as heaven.
- I was killed (unconscious) on an upside down cross and raised from the dead for the Luciferian group.

As you read these two lists, you can see how parallel the "Christian" or "Freemasons'" beliefs and the Luciferian beliefs are, just with different deities. Both groups sacrificed infants, and forced children to participate in murders and cannibalism. You will notice the references to blood giving power. Both groups embedded sexual abuse within a religious context. Those readers with backgrounds in Christian churches will notice how the "Christian" ritual abusers used ordinary hymns as part of their worship services, and how much of their doctrine was similar to that taught in many churches. Survivors of this kind of abuse who attend churches, or receive counseling or therapy from persons with overt Christian beliefs, will have alter personalities who assume that those in the churches or attempting to help them heal have the same beliefs (and perhaps, practices) as the perpetrators.

As Old Lady worked with this material to tell her story, her parts shared with one another. Initially they were very confused because different insiders worshipped opposite deities, and many of them were given the names of the Luciferian deities (she had several alters named Lucifer, Satan, and Beelzebub). The alters in the "Freemasons" group had not known the alters in the Luciferian group. As they shared with one another, they realized that there was only one perpetrator group who split parts off for both purposes, to serve their Gnostic theology of making light and darkness equal. And that the priest was also "Lucifer."

The main components of spiritual abuse are described below.

Simulation of religious figures and the afterlife

In countries where many citizens are Christians, it is common that God and Jesus are simulated. In ritual abuses based on Christianity, every aspect of the supposed nature of the Christian God is twisted: creation (creating alters through torture); judgment (rejecting and punishing the "evil" child), dying for sins (making the child hurt or kill "Jesus"), comfort (sexual abuse), forgiveness (forgiving through sex with a priest or someone dressed up as "God" or "Jesus"). Some survivors report being taken to a simulated "heaven" where "God" or Jesus rejected and verbally abused them and told them they were so evil that they could never be forgiven or enter heaven again. Children are put in graves with dead bodies, then "raised from the dead." Children and adults are abused while tied to upside-down crosses. Every Christian holiday has its perversion—killing the "baby Jesus" at Christmas, killing the adult "Jesus" at Easter.

In addition, the negative imagery associated with Christianity is exploited: a simulated "hell" is created with flames painted on the walls. Fires are used, dry ice is used to make "smoke", and people in devil or demon costumes hurt and rape children with forks or spikes. Children are encouraged to hurt others, being told that this (hell) is where they will have to spend eternity, so if they are on Satan's or Lucifer's side they will get to do the hurting instead of being hurt. What a choice!

Many Satanic and Luciferian cults have rituals in which "Satan" or "Lucifer" appears. "Satanic baptism" involves rape of a year-old infant by a man in a devil suit. "Marriage to Satan" involves dressing a child up in white to be raped by a man in a Satan costume with a spiked penis sheath.

Mind control groups that are not ritually abusive might simulate other kinds of gods. Trish Fotheringham, whose story is in Chapter Six, had a group of alters taken repeatedly to "the realm of the Gods" where Gods such as the Lord Almighty, Lady Luck, and the Three Fates instructed them to become the "voice of the gods". These gods later rejected them.

Blaming God or the child for the abuse

The inescapable nature of the abuse takes away any belief that the child might have that a benevolent deity will come to a victim's rescue. Later, survivors (and their therapists), depending on their belief system, have to face the reality of divine non-intervention, at least in any tangible sense.

This is often made explicit by the abusers. For example, a child being abused in a Satanist group is told to pray to God to come and save them. The child prays, and God does not appear. Then the child is told to pray to Satan, and a man in a Satan costume comes and tells the abusers to stop hurting the child. The child naturally assumes Satan is the benevolent deity.

The indoctrination goes one step further when God is blamed for the abuse. For example, one client shared with me that someone who was said to be God, and was dressed up in a white robe, physically and sexually abused her painfully at a young age, "creating" alters by telling them to split off. Another child was made very angry by the perpetrator group torturing her, then showing her a bearded man tied to a cross, who they said was Jesus. They told her that what was happening to her was all his fault. They gave her a weapon and told her to hurt or kill "Jesus."

These abusive groups explain divine non-intervention by making the children they abuse believe that God has chosen not to help them because they, the children, are evil to the core. One child was taken into the presence of "Jesus," tied to a cross. When she went to rescue him, he spat in her face. He said that he would rather die than be saved by her because she was so evil.

Forced perpetration

A large part of the post traumatic stress disorder experienced by war veterans is based on their having to harm or kill fellow human beings. This is not natural to us; it has to be drilled into military recruits, along with beliefs that dehumanize the enemy. Soldiers can go to war thinking they will be heroes for their country, and then have to face the devastating reality that they have killed someone just like themselves.

In the same way, one of the most heartbreaking parts of ritual abuse is the spiritual abuse that results from forced perpetration. Occult groups of various kinds force children (and adults) to participate in torture, rape, animal sacrifice, and real and simulated murders. To those who must take part, the murders are very real, even if the victim is not actually killed. And in some cases the murder is real.

Children love pets, and training in ritually abusive groups often begins with forcing them to kill a pet with which they have been allowed to bond. Because all contradictory emotions are split into different parts of a multiple, this creates a separation between the alters who feel empathy and those who are capable of perpetrating in order to save their lives.

The following are examples of what survivors have gone through in this regard.

- A little girl is given a puppy to pet. She is given a hallucinogenic drug, which causes her to see "waves" all around her. Then she is told her heart is being replaced by a black heart, and she sees a man holding a black animal heart; he hurts her chest and says he is putting it in her. Then he takes the puppy and at a signal the group pulls the puppy to pieces. The little girl is told it is because of her, her black heart sent out waves which made the puppy die.
- A two-year-old is allowed to play with a puppy, then is told to kill the puppy. When she refuses, her older brother is brought in and is made to kill a baby. The child is then told

that he had to kill the baby because she refused to kill the puppy. She is then told to kill the puppy, and complies.

Those of us who have not experienced this can only imagine how destructive such things are to the spirit of the child. The indoctrination that goes on around these experiences, with the purpose of "corrupting the innocent," makes it even worse. Children, who have a natural empathy for any hurt creature, are converted to "soldiers" or "priests," able to hurt and kill without experiencing empathy. The only way this can be accomplished is through dissociation.

As in war, the "choice" presented to the child is "kill or be killed." As you will see in Stella Katz's account (Chapter Seven), perpetrator groups know that many children will choose to die rather than to kill, but this really only results in that particular alter being "killed"—tortured to the point of unconsciousness—and a new alter being split off, until the child produces an alter who will do the killing. By now the child—the alter—is likely to kill robotically, with little or no awareness of what it is doing. Abusers will continue to train and refine the alters who do the harm, making sure that they do not feel compassion.

Adriana Green, whose full story will be told in a memoir, shares her experience of a therapy session regarding where such an event was addressed.

The strangers' house: Adriana Green

Maria is a small woman with dark eyes that witness the crimes of humanity. Her eyes reflect the capacity to believe, shine compassion when the need for kindness calls. I focus on staying the adult who moments earlier walked up the narrow flight of stairs of the historical building with its discolored runner, took off the blue duffel coat, embraced in greeting.

Five years have passed since Derek referred me.

"Good to see you," she says. I came to her in the latter part of her practice, with its long history of working in trauma recovery. She speaks publicly of mind control, teaches colleagues. She asks, "How are you?"

The past begins to stir, rises to the surface. I notice the subtle changes, the fuller mind, the shuffling about.

"This week has been more difficult."

"We are getting close to what happened," she says.

The small population within pushes forward, curious, listening for cues to come close. They are still getting used to the idea of moving to the top floor. For the past five years they have been walking down the narrow flight of stairs to Maria's office under ground level, where the windows ran high and narrow near the ceiling, footsteps hollow above our heads. Now we are perched high in a well lit room.

In this light, after all these years, I am still afraid of what might be seen at the core of me.

I do not speak this concern of mine. I know Maria's response without asking: *we must find out what happened. It is not enough to only feel, we need to know the entirety of what happened, so then you can finally understand.*

My headache comes in rapid waves, lasts seconds, interrupts me. I still want to trace the hurt on my face with my fingers, in search of understanding. But I refrain from raising my hands, and instead keep them interlaced on my lap. I know this to be a recurring memory, one that is linked to what is to be revealed.

Still, it stuns me.

"My face remembers."

Maria nods.

I sense someone else who noticed the hit on the face. He stands to the right of me, in my mind. I recognize him from last week, when he first appeared. He spoke quietly, making clear he was a boy. There's no protector to come and block his way, to refuse, punish the telling. A decade passed for him to learn there's help here. There's no need to stand separate.

I miss his rightful raging. I am still waiting for my anger to show.

This young boy believes he's an adult, a replica of the man who stood in front of him at the strangers' house. I have yet to learn why. Was it the utter loss of control? The confusion? Sheer survival? *What did they say to him to claim such a belief?* I do not trust him.

He wants to come forward, to break free from the forgotten place. I refuse to point him out. I'm afraid of what he knows. Everyone is afraid of him. He begins to fill the space beside me, leaves less room for me. I cannot keep his presence hidden from Maria. I speak loud, over the others, to make my position clear, that this moment is still mine.

I talk about hopelessness, not yet being able to connect the feeling to the small self. I say, "I wonder if this is where the healing ends."

"We need to look at what happened," Maria says. She understands the resistance, the progression to doing the work of recovery. She respects that I too, the adult, need time to speak. She listens as I try to talk it through. How can I go from mother and wife, to the child left on the strangers' doorstep, seeing the flash of grey of father's suit as he turned?

I wonder *why fight so hard to face that which can help redeem the self?*

"This is hard," I say.

"Yes. But he needs to share with everyone what happened," Maria says. "He is still back there, caught in time."

Many years have passed since I first remembered the pricking on the tops of the arms, the drugging, the slowing of body and breath. There was no story, only the effortless cry, the need to sleep.

The room swims in front of me, as if in water.

Now there's knowledge. Now we know this happened at the strangers' house. The memory resurfaces, persistent in saying *this too is part of the story.*

In my reluctance, I know too the boy's part will help complete the memory.

I'm afraid to remember, even though all the pieces are coming together, towards completing me.

"I would like to speak with him," Maria says.

"I can only see him." My voice slows, loses enunciation. I need to lay my head down, stop altogether.

"We need to let him know he's not bad, that whatever happened was not his fault."

I fill with insoluble confusion.

"Would it help to put the sleepy feelings away in a container while we go through what happened?" Maria draws an imaginary circle, describes the solid sides, the tight fitting lid that will keep the feelings at bay. "We don't have to remember all at once."

She takes care not to overwhelm the senses, knows this is the very reason for the existence of the others. "Can he come closer, show everyone what happened?"

I see the others far in the distance, their frozen cries. I do not want to know their pain. I do not want to know the crimes they are witness to, what secrets they still hold. But the dull of the sedation, being here with Maria, wise and familiar with the terrain of trauma, the intolerable wait—all this is enough to dismantle denial.

My head touches the soft mound of a pillow. And so comes the sequential telling with each step, the twist of story not grasped by the child's mind. But with patience and careful explanation, slowly the story forms, the thaw of then. When we arrive upon an empty space along the storyline, Maria will know a child, or a jagged edge of emotion, is missing. We need to find them, invite them here.

Maria asks questions in a kind investigative manner.

Everyone will listen, try to answer.

Sometimes no answer comes. *Not yet.*

At the center of the memory is the boy. He appeared last week in chain of recollection, promised to return today, to bring his part of the story. I wonder, is it the blank expression, the stoop of the shoulders, that Maria recognizes when she says, "You met me before. Take a look around. Those men are not here. They are probably long gone by now, or dead."

I don't want him to step to the front.

What is revealed may not give relief, in the glare of light and truth.

When Maria first met him, she said, "I like you." He heard the lightness of her voice, felt the warmth of her greeting flush across his face. *Could he matter in a different way than what he was created for?*

He wants to talk with Maria, to ease the pressure of keeping silent. If only he could, but learning what and how to speak takes practice, needs time and space. And these things, he did not know well.

The others stay their distance. He's not tempted to step towards them.

Besides, he's glad he's not a girl, for what happens to them.

He was created to come out in the world for only a short time. But what he did will take near a lifetime to shed the shame, to realize forgiveness.

"He doesn't like any of us," the eight-year-old tells Maria. "He doesn't like girls."

"Well, if nobody likes him, I can be his friend, until they get to know him."

"He's bad."

"I don't think he's bad. He's only five years old." She stretches out her hand horizontal to the floor near three feet to show how tall she suspects he might stand. "He's actually little. How can we find him? How can we let him know he can come out here today?"

"He did something terrible."

"There was someone who made him do what he did." Maria says. "I want him to look around the room, to see me. I will not make him do anything bad. I want him to know he's not there. He's here."

He sees with my eyes, looks for the men in the room, the one standing, the rest sitting nearby. But they are not here. He looks at Maria, and then looks around the room, takes in the painting of the lioness and her cub, the bright greens of foliage around their golden manes.

He takes a small breath now and again, wonders if they slipped through the door while he was taken by the color and light. He looks around yet once again.

But they are not here.

One night, when sleep would not come for the adult, he held firm the pencil, and drew a portrait of the stranger, with the long limbs and straight cut hair that stopped at his chin. He folded the drawing in four and brought the small piece of evidence to Derek, and said, "This is him." That was many years ago.

This is how long the memory is in the making.

Maria likes him. She told him this last week. She keeps one hand on his. Her one hand on his does not scare him. He watches her steady eyes, feels her calm. He notices that she's not afraid of him. Maybe he can stay a little while longer in the brightness.

The remembering begins to bubble upward. There's something on the ground he has to hurt, between him and the man who stands in front of him. There's a man behind him too. Large hands wrap around his to help hold the knife. The insides of his hands sting from the pressing.

He gave this memory of the stinging on the inside of the hands to the adult a long time ago, but she still does not know its meaning.

"It is all right to share what happened with everyone," Maria says.

There's a little girl that is behind him. She's still as a small statue. He came to do this for her, so she could live. They hit him on the face to keep him awake from the sleepiness. He feels the pull up and the force down on his wrist. His hands are squeezed together, the impression deeper than skin. The hands over his own leave, but he keeps on doing the up and down motion. He needs to vomit. But if he doesn't do this, the little girl who is quiet behind him will die. He came to be in her place.

Maria is still here, and he's glad for this. She watches his hands.

"Do you know what is happening?"

I need to believe he could not see what it was that he had to hurt.

"We need to be quiet," he says.

"Can you say why?"

"So nothing more will happen."

"Look around again. See? They are not here. Then what happened?

"The man says that I'm one of them." Maria's hand is still on his.

"You're not one of them," she says. "They only want you to believe this."

"I think I should be dead."

"I don't want you dead," she says, her eyes sad. He wants to believe her more than the man. But he believes in his badness, remembers being told about the balance between the good and bad. He had to be bad, just as he was to be good. He had to believe the man in front of him.

Maybe he can believe Maria.

Something wet is traced on his face—there's a fleeting sensation of fingers tracing downwards on his face, like a ghost passing through him. He wants to sleep, fade away.

"What happens then?"

"They put it on my face." He looks at her and wants her to know, without having to say.

"What did they put on your face?"

He can't say, only wants her to know.

"Do they say more?" He nods.

"I belong to them."

When I work through such memories with clients, I make sure to point out that there are likely to be many alters who refused to perpetrate before the abusers could get one who would do what they required.

These perpetrators go to great lengths to make children believe that they are so evil that nobody will want them except for the abuser group. There are often alters who are given the job of reminding your client that she or he is an evil killer or rapist who will be sent to hell when they die. They reinforce the message that someone who starts to remember or disclose being abused is not a victim, but an abuser. Abusers may teach that the child (later, adult) will harm anyone they get close to. For example, see the little girl with the "black heart," above.

A central aspect of our humanity is our ability to consider ourselves free beings who have moral choices, who are able to choose good over evil and to experience empathy for others. This core belief is certainly the target of mind controlling groups, in particular those with religious beliefs at the base of their practice. The mind control takes away the victim's free will. The forced perpetration takes away the victim's ability to choose good and act on that choice, and the splitting the personality system between "good" and "evil" alters allows the eventual committing of acts of violence without the empathy which normally prevents such actions. This systematic indoctrination allows such groups continue their existence into further generations.

The survivor who chooses to recover will go through the agony of knowing and taking responsibility for what she or he has done. In this way, survivors reclaim their humanity and spiritual purity.

We shall look more at questions of good and evil, meaning, and spirituality in Chapter Nine as well as Chapter Fifteen, "The unimaginable". Different therapists take different approaches, and there, I shall share mine.

Notes

1. Note that we only know what Old Lady remembers her perpetrators telling her about their identities and loyalties. Various perpetrators identified themselves as Freemasons, Nazis, GIs, Green Berets, MI6, CIA, and Luciferians. We do not know their actual loyalties.
2. We do not know that these people were really Freemasons; we only know that is what they told the child.

CHAPTER SIX

Military, political, and commercial uses of mind control

I t might be said that in some ways, all ritual abuse and mind control is perpetrated for power or commercial purposes. Some, however, arises specifically from government, military, or "shadow government" groups. Although this chapter focuses on the personal stories of two healed survivors of mind control who were used for military/political and commercial purposes, much of what they experienced applies to mind control survivors in general.

Trish Fotheringham was discarded by her abusers when she was in her teens, and never used again. This was probably because of her severe asthma and her rebellious nature. Some things that may be helpful for therapists to note in this story include:

1. The presence of one primary "handler" throughout;
2. The extremely complicated, intricate structure of her system;
3. The assignment of alter personalities to colors;
4. The simulation of the "real world" by artificial means, different for each alter;
5. The huge amount of stage magic, scenery and props involved;
6. The way in which hidden alters held emotions and other aspects of experience;
7. The deliberate creation of an "inner world;"
8. The use of age-appropriate play activities for training;
9. The sealing in of alters at ages where they could not tell reality from fantasy;
10. The internal filing system for training experiences;
11. The security system to prevent the survivor from remembering or talking;
12. The complex process of locking away the training memories and programming the child for a future of failure.
13. The deliberate creation of false memories to mask the existence of the mind control.

Mind control as I experienced it: Trish Fotheringham

I believe that I was raised as a demonstration model for mind-control techniques designed to provide the latest, most marketable form of human slavery of the time. I do not know the identity of the group who programmed me but it clearly had both a profit-making and a political agenda. From my birth in 1960, I was subjected to daily trainings and exploitations designed to create dissociated alternate personalities (alters) that could be programmed according to the needs of the buyer(s). This programming was instilled through the use of mind-control techniques, including ritual abuse-torture, that were built layer upon layer to form specific patterns of behavior within each alter. This resulted in alters that were meant to be perfectly controllable "slaves."

I was used as a child sex slave by individual pedophiles and cults, and also by pedophile rings, for orgies, rituals, child pornography and snuff films. I was used to write abusers' words, preach their agendas, recruit others, train other young children, and trigger others to action, record, and report. I was also used to steal and spy, for drug and arms trafficking, and for other common criminal activities.

As a demonstration model, I was trained to exhibit a multitude of personality profiles, any of which could be individually defined and selected for purchase and creation in others. Conflicting programs caused an increased need for adjustments and fine-tuning. Program deterioration and eventual breakdown were inevitable. When that occurred—on essentially a "built-in expiry date"—I was cast out and discarded. This conflicting training helped me to eventually break the programming bonds and bypass "failsafe" programs which are always a part of the programming package.

My mind-control programming included the use of:

- sensory/sleep/food deprivation; also sensory overload;
- confusion, fear, pain, terror, guilt, shame, humiliation and belittlement;
- theatrics, trickery, illusion, lies and coercion;
- physical, emotional, verbal, sexual and spiritual abuse;
- forced actions against self/animals/others;
- double-bind situations;
- systematic behavior modification and hypnosis techniques;
- drugs, lights, sounds, smells, special effects, film projections, hidden cameras and microphones;
- sets, props, actors, costumes and make-up;
- meticulously and elaborately designed role-play "characterizations" based on nursery rhymes, fairy tales, stories, books, movies and music;
- guns, electroshock, whips;
- shackles, chains and cages.

My handlers focused a great deal on creating dissociation. Their intentional use of traumatic situations (torture and electroshock) along with psychoactive drugs made it possible for them to selectively disconnect from my conscious mind aspects of awareness or experience; these were contained in dissociated identities, or alters, that they created. The alters would serve other purposes as well.

These abuses were carefully pre-planned. My trainers generally used only enough trauma to accomplish their goals. "Smoke and mirrors" (deception and illusions, assisted by drugs) made specific aspects of each piece of training attach to the correct alter identity in a predictable manner. For maximum effectiveness and potency, the science of child development was used to make training incidents age- and stage- appropriate. These trainings, which my alters understood as "life lessons," became progressively more frequent and more traumatic as I aged.

Although they had no real power, my alters were allowed or given just the right amount of apparent personal empowerment to fool them into never knowing they were being manipulated. *Their belief that their experience was real was the key.* Alters were called out into the body only for those experiences that would further their intended understanding of the world.

My primary handler, whom I called "Puffy," was present during my training throughout my life from infancy. Usually loving and friendly, stroking and kissing me, he was like my daddy, lover, sweetheart, and master all at once. He played with me and treated me like his precious little princess. He took me walking in his beautiful gardens, swishing me about, scooping me up into his arms. He danced alone with me in his bedroom to Johnny Mathis tunes, crooning the words to me as if I were his lover. I stayed the night so often at his estate home after various events that I believed I had my own bedroom, wardrobe, music box and porcelain horse collections, and that his servants were my servants. I even had "my own" horse in his stables for when the two of us went riding.

Puffy often filmed our time together. He taught me to ignore and not even see the camera, which was important in later trainings and exploitations. This created confusion initially in therapy, until I learned to "zoom out" to out-of-body alters who could give me the full details of a given scenario. Before that, I misinterpreted many memories. For example, at first I believed that a recalled series of Satanic events meant that my family were Satanists and that "I" had been married to Satan (red skin, horns, tail, and all). Later, an out-of-body alter enabled me to learn that cameras, wires, crew and staged settings had created these Satanic-themed situations as part of a series of porn and snuff films. The alters involved in the ceremonial events were never out anywhere else, so they naturally interpreted them as real life. Only this "zoomed out" perspective enabled me to recognize and distinguish the truth in all this.

During my first weeks of life, my handlers established as much controllable dissociation as possible, as soon as possible. Negative emotional states such as fear, helplessness, stifled anger, and loneliness, as well as positive ones such as pleasure, contentment and safety, were isolated into separate alters. Some of these splits initially involved trauma; all were developed by giving each alter experiences that locked them steadily deeper into their emotional state.

My deliberately created alters were all associated with particular colors, with each color representing a "path" or type of training. An alter who was being trained to follow a red path would only wear particular red clothing, be spoken to in particular ways, and have experiences in particular situations, with particular types of people. So little was left to chance that even the toys each child alter was allowed were part of the plan. This color training continued until adulthood, with additional associations added as I became older. Being dressed in particular colors helped me to know who I was at any given moment, right through to the end of therapy!

As much as possible, the color-coding was also linked to the seven primary chakra chi energy centers of eastern traditions. Their traditional meanings were given twists to make the associations fit each alter's color training. Colors were tempered by their shades—lighter shades (those with white added) tended to involve sensitive feelings, while darker shades (those with black added) tended to have only the angry, violent or power-seeking types of feelings, if they had any at all.

The first step in my color-coded training was to create the initial dissociative splits needed to form the foundation for my entire system of alters. The very first intentional splits were created through the use of trauma at the time of my birth. My birth cries were choked off by abusers shaking me violently while I heard my first words repeated loudly and angrily: "Don't cry! Stop crying! Be quiet!" This was followed immediately with very tight and brutal swathing, accompanied by the loud command, "Keep still! Don't move! Stay still!" These words had no meaning for me at that point, but thereafter they became important trigger phrases, used to develop these alters and to lock in crucial programming to obey, keep still, and keep silent.

Testing was initiated shortly after my birth to determine my natural, inborn aptitudes and interests. It continued through my infancy and toddler years. Many separate, color-based training paths were developed and "installed" over time, each built layer upon layer. Each color path was linked to a skill set, forging emotional and/or spiritual beliefs and control mechanisms or programs that created base belief systems.

Throughout my infancy and toddlerhood, trauma was used mainly to reinforce such commands as "Don't cry", "Be quiet", "Don't tell", "Don't move", "Be still", "Do as you're told", and "Obey", and to institute parameters for the alters' reality. An alter who "came out" when it wasn't his or her time, or who acted or spoke inappropriately, would be punished. Appropriate behavior was rewarded with praise and what appeared to be loving, encouraging treatment. Inappropriate behavior was met with pain and the withdrawal of love and affection. Alters who were supposed to be disconnected from people, such as the "mercenary soldiers" of the black path, had basic needs met if they behaved appropriately, and were given pain or deprivation for misbehavior.

By the time I was about six months old, splits, testing and training had already built a substructure of experiences, beliefs, attitudes, and behaviors in my earliest alters. The training then began to include more and more color links, progressively tying each color to sounds, then words, shapes, symbols, etc. These were linked to alter-specific feelings and meanings to produce specific and predictable results in alters' behaviors, responses, and actions. For example, by toddler age, when I was placed on a man's lap, my first red path (sexual) alter would do a lap dance, coyly and suggestively wiggling and giggling "just so".

From age six months to two years, my training focused on installing basic commands and triggers in the initial alters. Certain programs, such as Obey, Don't Tell, Be Loyal, or Internal Security/Alarms were created at the beginning and reinforced frequently as I grew. Later, my handlers would call forth these alters by using the trigger phrases or inducing the feeling states I had experienced the day of the initial split. Alters were each given "life experiences" to increasingly lock in their separate, distinctive understanding and experience of reality. Lights, colors, clothes and accessories, words, phrases, touch, smell, drugs, and quite specific color-coding were all used methodically. This enabled my handler and trainers to create and develop each alter's individual belief system and value structure, systematically shaping his or her conceptions and understanding of "how the world works", "the rules of life", and almost everything he or she thought, felt, said, or did.

For example, in order to familiarize red path alters with sexual treatment, feelings and behaviors, everything had a sexual aspect: the way I was (they were) touched, spoken to, held, and dressed all involved lots of stroking and sexual touching; sexy music was played in the background; and lots of light-hearted play and laughter was mixed in, so it was all just fun. When there would be pain, it was usually accompanied by soothing words, sounds and gentle touch, assuring me this was all for my own good and was preparing me for life. Hence, my young red path alters' understanding of love and relationships was woven into a complex, twisted sexuality. They learned a confused sense of play mixed with resignation, based on their understanding that some parts of life hurt and you just had to endure smilingly.

Until late in therapy, base alters took and held parts of my life. Experiences were therefore often fragmented at the time they occurred. Since only one alter could be "out" for an event, one or more of these base alters would siphon off the feelings, emotional states, and/or pain that went with whatever was experienced without truly being out in the body. Each alter's piece of the memory would have to be accessed and addressed before the whole experience could be considered reclaimed and healed. Yet, "I," the person who handled everyday life at home and in the world, was not aware that alternate identities held pieces of my life. Because it seemed natural to me for life to be broken into chunks, with missing pieces here and there, lost time went unnoticed. Since continuity was unknown, there was no sense of discontinuity. Nor was I aware that a dissociated way of life had been established and my brain's way of coping with difficulties was "wired in", to simply create another alter!

During the toddler period, training began to create in me different foundational understandings of reality, with specific color-coded patterns for the role and character development of each alter and each path. As each base alter had enough time "out" in the body, their reality steadily began to solidify. Dissociative barriers limited their awareness to only their own pieces of my overall life. Each alter had his or her own unique way of being, and, by the time I was two years old, each had a distinct identity, with basic color-coded identifications and associations. His or her feelings, thoughts, behaviors, actions and beliefs had been linked to color-specific situations, places, sounds, words, phrases, gestures, shapes, and symbols.

I was two years old when my trainers first used a special wooden chair with attached straps and helmet. It could rock, buck, rotate, and administer electric shocks. My trainers always told me it was a "magic gateway chair" that allowed me to "ride the rainbow" to faraway and strange realms. At first, the vibration and electrical stimulation of the chair, along with drugs and a fan blowing wind at me, would make me feel as if I were floating and actually moving through space. They gave the chair different purposes for different alters by naming different destinations, and then using props, sets, lighting and sounds or music to create specific moods and associations, specific foundational realities. The chair's bucking and spinning created internal tornados through little pulses and zaps. These added to the whole "wild-weather" feeling. When I "rode the rainbow" on this chair, lighting and special effects made me feel as if I were traveling. Later I was "repaired" harshly and punished by the same chair. Some of the final events which locked down my "inside people" and inner world happened in the chair.

Also at two, my handlers created a structured "internal world" to house alters when they were not actively "out" in the body. These alters always had the symbols and props required to ensure they remained programmed and controllable over the long-term. All of this was established and added to over time, using staged settings which were replicated in the inner world, to make the inner landscape, buildings, and items appear real and tangible to its inhabitants. Playful dress-up activities incorporated well-known nursery rhymes, songs, storybooks, TV, and movies. Every time I saw or heard these things in my daily life, outside of the formal training, my alters' beliefs would be subconsciously solidified.

My inner world was a luscious green magical fairy tale world, with hills, valleys, and a river. An ever-present murmur of sound was at first labeled "the whispering leaves;" later, I would refer to it as my internal soundtrack. This soundtrack consisted of words, phrases, songs, rhymes, and chants, such as "Be a good girl", "Do what you're told", and "Skip to my Lou my darling", all of which formed the instructional backdrop of my life. A core system placed in the center of the inner world served as a root or anchor, guidance system and overseer system all in one. This was a "Tree of Life", with branches for the general color-coded paths, and colored leaves for holding their specific memory and training links. Training thereafter was linked and built upon this tree.

The rest of the inner world was easily installed. Some of it was done outdoors, some in staged settings. "Weather phenomena" got into the inner world the same way everything else did, simply by my being told they were there, and being shown special effects. Like all children this age I naturally believed whatever I was told. Tornadoes, dustballs and whirlwinds were made with fans blowing wind at and around me when I was in the magic chair. At first I was taught to "control" them, then later to "be" them.

Rainbows were created in the air around and under me in the chair, apparently by means of light shining through sprays of water. I was told that the rainbows were multi-colored magic paths to other worlds. The end where the chair was located was fixed. The other end was "moveable," and so it could be "set" to the chosen destination. These other worlds were at first staged externally, then became sections of my inner world. Because the rainbows contained all colors, they could be used to call forth all the alters the colors represented simultaneously. Strobe or flashing lights were used for this later.

"Natural" phenomena and mind control images were coordinated with color coding. Green was grass, trees and whispering leaves. Blue was water, the sky, air, and wind, "the power and voice" of the whispering leaves and tornados. Yellow was the sun, a pot of gold at the end of the rainbow, pixie dust, a golden cup, and a "magic golden ball" of my externalized "dangerous true power". Brown was dirt, trees, "brownies and dwarves", dust-balls and whirlwinds that whisked things away out of sight. White was fluffy pillows and clouds, angels, and "heaven", the home of the gods and goddesses (who were simulated by actors). Grey was fog, smoke, confusion and illusion. Black was being alone, dark, silent, cold, scary, dirty, tough, mean and nasty.

Colors also defined the paths that were structured along the branches of my "tree of life." I came to call the nine branches "color paths", because each had its own particular color of leaf. These nine colors—red, green, yellow, white, pink, purple, multi-colored, brown, and orange—were everywhere as I toddled about outdoors in the autumn, so leaves on branches were easy foundational reference points to plant inside my mind. Once these foundational realities were solidly established, each of the foundational alters was assigned his or her own branch and leaf to keep track of his or her specific training.

The nine branches of the tree were assigned a combination of attributes that best enhanced each color's training path. These were the "virtues," based on actual virtues, such as kindness, obedience, loyalty, honesty, strength, wisdom, purity, cleanliness, order, truth, and justice. Each, however, was given its own twisted meaning. Some, like loyalty and obedience, were trained into all paths. Nearly all alters were taught to be "good", but the meaning of that term was tailored to their training path.

The nine foundational virtues alters were assigned their own branches and given a leaf of their color to keep with them at all times. With so many color paths, branches and leaves, my training was broader, more varied—and more conflicting—than most people's would be.

The virtues were developed through fun play with props and costumes with accessories, which were later used to control all of my alters. For example, a black purse or belt ensured that aspects of security training were part of the scenario, gold jewellery meant a degree of authority for the alter wearing it, and silver items created a spiritual connection. Metals and gemstones further defined complex role parameters. Each color-coded branch of training was linked with particular items, obstacles, warnings, links and guideposts for alters, most of which were given internal representations. An eyeball in a glass ball was the famous All-Seeing Eye, always watching and recording me. Brown dustballs and whirlwinds ("magical dwarves and brownies in disguise") came to "whisk things away" when a secret appeared in danger of being exposed, while a "wise" blue tornado whirled "safe words" into my mind as distractions. A golden cup, originally held to "open a channeling state," became an alter that was an open channel. All these things were produced in the external world and reproduced in the inner world.

For my red path alters, the virtues were initially developed by me being Little Red Riding Hood. The "good little girl in red" was in danger and had to watch out for the big bad wolf. She protected herself by being clever and coy while pretending everything was fine and normal. Playtime was a fun game, naked, with my handler Puffy being all scary and mean. "I'm the big bad wolf—keep me happy or I'll eat you," he said, his words accompanied by sexualized gestures and actions. He stroked and rubbed me. There was lots of bouncing, tickling, poking, laughs, and hugs. All my alter had to do to be safe was lick, kiss, wiggle and rub in the ways that made the wolf growl or purr with pleasure. Then she knew for sure she was a good girl. She would be the winner of the game too!

The red path alters' sex-focused virtue of "good little girl" was expanded over the years to include "good little hostess" and "proper little lady", along a path leading to madam-like responsibilities. The alters' experiences were designed to establish a comfort zone pattern of sex and sexual interactions as a necessary part of life. I had clients to satisfy. The skilled use of words, phrases, actions, body language and emotional response patterns was built in so that the clients' sexual experience was encouraged and enhanced. These alters only felt power and security when playing out familiar sexual roles.

My pink path alters were princesses or fairies. They were naïve and innocent, believing they were "in charge, powerful and entitled to be treated royally", as evidenced by much bowing and apparent subservience by Puffy and his servants and my trainers (who these alters thought were "private tutors.") Pink alters held fairy tale "all is good" beliefs and knew only good, happy feelings—that is, unless they didn't get their way and had a temper tantrum, whereupon all of their privileges were removed until "they" were able to "behave like proper ladies." They went to fabulous high-class parties; they were pampered, carried, "swished and flown about"; they knew daydreaming, light-heartedness, and the magical satisfaction of their wants and desires. Similar to red path trainings, as I grew, pink alters were taught the skills required of "ladies of high-standing"—how to dress, walk, talk, organize parties, be a hostess, etc.

Conversely, my dark blue and black path alters were tough soldiers (and a mean witch). They had to be forceful, calculating, manipulative, nasty, hurtful, uncaring. They must "not let anything stop (them)". Like a vicious, cruel version of normal boyish roughhousing, play for them involved much violence: sneaking up on and scaring people, tackling, kicking, hitting, nasty words, insults and putdowns. Their experiences established, for them only, a comfort-zone pattern of following orders and "thinking on their feet", with "doing a good job", anger, aggressiveness, violence and destructiveness as the only ways to feel powerful.

The white path was my main communication and word path. These alters learned to live in an outsider, observer point of view. Interpreting words, gestures and body language, they made note of people's needs. When I was about age two, a "cloud" alter was split off to "see, feel and be inside the clouds", far away from my body and unaffected by the cares of the harsh world. Not long after, a "bird's eye view overseer" was created to watch everything from an out-of-body perspective that saw "the bigger picture." Over time, through various alters, the entire white path learned to "hear the voice of the gods", "channel", "be an open vessel", and "let the visions guide." My handlers attached tiny speakers to my ears when I was drugged and used externally created film and holographic projections until just thinking of the "voice of the gods" in my mind would produce these visions without external aids.

While all of this was being established, each alter continued to receive experiential training. When my body was two-and a-half years old, my red and pink path alters' training had me in "an elite group" with other girls and boys. We were together in a class called "manners training" at an official local government residence, where we were taught "how to behave appropriately" in high society." We learned etiquette and manners, including such "necessary skills" as how to do lap dances. I learned to ballroom dance with my face provocatively buried in my partner's crotch in a way not clearly evident to any but him. We were also taught how to French kiss. Puffy was an important part of the manners training and "reward" dinner parties, at which we children were treated as pets. Men were partnered with girls, and boys with ladies. Dressed in grown up-gowns and tuxedos, we participated in fabulous dinners followed by ballroom dancing. These events included some big fat military leaders (whom I also knew in other settings along with Puffy) as well as members of the "circle of 12+1," the group with whom Puffy performed rituals.

As part of my training, names and other words that could identify characteristics of, or otherwise implicate my trainers, handlers or clients received special treatment. To protect against disclosure, every such memory was automatically shunted away to a secret place in my mind that was only known to the trainers and handlers. Eventually, entire special "code access only" storage areas were created in my inner world. Toward that end, from initial creation, all known alters were taught to not notice or be aware of (and seemingly not remember) such details. This was easily accomplished with simple, reality-denying statements such as "Don't be silly, that's not true, no-one like that (or named that) was here. You made it all up, stop lying". This invalidated and denied the alters' truth while creating and enforcing whatever false reality was needed. When that was insufficient, a hard slap across the face or some other quick, painful or shocking action would usually ensure that "what is forgotten remains forgotten".

If the security of the programming was breached, there were internal alarms. They were linked to the foundational leaf color of orange. The alarms involved pattern and word recognition, as well as the reporting and recording of information and experiences, both internally and externally. From the earliest lessons, orange connected the controller, storyteller and reporter alters to key trigger phrases like "Get the story right", "Don't miss anything", "Note every detail", and, "They're always watching". As usual, symbolic messages applied to what I said or did. Orange programs, like the first sign of the fall season, warned "the fall is coming," which was indicated that I was "nearing a fall", should "watch my step" or "be careful". Such warnings created terror in me, inducing a state of ever-present hyper-alertness over what would happen if I made a mistake.

This requirement of accuracy and attention to detail was also part of the white "word path" training. By the time the body was five, a little "scribe" or "scholar in training" alter had learned to make point-form lists for military leaders at their planning meetings. This was done initially through pictures, and then with words. (They believed the silencing programs were infallible at this point and found me entertaining in this role.) At first, the scribe kept track of who said what and what decisions were made. This progressed to detailed note-taking, followed by speech writing. By age ten I had been programmed with alters who believed themselves to be an oracle and a preacher, who, by channeling the words of the gods, roused and rallied the crowds. The message attached in my belief system was "People will suffer in these times of great change". By that time, a huge, previously installed inner world library held "ancient books and scrolls" that were the records of all "I" had listed, noted, read and learned. To this day, I still experience a scrolling marquee across the front of my brain, with my every thought plus the words I am hearing printed out in text.

Around the body's age of six, the integrity of each (known) alter's programming was subjected to tests of skill acquisition. My red path sexual alters were left completely alone with clients from start to finish, which included taking their money. Although they believed the test to be for their sexual skills and overall value, it was really a test of my trustworthiness: Would I talk/tell secrets, or try to run or escape? My dark blue and black path "soldier" alters were tested for their ability to be cold, calculating and cruel as needed, and to follow orders no matter what. The killing and dissection of a kitten was proof of the black soldier alter being able to "stomach the job", and a test proving "family loyalty" forced the dark blue alter to choose between letting my little brother get hurt and letting our pet rabbit suffer and die. These double-bind situations left me with crippling, soul-deadening shame, guilt, powerlessness and helplessness.

After the tests had confirmed satisfactory programming integrity, the inner world was sealed, trapping the foundational virtues alters inside with their programmed realities. These sealed-in alters would stay stuck at an age and stage of development that believed in fairy tales and magic, unable to distinguish between fact and fantasy. They were also completely unable to distinguish the inner world from the outer, despite living in both worlds, due to the internal dissociative barriers that the seals created. They were left with only their personal belief systems, personality traits and skills, and the safe, acceptable memories of their portions of my life. (This remained the status quo until "I" discovered the existence of the alters and inner world at the age of thirty-one.) Re-activation coding was incorporated so that my trainers would be able to open the seal at a later time and make necessary additions and other changes to my inner world. These codes consisted of the words, symbols, and actions to which alters had been trained to respond with certain previously installed instructions. It was not enough for me to simply remember the codes; a person outside myself had to say the words, show me the symbols, and make the correct actions (after I told them what to say and do) in order for the instructions to work.

In October, 1966, just after I entered first grade, the seal was solidly in place for all alters. At that point, the main focus of my training shifted to role responsibility and the steady acquisition of knowledge and skill. My red alters began to be used in a series of pornographic and snuff films (films involving actual or staged murders) with Satanic ritual themes, created in conjunction with actual local Satanic cults and pedophile groups. These alters, like all alters used in such films, believed the experiences to be completely real. One alter was proud to be the bride of Satan. I was subjected to increasingly nasty, painful, sickening aspects of my various training paths. My alters were taught to distract themselves when it was awful or yucky by counting or chanting, repeating a word or phrase silently, squeezing something tightly, or "getting lost in the music."

Another area of training occurred between the ages of five and ten, when Puffy took me to "military" planning sessions. I call them "Out of Time Rallies" because I was told they took place "outside of time" and the only way to get to them was by way of the "magic gateway chair". This was where the white scribe alter was developed and trained, taking notes for the fat old military leaders while also serving as a sexual entertainment tool for their orgies. These military men seem to have included sex in most things they did. At these sessions, I learned details of the "great leader's plans" and the intended role for my white path of "rallying the people", which greatly added to my underlying terror.

Puffy sometimes joined these men on a huge, glamorous off-shore yacht that was used for child sex slave trafficking. Here, when I was little, pink and/or red alters were passed around for lap dances and other sexual abuses, made to dance and otherwise entertain while being treated like little princesses. Here, my young dark blue and black soldier alters were sometimes forced to "do battle" with other young "boys" in soldier training, while the men placed bets to see which of us "had what it takes to succeed." As I grew older, pink and red alters were also groomed here for high society roles such as hostess and respected lady.

At some point, it became part of one red alter's job to help break down other child victims who were my age or younger, and then train them to be sex slaves. This use of me continued until I was twelve.

Often, I was taken to the yacht by my grandfather when he delivered newly acquired trainees. These were usually missing or unregistered children of all races and ages, who had been transported from other places in North America and were being readied for shipping and sale in other countries. I remember being in the boat with these children when grandpa was handing them over, helping them climb the ladder up the side of the yacht. Sometimes I would already be on the yacht, standing beside Puffy, who was awaiting grandpa's shipment. All the men in their dark blue military uniforms with their fancy insignia were standing in two-sided formal greeting rows beside and across. Grandpa (in the same uniform) would salute as he handed over the latest shipment. The ceremony included the formal military words of report, delivery, and handing over of authority. I even saluted back. I wore a formal gown to indicate that the children were being handed over to me for training. At the time, such pomp and ceremony made me believe this was legitimate and above-board, and made the other children (who were drugged, starved, beaten, confused and terrified) believe it too. This gave me clear authority over them as they were led, dragged or pushed through to their quarters and assigned bunks.

From ages nine to twelve, I was taught to take my place on "the stage of life," which not only existed in the real world of pre-teen peer pressure and media influence, but in my inner world as well. Staged and scripted scenarios, sometimes presented on the stage of a small theater, were instantly credible and completely believable to my now numerous alters. As my interest in popular fashions, teen idols, and hit parade music naturally grew, these things became powerful tools in the shaping of my alters. Many new storage and trigger mechanisms had to be created in my inner world now: clothes, purses, high-heeled shoes, make-up, and other feminine accessories for the red and pink alters; promotion-declaring insignias and more powerful weapons (such as a rifle) for the dark blue and black alters' cache. There was also much more. For proper program cohesion and function, each alter and each path had to have their own inner world stuff.

By about age ten, file rooms housing file cabinets had been established in my inner world. The cabinets were filled with folders of training and programming experiences. A fastidious grey file-keeper alter was created to keep the existence of the entire collection hidden, and also to hide the other alters' knowledge and skills from each other. This alter was able to order and reference files but not to understand what was in them.

From the start of my training, various self-destruct, booby-trap, and time-bomb programs were implanted, which I call "fail-safes". They became more detailed, involved and tailored to me and my alters, as time went by. My instructions were to never tell, to keep silent, to whisk knowledge or memories away, to keep the pieces separate, or to go crazy. Later, I was programmed to destroy my own credibility, sabotage myself, attempt suicide, or engage in addictions in order to cope or belong. The same instructions were imparted to the internal systems that reported infractions so that punishments or repairs could be done. These were the programs that made me crash or become flooded with unbearable feelings, that locked away certain memories, or that made a memory or programmed belief impossible to escape from. Like a spider-web, they were linked, woven together to intersect, support, and back each other up. This was done by repeating such phrases as "too much trouble," over and over. The same instructions were woven into many different trainings, so that a particular trigger phrase could set a cascade of programs into effect. The effects of the programs were designed to spiral, and to operate as a paradox. Thus, for instance, affirmations that work well with the average person might actually trigger increased problems for me. It was confusing for me and those assisting in my recovery that I would be getting worse when I was using methods that should make me get better.

One significant type of fail-safe programming involved "trip wires" which could trigger actual physical responses, such as an arm jerking or pain in the chest that felt like a heart attack. These began early. They were part of two separate aspects of my training: "flying" (for fairies, witch, and genie alters—done in a harness of the sort used in circus/gymnastics training), and being a "puppet on a string" (mostly to prove I was not in control of my own body). I was encased in wires and/or string (hidden from sight so the alters didn't know they were there) in a way that led me to believe my trainers controlled my movements from a distance through their magical powers. Over time, these wires were used to form a network of control points throughout my body, each of which had specific fail-safe body responses linked to it. Telling a secret produced the feeling of being choked. Ignoring an internal warning about a fall could make a knee buckle to make me actually fall, thereby enforcing the validity of the warning.

At small gatherings in the places I was abused in (most often on the yacht), my alters' abilities would be demonstrated to potential buyers. I would display some of the trainings specific to what the buyers wanted. However, certain things that I did in the "real world," such as organizing a protest march in a hospital for sick children, alerted my handler and trainers to the fact that my programming was deteriorating. This forced them to speed up plans for their last uses of me before my shutdown. They had me demonstrate my skills one final time.

I found myself in a large cage, on a stage, in a large military mess tent. Using their names and trigger phrases, Puffy called my alters out, over a loudspeaker. He would reach through the bars to give me a quick zap under my feet, or a flick of a whip or a poke with a stick—whatever helped trigger the behavior he wanted demonstrated. While I displayed various "slave trainings," buyers—rows of seated men in dark blue military dress uniforms—were told they could order children who would be trained for their purposes, as well as those already trained. My handler "switched" me rapidly from alter to alter, accompanied by different music and lighting for different alters, all to show the various trainings—from submissive sex slave to tough soldier to haughty princess to coy, provocative little girl to dominatrix to oracle to elf chanting programming rhymes and more. The men hooted. They jeered, laughed and catcalled. This enraged my rebel and activist alters, most of whom were shocked and confused to find themselves in a cage, even more so to be triggered in such a way.

I was in pain, drugged more heavily than ever by a new combination of drugs, and unbearably confused by the rapid succession of switches to alters with conflicting trainings, beliefs and feelings. Something in my mind snapped. I started screaming and swearing at the men from inside my cage while spitting, rattling and slamming myself against the bars. I was punished for this incident with a number of new splits, including an alter that lived in a cage.

Later, when I was eleven years old, I committed more major acts of rebellion, including putting poison in the ceremonial drink at a ritual. This, along with increasingly poor test results, proved that I was irrevocably uncontrollable. "Adjustments and fine-tuning" suddenly and drastically changed. Now, my lessons—drugged, brutally painful and confusing nightmares come to life—changed to what I call "shutdown" and "discard" programming. The plan was to severely and permanently cripple or destroy my credibility, my ability to function coherently and consistently, my sanity, and, if necessary, my physical body.

White alters, who had previously been taught that they were the "voice and words of the gods" (the scholar/writer, oracle, and preacher) were now "outcast from the realm of the gods." Tests were deliberately engineered for them to fail. These were followed by terrifying and humiliating belittlement about their inability to fulfill their responsibility to the gods and the people. They were accused of putting their loved ones and others in danger through their stupid, careless, selfish choices and actions. My perception and sensation were distorted by drugs, and I was exposed to initial shutdown scenarios through a combination of hypnosis, holographic projections, movies and scenarios acted out by actors on a stage. I saw masses of people rioting and being injured or killed because of my failures. Strapped in the now familiar magic gateway chair, my white alters "rode the rainbow" to "the realm of the gods". There, they were told by the "gods" (and shown, using holographic projections in smoke-filled air) that they were "no longer of value and had become too much trouble." They were cast out, tossed into a simulated hell and told that this was where they belonged. These experiences transferred into the inner world. One alter was left trapped in "purgatory", on the "outskirts of heaven", in smoky clouds of grey fog, hiding from the gods to avoid being sent back to hell.

My handlers used re-activation codes to open the seal. They individually called forth three of the original foundational virtues alters (red, green, and yellow). After receiving paralyzing drugs, these alters were "encased" in "webs" by my handlers, who systematically carved my whole body with fine spider-web-like lines which they painted red and/or black. When the paint dried and shriveled, the lines looked and felt like burning traps that had constricted. Then these alters were "thrown into the (inner) tunnels" (by throwing them into actual tunnels) and "left to rot". Thereafter, they were only allowed immobilizing, excruciatingly painful, restricted roles. This effectively silenced them. There were more shutdown and discard events, designed separately for the alters of each color path.

From the age of twelve on, each color path was taught that their only avenue to feeling good or powerful was to be "bad". Being stupid, scary, tough, weak, crazy, a hippie, a rebel, a partier or dropout were now good, necessary, and desirable. Alters were trained to embrace "wild times" filled with sex, drugs, alcohol, criminal activities and/or weird, flaky practices.

In order to give my personality system a new structure, a combination of four alters were to be simultaneously present in my consciousness at all times, though only one could actually be out at any given time. This would ensure two things: that I would always appear normal (not multiple) to the world, and that only the appropriate skills and knowledge base would be accessible in any given situation. A young alter called Pat memorized patterns for who should be out in each situation, and conveyed them to a Controller alter. The controller alter flipped the right combination of switches to bring the correct alters to "just below the surface" where they could then take their turns out as the situation warranted. Songs and rhymes continued in my head as instructions to the alters who were out.

At fifteen, a "stage-of-life" was created for the alters who were allowed to take part in my real life from then on, and each stage-of-life alter was individually called forth and given a false "memory shell". Thereafter, if they ever told tales, shared secrets, or otherwise broke the silence, their initial statements would be either false or fragmented and confused. This would discredit any revelations of truth that might manage to surface. These memory shells provided a common but false background of life experiences that naturally progressed to my programmed lifestyle and beliefs—those of the shutdowns, outcasts, and later, disables and lockdowns—making everything feel, and appear to have been, the product of my choice or true nature. The memory shells were created by showing each alter bits and pieces of "memory" that had been photographed, filmed, or otherwise recorded on a "brain imaging screen", spliced together with new clips of staged scenes with characters alters were told were them.

Finally, when I was eighteen, my handlers stopped layering more programs into my failed system. A "brain wipe" was done to erase everything that had been installed, and my memories were "rebuilt" over a period of nine months. These events occurred in a mental health center where I believed I was attending therapy appointments with a psychiatrist. I lay drugged on a stretcher, watching a screen which displayed photographs and films which I was told belonged to each alter. All of my experiences that were known to the mind controllers were included to the degree necessary for each alter or group to believe it was real. All alters (even those who had previously been made to disappear) had to sign contracts agreeing to whatever they understood needed to be "locked away forever." They were all regressed to infancy, and the ones who were to live my life from that point on were "re-grown" to my current age with newly implanted false memories.

In this regression part of programming that erased and rewrote alters' life experiences, my trainers told me about both the "false life" that was being erased and the new "real life" which was being installed, thus informing my file-keeper alter of which file to pull for whatever was to be done. In my healing, this helped distinguish what had actually happened to me from the fake life that had been created in installments over the years. Examples include "You were never or never did . . .," and "You did not receive . . . training," which really meant I was, and did, and had, and was now supposed to forget it forever.

New alters were created to guard the hidden system, including a "rear guard" and a "captain." After sufficient time for my body to recover, the control mechanisms were drastically adjusted and the controller was given new instructions yet again. Then I was taken back to the mental health facility, where the "brain imaging screen" was used to update the "memory shells."

After the final lock and seal was done I never encountered my programmers again, although they continued to have me watched and triggered by others when they felt it was needed. Calculated caution, along with terror of being locked up or trapped back in their control, has helped me get where I am now, integrated and able to write this paper. When watchers would visit me during the years of my recovery, I made sure to appear as dysfunctional as I had been programmed to be, and they would go away satisfied that the shutdown programming had worked.

I believe that I am still watched and occasional attempts are made to trigger me. But I really am free to live my own life now, the life my heart and soul chose, not the one they designed for me. Patterns can crumble. I am proof.

Trish has recovered to the point of full integration of her parts, and you can read more of her remarkable story in *Ritual Abuse in the 21st Century* or hear it on her DVD set.

Jeannie Riseman, a social worker by profession, is a mind control survivor and a pioneer in our understanding of mind control and how it works. She is one of the founders and leaders of Survivorship, an online resource for ritual abuse and mind control survivors. The following article describes what she has discovered about how her personality system was set up by her abusers/handlers. It does not go into her personal experiences, but rather describes the structure and articulation of her system.

It may be helpful for therapists to note:

1.   The geometric patterns in which the information is stored in her mind;
2.   The filing of information about training memories;
3.   The primary themes: death, sex, deceit, money, and cover-up (security);
4.   The use of "temporary alters", personalities created by combining fragmentary parts (Trish also had this);
5.   The inadequacy of our categories of dissociation to describe such a system, and the fact that one cannot ever assume that any survivor's experience of dissociation will fit into a preconceived pattern;
6.   The innocuous words used for access codes;

7.   The redundancy of the system, with information stored simultaneously in different fashions;

8.   The presence of esoteric cult information;

9.   The importance, once again, of the internal structure with regard to mind control programming.

A 1940s system of programming: Jeannie Riseman

I believe I was raised in an old-school "orthodox" Satanic family, of Scottish–English background. I was born in 1937, and thus the programming system used was developed before or during the Second World War. It is not based on multiplicity. I have never read or heard of any references to the kind of programming I have discovered inside myself. I want to document it for historical reasons, since I believe it has become pretty well obsolete.

I have five different systems of programming. Four may contain the same information, coded differently. The fifth contains historical information and the "control panel" for the other programs.

Programming for cult-controlled behavior

My four redundant programs are based on simple shapes: a sphere, a 3D star (like a starfish), a square with an X in it and a triangle on top (like a roof), and a web. The fifth program is an eye. I know most about the sphere, and will describe it in as much detail as I can.

At the center is a small sphere, with five lines leading to other small spheres, each with five lines leading to still others. This continues for many layers. Drawn in two dimensions, it looks like a string of neurons that have been chopped in half so that only one end branches. In three dimensions, the surface of the sphere looks like an orange studded with cloves.

Each of the small spheres is called a node. Each surface node can be traced back to the central sphere through the branching lines.

The first main line of branching nodes organizes information about death, the second about sexual activities, the third about deceit, the fourth about money, and the fifth about cover activities.

Thus, for example, tracing the death line: core–death–1. men; 2. women; 3. children; 4. animals; 5. plants. Starting at 4, for example: 1. dogs; 2. cats; 3. birds; 4. hoofed animals; 5. reptiles. It then branches into setting: home; ceremony; school; medical facility; other: then geographically pinpoints the area, then specifies the time frame.

In this way, any one surface node gives a set of instructions. Hypothetically, reading from the surface to the center: month/day/year/hour/location/setting/what/kill. Pulling something out of the air (I hope this is made up!): September/13/19xx/midnight/Chicago/basement/library/ceremony/goat/kill. The more layers (like an onion) between the core and the outer nodes, the more detailed information can be stored, accessed, and transmitted.

There are code words to signify that nodes are about to be accessed. Three or more nodes must be accessed at one time. Then there are code words to signify that the access is complete, seal the instructions, and order the action.

One can think of the groupings of nodes as coalitions that form temporary alters with the knowledge, skill, and will to perform a certain cult action. After the action is complete, the coalition dissolves, the nodes each disappear and five (I think) exact duplicates of the original nodes appear in their places. Looking at the outside of the sphere, there will be parts where the nodes are very dense, meaning that a certain cult-ordered action has been performed many times, and parts where the nodes are sparse, meaning that few or no cult-ordered actions of that type have been performed.

The sphere is divided into segments with lines, like longitude and latitude, with one original node to each segment. Thus each original node is uniquely identified by two numbers. These numbers are used to call forth the needed nodes (after the initial code words and before the closing code words). It would sound a little like a quarterback calling plays: "OK team? 17 46 11 69 22 99 hup hup hup!" and the players start the play.

The density of nodes also serves as a kind of cult resumé. With the proper cult code/command, the person can recite the number of nodes in each segment of the sphere, giving a totally accurate summary of cult actions performed, complete with dates and locations.

Access coding

The opening and closing code words (which I have not yet remembered) are socially acceptable, innocuous words, not unusual or bizarre enough to attract attention. Privacy is not needed to give directions. However, the opening and closing must 'fit', and there are different openings and closings for different combinations of nodes. The words must be pretty literate, they must have a certain rhythm, and the word combinations must be such that it would be highly unlikely that somebody could say them by mistake.

Often a word or concept is paired or echoed in the opening and closing phrases. Synonyms and antonyms are often used, as are puns, rhymes, or analogies, reminiscent of the sort of stuff you find in the Miller's Analogy Test or SATs.

(Relationships between ideas, puns, reversals, paradoxes, and jumping between systems of thought or ideologies are very common. Switching between math and language is common. Normally disparate things or ideas are connected in idiosyncratic ways. Up seamlessly becomes down, black becomes white, and reality is as elegantly complex as a Mobius strip. Language itself becomes a Mobius strip, floating between the Satanic and the cover world.)

The 3-D pentagram (starfish) works exactly the same way, with temporary coalitions of nodes, except that the numerical coding and the access codes are different. The starfish and sphere contain the same information, and after completion of the cult action, the nodes split on each surface. (If the sphere is accessed, the results appear on the surface of both the sphere and the star, and vice-versa.) This redundancy is built in; in case something happens to disturb one system, there is a back-up that is always kept up-to-date.

The house and web are, similarly, redundant systems. I can visualize the web in 3-D, like a crystal, with each node being a point of the crystal. I have not yet been able to see how nodes could fit into the house-like figure.

Number to letter or concept codes

Let's take a large rectangle, length and width segmented and numbered like axes on a graph, yielding a numerical grid with many cells. Then let's take the sphere, with its own numerical grid, flatten it, and make it transparent. Let's distort it, like silly putty, into a pre-determined shape, and place it over the rectangle. There are varying numbers of rectangle cells contained in the distorted sphere cells.

With sufficient distortion, up to twenty-six portions of rectangle cells can be in one distorted sphere cell. *Voilà!* Alphabet code. Knock out k, q, x, z and a few of the other rarer letters, and you get a simplified readable alphabet code with what looks like strange typos.

With less distortion, say only 1–9 rectangle cells to a distorted sphere cell, you could code to sequences of ideas. It would be pretty easy to identify a Bible passage this way, for example. Or identify a particular code from a master list. The intermediate step allows access to a large number of coding systems.

Back to the silly putty analogy. Just as silly putty can pick up newsprint, the distorted sphere could 'pick up' these coded instructions and 'remember' the message when returned to its undistorted state. This increases the flexibility of and usefulness of the original program.

Meta-programs

There are a number of programs which apply to all four of the behavioral programs equally.

One is based on the concept of the abacus and dictates cascading consequences for behaviors that the cult deems undesirable. There are two abaci: one for internal events, one for cult punishment or retribution.

Let's label the wires on the abacus A B C D E F and the beads on each wire 1 through 10. Wire A is the action the cult doesn't like. B is the first consequence. If bead A goes up, then Bead B-1 goes up, and A falls; i.e., the undesired action ceases. If bead A does not fall, then B-1 stays up and bead C-1 rises.

For example: A: I remember something I shouldn't: B-1: I immediately forget; C-1: I think I am crazy; and so on, all the way through F-1, which is suicide. Some of the undesired actions are: remembering, telling, cutting contact with the cult, disobeying or ignoring a cult order, acting bizarre and damaging the cover of social acceptability.

With these five contingencies and ten consequences apiece, there are fifty cells in the rectangle representing the abacus. This type of system is called grid programming. There are other meta-programs, some having to do with linguistic conventions.

The process program

The fifth program is represented by an eye. It contains theoretical information, operating instructions for the other programs, history, and theology. I suspect that not all members of the cult were taught all of this material, and that the amount taught depended on the role the person was destined for in adult life.

I have not figured out how the information is arranged, or how the mnemonic shape organized the information. These are some of the areas I know are covered:

1. Satanic liturgy, its meaning and history. Theology: 'why' the liturgy is a certain way. The purpose and uses of each ritual.
2. History and organization of the cult. What each role is, how it is filled, rules of succession. Blood lines and recruitment. How the cult changed over time. Old-world sources of traditions. Rules governing differentiation and consolidation of functions to meet changing circumstances.

3. Sociology and economics. How the cult related to other cults. Agreements to cooperate in certain areas. Information specific to certain economic considerations, including arranged marriages and economic ventures, both legal and illicit. Money management.
4. Teaching and programming. How to teach the material contained in the other four systems. Non-violent ways of teaching. Trance induction, amnesia induction. Child development. Comparative programming (analysis of methods used by other cults.) Curriculum development.
5. Methods to change the basic programming. For example, amnesia is a benefit during a member's early years and for low-ranking members. In order to control and coordinate cult life and ordinary life, amnesia is detrimental. The top leaders need to be able to be conscious of both lives simultaneously to run the cult smoothly. When leadership is passed on, many changes of this sort are made in the basic programmed instructions.

Models of the mind

This type of programming can be conceptualized as based on multiplicity, with extreme fragmentation of the core self. One alter is built from fragments and allowed to act as the host. Other alters are short-lived and only called into being for certain cult functions. Rather than having names, they have numbers, and they lie sleeping or dormant until the fragments are assembled.

These shapes can also be thought of as mnemonic devices to organize and simplify recall of cult information. They are not very difficult to memorize, certainly no harder than the multiplication tables. (It strikes me as interesting that elementary schools usually teach a maximum of five main subjects, with a few little extras like gym and art thrown in. Developmentally, small children could simultaneously be taught five programming systems, which would get more elaborate each year to match the child's intellectual development.)

These 'systems' can also be seen as post-hypnotic suggestions, organized in such a way that they are easy to activate. The abacus model of a series of increasingly self-destructive post-hypnotic suggestions is helpful in explaining escalation of symptoms as memories surface.

Clinically speaking, people today are generally dichotomized as multiple/not-multiple, or seen along a spectrum of dissociation. Either/or, with a clear demarcation, or a lot/a little, with gradations. What seems to 'fit' for me is a model that describes information as being stored simultaneously in different fashions.

In my office, I have much of the same information stored on the computer, on back-up disks, on paper in a file cabinet, and in a jumbled pile on the floor. There is a lot of redundancy. I could add audio or video tapes if I wanted, or CDs, and increase the number of modalities of storage. I could also memorize the whole mess, or make petroglyphs. The storage systems would be different, but the information would be the same.

I can also order this information in many different ways. By name, by icon, by size, by date, by author, by title, by the Dewey Decimal system, chronologically. The information can be translated into hundreds of languages. It can be cross-referenced. Given this plethora of systems, which is the 'real' system of organization?

So, with the cult information stored in my mind, I believe that all the storage systems are equally 'real.' I can simultaneously be multiple, non-multiple, a 'sleeping multiple', a potential multiple, etc. I 'am' whatever system I am using at that particular moment.

In a more classic sense, I can simultaneously store information both consciously and unconsciously. I can store it in action and in words. My body 'knows' how to ride a bike, and does not forget when I manage to put that knowledge into words to teach another person. Yet most of the time it is not in my conscious thought as I go about my daily life. There are many things that are 'really' conscious when I think about them, and 'really' unconscious when I don't, and 'really' pre-conscious when they are floating around in the back of my mind or on the tip of my tongue. I don't have to choose: the labels can be sequentially or simultaneously accurate.

Closing thoughts

No concrete elements of this programming system rely upon concepts developed after WW II, like video games or computers. The general principles, though, are certainly very familiar to computer programmers and can be found in post-WW II mind-control programming.

I have a hunch that one reason so few middle aged or elderly people are remembering, even given the social climate these days, is that this kind of programming is simpler than post-World War II programming. It has fewer moving parts to break down, so to speak. I also believe that it is dying out as a system, or is confined only to a few groups.

A couple of years ago I shared what I had discovered about my system by e-mail with a younger MC survivor. I was told that this looked like an early version of something called "blizzard programming" which was and is still used in Europe. In blizzard programming, the alters come together like snowflakes to form a temporary alter to do the task, then melt apart. The theory is that since the alter that did the job no longer exists, it is impossible for any part of the system to remember what was done or what happened. Total safety for the programmers and handlers.

As you can see, the personality systems created by non-ritual groups (military, political, organized crime) are quite different from one another. We have to learn from our clients about what kind of system they have.

CHAPTER SEVEN

A reversed Kabbalah trainer speaks

Stella Katz

WARNING

Much of the content of this article is really gruesome, so be prepared to be traumatized. I especially do not recommend that survivors read this, as it is likely to set off all kinds of conditioned reactions. For therapists, however, it provides incomparable information.

Editor's note

Survivor Stella Katz, who endured ritual abuse in her own childhood, worked as a cult trainer of little children, but was brave enough to leave the group and undo her own programming. This remarkable article gives us information which cannot be retrieved just from survivors' memories of their own abuse, and that you will need to be able to recognize in your clients, so it is important for therapists to study it. Remember that Katz was required to do what she describes here, and misled into believing that it was not the abuse that we, and now she, understand it to be.

Below is a list of important points for therapists to note, as indicators of these experiences are commonly found among ritual abuse survivors but have not been well understood to this point.

1. The experiences of babyhood and infancy, which are often very difficult for a survivor to recall because of the way baby memories are stored in the brain;
2. The deliberate disruption of the mother–child bond to prevent attachment;
3. The early splits and the Gatekeeper alter;

4. The categories or blocks of alters and how they are developed;
5. The way the initial (baby) alters are created, and how other similar alters are deliberately split off from them;
6. The "playful" way the system structure is built;
7. Garbage kids, doubles and reactivators;
8. Touch triggers;
9. The use of spinning;
10. Deliberate preparation of the body for sexual penetration;
11. First, second and third circles for recruitment;
12. The details of each major ceremony;
13. The creation and training of demon and animal alters;
14. The use of the Kabbalah;
15. Booby traps;
16. Rewards used in training;
17. The helmet and other technology;
18. Occult belief systems;
19. The context in which ritual abusers operate, so that we can understand their beliefs and the reasons for their acts.

The Kabbalah and its inversion

I want to make it very clear that not all Kabbalists are Satanists and not all Satanists train their children using the Reversed Kabbalah.

The true ancient Kabbalah is a beautiful thing that takes a lifetime of training to integrate and apply in one's life. It is an ancient body of spiritual wisdom. The Kabbalah has always been meant to be applied as a tool to bring clarity, understanding, and freedom to lives, rather than being merely "learnt." It teaches its followers how to navigate through life without pain, suffering, and chaos.

Kabbalah is a comprehensive philosophy that cannot be explained in a few short lines. Essentially, it teaches the person to integrate the spiritual with the physical in everyday existence. In Kabbalah, the person follows certain paths, using numerical codes and meanings in the shape of the Hebrew alphabet, to decipher the secret teachings of the Torah. As it does with all belief systems that it perverts, the Satanic version—or, perhaps, as it should be described, the "Satanic inversion"—bastardizes the practice of regular Kabbalah in a variety of ways. In the Satanic Kabbalah, the codes are still used, but they are taught using torture instead of meditation, and the Torah is twisted to make God the bad guy. To train children, Satanic Kabbalah trainers, in opposition to the practices of the regular Kabbalah, work from the feet up, rather than from the head down, their Supreme Being is Lucifer, and their angels are black angels.

I am a former trainer in a Kabbalah-based Satanic cult. I worked for them from 1971 to 1991. At the time I did this, I suffered from dissociative identity disorder. All parts of me except the host believed that they were doing the right thing in abusing children in this manner. I am now integrated, and have been filled with remorse at what those parts of me did. But I am also aware that I became DID in childhood from the same things being done to me.

The philosophy of the group for whom I worked was: "God is not the only one who can give. You do not beg Lucifer, you demand. You do not grovel on your knees, you stand face to face. Power is the most important thing in the universe. Without power you are nothing. Life is for taking, not giving."

I discovered that the only thing I did was grovel—that I had no freedom at all, no matter how high in the ranks I got. Everything I did and said was what I was told to do and say. Eventually, I became sick of hiding in the shadows. I was sick of death. I was sick of watching children being tortured and told that this was love. I knew that there had to be more to life than "kill or be killed."

I am writing this because I want others to know that freedom is a wonderful thing, and it is attainable. I want to help therapists who seem to be fumbling in the dark, sometimes doing more harm than good, not because they want to, but because they do not have correct information. I want to give back some of what I've taken. And most of all, I want these groups to know that no matter how much torture they put us through, and no matter how many chains they put on our bodies, they cannot imprison our souls.

Occult belief systems

Just as there are many different Christian groups, there are a variety of different occult belief systems. Not all are the abusive or dark kind that creates mind control victims. Magik is the occult practice of using a universal force or demons to get what you want in life. Death magik and sex magik are the two most powerful kinds, because they use the life force of a human for power. The magik used by witches or druids is basically positive thinking, drawing on the force of many minds and the universal force. Satanists do the same, but in the negative, using demons for power.

In both Luciferian and Satanist belief your spirit does not belong to yourself or to God, it belongs to the devil. In strict Satanism, the entire goal is to prove that Satan is more powerful than God. Since strictly Satanic groups use a system that is based on reversal of mainline Western religions, certain Satanic rituals reverse traditional Catholic ceremonies and symbols: the cross is turned upside down; the Holy Water is actual blood; instead of marriage to God, marriage to Satan; the Black Mass in place of the regular mass. Satanic abusers often meet in churches, and try to use as many sacred objects stolen from the church as possible in their ceremonies. This is to dishonor God.

Luciferians are more gentle than strict Satanists. They represent more of a religion than a revenge. Luciferians call upon Lucifer with the same respect as conventionally religious people give God. They focus less on attempting to prove God wrong and more on honoring Lucifer, and following his ways. More of the multigenerational groups are Luciferians. Like born-again Christians, who dedicate their lives and souls to their God, Luciferians do the same, but to Lucifer.

Some groups also incorporate ancient deities into their practices. Many of the ancient Pagan religions seem to share a number of lesser gods—a pantheon, as the ancient Greeks called it. Marduk, for example, was a lesser dark god, or a keeper of the gates to the underworld. In some religions he is a dark angel. Setians follow an older belief. Set dates back to the Egyptians.

Set is the God of Darkness. The belief is that Set is just another God among many, the God of the Underworld, the God of Death, the Mightiest of all Gods. Some men in the modern military follow Setian beliefs. Black Santerians, usually Hispanic, use black magik, demon magik, or Saints of the underworld. Black Santerians, like Satanists, practice a reversal of a positive religion.

When working with survivors, it is important to realize that the religious beliefs of the cult-involved alters are real. Trying to change them is just like telling a Catholic that everything they have ever known is nonsense. The magical aspect of the religion is also a very important part of the belief system and must be dealt with. However, the spiritual or religious basis of the group is only one aspect of how the dark religions influence their participants. The other is mind control, which is based on abuse and deception.

Rationale for deliberately creating dissociative disorders in children

From what we had been able to establish through reviewing old writings, it is obvious that the splitting of children had been done for many generations in certain of these religions to release greater and lesser demons through children. In the early days, when an alter emerged, it was seen as a certain demon by its behavior, and the group would call it by that demon's name. After a while the group could use the demon's name to purposely call it forth. However, when a demon came forth without permission—as most ended up doing—the child was usually subjected to exorcism by the church. Children that could not be exorcised would be put in an insane asylum. Eventually, as the dark cults developed a greater understanding of the process and consequences of splitting children, their activities and systems they created became much more sophisticated.

We (by which I mean the training group for which I worked) purposely split children because when a child splits on its own, without any guidance, the alters that are created are unlikely to become productive members of the group, and cannot be controlled. We knew that a child who had to bear all the pain and torture to which we subjected it would die unless it had parts to absorb the trauma. It was also important that the children whom we trained have a personality acceptable to the outside world, that could go to school and play with outside children without giving up the secrets.

Hierarchy of Satanic and Luciferian groups: first, second and third circles

The *First Circle* of the group in which I was raised consists of group members born of the First Circle or the higher echelon of the Second Circle. They are trained from birth in the ways described in this chapter.

The *Second Circle* consists of people not necessarily born into the group, but brought in at a very early age, usually before one year of age. For example, a child of a Third Circle member or a child recruited by a babysitter or neighbor. They also receive this training, though it may not start quite as early.

The *Third Circle* consists of people who have come in as teenagers or adults. If these people have children under the age of two, or very intelligent children up to age four, the children become Second Circle; children who are older remain Third Circle. They will become full-time breeders, prostitutes, or "gofers". They are never allowed to see all the intricacies of a ritual; they are kept in the back rows. Their bodies will form the outer circle but their backs will be turned, or they will be on the outside of the building. They might be told they are important because they must signal if someone comes around.

People who come into a group as teens or adults may not have dissociative disorders: after the age of nine you cannot split a person.[1]

Reversed Kabbalah training: goals, schedule, methods, and technologies

Reversed Kabbalah training is a carefully developed process, with elaborate goals, a schedule, methods and technologies.

Props and technologies used for deception and training

A variety of props and technologies help trainers in these groups to create the illusions and affects that help them accomplish their goals. These include:

1. *"Stage magic"* is used to create non-human alters and simulate various false scenarios, including murders. This includes bags of blood, tape-recorded cries, costumes, stage scenery, projectors, and so forth.
2. *Drugs*: Different drugs are used for different purposes, such as to aid suggestibility, to restrain the child, or to whip him or her up into fury. Injections of sulfur or Naltrexone will create pain all over (a punishment program). Curare will paralyze the body.
3. *Spinners*: see the detailed discussion of this in the section on infancy.
4. *Red light flashing machine*: One way of making an alter believe illusions is through the use of a machine that flashes red light on closed eyelids. The perpetrators believe that when the eyelids are closed, light seen through them confuses the mind so that the person is unable to tell the difference between reality and fantasy. You can tell such people that what they are seeing is a spaceship and that they have been abducted by aliens. You can tell them that they have had surgery, and that a device for keeping track of them is hidden under their scalp. With the correct use of this machine, the groups believe that victims will believe everything they have been told. For example, someone on whom a small cut or scar of some kind is done at the same time will believe that the eye of Lucifer has been placed in their stomachs to keep an eye on them, and they will believe it forever.
5. *Helmet*: The helmet is a piece of equipment used for imaginary brain surgery. Small electrodes in the helmet send small shocks to different areas of the head. This can be used as a form of punishment or to convince people they have had brain surgery. In punishment, these individuals are given a real scenario about something they have actually done (such as talk to an outsider), or an imaginary act, like killing a loved one or pet. Each time they deny it they are shocked. The shocks get progressively more severe as they continue to deny until eventually they admit to what they have done. The trainer will get them to repeat that confession numerous times, while recording their words. They will often then

be put on the light machine, and while the light flashes they hear themselves repeating whatever hideous crime they have committed in their own voices. At the end of the session they will believe they have committed the crime.

6. *Sensory deprivation room*: The deprivation room is a small soundproof and lightproof box. Sometimes it is lowered into a hole in the ground that is about two feet wide by three and a half feet high. The box has oxygen as well as stereo speakers. This is used for many different kinds of training, as well as for punishment. In training, the child will remain in the hole for hours at a time, with a tape repeating the same instructions over and over in a monotone. The child will then be removed, allowed to use the toilet, fed, and returned to the box.

    When the box is used for punishment, no sound at all is piped in, or there will be a high-pitched, screaming sound; the child must remain there for a day or better, never allowed to use a bathroom and given no food or water. This box is also used for tone training. Different tones will be piped in along with a specific word or instruction. This will teach the child how to read sound signals.

7. *Sound machine*: The sound machine is simply an audio machine, similar to the one that is used to test hearing. It is a sound-proof box with headphones that produce different sound frequencies. The child is strapped into the box, and the trainer, from a room outside the box, makes requests of the child. When the child does not comply, sounds are emitted. At first they are soft. Then they are louder and louder until the sound blows the eardrums, or almost does so. Survivors often have ear damage from this. The sound is initially used as a way to stop the "ignore reflex" in infants, at six weeks old. It continues to be used throughout the person's life as punishment for non-compliance or for talking to outsiders. All alters will be familiar with the sound used.

    The sound is often used as a booby trap, set to go off if the survivor does not comply with a return program or request. During training, the child is told she or he has so much time to comply; then a trap is created so that the child cannot comply even if she or he wants to. After a certain length of time, or after a certain date that has great significance, such as an anniversary or birthday, the trap goes off and the child is punished with the sound or a spin or an electric shock, or all of the above and more. Eventually the system learns the dates and what happens as a result of non-compliance, so the internal system automatically sets off the sound or other internal punishments.

8. *Electronic board*: This is a bed equipped with electrodes. It is used in teaching touch triggers. The child is hooked up to the electrodes. A small shock is administered that hurts but does not injure. It is accompanied by a repeated word or instruction. This lesson takes several months to complete. It will allow the child to be triggered by a simple touch, either given by an internal touch-trained alter or another person. Each time a person/alter touches one of these triggers with a finger in a specific manner, the child will feel the shock and will bring forward a specific lesson or specific alter who will carry out the lesson.

    The electronic board is used for many different things. Without a doubt it is the most effective kind of training. The touch must be done in a specific manner in order for the lesson to be triggered. This is so an outsider cannot set off the triggers accidentally.

9. *Virtual reality glasses*: These are a relatively new thing in modern day training. Since their invention, it has made illusion a great deal easier, especially for impersonation of therapists. (See Chapter Thirteen, "Boundaries and bonding: the therapeutic relationship".)

Role of the trainer

Most trainers of babies are young females, in their teens and twenties. The child has the same trainer for years—from birth to when they are "given," at age nine. During training, the baby is looked after by the trainer for two or three days at a time. The child is with the trainer for three days, home for three days, back and forth for months, until the mother is trained to maintain what the trainer started. If a trainer starts to bond with a child, she has to hand the child on to someone else. The trainer monitors the child in the home and at cult functions. The trainer is in an emotionless alter when she hurts and splits the baby, unless she is not multiple and is simply sadistic. Some trainers will smack the baby's face; some do not, because of the danger of brain damage. Some stab the baby's feet with extra sharp forks or fondue skewers. Exactly what is done when depends on the child's development.

The following describes what we did to the children we were training, and of course, what was done to me. It follows a chronological schedule.

At home during the first year of life

The child's primary guardian for the cult, who is often the mother but may be the father, another relative, or another cult person, must keep up the trainer's training at home. The trainers or programmers teach the parents what to do. The parents have to take notes, and are punished if the notes are not good enough. If the mother is too soft and cannot be trained to harm her child, the child is left to a specialized infant trainer until the age of two, then passed on to a trainer for older ages.

The following happens at home:

1. The child is neglected. The mother is not allowed to feed the baby consistently. Breastfeeding is not allowed.
2. The parent uses a home version of a spinner, like a baby weigh-scale, which spins the infant fast. It is a very smooth ride, and is not fast enough to cause shaken baby syndrome. Head and neck must be stabilized. This is used for compliance when the child will not stop crying on command, for example, or if the toddler will not stop touching something.
3. Colors made out of felt with little felt pockets are always kept in the crib. The mother has colored dolls made of hard foam (previously of cardboard) for the representations of the alters, and teaches the baby to put them in the pockets.
4. The parent shows the baby the magikal symbols in a game, and tells the baby what they are.
5. The parent uses touch triggers, especially Silence, taught with the trigger on the head and a hand over the baby's mouth.
6. The guardian calls out particular alters and speaks to them strictly in their own magikal languages. In the first few months, they are called out by using their name together with their unique touch.
7. The child is hurt without marking it. Its hand might be put over radiant heat, or it might be burned internally with a tiny probe.
8. The child is sexually abused with fingers and dildos.

If the mother cannot do these things because she has bonded with the child, the child is given to someone else, or the mother has to take it to the trainers.

Preparation for sexual abuse

Starting at about two months, fingers are inserted in the child's orifices to widen the openings. This is done very carefully, so as not to tear. Little boys' penises are stroked pleasurably until they are erect. Little girls are also stroked, with jellies used as lubricants. By eighteen months the vagina or anus should be wide enough to accommodate a full-sized penis. The trainer shows the guardian how to do this. Once the fingers are no longer large enough, a kit is used with a series of size-graded, smooth wooden phalluses. It comes in a leather binder like a musical instrument case.

The trainer is trained to think that by stretching the orifice in this way, she is protecting the child from physical harm and intense pain when the child is later raped. The trainer teaches this to the guardian. If the child comes back to the trainer bruised, the guardian is punished and chastised; the kit is taken from her and the trainer continues the job.

Bonding to group rather than family

Very little takes place in the first two weeks of life except the bonding with the parent and trainer.

The baby's bond with the mother and the trainer is established in the first two weeks. Then later the one with the mother is broken. The child is passed around among the group members, so that a bond to the group will replace the maternal bond. The child is taken out of the home, and cannot see the mother except at a distance. It is teased by being shown the mother at a distance, and told, "If she loved you, she'd be with you." The baby is made excited — "Mommy's coming!" Then Mommy comes and walks right past. The baby is kept away from the home for the length of time it takes to break the bond with mother. The child never really trusts the mother again. The trainer will always be the rescuer. A cult child rarely "makes strange" (that is, rejects strangers and clings to the mother) because it is accustomed to strangers and does not have an exclusive bond with its mother. It is passed from pillar to post. It is used to being in crowds, and will go to anybody.

Deliberate neglect

The infant up to six weeks of age is allowed to cry endlessly while its basic needs are ignored. Once the baby stops crying, its needs are attended to. During this time the child remains in the home unless the trainer feels that the mother cannot or will not do what is needed for the child. The trainer monitors this child daily to see how it is responding. As the baby becomes accustomed to neglect, it learns to calm down in minutes instead of hours. It is monitored during this process. A child of that age can be abandoned for up to two days, depending on its size. Doctors give their opinions on what the child can tolerate without physical damage.

The not-yet-split child is spoken to in only one language, the mother tongue. The child's name is used constantly. The main teaching between six weeks and six months continues to be that its physical and emotional needs are to be ignored. The child is still severely neglected, left to cry for hours. It is not fed on any specific schedule. It may be fed twice within an hour, and then left for twelve hours with nothing to eat or drink. It is left cold and without any diaper change, and it is not held or touched at all. Its hands and feet are bound so that it cannot comfort itself by sucking a thumb. During the first six months the baby is taught to dissociate its own pains and needs.

Milk and blood

The baby is rarely breast fed, as this creates too much of a bond with the mother. However, the mother's milk is used, as babies prefer the taste and will accept it more readily. The milk is mixed with small amounts of the mother's blood so the child gets used to the tinny taste. (Contrary to popular belief, the child is not fed whole bottles of pure blood, as that would make the child ill and unwilling to accept what you are trying to feed it.)

Fear training

Loud noises are often used to frighten the child, in order to see how long it takes to settle down. Frightening sound is used from Day 1 to get the child past the ignore reflex. The trainer wants the child to be frightened. The child is forced to listen to such a sound over and over, now and at a later date, to teach it to be on guard and fearful all the time. The child is given no chance to calm down; there is no real comfort, ever.

Color training

From birth the child's crib is surrounded by color. There is a black crib sheet on the bottom, a red panel on the right, green on the left, blue at the head, yellow at the feet, and white on top. Faces in black and white as well as magikal symbols are stuck to the color sheets.

Dissociative testing and application of results

The faster the child settles when it has been frightened, the easier training will be. This also means the less the child will have to endure in the way of pain. This begins the weeding out process, through which the children are chosen to lead or to serve. Just because a child is the first born of a member of the inner circle does not automatically make it High Priest/Priestess material. If the child tends to be placid it is trained easily, but from the perspective of the trainer it would be unlikely that such a child will be trained for the highest positions. The child with the strongest will is considered to be more intelligent. It was Lucifer's strong will that won him the position of Prince of the Underworld, instead of one as God's flunky. Therefore, the strong-willed child, who is harder to train at first, will be seen as a true child of Lucifer. Lucifer does not want anyone who is willing to bow and scrape. Remember, in Satanic prayer, the petitioner demands, s/he does not beg and plead. She or he stands on her or his feet, and does not bend the knees and grovel. Therefore, it is the children that are the hardest to break that will be the rulers of the underworld, and the right hand of Satan.

The first splits

Between six weeks and six months of age, the trainer begins to deliberately split the child.

The Firstborn

The physical child that is born is the "birth child". The "Firstborn", who is the same gender as the person, is "born", or created, from the first split, and will serve as guardian or caregiver to the birth child. It will forever know what is actually going on in the person's life, while being shielded from the pain that could kill the person. All other parts come from the Firstborn.

The Gatekeeper

The next part to be split off will be raised as Gatekeeper. He or she will always be present at the birth of a new alter. He keeps the records for the developing system and the order of the splits. The Gatekeeper is never hurt after his birth. He holds everything back, and observes everything that happens. He will raise the new parts if they seem worthy or junk them if they are not. The Gatekeeper is told that he is in control of the mind and all emotions. The only alters not recorded by the Gatekeeper are accidental splits which can become "floaters" or remain stagnant.

These two first split alters are the same age as the body. They grow up with the body because they do not receive further trauma.

The thirteen blocks of alters

The group that follows will be intended to remain children or animals or demons. The trainer builds on the infant's initial dissociative training and attempts to split the child further. The foundation created by the first splitting of alters usually consists of thirteen "blocks" (alters of particular job categories who will be the sources of further alters of those categories). It might also be based on a number divisible by three. The triggers to bring the alters "out" in the body mostly correspond to the chakras, as well as to stations of the Kabbalah.

The types of alters are: spirit, language, guards, touch, magik, sacrifice, pain, sex, demons, animals, re-activators, doubles, and garbage kids. The "locations" of these alters (the blocks), and the triggers to bring these alters out in the body mostly correspond to the chakras, as well as to stations of the Kabbalah, as follows:

1. Spirit—head, third eye (middle of forehead)
2. Language—throat, thyroid chakra
3. Guards—palm of right hand

4. Touch—palm of left hand
5. Magik—heart chakra
6. Sacrifice—solar plexus chakra
7. Pain—sacral chakra
8. Sex—genitals (sex chakra)
9. Demons—right knee
10. Animals—left knee
11. Re-activators—right foot
12. Doubles—left foot
13. Garbage bin—on the behind, tailbone area

How the child is split

To create the splits, the child is bombarded by constant annoying sounds, its feet are jabbed with needles, and small electrodes are placed in every orifice. Small shocks are administered, not to burn the child, but just to make it hurt as much as possible. The trainer watches carefully. It is believed that the moment of a split occurs when the child's cry becomes a hooting sound, similar to that of an infant going through drug withdrawal. Its eyes roll back in its head, and it becomes suddenly limp and silent.

At this point the trainer has a window of fifteen seconds to one minute in which to name the new child alter, and assign it a color and a magikal symbol. The trainer wears the color with a symbol in black on the trainer's shoulder or chest. The trainer then picks up the child and wraps it in blankets of the color it will be assigned. The child receives care for approximately one hour, in a very loving way. It is fed, bathed, changed and caressed. It is continuously spoken to in its own language, which may or may not be the mother tongue, using its new given name. Then it is rocked back to sleep. Once the child is asleep, it is returned to its mother until the next time it is brought to its trainer, which usually occurs two to three days later. This whole process can take a few hours or several days, depending on the child.

The task of the first few alters is to guard the "firstborn," who will not be not used again after the foundation is built. All of the other alters are told that without that firstborn, they would die. The firstborn is considered to be the body and soul; the others are "renting space".

Record keeping

All the child's data is recorded in a small book the trainer keeps. Data will include what was done, the exact amount of time it took to make the split, and what worked best to achieve the splits. The names of the child alters are recorded, along with the order of birth, the sex of the alter, what color and symbol was assigned, and what language they speak. A record is also kept of the type of "physical body" the alters have been assigned—human, animal or demon.

The Kabbalah on the body

An internal Kabbalah is installed when alters are split off. In most cases, binding and hurting parts of the body is sufficient for this. A cardboard cutout of a body, called "Kabbalah," is held where the baby can see it. Somebody points to a spot on the cutout while the baby is probed or stabbed at that spot on its body. The cutout is marked into layers. Initially, there are just three layers—from genitals down, genitals to throat, and head. As the child gets older the body is more differentiated.

The foundation of the first year

This includes:

- Original alters (blocks) with colors, names, touch triggers to bring them out, and locations in the body and in a cube.
- Compliance training.
- Spin training.
- Silence training.
- Training not to taste.
- Basic touch triggers to bring out alters, and to enforce compliance, silence, and not tasting.
- Some other triggers, e.g., sounds and smells.

Building the system structure

By the age of six months, the child should have at minimum 18–20 alters with distinct names and colors. This number is needed so that there will be some to fall back on if some of the splits are found to be untrainable.

Now, the visual form building begins. The child (each foundational alter) is placed in a box-like playpen with cloths of certain colors on the walls. Each wall cloth contains small pockets. Small cardboard figures are used for what appears to be a game. The figures are male or female, animal or demon. Each wears the color that corresponds to the name given. The names are printed on the chest and the magikal symbol is drawn on the abdomen. As the trainer shows each figure to the baby, the figure is called by name in the language that corresponds to the name. The little figure dances happily into its slot on the wall. "This is you. Where do *you* live?" The trainer talks with the child about the other foundational alters and where they all live. Each foundational alter learns the location of all the other foundational alters. Later, each foundational alter will learn where all those who split off from it live.

After a few tries, the trainer gives the child the figure, and helps guide the figure into the slot. The children are very responsive to this activity. It is fun for them, because it involves little figures, bright colors and a great deal of attention from the trainer. No torture is used in this game. This also makes it less likely that the person will remember it in therapy, as therapists tend to pursue discussion of traumatic events. Also, non-traumatic events from infancy are not available to explicit memory.

It takes a couple of months to build a base. The trainer tries to have it done by the time the child is 6–10 months of age. Internal structures are fixed by the trainer and the specific group. They are purposefully designed so that the trainers can easily retrain alters over time. Some groups use structures consisting of geometric shapes; others use trees; others use the Kabbalah. Each structure has a department head and workers. Colors and symbols categorize different groups of alters. Only the department heads know what the structure is based on. This is important for therapists to understand, as it is easier to go through the system once you know the physical look of the structure or structures.

In a reactive multiple (one not deliberately trained) any internal structure that exists is created spontaneously by the person for the safety of the system. It is not based on a hierarchy for the purpose of later use and is usually not elaborate. Most common are houses or boxes that serve no purpose other than as places for alters to live while inside.

Insertion of touch triggers

Once the child has a few of these little characters placed properly every time, the trainer can begin to inset basic touch triggers. Touch triggers are very important for the control of the children. A lot are put in during the first year. To the outside world, most of the program touch triggers look like loving touches.

The child is made accustomed to specific places on the body being made to feel more meaningful, being stroked, etc. These spots, at the acupressure points, are mapped out on the body as the child starts to learn her programs. Touch triggers are often taught through a combination of games and pain. Each program has a trigger in each sensory modality. A baby really begins to find parts of its body; those parts are intentionally hurt. Triggers are repeated over and over while the child is in a semi-conscious state from drugs and punishment. The machine that flashes red light on the child's closed eyelids is used here.

Silence touch

The first touch trigger to be inset is the Silence touch. If a child has had a slip of the tongue in public, the crown trigger, found at the crown of a child's head, is touched in a loving way by the parent or guardian. The child will fall silent. To create this lesson, the trainer gets the baby babbling any way s/he can. Then the trainer touches the child's crown and says "Shh." The touch is paired with putting a plant in the baby's mouth that makes its tongue swell, or with an electric shock. If the baby cries during training, the trainer repeats the touch and sound and covering of the mouth again using a louder voice. This is repeated until the baby figures out that it must be silent. It can take days, or only two or three tries. Another silence trigger is a little rub at the dip at the base of the back of the neck. An outside person observing the parent touch the child in this loving way would never know the child is being silenced through mind control.

The use of spinning

When a person is spun, he or she becomes ill and afraid, angry and thrilled: many different physical and emotional sensations are created. Spinning simply transfers these sensations to those alters best equipped to handle them, as alters tend to specialize in particular sensations. Thereafter, every time the individual remembers anything associated with that kind of abuse, they will be brought back to that original memory and have the sensation that they are spinning.

Compliance training

Spinning is meant initially as a form of compliance training. From the very beginning, the baby is taught compliance and obedience. The baby is spun in the small cot fitted with padding that resembles a baby weigh-scale that was mentioned earlier, on a spinning chair, or attached to a device like an electric potter's wheel. The baby cannot see out. It is prodded until it cries. The crying baby is placed on its side so that it does not choke when it vomits, and secured using rolled towels or foam blocks. It is spun slowly to begin with, increasing the speed as it goes. An annoying noise is made at the same time. When the child is exhausted from crying and has been sick several times, it stops crying. At that point the spinning is stopped. This process is repeated many times, using each alter. It usually takes several weeks before each alter has had its turn. This will be done over the next two years every time the child is disobedient.

Spinning teaches these children that they have no control over their own bodies. The child's head can flop, though their wrists and ankles are tied. Spinning makes the children physically ill, sick to their stomachs, but no help is given; they are spun until the screaming stops. The technique works better when children are not fighting. Small amounts of drugs are administered to calm children who fight a lot so they give up faster.

Sometimes mistakes are made in the spin training. These children can get "shaken baby syndrome" and can be killed.

Distributing lessons

After the child reaches the age of two, commercially available spinning chairs are used. A child is spun until it vomits while particular words are repeated over and over on tape such as *Die* or *Kill* or *Silence*. This is done to teach the child's alters to come forward quickly to take parts of the child's pain, fear, and nausea, or different illnesses. It teaches the alters to share the lesson being taught. Some lessons, such as suicide or homicide, must be held by more than one alter in order for the target behavior to take place, so that one alter cannot kill the entire system, or one alter cannot kill another member of the group. Because of this kind of security measure, the majority of people only injure themselves rather than die in their suicide attempts.

Basic lessons for each child

1. Total compliance.
2. Loyalty to the group.
3. Silence.
4. Do your job to the best of your ability.
5. Replenish the group through breeding or recruitment.

The first three lessons are taught when the child is under two years old.

Training not to taste

At ten to twelve months there is training to shut off the ability to taste. This is done (using little sniffs of ammonia) so that the child will not be able to taste sacrifices. The trigger is a little circular counterclockwise motion with a finger on the tip of the nose.

Satanic baptism

The ritual of Satanic baptism occurs when the child is between twelve and eighteen months of age. The child is starved and isolated for two to four days (depending on the size of the child). Following this, the child is bathed and anointed with fragrant oils. During the ceremony, a man in a devil suit rapes the infant, vaginally for a girl and anally for a boy. This is considered a great honor for the child.

Because the child has not given its body freely in its sexual encounters with group members (it is taken), it is still considered a virgin. When children give their bodies "freely" at age nine, they are seen as losing their virginity. All parts of all group members (other than their host alters) truly believe that this is the right thing to do.

Before baptism the child is not involved in worship services. After baptism, it is involved in all of them. It is "free to participate" in orgies. In these situations, adult participants can do anything they want to the child, unless an older child tries to protect it by taking it as its partner for the whole night. The women lick the infant's genitals and give it their breasts to suck. Usually the child is eased down on to an erect penis, and the rapist pulls out when he feels resistance. Those who have sex with upper echelon babies are all upper echelon, and know how to do this. (In orgies, everyone has sex with only their own level.)

Preparations for future indoctrinations and trainings

At around three years of age, preparation begins for the Satanic rebirth ritual. Starting at age three, the child is taken out to cemeteries, and put inside open graves or mausoleums. Dirt is thrown at the child, and it is told that it is dead. The child is taught that it is born of Beast rather than of man, that man is nothing and that Beast is everything. The child is also taught beginning magik spells.

Building foundational blocks of alters

The trainer concentrates on building one specific block of alters at a time, filling it fully. Each original block alter is split through torture,[2] usually administered to the part of the body where this alter resides. The system is built like a giant jigsaw puzzle.

After the blocks of alters are created (see below), they are trained using a combination of torture and pleasure for ceremonial and teaching purposes. Alters from different blocks work together to make events happen. Cutting the person's arms, for instance, involves somebody from Pain, somebody from Touch, somebody from Emotion, and the Gatekeeper.

Guard block

The Guard block is usually built first, when the baby is between the ages of twelve and eighteen months. The original Guard alter is tortured by burning or electroshock to the right hand to create a group of new Guard alters, in a number that is divisible by three (usually six). The new Guard alters are placed on the right hand in the reversed Kabbalah, and their representations are placed on the walls on the right and left sides of the child's box or crib, three in each color block. Their names will all be similar. Guards, usually male, are sometimes just labeled with numbers attached to the same name ("Michael#1, Michael#2", etc., M1 and M2 for short). Even though the child is too young to understand, these alters are told they are very important because it is their job to protect the body.

When these alters are older, they are trained using strength. Physical fights and beatings are used. The alters must not stop fighting their opponent no matter how badly they are hurt. Aggression is rewarded. A show of fear is punished.

This group's psychic ability is also trained. They are trained to feel others' emotions and to psychically see at long distances. The CIA started using this tactic several decades ago, calling it "remote viewing".

Language block

The next block, the language block,[3] is made between eighteen months and three years, depending on the child's linguistic facility. The language alter is split through torture to the throat, usually using plants that cause the tongue and throat to swell. Two alters are created for each language that the child will learn. They are placed in the thyroid chakra, and in the box they are placed on the wall behind the head. The language blocks alters are always given names in their mother tongues.

The block used for language is not treated as badly as other blocks that are created in this age bracket. Language is mostly taught with age dependent rewards. Younger children (1–3) are rewarded with affection and candy, older children (5–10) are rewarded with money, and young teens are rewarded with money and sex and favors such as having more honored parts in rituals or holiday celebrations. This block is trained like anyone else learning a new language. The faster an alter picks up the language, the more he or she is rewarded. Alters who are lazy or cannot learn the language are punished or replaced with ones who can learn quickly.

Touch block

The touch block is begun at eighteen months through dislocating the fingers of the left hand or making cuts in the creases between the fingers. Usually about fifteen Touch alters are created. The head Touch alter is in charge of being aware of exactly what it takes to harm someone else with a minimum of damage, and how to do such things as putting a nail through a hand or slicing a sacrifice with great care. Below this is an alter who is in charge of cutting or any kind of mutilation of the person's own body. The alters below that are in charge of setting off the triggers for harming their own body (by thought, not by actual touch). Some of this group are in charge of setting off self-harm programs in other people through those people's triggers. Names are similar to those of guards.

Demon and animal blocks

It is important to remember that not all of what is seen or believed by members of these groups is real. For instance, you know there are alters who believe they are cats or dogs or snakes or demons, although you also know they cannot possibly be real. But to the alter they are as real as you or I. Tricks, technology, and "stage magic" are used to deceive the child. These are regarded as legitimate parts of magik.

The Demon and Animal blocks are built before the age of five years from harm to both knees. Doctors are involved as consultants. The child, drugged with hallucinogens, is in an altered state.

For demon and animal alter creation, puppets are used to simulate demons. The puppets are operated from above, and some are spiked. Some are hand puppets; others are on strings and fly in the air. They come at the child, who then gets a shock. The child is strapped down and wired. Probes are used to create pain. Some demons appear to fly right through and inside the child. This is done in an empty room with white walls on which the demon pictures can be projected. Finally, the "Granddaddy of All Demons," a man or teenage boy in a costume, rapes the child. Little girls are raped anally as well as vaginally. Little boys are raped anally while the penis is manipulated, and then they are raped orally. The rapist is using a drug that maintains his erection.

This takes place during a long session, lasting through the night. More than one perpetrator is present. One operates the puppets. The trainer does all the vocalizations—making demon sounds, and giving each demon a name and a job. As many demons and animals are made as possible, from two to twelve.

After the rape, while still heavily drugged, the child is decorated with theatrical makeup and corresponding tail and horns. When he or she "comes around", the child alter is told that it is a puppy, pussycat, or snake, or a demon, gargoyle, or devil. The alter may be a demon in the shape of an animal, or just an animal. The child is shown a small "mirror" that is painted with the image of an animal or a demon, and told this is him or her.

For example, the "cats" are kept in a dark room, until their eyes become accustomed to the darkness. Objects are coated with neon paint. The children are then told that cats can see in the dark. A black light is turned on, and the objects glow in the dark, making the children believe they can see in the dark like cats do. When the child has been shown it is a demon, an image of fire is projected on to a screen hidden behind a wall of smoke. The smoke has been created by dry black ice that has a red lamp shining on it. These children are told the fire will not burn them because they are from hell. In their drugged state, they are walked through what they perceive as fire. "Snake" children are bound with gauze and plastic wrap so they cannot move their arms or legs, then are placed on the ground and told to slither like a snake.

The purpose of the demon alters is to keep the child in line and in constant fear of being grabbed and harmed by a demon. They represent actual demons, just as idols may represent deities in the Hindu faith. A total of thirteen demons are wanted, including the original one, and six animals. The job of demons is to come up during rituals and during times of potential disloyalty. If the child is about to disclose something to an outsider, a demon will come up and scare him, so as to ensure compliance. The demons are set up in a hierarchy. They are given names of actual demons. Animal alters are used for purposes consonant with that animal's nature, such as a cat for going through the bushes at night. The large animals such as dogs are also used for sexual intercourse with real animals. The child usually gets to pick their own animal names.

None of the children who are programmed to believe they have animal or demon alters are beyond the age of five years. This appears to be the best age in which to create these kinds of illusions. The group will be very careful to maintain the age of these alters. Beyond that age they would tend to question, and the illusion would be broken. If you come across a cat or dog or snake or demon when working with a client, remember that it is not likely to be more than five years old.

Painholder block

Built through pain (cramps) in the lower abdomen, the Painholder block includes three or four alters who inflict pain on the child's own body: three to six who block pain, and a smaller group of no more than three who inflict pain on others. Only one of each type of pain holder is kept in the Painholder block; the rest are shared among other blocks. For example, some might be put in with Demons, some with Guards, some with Touch, and some with Animals.

Sex block

Sex block alters are created through sexual torture. Once the splits are made and the names and jobs are given, the pleasure can begin. The child is taught to masturbate, and the trainer, guardian, and other group members masturbate the child. The child is taken for entire weekends of nothing but sexual pleasures. While sucking breasts, it is taught to enjoy being masturbated.

The number of Sex block alters depends on what echelon the child belongs to. Higher echelons (children destined for higher roles, depending on how they tested in infancy) have fewer such alters than lower ones such as simple breeders.

Little nymphomaniacs are created for prostitution. These include masochists and necrophiliacs. Some breeders are trained to become sexualized at ovulation time. Some alters are designed specifically for sex magik. There are also sexual perpetrators, including necrophiliacs, who are usually male alters even when the body is female. The masochists are also usually male. There are male-bodied breeders, used for stud.

Masochist and perpetrator alters

The perpetrator and masochist alters are trained between five and seven years of age. First, the masochists are taught to hurt themselves. Every time they hurt themselves sexually they are rewarded with treats, candies and praise. A Pain alter is brought forth to share the outside body with the Masochist alter, so that the child is not feeling the pain s/he is inflicting on his or her own body. Each time the child escalates the level of self-harm, s/he is given a bigger reward. Once the child reaches a specific level, other children his or her age are brought in to do things to that child. The perpetrator child is rewarded for hurting the masochist child, while the masochist child is rewarded for enjoying the pain. Both children have pain-holder alters co-present with the sex alters. Those of the perpetrator child hold the empathic, vicarious pain.

At a certain level of tolerance and enjoyment, masochistic alters are brought forth to abuse themselves on the altar to show their abilities. This is done in an official ceremony. The alter is praised by the whole group. Then the Grand Master or person in charge of the service is allowed to hurt the child sexually while the child enjoys it. This is usually accomplished via the vicious anal rape and biting of the penis for a boy, anal and vaginal rape for a girl.

The child is given sexual stimulant drugs during the orgies, and the sexual perpetrator alters are deliberately brought out. They see people having intensely pleasurable sexual experiences while harming or being harmed. They are allowed to go around and feel anyone's bodily parts. Masochistic alters are also trained during orgies. They are given pain-killing drugs, almost to the point of nerve blocks, so that the masochist feels as little as is physically possible until the physical stimulation (pain) reaches a certain level of intensity. These alters learn to need pain in order to achieve release, and experience it as pleasure.

Training to kill

The big ceremony for the perpetrator alter involves killing. The sexual perpetrator alters are also the killers. When these alters are first created some of them are put in the section with the Sacrifice alters. Prior to the ceremony, the alter has been taught not only to harm a masochistic child, but also to harm small animals, usually their own pets (such as kittens). They are allowed to have a pet for about two weeks, then have to kill it. Before killing, they have to sexually mutilate it. Ultimately, they are bonded for three to six months with a "disposable" child (an unregistered birth), whom they have to sexually mutilate and then kill.

Necrophiliac alters

The necrophiliac alters are taught with cadavers. A Sacrifice alter is brought out with them. They learn to slice a certain muscle in the male cadaver's abdomen, which can then be tugged to cause an erection. Then they mount the cadaver and have intercourse. The first time, the child has been sexually stimulated almost to orgasm before being put with the body. Oil of Wintergreen has been administered to the genitals, which then feel too hot, so the cold cadaver feels soothing. At age eleven or twelve, a necrophiliac alter is thrilled by intercourse with a cadaver; it is an honor. Earlier, they do not like it much because it is cold, but the child is praised a lot for this kind of performance, and by eleven or twelve vaginal secretions take the chill off for a girl.

Sacrificial block

The Sacrificial block of alters is created between five and seven years of age using torture to the solar plexus. Alters in this group are trained to do killing, cutting, and skilled dissection.

Alters of the Sacrificial block spend most of the time being tortured. They are put in a pit, starved, beaten, and taunted with little bits of food hanging down out of reach, having only rats or putrid things thrown in for them to eat. This makes them full of rage. However, the goal is for them to be trained to feel less. Rewards are given for showing little or no emotion. The more they can endure without emotion, the more they are rewarded. These are the alters who endure the worst kinds of torture. These alters will be put in small holes with rats, or in graves. These must kill their beloved pets or siblings.[4] By the "age of giving" (nine) they will already know how to skin and dismember an animal or fetus. No weakness will be tolerated in this block of alters. Any sacrificial block alter who shows one sign of compassion will be tortured for long periods of time, or "destroyed" (taken to the point of unconsciousness or temporary death, and never revived).

Re-activators, doubles, and garbage kids

Re-activators are alters created specifically to retrain a wayward alter who has forgotten his or her training or chooses not to do it. Doubles are simply "backup" alters, to be used while the original alter is being retrained. If the alter cannot be retrained, the double will stand in its place and do its job permanently, while the original alter is discarded. (Often if an alter "changes sides" in therapy, its double will appear to do the job it used to do.)

There is a dump—a garbage bin is a place in the mind, similar to a prison—for discarded or untrainable alters, called "garbage kids." Garbage kids are alters that would not comply in training, or could not learn quickly enough. The trainer either takes them to death point (via drugs or severe electric shock) and "kills" them (stops the heart briefly), or simply never calls them out again. The rest of the system may believe these alters are dead, or at least that they are not as good as the others and not worthy to be alive. Once in the dump, they never leave.

When trying to take apart any lesson, it is important to include any garbage alters (as well as doubles) who were present, or the lesson will simply be re-activated or regenerated.

Satanic rebirth ceremony

The alter that will head the inside world is created during the rebirthing ceremony. This takes place around the time the child is six. Children are prepared for the ceremony by learning chants and prayers. They are taught to crawl through a hole that has been cut in a piece of wood and fitted with a piece of tight flexible rubber. They are not told what they will crawl through for the ceremony. It will be the decomposing carcass of a cow, large goat, or sheep. These children are taught that they cannot enter the kingdom of darkness unless they are born of blood and beast. This is similar to, but a reversal of, the Christian belief that only those born of water and the holy spirit can enter the kingdom of heaven.

The child is drugged and placed naked inside the carcass. He or she is sewn into the body. Upon awakening the child becomes terrified and thrashes around. The hand of the deliverer is inserted and the child is brought through the opening in the animal. In the meantime, the child, used to splitting when frightened, has formed a new split. This child alter will usually be given a demonic name by the deliverer, who tells the alter that she or he is in charge of all the others. This new alter will control all alters of the cult side. The others will learn to fear and obey him or her.

If an already existing alter emerges during the rebirthing, it becomes the new leader. If that alter is strong enough to take the rebirthing without leaving the body, it is strong enough to lead the entire system, so it deserves the position.

Training from ages six to eight

Suicide training

Suicide is taught after the rebirth and is attached to Loyalty programming. Once children are old enough to understand the concept of death, they are told that if they are found out by anyone outside the group, they simply must die. This is why so many survivors who have never before attempted suicide begin these attempts once they get into therapy. This is also why so many kids in foster homes attempt to kill themselves or run away. For these people, suicide is not from "low self esteem," but because they have been told that the outside world is not as perfect as they are, so they must not allow themselves to be defiled by the filth of the outsiders. This viewpoint is similar to white supremacist beliefs. It is also important to remember that several alters have to be involved via a spin before an attempt will be successful (see the section on Spinning).

The group will only allow the system to successfully suicide if an "outsider" (such as a therapist) has been allowed to come too close to the core, or to tamper with a lesson that they should not have opened. The Kabbalah-trained alter will have many of these lessons throughout each important path. The system will also be allowed to die if the person, along with an outsider, reaches the angel at the end of a path, or if they tamper with the path. This is known as a booby trap. This will be discussed in the later section on walking the Kabbalah pathways.

Sexual training

During this time the child's sexual alters continue being taught how to sexually please adults, as well as themselves. The child is greatly rewarded for this by adults and other children, with praise, treats, and sexual pleasures.

Training regarding urine

Children are trained to hold urine for long periods of time, as it has been found that a full bladder actually aids in sexual arousal. Also, blood is mixed with urine, ashes, and wine for a Black Mass. The child whose urine is used is rewarded. During orgies, often a child will be asked to urinate on someone with that fetish, as a sexual stimulant.

Preparation for marriage to Satan

At age eight, the children begin preparation for when they will be given as brides and consorts of Satan. The head alter of the inside cult world will select the alter to become the bride. This alter is taught special prayers and chants in the chosen language, as well as spells in sex magik. Those children who are still physically too small to receive a full size penis comfortably will receive more physical preparation. Most of the ones who are not large enough are members of the second or third circle, who came in at an older age.

Marriage to Satan

Children are given as brides and consorts of Satan when they are nine years old. They take vows to Satan to love and obey Him, to give themselves to him freely in body and soul. This is the first time they "officially" lose their virginity. They are prepared physically by their trainer. They are bathed in special oils. They are taught prayers and chants. They are painted head to toe with colors signifying their rank and circle. The alter that will become a priestess or breeder is called forward. She is dressed in white and drugged with pain killers and hallucinogens. She is then walked to center circle where she takes part in a Black Mass. During the offertory part of the service the children are called forward and raped either by a member of the congregation dressed in a costume of Lucifer, or by the Grand Master or High priest, who uses a phallus with sharp spikes sticking out. After the service these children will become permanent parts of the circle.

Reaching "maturity"

Between eleven and thirteen, the female child will conceive for the first time. The firstborn male child is killed in a sacrificial manner during its first weeks of life. Simply put, this is what Lucifer demands. The belief is that the energy of the child's life force is given to those who encircle it.

At thirteen the child becomes an adult, and has something similar to the Jewish rite of passage for that age, the *Bar* or *Bat Mitzvah*. The cult version is celebrated with the child's first orgy, that is, the first one in which he or she freely participates as an adult. The adult gets to choose his or her partners instead of being taken by anyone, gets the say in what is done, and is given as much pleasure, without pain, as possible.

Beginning of Kabbalah training

After the sacrament of marriage to Satan, the children begin training on the Kabbalah. The Jewish Kabbalah, or "tree of life," is a structure like a tree, with pathways representing different aspects of sacred mysticism. It also represents the shape of the human body. The occult reversed Kabbalah groups use literal pathways and harm the literal body of the child. The Kabbalah, which was initially presented to the baby on his or her own body, is now represented in the training center both in that way and by pathways along which the child must walk. Most paths contain thirteen doors. Each path has a guardian at the opening and a black angel at the end. Doors on the first path always contain the first symbols of the major triggers of obedience, such as roses, sounds, smells, words, or music. The path is set up such that one door is the trigger, one door is a punishment, and one door is a pleasure. You may get two pleasures, one pain, and three triggers, or the other way around. The Trainer sets up the path according to a set law, but to the victim it appears to be completely random.

Twisted shapes of the alphabet as well as magikal symbols are used as a code of trail markers, and to bring forth specific lessons and alters. Different places in the body contain different lessons and codes. Only the Highest Jobs (high priest or priestess) will ever reach the head of the body, or be one with Lucifer.

Kabbalah levels and lessons

In each lesson of the Kabbalah, there is magik. Each spell accompanies a very important lesson. In therapy, it is important to remember the magik and the spell-work that go along with each path. Leaving this out would be the same as removing only part of a cancerous tumor. It would eventually grow back and spread throughout the entire system.

The bottom part of the body of the Kabbalah is for the Third and lower Second Circle. The mid section is for the higher Second and lower First Circle. The upper section, excluding the head, is for the rest of the First Circle.

The head is only for those who will become High Priest and Priestess, Grand Masters, or above. These children learn different lessons. They have to endure more physical and mental hardship and perfect their knowledge of secret languages. In the upper part of the Kabbalah, the child is taught a higher form of black magik and demon spell work, with the blackest magik, including the use of the Lords of Demons, being in the head region. The lower groups see this, but they are not taught how to do it.

It is here that the child will be broken, if possible. Only the strongest survive this level, and it is they who will become the leaders. The amount of abuse they must withstand is phenomenal. These children are the physically strongest and have the best coping skills. However, attaining this level has nothing to do with whether they are any more prepared or willing to do evil than anyone else. I was chosen, but I never liked doing evil. I often said no. The fact that I would stand up to them showed my strengths but also increased my chances for death.

Those who become members of the hierarchy are rarely so damaged that they cannot function in a very successful career. It is rare that they end up in therapy, unless they do so for other reasons. They also rarely have any visible marks on their bodies, and rarely ever physically injure themselves. They are, therefore, more likely to be invisible in society.

Most people will have finished their level of the Kabbalah by the time they are sixteen years old.

The Kabbalah pathways

People being trained in the Satanic Kabbalah travel down the paths of the Kabbalah. All paths consist of thirteen doors. Each door has a symbol and a letter on it. In each room there is another symbol. The lower paths have no magik; the higher paths have more, plus sacred languages. Without exception, every door divisible by three will contain torture of some kind. The last door (13) contains an angel who is a booby trap.

Example of a path

This is an example of a mid path, moving up from knees to waist, used in training a young teenager:

Room 1:   The symbol is A for Alef, or the Hebrew A, which is a symbol that means return. In the room is a single yellow rose. The word "Return" is played over and over.

Room 2:   B for Bet. In the room is a man with a candle. You enter the room, and the man burns your hand with the candle while a prayer of dedication is being recited.

Room 3:   G (Gimel). Two people hold you down and rape you, using excessively large phalluses. You will recite the sex magik spell.

Room 4:   Delet. You see red, yellow and white roses. The word "traitor" is recited.

Room 5:   Heh. In blackness, the only thing heard is a series of tones. In each tone is a subliminal command. It could mean anything from "Be there Friday night" to "Kill John Doe".

Room 6:   Vav is a room of terror. It is usually pitch black, and you stand in the middle while things poke you and prod you and burn you and shock you for no apparent reason at all.

Room 7:   Zayin contains an altar with a fetus on it. You have to dissect it or you will be beaten.

Room 8:   Khet contains a chair. It is a place of refuge and rest.

Room 9:   Tet is an electrode placed in the mouth with the word "silence" repeated.

Room 10:   Yod is a demon triangle, the meeting with the demon master, and a spell.

Room 11:   Kaf. Color and tone, with word "comply."

Room 12:   Lamed. The person is strapped down, raped, and beaten, while the words "love and respect" are played over and over.

Room 13:   Mem. A spell is cast for power, and it is the setting for the Angel of the sunset.

Angels and booby traps

Each path has set booby traps that will be set off if the person tries to break the code. Not all doors contain booby traps that are designed to kill, and neither do all pathways. Only the paths divisible by three are trapped to kill. However, other traps may cause such things as a crash in the system (which in turn will cause a total loss of memory), or fabrication of wild stories in order to make the person appear insane. One of the worst traps, beside suicide, causes the person to become completely catatonic and perhaps remain so indefinitely.

One booby trap is an overwhelming feeling of guilt and depression that causes the person to shut down emotionally or to kill him- or herself. Other booby traps cause such unbearable feelings that the person gets trapped in the emotion, or door, and cannot find their way back.

The angel[5] at the end of the path is a guard. If a survivor is trying to reverse the Kabbalah, and gets to the angel at the end of the path (in memory recovery or in therapy), it means she or he has gotten too close to the core. This will set off a trap of death by suicide or accident. The survivor who runs from the angel can avert the trap going off. However, the angel is enticing, and will call the survivor in. This angel is so compelling because s/he is so beautiful and peaceful, and s/he causes alters in the path to feel as if s/he is the only one who can take away their pain.

The memories that can cause these pain and depression booby traps are of the deepest kind. They include the death of a loved one, such as a brother, sister, or friend, or the death of a pet, especially by the person's own hand, or memories of abandonment, including being told they are unlovable, even by God. The children have been told, "No one wants you, you are worthless, no one can save you." Then the angel comes, and claims to be the only one who can stop their pain because s/he is the only one who loves them. This is so consoling that they want to go with the angel. The angel will help them stop the pain, but they must commit suicide, or die of a broken heart. This is very important. It is a double-bind, with no escape from fatal consequences. As hard as it is to resist the angel—and it is very hard—if the survivor does not, he or she *will die*, in one way or the other, within forty-eight hours.

Breeders, fertility training, and use of babies

Breeders are girls and women whose function in the cult is to give birth to babies for cult use. They are trained using rape and sexual torture to show sexual pleasure but feel none. A breeder who feels for the fetus she aborts is no good to the group. The fetus must have no more meaning to her than an ordinary menstrual period.

The young breeder, before she begins her period, is raped on a daily basis. If she does not show pleasure to her partner, she is beaten. She is given hormones beginning at age nine to make her periods begin early and to make her gain weight. The weight is to hide pregnancy. For the first year, her periods are monitored very carefully, so the trainer knows when ovulation takes place. Around the time of ovulation, the girl is given drugs to sexualize her. This continues for a year. After that, if the girl demonstrates she is sexualized when she ovulates, the drugs are stopped; if she does not, the drugs continue until she is sexualized at ovulation. For some, this can take as much as three years. The girl's first few abortions are done with the use of drugs, so that she does not feel the procedure. As time goes on, less and less medication is used, until she needs none at all to abort. If the pregnancy is beyond twenty weeks, the girl is given ergotamine for several days to make her abort naturally. As time goes on some of these girls can actually abort at will. It just takes visualization for a day or two to begin contractions. A natural abortion is prized more highly than one done with instruments.

A girl who is destined to be High Priestess is also trained to become sexualized at ovulation. This is to ensure that her children are fathered by a High Priest or her mate. The fetus of a High Priestess is prized more highly than any other. Impregnation during ovulation helps to time a pregnancy so that the abortion falls on a Holy day, such as Imbloc.

It is considered that sixteen to twenty-three years of age is the best time for breeding, and that the infants that result will be of better quality. These babies are rarely killed. They might either be raised by the group to be future leaders, sold for large profits to other groups, or put on the baby black market. Most often, the firstborn healthy child is adopted by a member of the group residing in a different part of the country, or another country altogether, to be used as a pawn that will help control the mother later in life.

Internal calendars and dates

Internal calendars are used for special events such as birthdays, recall dates, and other such special events.[6] These are usually learned by alters in a normal everyday way, just as you would teach any child its birthday, or what day Christmas falls on. The outside person ("host" or ANP) does not know that cult holidays are significant.

Children in Luciferian cults are taught that in the Millennium (the year 2012) Lucifer is supposed to return. The teachings that these people have received say this: *We will all be called to account. Don't forget we owe our souls, so if you have been a good little Satanist, you will be rewarded; if not, you will be punished for eternity.*

Satanist and Luciferian Groups celebrate both Christian and pagan holidays. Although many of these holidays correspond to the traditional pagan holidays the witches, druids, or Wiccans celebrate, you should not confuse these groups with Satanists. Traditional Pagans do not worship Satan, as they do not have such a deity in their belief systems; "Satan" is strictly a Judeo-Christian manifestation. The fact that Satanists also celebrate Christian holidays does not make Christians Satanists.

Rewards used in training

In Satanic Kabbalah, the rewards given for compliance depend on what the individual responds to. Some want money, others sex, and all want power. Those in the situation do not even consider other rewards, such as having loving relationships, since these are not possible. They know what they will be rewarded for or what they will be punished for. So much of Satanic Kabbalah has to do with "double binds"—putting people in the position of having to choose the lesser of two evils. Pain or less pain? Power is preferable because it means being hurt less often and less severely. (Of course, the alter who lives in the "real world" is unaware of all this.) The highest levels of the Kabbalah contain the most rewards, balancing out the torture.

The rewards of ordinary life can seem very mild compared to those given in the cult. But I know the value of what I now have: freedom of body and soul. I am no longer a trapped soul; that is worth it.

*   *   *

We shall hear from Stella at other points in the book regarding her own experiences both in childhood and in recovery. Her documentation of the training given to children from the perspective of the abuser group, in particular the training center, is very valuable for our understanding, as no one but an adult perpetrator is able to give us the information regarding what is done to infants. Many survivors' accounts, from many different locations, reflect the kind of experiences that Stella describes here, although they often do not know the purpose of those experiences. It is similar with the experiences of ritual abuse and mind control described in Chapters Five and Six. Many specific details and themes are constants, even though the survivors were abused by different and unrelated groups in different places. The selections from survivors in this book should be seen as not just the experiences of one or two, but as representative of many, voiced by these brave and articulate people.

The contents of this chapter in particular illustrate why therapists MUST be careful to do things in a particular order, rather than just responding to whatever their clients present at any given time.

Notes

1.   Editor's note: Nine is a bit older than we have been taught to believe as the upper limit at which DID can be created.

2. Editor's note: The torture and training described in this section are gruesome, so reader beware.

3. Editor's note: Occult groups use various magikal languages, such as Enochian or Latin, in their rituals, and members have alters who are trained specifically to use these languages.

4. These memories, as well as those of perpetrating, often come up as soon as the client makes significant disclosures to a therapist. They are part of the "booby traps" to induce suicide attempts if security is breached.

5. Editor's note: In the angel booby traps, an alter has the job of making those who try to work through a memory feel that the angel is present in the here-and-now, and invites them to join the angel by suicide.

6. In addition to Appendix 2, a Satanic calendar authored by Stella Katz, a more detailed calendar for each year with holidays for a number of different groups can be found on the Survivorship website.

CHAPTER EIGHT

The programming: indoctrination, lies, and tricks

It is widely known that mind control is produced through a combination of hypnotic suggestion, torture, threats, and double binds. But the most important thing for you—and your client—to know is that the mind control created in children, whether by cults, military or government groups, or organized criminal groups which use children as sexual slaves, is based on carefully designed and meticulously executed deceptions.

Abusers create false beliefs by setting up certain scenarios, using trickery (stage magic and illusions), reinforced by the effects of drugs, and, when it might be helpful, torture. You will see further elaboration of this process in Chapters Nine through Fourteen; this chapter summarizes some of the most common lies told by these abusers, the purpose of each, and the methods abusers use to make children believe them.

The most crucial lies are those that create lifelong obedience and loyalty in the survivor and those that maintain the secrecy and security of the perpetrator group. Other lies are told to get alters to do their "jobs."

In my experience with these survivors, I have found that there are many lies and tricks that might be called "standard." (Some "deprogrammers", such as Steve Oglevie, say that they can recognize the abusive group by the way the personality system is structured and then know what specific deceptions are practiced by that particular group.) Spontaneous DIDs do not appear to share such commonalities.

Alters who are split off at different ages are told lies that are effective for the ages at which they were trained and stopped maturing. So, for instance, four-year-olds will be told about the "magik" powers of the perpetrators, and will see these demonstrated; eleven-year-olds may be told about the extensive power of the perpetrator group to infiltrate every organization, spy on everyone, and use sophisticated technology which has not yet been released to the general public. Both these lies serve the purpose of causing the child/survivor to believe there is no way to escape the perpetrator group. An adult survivor may have many different alters, each of whom believes the lies they were told at the ages when they were trained.

The fact that there are alters who live most of their daily lives and function socially in the outside world, alters who often do not know of the beliefs, training, or even the existence of the other alters, allows for the lies and tricks to be effective.

It is interesting to observe how many of the themes found in the primary lies told by the mind controllers are devoted to reinforcing the basics of the belief systems of dangerous cults as listed by Bonewits (see Chapter Two). These include the leaders' wisdom and knowledge, the leaders' power and control, the correctness of the belief system of the group, the need for sexual submission to whomever the group designates, the importance of censoring communications with the outside world and of isolation, the wrongness and danger of leaving the group, the rightness of violence, the dangers of the outside world, the importance of surrendering the will, and the importance of appearing "normal" and maintaining a double life.

Lies about the abusers' correctness, superiority, and wisdom

- Children are told that the way of the abuser group (worshipping Satan or Lucifer, or the Third Reich, or the white American way of life, etc.) is the only right way and its leader or deity deserves obedience and loyalty.
- Children are told that they can trust the abusers because the abusers are their "family," but they cannot trust anyone else. Only this cult defined "family" cares about the children.
- Children are told that the group performs these abuses for the child's own good (rape confers forgiveness; torture or being forced to harm or kill someone else makes a person strong).

Methods of indoctrination

How are these lies conveyed? Intense, abusive religious or military indoctrination forces mind-controlled child alters to adopt the belief system of the abusers. These beliefs are hammered into the child's mind over and over, through religious ceremonies, military drills, songs and chants and rhymes, severe punishments, and rewards for compliance or memorizing the correct beliefs. At night or during breaks from real school, cult children attend "cult school." Children are coerced into making vows of loyalty and signing official documents, sometimes in blood.

Lies to induce obedience to the abusers

- Children or alters are told they are "good" if they obey the abusers and "bad" if they disobey.
- Children are told that they have to remain loyal and obedient to the abusers, because they made vows or promises of loyalty.
- Child victims or trainees are told that they are robots, or computers, or sex machines, or killing machines, not persons. Or that they have robots inside who control their minds and bodies.

- Children are told that someone who fights back against the abusers is a traitor and should and will be punished. (Such alters become discarded "garbage kids.")
- Children are told that all "inside people" were created only to do the jobs assigned to them by their abusers, and if they do not do these jobs they will have no purpose and will no longer exist.
- Children are told that all "inside people" must stay in their "places" in the inner world or structure.
- Child victims or trainees are made to believe that they are soldiers whose duty is to obey without thinking. Thinking for oneself is viewed as wrong.

Methods of indoctrination

Children being taught that they are killing machines or sex machines or robots are put in positions where they lack control over their own bodies, which are made to perform the desired actions even against the children's will.

To make alters believe they are soldiers, abusers dress the children up in uniforms, and uniformed adults who call themselves generals or commanders or captains use their power, their size, and their loud voices to frighten the children and make them obey. The children are forced to engage in training just like adult soldiers. The "generals" make them watch movies of soldiers marching or fighting. They talk about pride in fighting for their glorious cause, and dying for it. They give fake promotions. They shout at the children and tell them to obey and not think for themselves. Children who cry, vomit, show fear or sadness, or show compassion for others who are being hurt, are punished.

Lies that create loyalty to the abusers

- Children are told that a disloyal group member is a traitor and deserves punishment by rape or torture or death.
- Children are told that the abusers can kill the child or take him/her away at any time and no outsider can stop it happening, because the group has infinite power.
- Children are told that if they disobey the group, someone they love or another vulnerable child will be punished or will die.
- The alters whom the abusers put in charge of the other parts are told that they must always make the other parts obey, and punish them if they disobey, or the abusers will find them and punish them severely.
- Children are told that if they do as they are told, they will rise to be the highest members of the coven or to be generals in the army.

Methods of indoctrination

Children being shaped to these beliefs are punished for minor infractions. They are also rewarded (by drugs, sex, or being allowed to harm someone else instead of being harmed) for compliance. They are given "promotions" in the cult or the military organization, with stripes or rings or some kind of token of the increased status.

Each child is usually put through a scenario in which he or she watches an alleged "traitor" being tortured or apparently killed, and is told this will happen to him if he is a traitor. He is given a sample of what this feels like, such as being stretched on a rack, or severely electroshocked.

Lies about the abusers' power and knowledge

Children are told that:

- The walls have ears (taught to a young child in a room with plastic "ears" glued to the walls. The abusers said the ears would always be there in any room but will not be visible.)
- The all-seeing Eye always sees you even when you cannot see it (taught with a plastic eyeball in a glass case, or even an actual eyeball from a dead creature).
- The stuffed animals (some given to the child by the perpetrators) report on the child to the perpetrators.
- The abuser group are always hiding in the shadows or in the walls (taught through an actual experience where this was the case). (You may note that not all tricks require the same level of detail, depending on their context.)
- Mothers have eyes in the back of their heads.
- The crows or the spiders or some other common creatures report to the abuser group.
- "Satan's eyes" are always watching (simulated with flashlights in the dark).
- There is a microchip implanted in the survivor's body that tells the abusers where s/he is and/or what s/he is thinking.
- There is a device implanted inside the victim's head that sees and hears everything and reports it to the abusers.
- The abusers have sophisticated state-of-the-art technology to listen to the survivor's phone conversations and read his/her emails and see where s/he is at all times.
- The abusers know things and do things by means of real magik.
- The abusers always know if someone is lying, so the child must always tell the truth to them.
- Everyone the survivor knows is linked to the abuser group and knows his or her every move, and will report back to your abusers.

Methods of indoctrination

Mind controllers want and need their victims to believe they are all-powerful, all-seeing, all-knowing, and able to appear at any moment to punish disloyalty. These lies are basic to the "access programming" we shall discuss later, as well as the "silence programming" which prevents survivors from disclosing their abuse.

The most basic lie is that the perpetrators always know where the survivor is and what he or she does, says, or thinks. To prove this, they commonly use their deity or deities, "God" or "Satan" or "Lucifer." Those of us who attended church or Sunday school will recall being taught that God is omnipotent, omniscient, and omni-present. There is nothing like an invisible, omnipotent watcher to make children behave in the desired manner when no one is really supervising them. This is especially effective if that deity has already been simulated by a costumed person who punished the child for disobedience with rape or torture.

Punishment and trickery are used to convince the child of these lies. A situation is created in which the child is likely to hide, to talk to someone about the abuse, or to disobey. A hidden microphone or a one-way mirror permits the group to see or hear what the child is doing or saying. The group punishes the child for what s/he did or said when the child thought s/he was alone or hidden. Some of the details of the tricks are in the examples given above.

Lies used to keep the survivor in contact with the abuser group

Abusers must make sure that the survivors do not begin disclosing the abuse once they grow up and leave the area. In addition, some groups want to continue to use some survivors. For instance, ritualistic cults expect the children they abuse to become adult cult members who will transmit the group's values and practices to the next generation (Stella Katz, the author of Chapter Seven, was such a member.) Military/political groups continue to use some adult survivors of their training as spies, assassins, or drug couriers. While they "close down" the programming of some survivors, as they did with Trish Fotheringham, they keep others in active use. Child prostitution and pornography groups probably allow survivors to leave when they reach adulthood, unless they are also involved in the adult versions of the same things.

There are many lies designed to keep the trainees or group members involved. "Return" programs are based on lies that invoke the necessity of returning at specified intervals or for specified events. "Come when called" programs involve the necessity of responding to callbacks by perpetrators. "Report" programs address the problem of members giving away secrets by forcing those who have done so to return to or contact the group of their own volition. Particular groups of alters are given each of these types of training. In Chapter Eleven, "'Stabilization' takes on a new meaning", we will look in more detail at how these beliefs are induced, and what to do about them.

Lies to ensure the survivor returns to the abusers (return programs)

- Children are told that if they go to the abusers when they are supposed to, they will not get punished, but will get a special treat.
- Children are told that if they do not return to the abusers on birthdays and other special dates, they will be hunted down and punished severely.
- Children are told that if they do not return to the abusers on birthdays and other special dates, the group will hurt someone else.

Methods of indoctrination

These lies about what the survivor can expect to happen throughout their lives are all established through tricks that happen in the person's childhood. In one scenario, children are unable to attend an event on time, and are then taken to the event and forced to watch some-one else being punished on their behalf. In another setup, one child is told that he or she is the only person that can save another child from being hurt, but is prevented from arriving in time to do so. Other setups involve rewards for coming on time.

Lies to ensure current contact (come when called programs)

- Children are taught that they always have to answer the phone, or something bad will happen.
- They are taught that even on the phone, alters have to come out if they are asked for.
- They are taught that they always have to answer the door and open it, even if they do not want to see the person who comes to the door.

Methods of indoctrination

Children are trained to accept the false belief that they must always be available to their abusers—that is, they must respond to their abusers and come when called. These lies result in programmed, immediate responses. They are reinforced with such things as painful electric shocks until a child picks up the phone, and doors kicked down by violent abusers. Children are also deliberately given opportunities to run away, only to be caught and violently punished repeatedly while they are given the message that they cannot run. (See Chapter Eleven for details.)

Lies to ensure the survivor reports any disclosures or relocations (report programs)

Mind control survivors learn the false belief that the abusers always know where they are and what they have said and done, and will hunt them down and punish them severely for disloy-alty. One or more alters are taught that they must report to the abusers any time the child disobeys or discloses secrets. These "Reporter alters" are also told to report any relocations, so that the abusers always know where they are. The paradox of this situation is that the alters who report to the abusers do so because they believe the abusers know everything and will punish them if they do not report, while the secret reporting and its consequences provide evidence to the rest of the system that the abusers know everything.

Methods of indoctrination

The alters who do this job are created when children are forced to watch other children being tortured until they disclose to the perpetrators something they have said to outsiders. Then they are put in a position to receive a milder version of the same torture, accompanied by a warning about what will happen if they do not tell the group what other alters have told outsiders.

Reporter alters are tested and trained; they have backups. It is important to the abusers that the rest of the survivor's personality system does not know about the reporters, so they will all continue to believe in the magic or technology which enables the perpetrators to know everything, so survivors can never escape or be free.

Lies about the child being evil

- The children are told that they are evil and are perpetrators rather than victims, just like the abusers.
- The children are told that God hates them and will punish them because of the evil they have done.
- The children are told that they are children of the devil and belong only to the coven and to the devil.
- The children are told that they are going to hell, and their only choice is whether they will be hurt there or will hurt others.
- The children are told they have special powers that can at any time destroy people's lives.
- The children are told that they will harm anyone who gets close to him or her.

Methods of indoctrination

Mind controlling abusers isolate survivors from the rest of humanity through forcing children (and adult survivors) to perpetrate various abuses. In ritually abusive groups, this means taking part in animal sacrifices and in real and simulated human sacrifices. Initially the child's hand, holding a knife, is forced by the hand of an adult to stab the victim. Once the child realizes he or she cannot resist, an alter is split off who will do the stabbing without being physically forced. The child is similarly assisted to participate in rapes. For a girl, this is done with objects. Military/political groups train their little assassins using standard military indoctrination and training, praising children for being skilled "soldiers." However, these children are generally tortured to produce these alters, who are then forced to commit acts of extreme cruelty. We can see this kind of training in the Ugandan "Lord's Resistance Army," known to engage in both ritual abuse and mind control, though these terms are not always used in news reports.

Persons who steadfastly refuse to perpetrate are subjected to scenarios wherein others harm someone or kill an animal, and the person is told it is their fault. A child might also be told that she or he has the capacity to kill someone psychically, followed by a simulation of this killing. This forced perpetration, real or simulated, is immediately followed by teaching about how evil the child or group member is and how no one else will ever want him or her. Sometimes the message is heightened when scenarios are enacted in which costumed actors pretend to be God or Jesus and either abuse or reject the child.

A child may also be convinced that something evil is put inside him or her. In "brain transplants," the brain of an abuser or of a despised animal, such as a rat, is supposedly put into the child. A child who is made to believe she or he has a "black heart" sees an animal heart and then feels a pain in her chest while it is supposedly inserted. Alters are told that they are demons or monsters or aliens, and other alters are created as internal copies of an abuser whose "seed" has been implanted by means of a rape.

Lies to isolate the survivor from the outside world and prevent disclosures

Like all dangerous cults, these groups teach the persons they indoctrinate that they are only safe within the confines of the group, and being involved with any people in the outside world will harm either them or those they get to know. Because the primary victims are children, these lies have enormous effects on the children's development, and lay the groundwork for dissociative disorders as well as attachment disorders. This group of lies includes both general ones about not trusting or attaching to people, and specific ones targeted at such people as therapists, police officers, and medical professionals. Children's beliefs that they are perpetrators rather than victims also adds to their isolation.

Lies that destroy children's ability to attach to other people

- Children are told that they can never trust anyone who is not part of the family or the abuser group.
- Children are told that people they know and like or love will always leave and will end up hating them.
- Children are told that anyone they tell about the abuse, as well as their families, will be hurt or killed.
- Children are told that if they get attached to people, something bad will happen to those people.

Methods of indoctrination

You will notice how the victims' altruism is used against them. As with all the mind-controlling lies, scenarios are set up to "prove" the "truth" of these statements. For instance, a young child is asked to choose between two groups of people, one group wearing hooded black robes, the other group wearing ordinary clothes. Naturally, she chooses the people in ordinary clothes, and they attack and abuse her. She is put back in the choice situation, and chooses the robed cult members; they welcome her lovingly. Now, this child alter will bring on fear inside the adult survivor if she begins to develop friendships with regular people.

A worse scenario occurs, in which a child is paired with a "disposable" child, is allowed to become her friend, and then is forced to participate in the real or simulated murder of that child. Even worse is one in which a child is forced to participate in what she believes was the killing of the only woman she trusts (or, more likely, someone impersonating that woman). The woman then rises up and sexually assaults the child, telling the little girl that she, the child, is responsible for making the woman evil, because when you die you become evil.

Though not consciously remembered, this indoctrination into an "upside down" system of reality prevents the child (and later, the adult survivor) from breaking free from the group and developing real friendships with outsiders.

Lies to prevent disclosures to professionals

- Children are told that if they show physical evidence or tell the story of their abuse to any professional, that person will not believe them and will lock them up in a mental hospital, where they will be drugged and abused.
- Children are told that any therapist they talk to will sexually abuse them.
- Children are told that if they disclose to law enforcement professionals, they will be arrested, charged with crimes such as murder and rape, and put in prison where they will be abused by guards or inmates.
- Children are told that if they tell anyone about the abuse, a bomb will go off inside their body, or an animal such as a rat or a snake will eat them up from inside.

Methods of indoctrination

These perpetrators pay special attention to disrupting their victims' potential relationships with therapists, doctors, and police officers. Members of ritually abusive cults have almost all been invited to talk about the abuse by people posing as these professionals, only to then be sexually abused by them. Stage "psychiatrists" or "psychologists" will tell children they are crazy for talking about such things, lock them up in restraints in a "mental hospital" or "loony bin," and administer strong drugs which make them feel ill and unable to think. The children may also be assaulted by the "inmates" in the loony bin or mental hospital. The "police" either beat and rape these children themselves, or put them in "prison" where inmates claiming to be killers or rapists do so.

Another technique to keep survivors from talking is the staging of simulated operations. For example, a four-year-old child is put on a stretcher or table and prepared for surgery. The child is told that the abusers are putting a bomb inside her or his stomach, and if he or she talks about what has been done, the bomb will go off. The child blacks out, comes to, and is shown the bandages and an X-Ray of the supposed bomb inside his or her belly. Later, this alter's fear will be enough to prevent the adult from speaking out even if there are recalled memories to talk about.

I have encountered this "bomb" with sufficient frequency among my clients that I have begun to joke about it with some of them. I say something like, "Oh, that old X-Ray again. It must be starting to wear out by now. I think they use it on all the kids. I wonder whose stomach it was really in the time they took the picture." The client, who has told me in hushed tones about the bomb, looks at me in amazement, but begins to feel some reassurance because she realizes that I know about this, and it is a trick. (A macabre sense of humor may be a requirement for this work. When survivor clients demonstrate this kind of humor, it indicates perspective, and I know they are really recovering.)

In other versions of this technique, military/political mind controllers claim to implant small devices that will record everything the child thinks or says and transmit it to the abusers, and/or to explode when the abusers become aware that the survivor has "talked;" ritualistic cults insert snakes or rats in a small child's vagina or anus, declaring that if he or she talks, the creature will devour him or her from inside. They then switch the child to another alter, who is told he or she has "given birth" to this creature because s/he is so evil.

Remember that the alters on whom these deceptions are perpetrated are deliberately maintained at the ages at which they believe such things and accept the "proof" of them provided by their abusers. If a survivor attempts to find out what happened to him or her, the fear coming from these young alters will flood the person, no matter what their actual age.

Lies to induce suicide

- Children are told that it is honorable to die for the cause of the abusers (common with "soldiers" or religious alters).
- Children are told that since the group knows what survivors have said and done, traitors must kill themselves quickly before the group finds them and kills them slowly and painfully. (Note the theme of double binds.)
- Children are told that their lives will always be so unbearable that it is better to die.
- Certain alters are told that if they kill the body when it is traitorous, they will be rewarded in the afterlife. (This is similar to the belief of extreme Islamic suicide bombers.)
- Demon or alien or ghost alters are told that they can kill the body without themselves dying, or that their special powers will bring them back to life.

Methods of indoctrination

One of the ways that organized abusive groups guarantee secrecy is to train alters to commit suicide if someone is no longer of use to the group and begins remembering or disclosing the abuse. Abusers use anaesthetic drugs to make the "non-human" alters responsible for suicide unable to feel anything in the body, thus convincing them they do not belong to the body. Sometimes there is a reward promised them for killing the body. Other indoctrination discussed earlier, such as watching an alleged traitor be tortured or killed slowly and painfully, convinces other alters that they would be better off dead if the person is a traitor.

Suicide and self-harm programs will be addressed further in Chapter Eleven.

Lies that cause survivors to deny or recant abuse memories and experiences

- The alters who are designated to live in the "real world," going to school or college and holding jobs while interacting with others in adulthood, are trained, usually at home by parents, to disbelieve any memories that might come up.
- Children are taught to believe that they got the idea that they were abused from something they read or saw on television or from someone else's experience or from a therapist. (This is a basic argument of those who attempt to discredit these experiences in the public eye and among professionals.)
- Children are also taught that if they experience flashbacks of awful abuses, those must be dreams or imagination or signs that they are crazy. Nothing bad really happened to them.

Methods of indoctrination

The group might "prove" the unreality of the child's memories through simulated murder events that the child attends, or in which the child is forced to participate. The next day, the child sees the murdered person alive, and if she or he asks questions is told that the awful event was a dream or a product of imagination.

Since survivors of extreme abuse often do not remember much of their past, it is very easy for people who have power in their lives, such as their parents, to convince them that nothing bad happened to them. Everyone wants to please their parents. Parents involved in the abuses of those who have a dream, a flashback, or a memory of the abuse in childhood will tell them that they got the idea from somewhere else. It is reassuring to these children to believe it was not real.

Chapter Twelve, "Maybe I made it up", addresses these issues in more depth.

Therapy to address abusers' lies

Cognitive therapy of mind control survivors is an important part of treatment for these lies and deceptions. This needs to be done both individually with particular alters, and also with the personality system as a whole. Therapists can provide an alternative explanation to that given by the abusers. For example, if an alter personality was told that he or she is not part of the body (and therefore can kill the body without the alter dying), a therapist can discuss making a mark on the hand of another alter, and then the alter who believes he or she is not part of the body can come out and see whether or not it is also on his or her hand. The alter will stare in amazement and ask how the mark got there. In a few cases there will be another alter inside who creates an illusion of an unmarked hand, and it may be necessary to ask this one to stop creating the illusion so that everyone inside can see the truth. In most (but not all) cases this will be effective. I do this in a playful way, engaging the child alters in showing their power by turning the illusion on and off again.

Unmasking the deception can be very powerful. Often this is done using the abuser's type of trick, without any abuse. For example, I induced an alter who believed he had no body to come out into the body. He was invisible to all other alters. He explained to me that he did not have a body. I asked what was in his hand. A cup, he said. I asked how he was managing to hold it. He looked in amazement at the cup, and slowly began to move the hand. He did not understand how he could be doing this. I asked what he looked like. Nothing, just blackness. How did he know this? He said that he saw himself in a mirror, and it was just black. I showed him his (that is, the person's) face in a small mirror. Then I put a piece of white paper over the mirror, and asked what he saw. Just whiteness. I assisted him to move the paper on and off the mirror, so he could see it was just covering the real image. He said that he was not white, he was black. I used the black plastic cover of my notebook to cover the mirror, and he said yes, that was it. With the help of another alter, who informed him that the abusers had put a black cloth over the mirror, the illusion was dispelled, and the alter realized how he had been tricked.

It is most effective when alters who were deceived receive information directly from alters who know the truth. Since alters whose mothers were involved in the abuse commonly believe that their mothers can use magik to always know everything, it comes as a shock and a relief when another alter reveals having had the job of tattling. So when new alters emerge, I always ask them to get information from others in the system rather than just from me. Why should they trust me? But the others can give them actual memories. I tell my clients that when all their internal parts share information with one another, they can discover the lies and tricks perpetrated on them.

Similarly, groups of alters together might be invited to view the whole memory of an event in which they were deliberately deceived. For example, you recall a recently described trick wherein a ritually abusive group inserts a rat into a girl's vagina, telling her it will eat her up from inside if she talks about the abuse. They switch the child into another alter, and then extract the rat, telling the new alter that she has given birth to a rat because she is so evil, and no one but them will ever want such an evil person. If both these alters view this event together, they will see how they have been deceived. This intervention is even more effective than one alter telling the other what they know, but it cannot be done until the personality system is ready for memory work, and prepared with a way to handle the emotions and physical pain of such horrendous memories. This information will be found in Chapter Sixteen.

Many alters can be "stuck in the past" and still think it is 1968 or 1987 or some other year when they were still physically a child and the abusers were in charge of them. The parts who were put in charge need to be fully informed about the situation, and if they realize they are no longer in danger (when this is an accurate perception, and current contact has been addressed) they can stop punishing the others and learn to work together with all parts, for safety and healing.

It will empower your clients to understand that there are lies which they do not have to believe any longer. You can tell them that when they share information and emotions between and among all their parts, they will know the truth. They now have choices that they did not have in childhood. As they question what they were told, and consult with their inside parts to discover the truth, they will regain their freedom and control of their own lives.

My car has a bumper sticker that says, "I think, therefore I'm dangerous." One of my mind-controlled clients, who was told repeatedly never to think, bought me two more of these stickers when I replaced the car. It meant a huge amount to her. And it is a delight to see her alters begin to think for themselves and recognize the truth of past and present. She has requested that I ask therapists to give their clients the following message:

Think for yourself, now that you are an adult, and critique the information the abusers gave you to see whether or not you now think it could be true. If something is really true, it will resonate as a truth for you. You might find that when something resonates this way, you feel angry or sad, and you might want to avoid thinking about it any further. If this is the case, it will be helpful for you to follow the thread of emotions and thoughts and ask yourself why you are avoiding this. Shed light on it so that you can find the real truth, which is the only way you will be able to heal and to move forward in life. Recognize that if you were deceived, you were a child, so it is not your fault you were deceived. Be determined to get at the truth. If one thing the abusers said to you was a lie, then perhaps other things that were said to you were lies or tricks (fabricated events). You can find out, and you can regain control of your own life and be free.

CHAPTER NINE

Understanding and working with alters' jobs and hierarchies

W hat is usually known as a "program" is really the job that an alter, or an orchestrated series of alters, has been trained to do. The alters in systems created through mind control function within specifically designed internal structures, as we have seen. They are also arranged in an internal hierarchy, which is another of mind control systems' most distinguishing features. In this chapter we shall look at these alters, their jobs, and the way they relate to one another. We shall also address treatment issues particular to the programming and arranged roles of your client.

Basic rules and arrangements for alters

Unlike the more random arrangements found in "spontaneous" multiples, the personality systems of most cult children are structured with a strong dividing line between the left (cult) and the right (ordinary life) sides. The alters are told by the perpetrators that this is where they live, but this division is unlikely to represent the actual physiological differences between them, since alter personalities reside more in circuitry than in specific brain locations. The left/right division is not the only way that alters from organized abuse are separated from those from "regular" abuse in the home. Many mind-controlled systems also have internal walls and barriers to segment groups of alters. Sometimes groups from a particular kind of abuse are hidden "underground" beneath other groups. So, for example, Ku Klux Klan alters can be hidden beneath ritual abuse alters. It is easy for a therapist, even if he or she discovers ritual abuse, to completely miss the hidden mind-controlled alters from child pornography or military/ political abuse.

All of this is done to ensure that mind control alters remain hidden—from everyday alters, and from the world. Memories from the alters involved in the organized abuse do sometimes "leak" into the ANP or other alters from everyday life. When they do, they cause terror, as the everyday life alters have no idea that any of these horrible things that they are "seeing" occurred. More commonly, it is emotions that will leak through to an ANP, who has no awareness of what is causing them. This can be the basis of the depression, anxiety disorders, or obsessions and compulsions that drive some survivors to therapy.

It is easy to miss the real cause of such symptoms and treat them in standard ways which will be ineffective as long as the memories and the alters involved remain dissociated. For example, one of my clients originally went to therapy for an obsessive fear that she would harm her child with a knife. It took many years before the ritual abuse at the base of this became evident, which might never have happened had I not been open to the existence of these issues and able to work with them. Her previous therapist was unfamiliar with ritual abuse, and believed that allowing "body memories" to surface without knowing the associated events would be sufficient to resolve her trauma. It was not.

There are rules that abusers require to prevent the emergence of alters and memories. These are:

1.   Silence—do not disclose the abuse to outsiders.
2.   Maintain a façade of normalcy, or of craziness if you have been discarded by the abusive group.
3.   Obey all past and present abusers, and obey the alters in charge of the system.
4.   Be loyal to past and present abusers.
5.   Do not develop close relationships with outsiders ("Isolate").

Each alter personality in a mind-controlled system either takes pride in the job they have been forced to do, or is terrified of punishment if he or she fails to do it. For alters low in the hierarchy, the punishment comes from alters higher up. Alters higher up fear punishment that can come from the actual adults who abused them, who might or might not be still involved in their lives, but who they believe can find them ("hunt them down") and kill them if they disclose the abuse. Hidden parts of the personality system who believe they are demons or ghosts or aliens have the jobs of frightening and punishing higher-ups to keep them obedient. (More about these alters later in this chapter.)

In treating these survivors of extreme and organized abuse, remember that it is important to treat whichever parts are put out into the body to speak with you with respect, kindness, and gentle curiosity. In the early stages of therapy, your job is to ask who the part is, what their job is, and why they are present at that moment. Later you can ask to speak with specific alters. Do not ask leading questions.

It is often wise not to ask for the names of the alters, as abusers use names to call them out for torture or punishment. They may have no trouble giving names, but do not assume they want to. I sometimes suggest that they might like to give themselves new names, an idea that they often welcome. Thus, one client's "Satanic Legions" have become "Alicias," and another client's "Satans" have become "Simons." I remember when first working with Tony, I encountered an alter who announced he was "Almighty God." I told him I had a bit of difficulty calling him that, so was there another name he would be comfortable with. "Well, I always liked Geoffrey," he replied.

If you received standard training for treating DID, you may have learnt that you should map your clients' whole personality systems. However, horizontal identification of the parts is not your goal; vertical navigation up the hierarchy is what you need to do. With one of my first ritual abuse survivors, I spent a couple of years working my way through what I believed to be the whole system, mapping it out with her, and then discovered that this was just the first layer. Generally, the structure (if there is one) is intended to be kept secret. The main thing is to get an idea of the size of the system, the number of layers, and the number of alters. Then you work with parts who have more power and more actual content. Often, ritually abused and mind-controlled clients are described as being "polyfragmented," with hundreds of alters or more. Do not be overwhelmed by the number of parts. Many are just memory fragments.

Integration, or fusion, is not a big deal if you do not make it one. If the client chooses to integrate, it will happen naturally when they are ready. Talk about walls between "inside people" no longer being needed. Do not talk about the "people" disappearing. Alters are afraid that if this happens they will die. In my experience, as alters share experiences and memories, the walls between them dissolve, either gradually (when they are co-conscious a lot) or suddenly (during a major abreaction). Do not talk too much about integration or fusion between alters, especially at the start. Respect their choice not to fuse until—and unless—they are ready. And never, never, force an integration on a client.

Alters' jobs

Certain "jobs" are commonly assigned by mind-controlling abusers. You can also consult Stella Katz's account in Chapter Seven for the categories of job assignments created by cults, which include the following.

Internal organizers

- Keeping track of training memories; organizing these as files or tapes or videos.
- Keeping track of alters and making sure the wrong ones do not come out.
- Switch control—turning "programs" or training effects on and off by internal switches and buttons which have specific effects, like putting alters to sleep, or making them suicidal, or creating hallucinations.
- Recycling memories, keeping parts of them separate so that programs cannot be destroyed by memory reintegration.

Internal enforcers

- Making internal threats, sounding like the abusers or like demons.
- Punishing disobedience.
- Harming or killing the body.
- Putting the person to sleep, scrambling their memories, making them "crazy," upsetting other parts so they harass the therapist, distracting the therapist and setting off other behaviors which can interfere with therapy.
- Spinning internally to distribute feelings or impulses through the system.

Alters who deal with perpetrators

- Memorizing and responding to triggers from the outside world.
- Observing the person's behavior and thoughts and reporting disobedience to internal or external bosses.
- Reporting to the abusers.
- Returning to the abusers.
- Engaging in trained sexual behaviors.
- Killing, cutting, and sacrificing.
- Fighting, spying, and other military duties

Using the alters' jobs to assist in recovery

Many alters define themselves by their jobs, and do not know who they will be when those jobs are gone. This can make them resistant to therapy. They usually have special skills related to those jobs, and in some cases, the jobs can continue to be useful long into the course of therapy. As you meet various alters, it is advisable to ask them about their jobs, and show appreciation for their skills. Then, help them find other ways to use their skills in the service of making the whole personality system healthier.

For example, some of my ritually abused clients have alters who can put other alters to sleep. If we are in the middle of processing a traumatic memory, the alters involved in that memory agree to be put to sleep until the next therapy session so that the memory and its feelings will not leak out between sessions. Another client has bad flashbacks and nightmares, so I contacted the Gatekeeper, who has the job of containing the memories, and asked him to please do his job more thoroughly. A client with military training has her soldier alters involved in exercising to keep her body healthy. This was their own idea.

In many cases, the alters can change their jobs to other functions which employ the same skills in the service of their recovery. File keepers have access to the training memories and can bring them up when the system is ready to process and resolve them. Observers and recorders can watch the present life to make sure the client is safe. Spinners can spin peaceful and calm feelings when others in the system are anxious. Some alters may know how to remove pain. An alter trained to make the others forget events can make the alters who are supposed to report to the abusers forget having talked about the memories. Internal leaders assigned by the abusers can remain in leadership of the personality system, maintaining order, until that is no longer necessary. When new alters emerge who would destabilize the system, these leaders can take charge and make sure they do not do any damage.

Survivor Jen Callow's experience regarding her alters' jobs demonstrates the benefits of helping alters find new jobs:

> It was important for our parts to find a purpose beyond the one our abusers assigned to them. For many parts, running the programs and keeping constant vigilance over our system had been the only way to feel powerful and to avoid feeling physical or emotional pain. After we'd processed a memory, our therapist made sure to help each part find a new job and purpose inside, including the children, if they wanted (children need the time to grow and play, but we found that often

they liked to take on a smaller job of their choosing). For example, we had a group of inner soldier parts terrorizing our system. Our therapist talked to the soldiers through a host part and eventually determined they were scared children, wanting to feel powerful. After working with them and their memories, she talked with them about their talents and skills. Many of them had no idea what they liked or disliked, or what life was like beyond being a soldier. She encouraged them to spend time exploring our inner world, and asked for other parts to volunteer to show them around. We also needed to create a space for them to live and eventually reassigned them to jobs such as security (keeping us safe in the outer world), record keeping (tracking the memories we'd processed and filing them), and even maintaining the soccer field (one of them likes the discipline and precision this requires). Their responsibilities inside grow and change as they do, with the intent that they enjoy their work.

The enforcers: the key to unlocking the system

The persecutor/protector alters who are found within virtually every person with DDNOS or DID are the key to unlocking any personality system, particularly those of clients who have experienced mind control or ritual abuse.

In his study of the features of DID, Ross (1997) found that 84% of 236 DID patients said they had internal persecutor alters. As he describes them, "On first meeting they will be fearsome, loathsome, demon-like entities totally committed to the malicious harassment and abuse of the patient" (p. 115). These parts are aggressive exaggerations of the more common "inner critic" which almost everyone experiences. They tell the person not to talk, they threaten consequences for disobedience, they alienate friends and family, and they may harm or even attempt to kill the body.

Here is the perfect example of how the mind controllers and ritually abusing cults build programs that are destructive to the person by deliberately exploiting survival and self-care motives. As abusive or destructive as they appear, particularly in ritually abused or mind-controlled systems, it is very important to recognize that these alters are no different from all other alters, in that they doing their job of serving the survival of the person. They persecute in the service of protecting. For example, a client with a very angry, critical mother might hear her mother's voice telling her not to do something, or reprimanding her harshly if she did something her mother had not permitted her to do. By influencing her behavior, the alter protected her from very real abuse from the mother.

Goulding and Schwartz (1995) list these protective goals: looking for present dangers, using self-injury as protection (for example, to relieve pressure or nullify pain), being keepers of pain and badness, imitating the abuser or pleasing the abuser to avoid punishment, feeling tainted and damaged and only able to excel at being bad, distraction, trying to stop memories, and trying to protect other people from the survivor.

Some persecutor/protector alters actually believe themselves to be the person's real-life abusers. There may be more than one internal representation, for example, of a parent. This happens spontaneously, and its tendency to happen is exploited by mind controllers. For example, an abuser will rape a child while saying he is "putting himself inside her". The resultant alter believes itself to be the perpetrator.

Some alters have been deceived into believing they are demons, devils, Satan, or animals, such as Stella Katz described in Chapter Seven. They are very young (around age three) and imitate "demons" or animals they were shown to frighten them. Other deliberately created alters are responsible for the programs to cut the person's arms as a punishment, to flood the system with despair, to prevent a memory from being completely processed and put together, or to stop the person from talking by making him or her mute and terrified. Particularly because of these jobs, the persecutor/protector alters are the key to unlocking a mind-controlled personality system.

Early interventions with persecutor/protector alters

Uneducated therapists often have an inability to cope with the behaviors of persecutory alters. They commonly focus on helping one side of the personality system and battling with the other side. When "Satan" or some similar part talks in a deep scary voice to you or to the client, it is easy to think this is a nasty perpetrator or a supernatural being, and to oppose it or fight with it or try to banish it. However, if you do this, you will engender the hostility of this part, who has probably been very badly hurt and told a lot of lies. You will foster internal splitting in this way, and get nowhere fast.

Once you recognize that these alters have a protective intent, you can see that working with them involves enlisting them in the service of healing, just as they were originally enlisted in the cause of safety.

You will see examples of these kinds of errors, which often result in clients leaving their therapists, in survivor LisaBri's story:

When therapists make mistakes: LisaBri

In the early 1990s, I was diagnosed with everything from schizophrenia to pre-menstrual syndrome. I was told to get a hobby, to not drink in the evenings, and one psychiatrist pulled a packet full of white pills from his desk drawer every time I showed any kind of emotion. Every therapist, doctor and psychiatrist I had ever seen wanted me to stuff the feelings away. But where could they go? The more I 'stuffed,' the worse I became, until I landed in a locked ward of a psychiatric hospital. I sobered up, threw away the drugs and alcohol and finally found a therapist to work with. I arrived battered and worse for wear, ready to do anything to curb the intense feelings I was experiencing. I was quickly diagnosed with DID, and during the next five years, hospitalized frequently.

With my new therapist, I discovered that I had been ritually abused. I soon learnt to substitute the process of stuffing feelings away with stuffing away 'bad' inside parts. This was what my left side alters were labelled—evil. They needed to be dealt with harshly, I was told. They were 'sabotaging' therapy by creating chaos in the system, preventing any healing. Today, we bear the scars caused by these early misinterpreted inner parts. They were just doing the jobs assigned to them by our abusers. (At this time, no one inside understood that we were safe by then, as the core of the cult was dead.)

In order to make our right side more strongly defended against the left side, the therapist attempted a forced integration between the host, Lisa, and the strongest defender of our system, Brian (Bri), by creating a hypnotic integration ceremony that took place in an imaginary forest.

It appeared to work, and the therapist was ecstatic, but it was too confusing inside. I tried to talk, but I couldn't find the proper words. Julie, a five-year-old part from abuse by my father, had appeared just as we joined. At that moment, we were a threefold alter who had no idea on how to live in this singleton world. I tried to convey that there was a complication but the therapist didn't listen. We finally made it out to the car and stalled it all the way home as we couldn't operate the stick shift. After three days of not being able to function and carry out simple tasks such as unlocking a door or preparing a meal, we broke apart, but not before deciding never to integrate again.

It felt as if our core strength, Bri, who had been the basis of our survival for so long, almost crumbled because of a botched attempt by an outsider to gain control of our personality system. This therapist was wrong. An outsider can't revamp a system that has been in place for forty years and make it work, no matter how logical it seems or how right the therapist believes herself to be.

When we discovered an inside part whose main function was to hold pain arising both from the present day and from traumatic memories, the therapist felt it only right for her to be banished and isolated from the rest of the system. Miss Pain was sent away to an internal imaginary beach, alone with all her pain. She had no one to talk to, cry with, or hold. Years after that therapy we attempted to find her, hoping to tell her the world had changed, we had changed, and we wanted her back. I am happy to say that we found her, and, to our pleasant surprise, she was in better shape than we could have hoped. She was smart. Those years at the beach were spent ridding herself of the pain that so often led to self-harm. She revealed to us that when the tide came in at her beach, she took a little piece of pain and put it in the tide. When the tide went out, the pain went with it, making her isolated life just a little more tolerable.

The therapist eventually terminated therapy with us. Since she was unable to get rid of our left side alters she became convinced that we were evil. We were rerouted to a psychiatrist who practiced hypnosis. Due to our ability to dissociate at any given moment, we were highly susceptible to this type of therapy. Unfortunately, this doctor also set the goal of banishing the 'bad' parts. He had the strongest right side parts gather all the left side parts, many times forcibly, put them into a rocket and send them over the highest imaginary mountain into space. We did this routine with him once a week for over three years.

After some other unhelpful therapy experiences, I found our current therapist. Our first session scared the hell out of me. She said, "I will work with your right side; however, we need to do a lot of healing with the left side parts. This is going to be my starting focus."

She wanted to *work* with the left side, the inner cult parts. Was she crazy or what? After spending almost a decade with doctors and therapists doing all they could possibly do to get rid of those parts, this took me by complete surprise. But that's what I needed. Finally, I could heal.

It is not acceptable to hide or banish inner parts for whatever reason. Labeling alters 'good' and 'bad' has to be eliminated. All parts are equal and all deserve the respect of the mental health community.

I did not write this to bash therapists, but to help them help their clients.

LisaBri's experience reflects several mistakes that untrained therapists working with these clients often make. Avoiding treatment of certain alters may seem to be an efficient way of helping mind-controlled clients, but it is unwise, and damaging to the survivor. It takes patience to work with alters who appear to be destructive, or who are overtly hostile, but it needs to be done.

What LisaBri found most helpful, and what is the most effective approach with persecutor/protector alters, is to immediately engage these personalities in a therapeutic alliance. As with any alter, you need to be aware of their ages, and of how much they know about life in the present. Empathize with the dilemmas they have faced and mirror the importance of their protector roles. Then you can help them to protect in more effective ways for present circumstances.

Sometimes, before you talk with these protector alters, you first have to overcome the resistance of *other* protectors who believe these parts to be dangerous or even just "improper" in their speech. Often, the ANPs, for instance, are "meek and mild" people who do not swear or say things bluntly, and they hold back alters whose words they consider rude. The internal censoring can get in the way of the therapist knowing what is really going on. I do not know how many times I have told dissociative clients I have heard those swear words before, and I want to speak directly with the alters who are saying the bad words in their head anyway.

After you overcome the language issue, you need to talk with the alters who would keep you from the "abuser" alters, explaining (with the knowledge that the inner abusers are covertly listening) how the abusers are actually protectors and are trying to keep the person safe. You can reframe the abuser alters' actions as protective or nurturant; they are trying to contain overwhelming memories, control rage, or ameliorate the fear of abandonment. You can point out the protective intent by asking about the effect of this behavior on the person's life (Goodman & Peters, 1995).

Remember that these parts are actually lonely because they are internally isolated, and they long to be accepted into the internal and external community, so just talking to them and listening makes a great deal of difference (Blizard, 1997). When first talking to persecutor/protector alters, it is important to reinforce their strength and self-sufficiency. If you fight them or try to weaken them, they will demonstrate their strength by attacking. Do not talk about their needs for comfort or help at first. This comes later. I often find it effective to challenge them to come out, and talk "tough" with them, not in opposition but in alliance. They think other parts are wimpy, and they can often tolerate large amounts of physical pain, but not emotional pain. They see the expression of vulnerable emotions as a sign of weakness. They simply do not feel emotional pain; it is diverted to other alters—though they might feel anger.

In some personality systems, each "tough" alter has its own "inner child" to hold the vulnerable feelings. Yes, alters can themselves be multiple. And multiplicity often is experienced by more than one generation, particularly in mind abusing families. One client of mine had within her the entire personality system of her mother, complete with mother's "host" and hidden alters underneath that host. When I asked to meet her "mother" alter, she went out to the waiting room and returned to the therapy room as her mother, ready to discuss the daughter's problems.

It is important to find out why the persecutor/protector alters do and say what they do and say. If the client is ritually abused or mind-controlled, at least some of these alters will be doing jobs which they were required to do by their abusers on pain of death or serious bodily harm. They may not understand the effect of doing these jobs on the body or the rest of the personality system. Persecutor/protector parts believed the aggressors' verbally abusive statements and threats, so think they have to keep the system in line to prevent bad, or worse, things from happening. This is not always a false belief.

Finding out the content of the threats from these alters is very important, as it is for most alters. Disclosing the nature of the threat is less likely to stimulate harmful behavior than disclosing the abuse memories, and so is a basic strategy in working with all alters, and persecutor/

protector alters in particular, whose actions can be unintentionally hurtful. Ask them what will happen if they do not do their jobs, or if the system disobeys the abusers. Then you can give them a reality check on whether or not those things can happen in the present. It is, of course, important to check for current contact with abusers, because in that case, certain actions are protective in a concrete and real way. In some cases, clients will have contact and not know it; in other cases, they may have had no contact, but the protective alters might believe they have.

Once you have got to know persecutors a bit, you must empathically join with their underlying emotional states. This may challenge you as a therapist, because they are likely to feel pleasure at being aggressive and powerful, but it will yield many benefits. Frankel and Ahearn's "ghetto model" of the personality system (1996) may be helpful here. They explore the similarities between the organization of eastern European ghettos during the Second World War and the personality systems of persons with DID. This analogy helps us recognize the dilemma of the internal leaders of a personality system, so we will not be so quick to judge those who are loyal to the perpetrators. These are people who were held prisoner and abused throughout their childhoods, so it is no wonder they have parts who cooperated with the "guards" to get a few privileges. Now, you can carefully express empathy for other feelings, such as pain, exhaustion from hard work, and anger at abusers *and at the ANP*. Underneath these emotions are love for the ANP and the hurt child alters, loneliness, and desire to be loved and to belong. Joining with the whole range of emotions helps your client develop ambivalence (which multiples are prevented from experiencing because their opposing feelings are contained in different alters) and co-consciousness of different affective states. Often, persecutors switch quickly to positive, helpful behavior. Transference is really important for these alters, who are so "identified with the aggressor". Only when these clients have an attachment to the therapist can they let go of the attachment to the abuser(s).

Once a working alliance is established, the persecutors, the ANP(s) and other alters must negotiate their differences, resolve long-standing conflicts, and overcome past hurts, both real and imagined. This is often difficult, as other alters are terrified of the persecutors and will not go near them. It takes time to change this situation. Do not take sides; your job is to facilitate a negotiation. Ask what each part needs, and help them listen to each other. In encouraging internal communication, sometimes "deals" can be made, for example, the persecutor will not create flashbacks if the little ones do not talk about their abuse. Agreements are very helpful, as is homework, but make sure you dot every "i" and cross every "t" in an agreement, as young parts can be very concrete. You can understand this in the framework of negotiations. Agreements between alters or between alters and the therapist are not the same as the contracts advocated by some therapists engaged in DID treatment. I do not make contracts with multiples, since they can rarely guarantee that the entire system will agree to something.

Later in therapy, you can help abuser/protector parts do their jobs of protection better, or change their jobs to help the person instead of the abusers, especially when the abusers gave them their jobs.

Alter hierarchies

In the hierarchies of mind-controlled clients, a new layer is usually created every year (often on the person's birthday). This means that some alters have the power, internally, and others fear and obey them. Some believe themselves to be demonic entities. Military/political mind control survivors also often have systems dominated by introjects of the abusers (e.g., doctors, priests, generals and commanders), as well as internalizations of important figures in the belief system, such as Hitler, if the person was abused by a Nazi group.

The most important alters for the therapist to communicate with in a structured system are those who keep the others in line. These are higher-ups in the hierarchy, the ones who issue threats and punishments to those who disobey or order other alters to punish those below them. These important alters are generally aware of what happens in therapy in terms of disclosures or disobedience. They are often not aware of what is going on in the person's everyday life apart from therapy: for example, that the person has not seen the abusers for twenty years, or that the abusers are dead. They have been taught in childhood to believe that the abusers always know what is going on with the person, and that if they do not punish the other parts the abusers will punish them.

Be aware, however, that these parts are keeping track of what you are doing for their own purposes, not just on behalf of the abusers. They are watching you to determine whether you are trustworthy, and whether you are strong enough to receive their disclosures. Their experience is with the abusers, who switch into other states of being, who torture and punish. For a long time they may think you are one of the abusers testing their loyalty, since this kind of trick has been done to them. In most cases, they have been conditioned against you, warned against people who try to find out the secrets and express caring or empathy for them. They will be very cautious—as they should be.

Here is how Svali, who was a programmer for a cult which she calls the Illuminati, explains hierarchies:

> The cult itself is very hierarchical, and puts this hierarchy inside the person. What better way to inspire loyalty to leadership than to put the leadership inside the person's head? . . . The survivor may be horrified to find a representative of one of their worst perpetrators inside, but this was a survival mechanism [because] people will be less likely to punish someone who mimics them but will look down upon and punish a weak crying person . . . The survivor may mimic accents, mannerisms, even claim the perpetrator's life history as their own . . . The ultimate form of internalization comes with internalizing hierarchical councils . . . [which] will correlate roughly to the outside group . . . The[y] will be seen as holding power of life or death, and the child or youth will do anything to gain their favor. The trainer will help with the internalization, using photographs or holographic images of the people to "burn them in". [Svali, 2000]

Svali also writes about the hierarchies created by military programming:

> Military alters inside are extremely hierarchical. They will often be ranked inside, with lower "foot soldiers" accountable to inside alters with increasing rank. . . . A soldier with no rank may not have much knowledge about, or pull, inside the system. Its only job is to blindly obey others, after years of conditioning to do this. Ranking officers inside will often be modeled after outside perpetrators, officers, or trainers. An internal General will often have much more knowledge than lower ranks, and should be befriended, as they can help with therapy.

She points out that these internal officers have strong loyalty programming, including training to die an honorable death rather than betray the group. It is very important to be aware of this programming. Reason with the higher ranked members, respecting the loyalty, bravery, and sense of honor involved in their misguided allegiance to a perpetrator group which deceived them about its purposes. If they change their allegiance, they can be excellent protectors in the present from outside perpetrators.

The higher-ups

The higher-ups who are in charge of the internal hierarchies enforce the loyalty programming, which the rest of the alters obey. They are also the ones whom most of the rest of the system will still obey if they decide to work for healing.

The higher-ups' loyalty training

Higher-up parts have received some of the most horrendous spiritual abuse, in that they have been forced to perpetrate. Here are some examples of loyalty and obedience training that clients have shared with me (once again, a warning about disturbing material).

- A child has to watch another child stretched on a rack until he is pulled apart and dies. She is told to drink his blood, and when she balks she is put on the rack until she agrees to do it. The lesson is, "Never say no."
- A child (on her birthday) has to harm another child to prove she is worthy to receive a demon. She is given a hallucinogenic drug, and as it takes effect, demons are supposedly collected through a spell. She is hit on the head with a hot poker until she invites a specific demon to enter her. With the aid of the drugs, she feels "possessed" by the new demon alter. The demon alter has to say vows of loyalty to Satan.
- A child observes a woman refuse to keep her promise, made before she had children, to kill her own child. Because the woman does not keep her promise, the woman's child has to (apparently) kill her, while the children witnessing the event are instructed to keep their promises.

When a survivor is re-contacted by the abuser group, there are reminders of these trainings. Often the higher-ups are forced to perpetrate on another person, and then told they will always be part of the evil group. They have to repeat their loyalty vows, or sign them in blood. For example, the survivor is kidnapped, and raped and tortured with electroshock until alters agree to listen and repeat their vows of obedience. She is made to hurt another victim to prove her obedience. The cult threatens to kill someone she loves, and/or her therapist, if she disobeys.

When a person has parts who have been through experiences as heinous as these, they also carry considerable shame. When you think of the shame carried by a child for being sexually abused, you can only begin to understand how much shame a person carries if she or he has been forced to participate in the sexual abuse of others, or in what she believes are murders.

Your client will be afraid to disclose these experiences, and very afraid of the perpetrator group that does them. Alters who have been through these things are afraid of their own memories, and afraid you will reject them if you know what they have done. You need to be ready to accept them, no matter what they have been forced to do. You will need to explain to them, in ways they can hear, the coercion which was involved in their past behavior. You must be patient. Your own need to have the client free herself of undeserved self-hatred cannot replace her own process. And you must understand that her guilt is what distinguishes her from people who really are evil. I often say to such clients, "If you were truly evil, you would not be feeling this way. Evil people do not feel guilt for what they do."

Rewards given to the higher-ups

The parts in charge of the personality system, who hold the power over the others, have also been given rewards. Rewards include pleasurable sex, pleasurable drugs, and getting to do the hurting instead of being hurt. If they are supposedly demonic, they may have been taken to a simulated hell, and given the choice of being tortured there or being in charge of the torture of other children. Since they believe they are going to hell for eternity anyway as a result of the crimes they have committed, they might naturally choose to be the ones doing the hurting rather than the ones receiving it. Note that these parts have been split off from other discarded parts (garbage kids) who refused to cooperate with the abusers. When the higher-ups confess their guilt to me, I ask how many different alters refused to do the heinous act before they finally agreed to do it. I point out that the perpetrators would not actually kill the child even if s/he chose to be killed rather than do what was required. It takes time to convince them about how they were coerced and tricked. Stockholm Syndrome is a reality, and organized child abusers deliberately exploit it.

Sometimes when these parts watch what you are doing, they can surprise you. For example, one long-term ritually abused client of mine recently discovered she had a hierarchy on the right side (home alters) as well as the left side (cult alters). But it had given us no trouble, because the alter in charge of it, called Mother, had earlier decided to become disloyal and renamed herself Mother-F——er!

Working your way up hierarchies

Svali has this advice on how to deal with internal leadership councils, the alters at the top of hierarchies:

> Internal leadership councils will often be some of the most resistant to, and hostile towards therapy, especially in the early stages. They will verbally banter with, or refuse to speak to, the therapist, as being "beneath their notice." They are mimicking the haughty, hierarchical attitudes they have been exposed to all their lives.

> They also have the most to lose, if the survivor leaves the cult, and may fight this decision tooth and nail. They will often be the alters with an "attitude."

> Both the survivor and therapist need to recognize that these parts had powerful needs that were met in the cult setting. To ignore this and argue with them will only entrench their belief that therapists are stupid and unknowing people. Acknowledge their internal role while gently pointing

out reality. Try to enlist their aid in helping the survivor strengthen. Discuss honestly the pros and cons of leaving the cult. These are highly intellectual alters, and they need to express their concerns and doubts. Setting good boundaries and not allowing verbal abuse of the therapist is important. These alters are used to "pushing people around" verbally, and have been rewarded for it prior to therapy. Now, they need to learn new coping skills and behaviors, and the process may take time. Allow them to vent their anger, displeasure, and fears about the decision to leave the cult. Offer them new jobs inside the person of leadership over safety committees, or even decision making committees.

Sometimes, a system that has broken free from the cult, and has no external hierarchy that they are accountable to[,] will go through a short period of chaos as word gets out: we're free, and don't have to do what the cult tells us to do any more! Hundreds of internal arguments may break out as to: what do we do for a living? Where do we live? What do we eat? What hobbies will we have? Everybody wants to come out, see the daytime, and live this new, free life. But the freedom may cause imbalance with all of the switching going on inside. Enlisting the aid of the internal hierarchy, and creating a limited democracy, with ground rules, may help during this time. Don't dismantle the internal hierarchy overnight, or the systems will be rudderless. Enlist their aid in helping direct which direction the survivor goes. Things will settle down after a period, as the systems learn to listen to each other, vote on ideas, and begin going together in the same direction. [Svali, 2000]

Be aware that as you establish rapport with the "lower-down" parts, the higher-ups will make their presence known, either by coming out and objecting to what you are saying or by creating symptoms or by voices in the person's head. If your client appears to be hearing something scary, you may ask what she is hearing, and then ask who is saying it, and then ask whether you can speak with them. If the client goes through a flashback or body pain, you can ask to speak with whoever is causing it. I have one client whose right hand I take when establishing rapport; after a few seconds her left hand moves forward to remove my hand, and I take a gentle hold of the left hand too, letting those "left side" parts know that they too are welcome to be with me. Even though they usually pull away (and I let them go) the message has been given.

With my most recent mind control client, I began working my way up the hierarchy immediately. Each week I meet a new part whose job is to sabotage any healing by the other parts. I emphasize that they can all now be brothers and sisters, equal partners in healing. I meet "Hitler" or "God" or "Beelzebub," greet them in a friendly manner, and invite them to work with the others towards healing the whole person from the abuse and eventually helping other hurt children. Several of them have decided to change their names. They are enthusiastic about having a purpose other than the one they were given. They are delighted to discover that they were not "created" by the abusers, but were simply split apart from the other parts by the pain the abusers had given. The ones with important jobs have learnt to respect the "blue pile," the bruised and beaten parts who resisted doing the jobs and were discarded by the abusers. Later, when we work through memories, we will involve the blue pile too, so that they will heal from their pain.

In getting to know such a system, I frequently ask each alter if someone else is threatening them or giving them orders, and then ask to talk to their boss. This expedites the process of working my way up, and if they decide to change sides it makes the work much easier.

Survivor Jen Callow (See Chapter Seventeen) describes the new job description adopted by her Council, once they were enlisted in the service of healing:

> The Council was often able to suggest which programs were safe to work on and where inner booby traps and the like were a concern. Rather than stay a dictatorship, which would have been detrimental to our healing work, our Council chose to become an active part of our system. They disbanded several years ago, as they weren't needed in that role anymore. Many of them now assist our system in other ways and participate to varying degrees in our outer life. Some have integrated over the years. In the end, the parts designed to be the most loyal to our programming turned out to be some of our greatest allies in healing.

Backups

If you manage to gain the cooperation of the higher-ups, and therefore of the primary personality system, you can expect some trouble for a little while. All alters with jobs, including those in charge of the system, have "backups," alters who have received the same training and are supposed to take over the roles of any alter who becomes disloyal. Do not be discouraged. This will be manageable. Backups are pretty easy to convince to change sides, if the primary higher-ups have already decided to work for healing. Backups do not have much real life experience and are hollow compared to the alters they are backing up.

Work your way up the hierarchy, getting to know resistant alters, until you have at least some trust from those in charge of the system, who have until now been identified with the perpetrating group. If disclosures are made prematurely, you can expect that the client will have flashbacks and engage in self-harm and suicide attempts, plus there is the risk that alters will report to the abusers that s/he is disclosing, and they will make moves to stop her. This may take several years, or only a short time, depending upon the individual client. In the meantime, you can explore in the inner world, and intervene to make it more pleasant for the parts, and you can work on helping the client achieve safety and stabilization, all of which will be discussed in the next few chapters. Only after you have good cooperation from the personality system can you begin your work with traumatic memories.

Outliers

Outliers, as I call them, are outside the main personality system. Their job is to keep those in the main personality system in line. Outliers may be located in a structure separate from the main structure. For example, two of my clients programmed in Ontario both had their main alters in an inverted pyramid, and their outliers in rings around the outside of the pyramid. As you have seen, survivors of ritual abuse often hear voices, alters who are often viewed by themselves and other parts of the system as demonic beings, ghosts, or other evil and generally non-human entities. (They may also purport to be other people, living or dead, or God or Jesus.) This identity gives them more power over the alters who are supposed to run the system. However, they are just alters like everyone else, with a job to do; their job is to keep those in the main personality system in line. One such group that I encountered led to a delightful resolution, as described below.

The Woo-Woo Kids

The client left me a message: "I went to bed really early and woke up at 12:45 a.m. and can't get out of my head. I keep replaying everyone I know who is dead and they are taunting me, telling me that I'm making it all up and they are watching me and know that I'm a liar." She managed to calm herself with medication until our next appointment.

I know this client pretty well, and we have worked through much of her training and abuse memories. So I did as I usually do with her. I requested she ask the part named High Priestess 9, who was the main alter in charge of the system, whether she knew who inside was making my client hear these voices. I was assuming that the voices were neither real dead people nor memory fragments, but something some alter personality had been trained to do.

The reply was that High Priestess 9 was also affected by hearing the voices of the dead, as was Satan 9. I knew these two well. It had taken me about a year to work my way up to High Priestess 9 and convince her that I wanted to work with her, rather than against her. The left side of this client's system had nine layers, and each one had a high priestess, a Satan, and a complement of deliberately created alter personalities.

I remembered a group of three alters I had worked with about a year ago, the Big High Satan and two others called the Entities. This little group functioned to keep the alters in charge of the system in check by frightening them, Big High Satan frightening the rulers on Level 9, and the Entities in turn frightening him. It had taken some convincing for this client's system to let me actually meet the "Big High Satan." Did I not know he was the real Satan, implanted in her at a ritual? The alters knew by now that all the other Satans from ages three to twelve were just alter personalities. But this one was the *real thing*. That was in line with what many survivors and therapists believe, that somehow real demonic entities are attached to the personalities within a ritual abuse survivor.

I reminded her that little Satan 1 had thought Satan 2 was the real Satan, and Satan 8 had thought Satan 9 was the real Satan, and so on. Why should this new situation be any different? And, sure enough, it was not. The Big High Satan, who was all of eleven years old, boasted about how he was the one *really* in charge. We worked through some of his memories, and he became, for the most part, a cooperative part of the system.

This new problem sounded to me as if it might originate with our young Big High Satan. I asked to speak to him. He came out. "I'm the only one who can make those voices," he bragged. I asked why he was doing it. Because Stan was telling him to.

The problem with this was that Stan was not an alter. He was an actual high priest and the uncle who had abused my client. And he had died of cancer several years ago.

I asked the Big High Satan whether he thought anyone inside could be impersonating Stan, since he himself was impersonating several different dead people. He was indignant. No, he was the one really in charge, and he was the only one who could do the voices realistically. I reminded him that the Entities had been split off from him in order to control him, just as he was supposed to control the rest of the system. Oh, yeah: then, he guessed, it could be them. I asked him to check it out. He reported that he heard laughter. They were laughing about how they had fooled him.

We all laughed together about how the Big High Satan went "Woo-woo" and scared the rest of the system, and how the Entities had done the same thing to him. We decided to call them "the Woo-Woo Kids" from then on.

Conflicts in the field regarding "outliers": demons, ghosts, and "attachments"

There is disagreement in the field about how literally to view alters who see themselves as demons. Should they be seen as "attachments" or intrusions from a spiritual power?

I believe that this issue affects the proper psychotherapeutic treatment of our clients. To address it, I must challenge certain Christian perspectives. I want to point out here that my criticism is of the way in which these beliefs are applied to our understanding of the internal structures of survivors and what is required for their recovery, rather than of the beliefs, *per se*. I certainly do not have the right to criticize anyone's religious beliefs. In fact, I would like to point out that I am not even criticizing what might be seen as the extreme beliefs that are the subjects of this book, but the *practices* that hurt children and others. However, certain beliefs lead inevitably to cruel or unethical practices, and I believe it is important to challenge those beliefs. For example, Nazism is inextricably involved with the idea of the superiority of the Aryan race, and therefore the right of Aryans to exterminate those of other races.

Many survivors who experience "demons" seek a spiritual remedy for their experience, and a way to battle them, in evangelical Christian churches. In some such churches they do find helpers willing to work with them from a specifically Christian standpoint.

Among those professionals who have written about these issues from the conservative Christian perspective are the late Pastor Tom Hawkins of Restoration in Christ Ministries (2010), and Reverend Tom Ball (2008). Both of these men have extensive knowledge of, and experience with, dissociative disorders, in particular those which result from ritual abuse and mind control.

As you have seen, survivors of ritual abuse hear voices purporting to be demons or other evil entities (and might also hear voices purporting to be God or Jesus). Like other evangelical Christians who work with ritual abuse, Tom Ball makes the assumption that some of these demons are real entities which have been "attached" to the alter personalities through curses, etc. He recommends treatment in which the demon is told it has no right to be in the person and is commanded to "go directly to the throne of Jesus for Him to do with you as he will" (p. 441). Ball states that for him the best proof that real demons have been expelled is demonstrated "when the demons are prayed against authoritatively and commanded to stop bothering the person and leave [and, as a result] the upsetting feelings, ideation and symptoms do in fact stop quickly" (p. 435). He notes that other Christians working in the field "assert the best method [by which] to be sure a demon is present is to exercise the gift of discernment of spirits" (p. 435).

Hawkins went further. He saw ritual abuse not merely as a treatment issue, but also as a religious war. From his perspective,

Most [ritual abuse survivors] were forced to engage in rituals that included vows, oaths, sacrifices, or covenants made with the evil spiritual realm. These 'legal transactions' gave evil spirits, or demons, the right to 'attach' to the specific alters involved and to exert varying degrees of influence and control over them. They may play a role, for instance, in enforcing programming; blocking memories; and re-traumatizing any alter who fails to fulfill cult purposes, tells secrets, or seeks outside help. These demonized alters have essentially been brought under bondage to Satan and his agenda. . . . Connections can also be made to evil entities of a higher echelon than demons . . . Many of the more sophisticated cult perpetrators also claim that dissociated identities can be taught, or coerced under conditions of severe duress, to enter states of transcendent consciousness that connect them with what we have come to call the 'second heaven,' referring to the 'kingdom of the air' over which Satan is the reigning 'prince' (Eph. 2:2). Here they can seemingly be held 'captive' by evil cosmic beings and covertly used in Satan's worldwide agenda that is being directed from the spiritual realm. Within the person's system, these alters generally maintain a seemingly out-of-body perception and may be considered absent or even 'dead' by the other identities. [2010, p. 62]

This belief system has been influential over many Christians and even secular therapists working with ritual abuse survivors. While Hawkins said that "A therapist must always respect the worldview of the client" (p. 63), he also stated that

Successful resolution of the major spiritual bondages occurring in RA survivors requires . . . an understanding of the spiritual principles relating to the cosmic struggle between the forces of God and the forces of Satan as found in the Bible. While the secular community is well-equipped to deal with many of the psychological issues involved in DID-RA, releasing the person from bondage to the spiritual realm can only occur through the power of God. Therefore, this part of the process needs to be facilitated by a pastor, Christian counselor, or prayer minister who has thorough training in working with the dissociative disorders. [*ibid.*]

How did Hawkins reconcile his respect for the client's world view with his own view that these spiritual bondages require spiritual interventions? In an email to the Ritual Abuse and Mind Control Special Interest Group of the ISSTD (used by permission), he made it clear:

Since I am coming from a Christian perspective I make my own perspective clear (usually that is why they seek me out) but at the same time I work hard to not impose my views on the clients. A major component is encouraging them to come to a place of safety to express their anger and disappointment, including "anger with G-d".[1] Nearly all of them have parts with conflicting perspectives and respecting their internal diversity allows for them to solve these conflicts and come to their own conclusions with a cohesive internal view they can own. If spiritual issues are not dealt with in a balanced manner it actually fosters more dissociation, in my perspective. [personal communication]

I see several problems with Hawkins' position. His analysis and recovery plan might be all very well for those therapists with the "correct" religious beliefs, especially if they only see clients who specifically seek them out for that reason, but it leaves the rest of us out in the cold. How can we help ritual abuse survivors effectively if we do not subscribe to these beliefs, or if our clients do not? And how can we intervene in a religious way if doing so violates our professional codes of ethics?

Hawkins was aware of this problem, and stated in a footnote,

Dealing with spiritual issues of any kind can sometimes put a licensed therapist into a difficult situation. I encourage those with licensure to seek good counsel and get a clear understanding of their legal responsibilities under such licensure." He then suggests that we therapists work together on a team with what he calls "spiritual leaders".

This is, presumably, to get around the fact that the ethics of professional licensing bodies (who disapprove of imposing beliefs on clients) differ from those of religious organizations.

He introduced another complication: "Disconnecting RA survivors from the spiritual entities holding them in bondage is not a simple process. The specific legal rights claimed by the demons and/or evil cosmic beings must be ascertained and renounced by the identities involved" (2010, p. 63). (At the end of Volume 1 of his book, Hawkins has a table containing "Renunciations and Affirmations" designed to deal with this. He intended Volume 2 to go further into the spiritual dynamics.)

In my opinion, this collusion with the alleged validity of such agreements is unwise and therapeutically inappropriate. The notion of "legal" agreements and rights is used a great deal by mind controllers of all kinds. Children are often made to sign such agreements in blood and are told they are "married" or are bound for ever. Rather than simply accepting that these are genuine legal agreements made in some heavenly or hellish court, therapists should explain that such agreements, especially when made by under-age children under coercion, are not legal or binding in any way. Once the victim lets go of his or her belief in them, they are meaningless. Hawkins stated that "The specific legal rights claimed by the demons and/or evil cosmic beings must be ascertained and renounced by the identities involved" (*ibid.*). In light of what we know about how they were actually created and the alters who maintain them, it could indeed be helpful to take time to renounce agreements which were made, but simply as a statement of the survivor's free choice, not because they are actually legal agreements. One client of mine "divorced" Satan, but even this creative act might ascribe too much credibility to such agreements, the acceptance of whose legitimacy and power I believe to be detrimental to recovery.

Steve Oglevie is a well-known and self-described "deprogrammer" and expert in different mind control systems who gives workshops on the different kinds of mind control programming. Many therapists have attended these trainings. Here is how one day-long event is described:

Recognizing Spiritual Evil, Recognizing Dissociated and Disembodied Foreign Human Spirits and 'Installed' Personalities. Understanding of Spiritual Evil and how it Interferes in the Therapy Process. The therapist will be introduced to the very complex field of dissociated and disembodied foreign human spirits including their level of attachment to the client and ways in which they can be successfully disentangled from the true humanity and sent away. Therapists will be introduced to understanding installed personalities and how to differentiate between installed and genuine personalities.

Such trainings have a strong effect on how the therapists view the problems they are dealing with, and I consider their being labeled as "psychotherapeutic" training to be unwise. If a person working with a mind-controlled client subscribes to such a definite belief system, one which influences what they believe about what is wrong with the client and how it has to be fixed, there is not much room for the client to determine his or her own world view. This is of great concern. Such strongly held beliefs—developed to the point of being "absolute truths"—have an even greater potential to influence our clients even when they are not made explicit.

Prayer, beliefs, and treatment

In his chapter in *Ritual Abuse in the 21st Century*, Ball (2008) reviews several different Christian methods of "inner healing." His favored approach is Theophostic Prayer, which involves asking Jesus to take the client to the origin and source of a troubling emotion, then having the client look around and describe the memory all the way to the end, find the lie embedded in the memory, and ask Jesus to bring His truth to that lie. In Ball's experience, this brings rapid release and freedom to survivors.

If you break it down, in many ways this part of his approach is not different from the memory work I recommend, which many therapists have found effective: having the survivor watch a traumatic memory from start to finish, and see the lies and tricks embedded in it. It can be done therapeutically, without the explicit presence of Jesus, which certainly makes it easier for survivors who are not Christian or those whose ideas about Jesus have been severely distorted by their programming. For survivors with a strong ANP who is explicitly Christian, the addition of the prayer and the visualization of Jesus probably creates an easier and more comforting way to view the traumatic memories.

In a 2010 post to a ritual abuse and mind control discussion list (used by permission), Ball offers this useful caution to those wanting to make specifically Christian, or spiritual, interventions with this population:

> I have recently learned how absolutely important it is to take my cues from the survivor about using language when referring to anything spiritual. Terms I take for granted, I now understand, may actually cause internal pain to some parts of the personality stuck in programs related to certain abuse episodes . . . because those terms may have been used as part of the abuse/programming. But, by asking the survivor to pay attention inside, and then testing out a spiritual term that feels intellectually honest to the survivor and really does reflect the intent of the survivor, I find we can easily come up with a word for G-d that does not upset any parts inside, but that allows the survivor and me to draw/call on that spiritual resource during sessions.

Old Lady's ritual abuse experiences, described in Chapter Five, illustrate both a Satanist or Luciferian world view and a fundamentalist Christian world view, believing in specific controlling deities and other entities who interfere in human life and expect loyalty and obedience. The primary difference between these "mirror image" world views seems to concern who will win the battle and control the universe—God or the other side—and who is right and therefore deserves people's loyalty.

But what about those who do not have this particular religious perspective, or who do not have religious beliefs at all? For them, the insistence on having Jesus involved might easily feel alien, or even alienating. It can also feel like yet another violation of their autonomy. A point stated earlier should be highlighted here. Even if their personal position is not explicitly expressed, therapists need to be careful to avoid influencing their clients' development of their new world view—or even appearing to want to. This is particularly relevant for mind control survivors, who often assume that the therapist is their new "handler." My clients often wait for me to tell them what to believe and what to do. I tell them that I do not want them to obey me or believe what I say; I want to help them regain the freedom to choose their beliefs and their behavior. When I explain that I do not intend to try to control them in that way (or in any way), they look at me in shock and say something like, "That's not possible." But of course it is: that is what recovery is all about!

Let us look at how, by examining one particular consequence of the fact that survivors of these abuses all have dissociative disorders. My client, Tony, had an ANP who was a very strong Christian; his alters called him "religious Tony." Tony was a religious Christian, but among the alters who controlled his personality system were Satanists, who believed as they had been taught, and others who disbelieved everything. If I were to work with Tony from an explicitly Christian world view, I would be supporting the ANP but possibly violating the rights of, and the potential for any empathic bond with, the other alters. I would also be reinforcing the view that Tony's abusers imprinted in him: that life is all about the battle between God and external demonic forces. Tony was also filled with religious delusions, including having an alter named "Almighty God." How could a person like this come to develop a unified world view, and make meaning out of his horrendous history? Surely it would begin with internal communication and beginning to think for himself. The beliefs of the conflicting "selves" he carried were something only he could resolve, a challenge that required absolute impartiality on the part of his therapist. Even if a "Christian" client, such as Tony, deliberately comes to a religious organization for help, and receives this team service, what would the team do—and what should they do—about the fact that different parts of Tony have different beliefs?

Not all therapists who use the methods taught by Oglevie and other deprogrammers do so from a personal belief system. While not taking a personal position of endorsing these recommendations, some therapists maintain a perspective of "objectivity." They suggest that one should not take a stand either for or against such belief systems, but should support a client's belief where it exists. In my view, however, even this ostensibly "non-judgmental" position also has serious drawbacks.

Psychologist Ellen Lacter (2011), whose ritual abuse and mind control web page was mentioned earlier in Chapter Two, offers a perspective that might be seen as typical of this school of thought. She describes what she sees as the benefits of working within the client's own cultural world view without taking a position about the "reality" of any such belief system:

> When clients perceive the presence of spiritual evil, internally or externally, I usually work with that perception, rather than initiating dialogue about whether the perceived evil is real or not. If I were to try to convince a ritually abused client that human spirits or entities are not real, to try to reduce their fear, etc., I might stand a chance with some hosts, but no chance with self-states raised in Satanism or abusive witchcraft. Those self-states were raised in cultures rooted in theologies that [assert] such entities are more powerful and enduring than human life. And these self-states are barely orientated to the outside world. Programming is most deeply resolved when it

succeeds in changing the reality of programmed alters in the inner world. Whether such 'evil' is spiritually real or not, it is psychologically real to these self-states, and I believe it can only be dealt with as such. [pp. 128–129]

Reading this, one issue that immediately surfaces for me is the character of the belief system we are talking about here. Is it wise to "work within" the cultural world view of someone raised as a Satanist or a Luciferian, or a Nazi? Once we acknowledge that, we need to address how the belief system was installed—with abuse, tricks, and lies to our clients. In my view, we need to weaken the entire belief system so that the client can recognize they were told many lies. I told my Nazi-raised client about Barack Obama being the U.S. president. I told the internal "programmer" of a client raised by Satanists that "Satan" (that is, the man who dressed up as him in the rituals) was dead. He was shocked, as he had been told that Satan never dies. Yes, and that *he* would never die if he killed his own body. This was a good opportunity for him to discover that the abusers lied.

When Lacter describes her treatment protocol for "demonic" alters, she is on the same ground, albeit with different language, as Tom Ball and myself, but these similarities occur in spite of, rather than because of, her theoretical base. It is at the conclusion of her statement that she acknowledges what I see as the real mechanism for recovery:

I have found that to achieve 'separation' of perceived attachments, whether this mechanism is partly spiritual or only psychological, survivors must recall the rituals in which 'transfers' and 'captures' were perceived to be accomplished, and then assert their will to reject each act. I tell survivors that I believe that any act intended to spiritually control children, who are not aware that they had any choice to the contrary, can now be opposed and 'separated' spiritually and psychologically by a simple act of one's will, that we each have control of our spiritual self. I believe that an overwhelmed, frightened, and abused psyche is what permitted the perceived 'admission' of these entities and introjects. *Making the trauma conscious and the exercise of free will is what allows for their rejection and separation.* [ibid., my italics]

In my view, it is making the trauma conscious that creates the healing, along with the exercise of the client's free will. True, free will can be exercised in rejecting and separating perceived attachments, but it can be exercised just as well by the whole person asserting that she or he will no longer be part of any religion or belief system which does evil, without all the complications I have described.

Furthermore, the theoretical base of Lacter's discussion, which defines some alters as "attachments", builds in a real treatment limitation, which can best be understood through the review of how "demon parts" are created. The therapeutic review of these traumatic memories needs to include the parts played by all of the alters who were involved. This includes the "garbage kids", who were discarded because they refused to perform the desired evil behavior, as well as those parts who came forward to assume the responsibility of doing the lesser of such evils as, "You kill this rabbit or we will kill your baby brother," or, "You stick this cross into this person or we will do it to them and to you." The child is told that these alters, who split off to do this evil act, are not part of the child, but are "demons" or some other kind of attachment. And one can easily see how these tormented and victimized helpers could well be the alters that Lacter describes in her discussion of how the parts seen as demonic attachments can be identified:

Many survivors easily differentiate self-states from perceived introjects or entities. For others, the therapist can help the survivor differentiate these through dialogue. Self-states, even those with a hostile veneer, usually desire some human connection with the therapist, are motivated to feel 'better', and their hostility has a quality of underlying fear and pain. Perceived introjects and entities generally do not establish a 'felt' human connection with the therapist. Instead, they demonstrate scorn for the survivor and intense hatred for the therapist. [*ibid.*]

Similarly, some of the sources Ball cites suggest that you can tell a demonic spirit if it slithers like a snake or has rolling eyes or looks hateful. Ball, however, is wise enough to recognize that a hostile presentation does not necessarily mean a real demonic entity. After all, any alter that has been told that it will be destroyed is going to be hostile.

I have one client in whom it took years of therapy before the cult alters could accept that I was not just another abuser testing their loyalty. (Such tests are common in the training of cult alters.) An alter in another client, whom I met very recently, was very hostile, and very much acted the role of a "spiritual attachment." It demonstrated the "scorn for the survivor and intense hatred for the therapist" that, according to Lacter, define demonic entities. I wondered why. I asked the alter whether it thought I was a member of the cult and was testing it to see whether it remained loyal. *Yes, of course.* This alter simultaneously believed that I was an outsider who would destroy it, and that I was a cult member who would punish it if it showed any signs of disloyalty. What a set of feelings to juggle. I got the system leader to explain to it why she had become a "traitor," and that she had known me for several years and they really were safe. Then it relaxed.

These parts may be the ultimate challenge to the therapist's understanding of dissociative self states but, in the end, they are no different from any other part. You cannot judge that some part is external to the personality system just because of its behavior, no matter how "evil" that behavior, or its attitudes or self-identity.

In my view, the way to interpret what Lacter describes is to see those parts with an extra dose of compassion, not a willingness to collude with the client's view that they are evil. It is not hard to see that such reactions are normal for an alter who has been told (1) that it is not part of the body and should kill that useless and traitorous body, and (2) that it is an evil spiritual being and if it talks to a therapist it will be destroyed. It takes patience, persistence, and kindness to break through their defenses and help them know they are now safe and do not need to continue to do their jobs.

Restoring the human dignity of alters who have been forced to perpetrate is one of the most important and difficult parts of therapy with ritual abuse and mind control survivors. For this to happen, the alters who performed the evil acts need to see how they came into being and the double binds involved. But if these alters are rejected and ousted as demons or "attachments," they lose this chance for recovery. Certainly it is possible that in some cases, with wise Christian therapy, they can come to believe that they are simply alters to whom a demon was attached, and they can get rid of it. But if the abusers told them that they *were* that demon, and they, along with the rest of the system, believe it, recovery will not take place.

Lacter does not see this conflict. She says that this approach yields successful outcomes, and says that she has "consistently observed that when affected self-states perceive spirits and entities to be gone, the survivor experiences tremendous relief." In fact, she says, "To date, no survivor I have worked with ever felt that they had separated a part of the self in the process" (*ibid*.).

Perhaps this has not happened to her. But it has to me. At my client Teresa's request, I experimented a few times with removing such parts from her, following a protocol such as that of Hawkins. She also had exorcisms in churches. The alters *always* came back. In LisaBri's story you saw the chaos in her system caused by her cult-aligned alters (including several "Satans"). After these parts were banished, they became even more destructive and dangerous, continuing to do their jobs but now in hiding. Suicide attempts, self-harm, and flashbacks continued, but the ANP was not aware of the causes. Those who approach such alters as demonic may be similarly unaware of the negative consequences of their recommended interventions.

What if you are a therapist who happens to be a Christian, reading this? Must you accept the approach recommended by the most vocal Christians working in this field? I do not believe so. Many Christians do not believe in "possession" as a literal fact, or in "legal agreements" between coerced children and external spiritual entities. Even among those that do, you will find Christian therapists who, like any others, can learn to detect "sheep in wolves' clothing," child alters who have been told they are evil spiritual beings, and have been forced to perpetrate through being placed in double binds. Jesus' teaching is that "by their fruits you shall know them"—in other words, an evil or a good being is distinguished not by its appearance or its supposed loyalty, but by its actions when it has an actual choice.

In twenty years of working with ritual abuse survivors, I have seen several integrate fully, and several others achieve healthy co-consciousness. I have never met a single real demon or attachment. It is true, as both Tom Ball and Ellen Lacter also point out, that putting together the memory of the events that created the belief in possession is crucial. But I disagree with the assertion that we need to believe that the possession itself is real, or to go along with the client's belief in the interest of cultural appropriateness.

As we work with abuse that is so clearly evil, it might be difficult for some to accept the fact that we will never all be able to share a position about whether evil spiritual beings exist. But what we can all agree about is that evil is about what we do, and its essence is doing harm to other people and living things. Raping little children and teaching them to kill are evil. It only muddies the waters to add notions of external forces to the treatment conversation. Evil done in the name of Jesus, or Mohammed, or Buddha, or Hitler, or Stalin, or Satan, or the "free world," or democracy, is still evil.

When we apply our theories to the question of evil, we should remain mindful of Occam's Razor, a well-known scientific concept: "One should not increase, beyond what is necessary, the number of entities required to explain anything." Dissociation offers a powerful explanation for the existence of relatively autonomous and destructive entities within someone's mind. An alter, a part of a person, separated from that person's capacity for empathy, is more able to do evil than an integrated human being.

Even the ritual abusers, who might for centuries have believed they were attaching real demons to children, now recognize they are creating dissociative disorders, as Katz states in Chapter Seven. They still *tell* the children they are attaching demonic spirits, or their own spirits, or the spirits of dead relatives, but they now know they are actually splitting children and naming and training the alters. Should we continue to subscribe to the belief system the abusers have implanted, even when they themselves know that it is dissociation that gives them power over their victims? Our responsibility is to help those desiring to recover from such evil to be able to do so. The answer lies in psychotherapy techniques and practices that are appropriate for mind-controlled persons with dissociative disorders. It is our job to assist our clients in moving toward a state of wholeness, whether or not it comes in the form of literal "integration." In my view, to approach evil as a set of disembodied evil entities that are attached to our clients interferes with our ability to achieve that goal.

> The belief in a supernatural source of evil is not necessary: men alone are quite capable of every wickedness (Joseph Conrad).

> Ethics . . . are nothing but reverence for life. This is what gives me the fundamental principle of morality, namely, that good consists in maintaining, promoting, and enhancing life, and that destroying, injuring, and limiting life are evil (Albert Schweitzer).

Note

1. Note the use of "G-d", which is commonly used in online survivor discussions because the word "God" is frequently triggering to survivors.

CHAPTER TEN

Dealing with programming: alternative strategies

Some programs are triggered deliberately; some, accidentally. Some programs reveal themselves early, as they are part of the abusers' plan to sabotage therapy. This can alert you to the fact that your client has mind control. Once that fact has been established, the therapist knows s/he must consider that a particular issue may be due to the activity of trained alter personalities. Instead of wasting time suggesting that the client take soothing baths to promote sleep, you can search for the alters who are responsible for the insomnia. If the client were cutting her arms, you can find the alters involved, ask how they were trained to cut and why they do it, and eventually work through these training memories. You can use whatever has been triggered to search for the trainings involved. Then, you can take care of them in some way, and eliminate or arrest the problem behavior.

Learning from what is triggered

A client of mine was triggered by an incident in which her cat caught a fly, which made a loud buzzing sound. All her alters went deep inside and hid for a week, until I saw her. Two different things were going on. In one, child parts who had been put in a pit with rotting meat and dead things and flies now began to think they were back in the pit. I had to give them a little biology lecture about flies, and make sure they knew they were safe in my client's apartment. The buzzing of the fly also brought out an alter who had been trained with electroshock administered (with a buzzing sound) by a helmet. The alter made a buzzing sound himself, which frightened all the other alters who had worn the helmet. I had to bring him out and show him that there was no helmet on his head, and he was in a safe place; he could let the others know that. I then had the alter in charge of the memory storage put the memories of the pit and of the helmet safely away, so those affected would no longer have flashbacks.

You will make your decision as to how to address a triggered program based on your treatment agenda. In treating mind control, it is wise to be systematic in your approach to therapy. Generally speaking, memory work comes only after a good deal of groundwork has been laid. (This will be discussed further in Chapter Sixteen, "Working with the traumatic memories".) In this example, it was not time to do memory work. Since we did not need to work through all the memories of the "pit" or the helmet when we found what was triggered by the fly's buzzing, we just had to put them away. Sometimes it is preferable to just turn off and put away what is triggered, and continue to work with whatever you have made your priority. However, when the triggering has produced a dangerous behavior, such as severe self-harm, it is smart to make it a priority to work through the memories of the original training, once the client is ready for memory work.

It is possible for a therapist or client to use perpetrator-group-created programs for helpful purposes. For example, an alter trained not to feel pain can reduce the pain resulting from a re-abusive group contact. An alter trained to put other alters to sleep can put to sleep alters who are programmed to go to group meetings or to harm the body. An alter trained to make the others forget events can make the alters who are supposed to report to the group what they have disclosed forget having talked about the memories.

Asking, negotiating, and commanding

Many interventions that are not useful or even wise in therapy with non-mind-controlled clients are helpful and even necessary with survivors of mind control.

Therapists may affect programs through asking, negotiating, or commanding. Naturally, I prefer to ask or negotiate before attempting to command.

But with some personality systems, asking and negotiating does not work, and verbal commands are necessary. This is because you are speaking with very young alters who are trained to respond only to commands, often phrased in a particular way. They are concrete and literalistic. They are not offended by commands.

The three little words, "Turn it off," can have profound effects. One client would leave me telephone messages, and when I replied would not pick up the phone. However, I would leave a message giving the order "Turn it off," and without the client understanding why, the problem would be alleviated.

With another client, I had to add "in the name of Satan" in order to get the young alters to comply. Since I had difficulty with that phrasing, I added "whom I don't believe in," which apparently did not give them any difficulty. So I would say "Turn off the Pain, in the name of Satan, whom I don't believe in." You can say firmly "I command you in the name of Satan, whom I don't believe in, to stop, turn off, and put away the Suicide Program" (for example). If you and/or the client are Christians, you may add "And I ask you in the name of Jesus, whom I do believe in, to stop, turn off, and put away the program."

With some clients, a general command will work, as internal programmer alters (that is, those that are trained to activate the memories which will produce symptoms) are always listening. With other clients, it will only work if you know the cult-assigned name of the internal programmer alters, and command them by name. (They do not have to be cooperating with you, and do not have to be "out" in the body, for this to work.) Internal programmers are controlled by strong obedience programs; that is why they often do not want their names known, because they do not want to be commanded by name.

One danger in doing this is that some insider alters will believe you are a member of the perpetrator group. So, if you use commands, be sure to explain to the whole system that you have learnt this from other therapists, and that you are not one of the abusers. This applies even more strongly to the use of triggers deliberately installed by the perpetrator group.

When you search for alters who are creating these problems, keep in mind that their training probably included threats of punishment to them if they did not comply with the abusers' instructions. Usually there are other alters who are supposed to punish them if they do not comply, and backups who will do their jobs if they become disloyal. You can search for the punishers and the backups and dialogue with them until they agree to turn it off. You will need to update any alters you speak with, explaining how the perpetrators can no longer hurt them (because of time and/or distance), or if the group is local and still harassing the person, the group can only hurt them if it gains access to the body.

Generally, however, as long as the trained behavior has been performed, it may be all right to turn it off, though it may be turned on again in response to a cue or to other alters' disobedience to their instructions.

With programs such as flooding of emotions, the alters involved might not feel safe in turning the program off. But you might be able to negotiate that they turn it down so that it is barely noticeable. Or you could ask the spinner alters to spin in the opposite direction, so that they spin the effects back into the original alter rather than out to the rest of the system. Or you could find a way for them to implement the program without doing harm. One client of mine used to come into therapy sessions with instructions to harm me. She would take a thumbtack from my notice board and prick me lightly with it once. Then she would say "Okay, I've done my job," and we would have no further problems. Similarly, you can have the child alters draw on their arm in red ink rather than cutting it to draw blood.

Use of perpetrator-created triggers

Most programs, if they have "on" triggers (cues which trigger trained alters to do their jobs), also have "off" triggers. Sometimes you can convince alters to show you the "off" triggers and, with their permission, can use them. Note that you do not have to know alters' names for touch triggers to be effective.

Psychologist and ritual abuse expert Randy Noblitt uses such triggers, with the client's permission, to assess whether or not they have been subjected to ritual abuse or mind control, and also to help insure the safety of survivors. He has written a monograph on those triggers which he believes will access alter personalities safely. He obtains a general informed consent where he asks the client's permission to "explore his/her mind" (Noblitt, 1998). He makes a video recording of the session that becomes the property of the client so that the individual knows what has transpired and can be assured that no further victimization has occurred. He uses benign triggers for this purpose, ones that will elicit child alters or protective, knowledgeable alters. After what he calls "dissociation of identity" occurs (and it always does to some extent) Dr Noblitt explains what occurred in terms of the individual's response to triggers. The individual has the video to study, to see how he/she was triggered and develop self-defensive responses to triggers. Dr Noblitt is always happy to explain how he obtained his knowledge. He is the first to admit that his information is not all-inclusive. The reader might have concerns about his use of this technique, but Dr Noblitt's willingness to learn, courage to employ it for the individual's benefit, and encouragement for the individual to become empowered and self-advocate make it clear that he is not a "bad guy." He has never had any response other than relief that someone has been able to unlock the door and let the secrets emerge.

I do not want to list all the triggers that I know in this book, because they could be misused. However, I can mention three that might be useful.

1.   Grasping your client's arms firmly and briefly halfway between the shoulders and the elbows will turn off a spinning program temporarily.
2.   Holding your hands out in front of you, palms upward, then drawing them quickly towards your chest and closing them will temporarily turn off all programs.
3.   Running the fingers of your left hand down the left side of the face from the cheekbone will cause the person to forget whatever memories or flashbacks s/he has just experienced. I noticed two different clients doing this to themselves spontaneously at the end of sessions where we had dealt with traumatic memories. This enabled them to go out into the world after these sessions without being still in a state of shock from the traumatic memory.

I do not know how widespread these particular triggers are, but I have found them effective with many clients.

If you use triggers (e.g., special touches or hand signals), make sure that your client has confirmed what effect they will have on him or her and agreed to allow you to use them. Also, explain how you learned these triggers. Otherwise your client may believe that you must be one of the perpetrator group to know such things. One client finds it effective when I do these triggers on my own body. Without having to touch her, I am able to use some of them when I believe they will keep her safer. For example, I used a signal (tracing a line down the forehead) to keep her "left side" (cult-abused) alters separate from her "right side" (everyday life) alters, when the left side alters were increasing the suicidality of the right side alters.

Some triggers are common to many survivors, but some are unique. One thing that all touch triggers have in common, according to Stella Katz, is that they are installed at acupressure points. (For this reason, acupressure techniques can cause unexpected effects in this population.) The same trigger may activate or turn off different behaviors in different survivors, so be careful in using triggers. Turning off a behavior through a trigger does not mean it will not recur. Permanently deactivating the training can only be done by working through the training memory with all involved alters.

It must be remembered, however, that use of perpetrator-installed triggers by the therapist, or the use of force by certain alters of the client on other alters will be experienced by the client as coercive if the alters being triggered do not consent. Cooperation is always to be preferred to coercion, and can often be achieved. For example, an alter who is trained to harm or kill the body may agree to be put to sleep or internally isolated until the next therapy session, when the self-harm program might be undone. It is preferable to convince the internal alters to do these things rather than having the therapist do it via triggers. If and when it is necessary for the therapist to use touch triggers to turn off dangerous behaviors, an alter should first be out who does not mind being touched, and who understands that the therapist is not a group member just because s/he knows about triggers.

Program codes

Another way that alters can be helped to change their jobs is through their program codes, which are the sequences of letters and numbers which, when spoken by the correct person or in the correct manner, will turn programs on or off, or even destroy them. These are spoken signals which are taught to alters, and which alters are expected to obey. They might best be understood as similar to the touch triggers discussed in Katz's chapter. The concept is simple, but the sequence can be quite complex.

For instance, one of my mind-controlled clients had assassin programming, the codes for which were songs on a particular record album. Each song brought out a particular alter, in sequence, the second last being the assassin, and the last being one who was supposed to stand around to await getting caught, appearing crazy. The "off" code for the program was all the lengths of the songs on the album. The "off" code for a program to make him smoke was the chemical formula for nicotine.

Knowing codes and saying the "off" codes can help in undoing programming. Since it did not remove the trauma that had created the programs in the first place, it simply meant that the alters involved no longer had to do their jobs. Neutralizing the programs can be helpful, as they will then not get in the way of the therapy. The time period during which a program is turned off can allow the survivor to work through the memories of the abuses that these programs represent. Be aware that programs which have been turned off through codes sometimes get turned on again, perhaps after a time lapse or because an internal programmer alter has discovered they are turned off and turns them on again.

I do not know whether some program codes are universal, or at least universal for survivors of the same organized perpetrator group.

I do believe that it is wisest to obtain such codes, if you use them, from your client rather than from elsewhere. One client wrote down the codes for a particular set of programs, and I spoke them to her. If you use codes which the client has not given you, they might have unexpected effects, and they might alienate alters in charge of the personality system. If you have worked with your client for a long time, you might inquire whether there are any codes that could hasten the therapy process. But the psychotherapy remains to be done, even if codes have been used.

Using program codes to disarm programs can be a useful shortcut, but it does not resolve the trauma, which still must be worked through for complete recovery to occur. However, survivors of ritual abuse and mind control have suffered such extensive and traumatic abuse over such a long period of time that therapy can go on for their entire lives. Anything that can make such persons functional in a shorter period of time can be very helpful. It is up to the survivor to decide whether or not s/he wants to work through all the traumatic memories in order to have full healing, or whether s/he prefers to become relatively functional (if that is possible) without doing all this work.

Use of internal programmers for program charts

You might have heard of survivors having "internal programmer" alters. Do not be intimidated. These are alters who have been trained to turn programs on and off, in response to environmental cues. When someone speaks a program code or does a touch or sight trigger, it alerts an internal programmer to turn a program on or off, usually through flipping a switch. The programmers usually do not know what effect their switches have, but are heavily trained in obedience and in memorizing signals. In most such systems, the switches are located on control boards, such as would be found in an electrical circuit-breaker box. Every switch is labeled, usually with some kind of shorthand representing what the training was, when and where it was done, and how many times it was repeated at what ages. The labeling is similar to Jeannie Riseman's description of her inner structures in Chapter Six.

Most deliberately structured personality systems have some kind of control system for the programs. When a client has reached the point where his or her personality system is working together effectively, the therapist may ask the internal programmers to put together a chart of all the programs existing within that system, based on the labels on the switches. Once that is done, it is possible to work through the programming memories systematically to permanently disable the programs and rescue the alters from their traumas.

As an example, here is how one client's internal programmer described his instructions:

1.   To turn on a program, hit the black button, speak the program, and then press in the two-numbered code.
2.   To close the program, hit the red button, speak the program, then press in the reversed two-numbered code.
3.   The first number or numbers followed by a comma is the Programmer level that can activate that code. (There was a programmer alter on every level of the system: levels 1 to 9 reflected ages five to thirteen, and level 0 meant every level.)
4.   The numbers after the comma are the numbers in the alphabet of the first letter of words except the last, and the last letter of the last word of the program title.

So, for example, the code for the program "Watching You" was 0 – 23 – 21. The number "0" meant that programmers at all levels held this program. The numbers 23 and 21 after that were for the W in Watching and the U in You. I would not have to speak the level numbers, but if I were going to dismantle the program by going through the memories with the client, I would have to make sure to deal with all nine instances in which the training was given.

Each program also had a spoken code, which would turn the program on or off if spoken. For example, one program to make the client go home was triggered by the words "butter tarts," which were innocuously inserted into a letter from the client's aunt. To turn this program off I would have to say "Butter tarts 19 – 2." The program to make the client go with someone was triggered by the word "cigarette."

There were around 200 programs listed. Their content was similar to what we discussed in Chapter Eight. Some interesting titles were "therapist no clothes", "drive fast," "act insane," "show mother's face," "jam thoughts," "miss family," "shoot outsider," and "little ones explore sex."

With a list and chart like the one this programmer gave me, it is possible both to turn off programs that have been triggered, and to identify the programs for working through the memories. It should be noted that another inside alter (hidden as a sub-alter of an alter with a different job) controlled a different set of programs.

Creating program "wiring diagrams"

The abusers of my first four survivors, who were involved with the same Satanic coven, began to instruct their alters about what to do if I attempted to work through programming memories in order to destroy the programs. Each program that I attempted to undo (through working through the memory) was attached to another program, which was turned on as soon as I interfered with the first program. Some personality systems have this connection between programs built in. For example, if we attempted to undo a suicide program, it might trigger a program to harm the therapist, and if we attempted to undo the program to harm the therapist, it might trigger a program to not understand English, and if we attempted to undo that program, it might trigger a program to fall asleep in the session. Sometimes the wiring was circular: for example, in the above scenario, working through the "Sleep" program might trigger a suicide program.

To battle this, Jennifer learned to bring "wiring diagrams" to sessions, describing what program would be set off if we interfered a particular program. Jennifer and I would examine the wiring diagram together and select the weakest link; this would usually be a program we had already worked through, or one that was minimally harmful. We would start there, and work our way through the sequence backwards.

The key to dismantling or neutralizing programming is in the work with the personality system. We will look at this in the next chapter. In the following sections, we will address the first step of the process: unlocking your client's mind-controlled system.

Is "deprogramming" effective?

The term "deprogramming" is used in various ways. "Deprogrammers" such as Steve Oglevie who work specifically with ritual abused or mind control survivors appear to know a great deal about the specific illusions implanted in the minds of survivors programmed by different groups, and the program codes which have been implanted by these groups. Deprogrammers such as Oglevie attempt to discover the type of structured personality system, speak the codes, and rescue the alters from the perceived abuses or internal situations in which they are trapped. (Oglevie, for one, also believes in removing spiritual "attachments" from such survivors. This will be addressed at the end of this chapter.) The deprogramming is conducted over a period of several days.

Therapists who have taken their clients to such deprogrammers report mixed results. It appears that the client's stage of recovery, along with his or her trust in her therapist, has an effect on whether or not such deprogramming is effective. Randy Noblitt has done some of this work, and he sees this strategy as the equivalent of using temporary shutdown codes. He posted his concern to the Ritual Abuse and Mind Control Discussion List (reprinted by permission). He does not "deprogram", he says, because ". . . people are not computers even though they may be abused and under traumatic circumstances they may come to believe that they have computers installed inside them. . . . I do not believe any of us can 'deprogram'—the brain is not a programmable/nonprogrammable computer."

Noblitt is also critical of the process because in his experience it leads to complications: ". . . it only [gives] a temporary but false sense of recovery to clients (comparable to premature integration)." After applying a method he had learnt to "deprogram" robot alters, he found that

> . . . the method worked but it kept me and the client in an interminable loop of deprogramming rather than attending to the necessary therapy. For example . . . It took about 20 minutes for each robot and I could "remove" the robot alters one at a time. However, my client had 1,000 robot alters. Had we continued with that goal in mind we would have been sidetracked and missed the important therapy that she needed.

In fact, Noblitt found that for his client, deprogramming was not even a shortcut. He developed a way to integrate these "robots" in "less than 15 minutes", without codes or passwords. In the end, he cautions, "Many of the tunnels, mazes, computers, files, etc. [found in these clients] can keep a therapist and client distracted from the work of therapy for a long time."

Effective shortcuts

As Randy Noblitt reminds us in his previously cited post, "In order to become psychologically healthy[,] the survivor needs to access the parts, hear their stories, integrate affect, memory, sensation, behavior, etc."

So, are any shortcuts really effective? Some are. One of my mind control survivor clients developed his own shortcut. It was "Whatever they told you to do, do the opposite." He spent several years actively psychotic while many bizarre programs were set off. Once he got his inner kids to "do the opposite," his system settled down, he began to access the significant abuse memories, and he is now much more functional.

The key to either using a pre-existing shortcut (e.g., finding out program codes) or developing a new shortcut, like this man did, is for the whole personality system to work together in the service of healing. The alters in charge need to decide to do this. If they do, many things are possible. This survivor is not fully healed, but he has become functional, which is a huge step forward for him.

This may well be the key to all effective shortcuts. As therapist Arauna Morgan wrote to the Ritual Abuse and Mind Control Discussion List (reprinted by permission),

> Of the survivors I know, one common thread seems to be that they finally decided that they have had enough. Some of the most impressive deprogramming I have seen was various ways of stating just that, "I have had enough and I no longer accept . . . (fill in the blank)."

Survivors' self-help strategies and other wisdom

Jeannie Riseman, MSW, has been a leading light in the ritual abuse and mind control survivor community for many years. We saw her perspective on mind control in Chapter Two, and a description of her own programming in Chapter Six. In the following contribution she offers her own expertise, as well as that of another survivor, C. "Cheryl" A. Beck, supported by the power of their creativity, experience, and humor, about how to deal with programming. Your mind-controlled clients are not passive patients who merely receive treatment. They can be, and are, quite active participants in identifying and changing their own programming. You will see examples of this throughout this book, and especially here. Not only does Riseman personalize this issue, but, in my view, the strategies and understanding of her selves that she developed can provide invaluable information and ideas, as well as reassurance, for therapists.

Programming. taking the wind out of its sails:[1] Jeannie Riseman

Finding out about the programming

In a group I attended years ago, we were asked to pretend that we had been molested and write about the experience in detail. Some amazing things came out, because the "it's just pretend" framework helped to bypass the inner censor. I remembered doing this, and said to myself, "I'm going to pretend I'm multiple and draw my system." Simple technique, but the system was so complex it took three months to get all the information.

Dealing with programmed thoughts and urges

Here's a very simple technique that I often use when I do not have the faintest idea what is going on. It is the same method I used for dealing with my ordinary internal prejudice, a technique anyone can use for dealing with conditioned thoughts and responses.

When I have a thought or urge that seems cult-related

1.   I name and label it as soon as I become aware of it.
2.   I refuse to act on it.
3.   I let the issue go—I do not brood on it.

To name a thing is to take away some of its power. A name is like an anchor in my mind. Labeling a thought "programming" clearly brackets the thought that I find undesirable and separates it from the "me" that I value. It is now something that was taught me without my permission, not my own thinking.

Steps two (not acting on it) and three (letting it go) are weakening the programming by not reinforcing it. Refusing to act on it—refusing to cut, for example—is avoiding reinforcement and avoiding buying into the perps' value system. And refusing to brood on it, to beat myself up over it, is equally an avoidance of reinforcement. If I spend three days agonizing over having had a suicidal thought, that is three days of driving that thought deeper into the grooves of my mind.

Note that this is not the same as denial. I am not shoving anything under the rug. I acknowledge it, deal with it, and move on. If I slip, I make amends to myself and move on. But I do not solidify the programming by thinking about it all day and all night.

Here is how I used the technique to deal with a cult-implanted "don't talk" program.

At one point I told my therapist something I was never supposed to remember, let alone talk about. The internal backlash was something fierce. I was haunted by strong urges to suicide, mostly in particularly revolting ways. So I tried thinking "programming" every time I spotted a self-destructive thought.

What happened? For starters, it seemed like every third word I thought was the word "programming." I had no idea that the "kill yourself if you tell" program was that compelling. "Wow! They really did a number on me, didn't they? I wonder how they did it?" My mental attitude changed from fighting suicidal impulses, trying not to think those thoughts, to curiosity about the past. Which was great, because trying not to think something is a losing battle, and consumes a vast amount of energy, besides.

Step two. I gave my kitchen knives to my best friend to hold and re-committed myself to not acting on suicidal urges. Just let them be. If I act on them, I will never get a chance to understand where they came from and what they mean. I am sure I would have experienced some relief if I had cut, but I chose to stay with the thoughts and feelings and see what happened.

Step three. After I labeled the suicidal thought as programming, I turned my attention back to everyday activities. No point in hanging on to it, for surely it was going to come back by itself. Meanwhile, might as well get something accomplished.

I walked around my home describing all the things that were mine. "This is my refrigerator, and I can buy and eat anything I want now. I don't have to eat what I am told to, like in the old days. I can eat spaghetti or ice cream for three days straight if I feel like it, or I can stir-fry spinach with olive oil and a whole head of garlic. I can do whatever I damn well please. Isn't that great?"

And so I "out-Zenned" the program, rather than fighting it, and it ran its course and faded. I emerged from the situation feeling more empowered. There was more of "me" and less of the programming. The next time a suicidal program kicked in, it was less intense and lasted a shorter time.

I then proceeded to fine-tune this simple technique. I tried talking to the program as if it were an alter. I praised its strength, intelligence, and sophistication. I could almost feel the programming smile. (Of course, I was not really talking to the program, I was talking to the alter or to that part of my mind that had learned the program.)

I also spent some time telling that part that nothing bad would happen if we broke the rules now. I explained that there was nobody around to enforce the old rules, and so they did not really apply any more. They had stopped being rules. We were free!

Educate. Accept. Do not arm-wrestle with programming. Work with, rather than against, my parts and my programming. Cool.

Dealing with the programmed parts rather than the programs

I would like to share this contribution from one of my heroines, C. "Cheryl" A. Beck. She wrote about dissolving a complex mirrors/everything backwards/matrix program by talking past it to the underlying parts that had been programmed. I am paraphrasing from her e-mails with her permission.

> I had a diamond matrix. The front side opened like butterfly wings. This was the open access side, which I could enter easily. It was composed of RA stuff like complicated belief systems such as the Kabbalah. I could've spent a lifetime confused and lost trying to figure it all out.

> The ever-present threat looming in the background was Draco the Dragon that patrolled the "Dark Side of the Moon." This was the backside of the diamond where the real MC programming was stored. The rest was just a cover. This part of the matrix fell under "Draconian Law"—death to me and my family if Draco reported disobedience by me to my MC handler. Draco was the ultimate internal perp. There were also others like the Iceman, who froze me if I got too close to an MC memory.

> The facets of the diamond were mirrors which multiplied one image and made them into dozens. This was all meant to confuse and overwhelm. In fact the mirrors were alter fragments doing a job to keep me safe, to keep me away from the MC memories. What worked for me was simply to congratulate them on a job well done and to find something else for them to do. My fragments usually just threw away their jobs and blended with a protector alter.

> The need for backwards communication and pairing of opposites was also a way to keep me safe by confusing me and leading me away from the MC memories so I didn't have to be accessed and re-trained by torture. I communicated internally that I was a competent adult free from the cult/MC world now, and I had no need for that type of "safe communication" anymore. I promoted those fragments from that type of confusing communication to straightforward reconnaissance. Whatever the fragments understand and desire to become works.

> After a while I "got it," from head knowledge into my very "knower." It was my mind that created all this. They didn't insert a matrix into my brain. All material constructs and figures and images were actually little kids—alters or alter fragments imitating perps, dragons, colors—all in the interest of keeping us safe from further harm or torture. When I got it on a gut level, the construct came to an end quickly. It literally blew up and freed all the alters, instead of killing them in the explosion, which was the lie they had believed.

> Lying fuckwads.

It was very reassuring to learn that the same technique worked for Cheryl and for me. Maybe my instincts were right after all! I just knew in my bones that it was not necessary to get all fancy and complicated to deal with programming, no matter how complex it might be. It just felt right to use simple, proven, everyday, common sense techniques. It also felt instinctively right to use love and respect and friendship to counter the mind-fucking that had been done to me.

Look at it this way: I spent many long years of hard work learning Latin, which is a highly complex language. I learnt it very well, too. Got straight As. But I do not have to think or speak Latin today. Just because I learnt it does not mean I have to use it. I prefer to speak English. Of course, the difference is that no part of me ever believed I had to use Latin for the rest of my life, while many parts of me believed that I could never escape the cult system and way of thinking and behaving.

My complex programming initially frightened me. I thought it was so exotic, so other-worldly, that I did not have a fighting chance against it. It did not help that the system contained no recognizable alters. Everything was geometric patterns and mathematical codes, and I had no idea how to talk to non-Euclidean geometric figures. What could I say? "Nice figure! You are really flexible!" I was totally snowed. How could I unravel it if I did not have the codes? The codes would let me remember, but I had to remember to get the codes. Impasse.

I soon realized that I was thinking using the premises of the programming. It had been designed to block me, and as long as I thought in *its* terms, I was, indeed, blocked. I had to think outside the box.

I have come to believe that it does not work well to use the perpetrators' framework. By doing so, you are buying into their belief system and reinforcing it. Just like I cannot see how to teach children not to hit by hitting them. Or teaching people not to kill by killing them. All it teaches is that the strong get to do what they want to the weak. Besides, if I use the perp's weapons, I feel like a perp myself. I do not like it. I usually feel miserable enough as it is without purposefully adding to those bad feelings.

It dawned on me that a sentient part of me must have been present when my mind learnt all that mysterious math junk. I decided to work with the part or parts of myself that had learnt all this stuff. Back then, I had been an everyday child, with likes, dislikes, fears, dreams, head colds, and much-hated brown socks. I might not have the vaguest idea what to say to the programming, but I sure as hell know how to talk to an eight-year-old.

I started to talk past the system to the child I had been, and still am in some frozen part of my mind. "There's nobody around who will hurt you. They hurt you back then, but now is real different. They aren't here anymore." And for the very little parts, "Bad guys all gone bye-bye!"

With my biological children, especially when they were young, I would over-simplify whatever I was talking about. As they caught on, I made things more complex, matching my explanation to their developmental stage. I figured that it was worth a try working with myself and assumed that there were parts of my mind that were still operating on a child-like level. Even if it did not work, I was convinced that the very fact that I was using commonsense things that any teacher or mother knows instinctively would help me cut the mind-control programming down to size in my own mind. I was no longer paralyzed when thinking about it. I had a plan and some hope.

Looking back, I see that instinctively I did three simple but effective things.

1.   I set the stage for respectful internal communication.
2.   I educated myself internally about the present and about the past and its effects.
3.   I offered opportunities, but did not try and change anything internally

Step One: Setting the stage

I start by giving permission to my parts to learn, without being coercive. "Anybody who wants to listen can. Nobody has to. Anybody who isn't listening can ask others inside about what I said. And I will explain again, too, in case you want to listen later on." I've snuck in the idea of freedom of choice.

"Anybody who objects to or doesn't like what I am saying can let me know if they want to. Anybody who wants to give me information may, as long as it's okay inside."

I try to keep it casual. I do not want to sound frantic and scare my parts or make them feel as if I have a heavy agenda.

(As an aside, I had a friend who spoke to his alters like this, "Listen up, ass-holes!" He did not get a lot of internal cooperation by being rude. Exorcism does not encourage internal cooperation, either, in my opinion. It just scares alters and sends them into hiding.) [*Author's note: This parenthetical observation mirrors the conversation in Chapter Nine, on attachments.*]

Step Two: Then I educate and explain in simple language

I explain that we were raised by people who liked kids to obey and liked to hurt kids. But those people are not around any more. We do not have to follow their rules. We do not have to agree with them any more. We can make up our own rules. We can change our rules any time we want.

I steer away from words that have a weird connotation to me. "Safe" for example, means to many of my parts that I am locked up, and that therefore I cannot hurt anybody or anything. I am "safe" because I am imprisoned. This is not a message that I am trying to convey inside, so I avoid the word and find words that were not used back then. "Okay" is a fine substitute, as my perps were too proper and snotty to use that word. If I find that I am getting anxious or panicky, I take a look at the words I have just used and apologize inside and ask if I need to add to my list of double-meaning words.

I describe my present life. "This is my bed. These are my sheets and pillowcases. I bought them myself because they are pretty. I sleep alone in my bed. Nobody comes to my bed to bother me. Never! Those days are all in the past. I can sleep with stuffed animals if I want. This is my purple frog. I can go to sleep whenever I want and I can sleep as long as I want. I can get up in the middle of the night to pee if I want. I don't have to ask anybody's permission."

I explain all the psychological things I have learned about PTSD and dissociation. I explain *amnesia*, *alters*, and *flashbacks*. Again, I keep it simple. The young parts can understand.

"This is a flashback. It feels yucky. It's something we are remembering. Once long ago we forgot it, and now we are remembering. It isn't happening now. It just feels like it is because the memory is so strong. But that's okay. It's like the mind is burping up a memory. Burp! Feels better after you burp."

I do this at random times during the day when I am relatively calm, as well as in an emergency. Years ago, when all this was new to me and I was flooded, I held a stuffed rabbit and patted it, saying, "Of course you're afraid. You'd have to have rocks in your head not to be afraid. It's okay to be afraid now." Day after day I repeated the same message. In time, with repetition, it got through. My feelings had been normal, there was nothing wrong with me, and I was in a different situation now, one where I could feel my feelings.

Step Three. Without trying to change anything inside, I offer opportunities

"Would anybody like to learn how to make an omelet? There is a pretty nifty omelet maker around here, and maybe that omelet maker would enjoy teaching you all. Nobody has to learn, but you are welcome to watch and learn if you want." "Anybody there who never got to choose what kind of ice cream to eat? Yeah? How would you like to choose what kind we're going to buy today?" I think what I am doing is expanding the number of jobs and skills each fragment has, without challenging their fundamental sense of self.

I also explain things to my drivers. "We'd like to drive carefully and calmly. We will watch all the traffic signs, the cars, the bicycles, the pedestrians. Under these conditions, anybody can drive who wants to." (I do not use negatives, like "we won't hit anybody," because the unconscious tends to ignore the negative and hear "hit a pedestrian.") And I thank them afterwards and say it was a great job.

This worked with my biological children, by the way. If they knew how they were expected to behave, they did, as long as there were not any disconcerting surprises. It was usually ignorance and confusion that made them behave inappropriately.

I have been talking about building relationships inside. The same principles, however, apply to interactions between alters and a therapist, partner, or friend. Giving information about the present is very useful, as long as it is offered gently. It is never a good idea to be pushy. The idea is to avoid arguments, to offer information in a non-threatening manner, and to convey an attitude of respect and interest.

Frightening alters are usually acting that way in order to save the system as a whole from real or perceived harm. It's not personal! Compliments often help make a connection. "Gee! You are really fierce! I bet you would be wonderful at protecting others from harm. Has anybody ever told you that? One of your friends, maybe?" Aggressive alters are generally feared inside, and this may be the first time somebody has had a calm conversation with them. They might tell you sadly that they have no friends.

Information can be tailored to match the alter's age, previous experience, and interests. Simple things, like offering choices in the present (chocolate or vanilla ice cream?) can introduce new and earth-shattering concepts, like freedom of choice, learning new things instead of being frozen in one rigid mold, and respect and reciprocity.

It is not always easy going, of course. When things get rocky, alters appreciate an honest apology and an admission that they have not been understood. There will be many misunderstandings, but as long as they are treated with and respect and caring, relationships can be created.

To summarize how I work with my parts: I talk to myself, respectfully, reassuringly. I educate. I open doors to new experiences and viewpoints. And I try never, ever, to be coercive, or know-it-all, or bossy. I want to be as different as possible from my perps. I try to accept and work with, rather than against, my parts and my programming. I do this even though I do not have conventional people-like alters inside. It does not seem to have done any harm, at least so far.

Within this simple framework you can add almost anything you can imagine. Some people make an internal "healing pool" for newly awakened alters to wash away the hurt and pain. Some make a special place where there are kind and competent alters to take care of the wounded ones. Some find relief in making small internal changes, like laying an hourglass on its side or giving a frightening fire-breathing dragon the job of lighting a fire for coffee every morning. The number of ways you can adjust things to suit your system is limited only by your—and your therapist's and friends'—imagination.

Start simple, see what works and what does not, and then tweak my technique. Accept. Educate. Work with, rather than against, my parts and my programming.

*   *   *

Working with the inner world

People's inner worlds are not all the same. Some, like that which Trish Fotheringham described, have magic castles and woodlands; others have prisons and fortresses and control rooms and various military installations. Some have places they describe as different worlds and other planets. People with spontaneous, self-created DID often have internal "houses" in which alters live, often copies of the houses they lived in when the abuse occurred. Or they may simply have no inner world, and the alters disappear into blackness when they go inside. In ritual abuse and mind control survivors, however, the alters are arranged in a hierarchy, and often reflect whether their abuser group is military, Satanic, Kabbalah, etc. It may be possible to identify the type of abuser group by the type of inner world they create.

Here is one survivor's highly detailed description of an inner world which is very different from those we have looked at so far, how she worked with it, and how she managed to dismantle it.

Dismantling my inner structures: Robin Morgan

The purpose of my programming was to create alters who were trapped or imprisoned in an internal structure that could be seen by the system internally, if they knew where to look. Alters were only released long enough to perform a prearranged function, then they returned to the structure. In my inner world, every part of the structure, even the booby traps, was an alter, programmed to be something else.

Deep inside, there were walls containing the only alters that had not been programmed. If I talked to them, the wall would dampen not only what they said, but also the emotions they projected. I learnt to thin the wall in order to communicate with them. The cult had discovered these alters, sometimes years after their programming was done, and just neutralized them by enclosing them in walls. There was gold in those walls! Those were the alters that would later help rescue programmed alters and dismantle the program structures.

In my system there were entities that would attack if not appeased in a prescribed way. After all of the entities were pleased and calm, no traps would be tripped. At one time, I thought the entities were not part of my system, so I tried to send them away. I found that they kept coming back; they no longer attacked, but were still there. I learnt that when something does not go away, there is an alter in it somewhere. There were often shells that contain alters. The shell could look or act like anything that can be imagined, even a real alter, but they were not themselves alters. There were layers of shells.

I noticed that all shells would start to lose definition and turn into blobs when separated from their original placement by the programmer. I had an internal safe place where I put all rescued alters. There was one alter that I pulled out of a cement floor. The alter looked like a fetus. It did not move, but I knew it was alive. I could not help that alter right away, so I left it in the safe place, while I tried to figure out what to do. A week later it had degraded into a blob. I thought it did not belong and tried to send it away, but it would not leave. I finally opened it, as one would unwrap a present, and there was an alter inside.

My programming would be "unlocked" by a programmer to improve upon the training of an obedient alter, then would be "locked" by the programmer to trap alters within the structure if they were no longer useful to the cult. Alters who were designed as mythical creatures were created at the top and bottom of the Tree of Life. Then an alter was created with the sole purpose of antagonizing the two creatures and turning them against each other. In my system there were several such scenarios where I had to convince the alters that the true enemy was outside and we needed to cooperate to be able to better our lives.

I took apart one structure by myself, using my primary alters as caregivers for the rescued alters. Then I was ready to take a break before diving into the next structure, but my primary alters did not wait; that night and every night thereafter, they worked at dismantling structures and rescuing the alters that were trapped inside. Daytime was reserved for me to remember exactly what the programmer said for the part of the structure that we worked on, to be able to finish dissolving the structure and freeing the alters inside.

My primary alters are very helpful and often work on problems on their own. Most of the time I am aware of what they are working on, because I have asked them for help and I feel slightly dissociated while they work. They dismantle the programming structures at night, so I do not get a very good night of sleep when this occurs.

The last and very necessary step of dismantling the structure, for me, was to remember exactly what the programmer told me and the imagery that I created from this; once I realized that the structure was that way because of what someone told me, I was able to dissolve it permanently. Strangely, just knowing that the programmer told me to make it that way did not work; I had to remember *exactly* what he said, and what I did in response. What I did in response to what they said was just as important as what they said for me to get rid of the structure.

* * *

As you see in this example, much can be discovered about the nature of the personality system and about the abuse by exploring the inner world. And much healing can occur by the client's making deliberate changes in that world.

Exploring the inner world, detecting the ways in which alters are trapped there, and then improving the conditions for the resident alters—who, after all, are just dissociated parts of the survivor—can go a long way to assist your client in healing. The preceding articles may be shared with survivors, who often seek, and share, recovery tips and stories with other survivors. As a therapist, you can gently facilitate the process. You can inquire—perhaps more through "wondering aloud" than directly asking—about where the alters are housed in the inner world. Often there are alters in dungeons, cages, and other unpleasant places where their real body was placed during the abuse. When those alters are discovered, you can work with the personality system to help bring them up to date, and internally provide anything they might need. Often alters represent unmet needs of the person from childhood; some of these needs can be met by internal caregivers; friends can also provide caring, acceptance, and play. We all need play. In her inner world, for instance, one of my clients has little ones bouncing around in "space suits" that prevent emotions and body pain from leaking from one alter into another. The wonderful thing about an inner world is that it can be redesigned to give all insiders whatever they need.

Many survivors, especially of ritual abuse, have programming for internal world disasters. An inner world earthquake is created by shaking up both the model of the world and the child. A tidal wave is created by flooding the world model and simultaneously almost drowning the child. Tornadoes are created with a leaf blower or wind tunnel, and you can imagine how inner world fires are made. An alter is instructed to set off these programs in response to certain triggers, and the rest of the system then experiences the destruction of the inner world by whatever means was used in the program. Often alters are believed to have been "killed" internally, presumably suffering whatever the child suffered during the original programming. It is important to be aware of these programs and to anticipate them by speaking with the alters in charge of them. In my experience, their use is reserved for cases of serious disloyalty. If alters have been "killed" internally, there is nothing to stop the system from creating a magical river in which they can be placed to revive them.

As alters in the inner world leave their original places and begin to interact with others, there may need to be some rules, like no abusing other alters. Those who have always been in charge may need to learn new internal parenting methods, as often they can be authoritarian and critical or even abusive, copying what they saw in the outside world. They can learn, or they can be relieved of their duties and do something else that they like, while other alters can take over the parenting or management of the inside world. With your help, you client can create a functional inner family to replace the one that the abusers made in their own dysfunctional image. You will learn more about this in Chapter Seventeen, "Successful resolution: co-consciousness or integration".

Note

1.   Adapted for this book from Riseman's articles on the Survivorship website and her talks from the SMART conferences.

CHAPTER ELEVEN

"Stabilization" takes on a new meaning

Destabilization is characterized by traumatic intrusions such as flashbacks, nightmares, body memories, emotional states of sadness, anxiety, and despair, and, sometimes, PTSD-related symptomatology suggesting bipolar disorder or psychosis, all of which are severely disruptive and painful. Self-harm and suicide attempts are often methods survivors use to try to reduce these unbearable intrusions. Dissociative disorders are a defense against trauma-related overwhelm, and therapists walk a fine line, trying to balance between the denial and numbing which impedes recovery and the horror of post-trauma flashbacks. The commonly recommended approach for treating people with dissociative disorders is that the therapist should achieve stabilization, and then begin working with the traumatic memories.

Survivors of ritual abuse and mind control experience these symptoms, but not for the same reasons as other survivors and often in the extreme.

Ritual abuse and mind control survivors often continue to be at risk for dangers in later life, such as harassment of survivors, family members, and pets via physical and sexual abuse, poisonings, and break-ins. Therapists are also sometimes affected. Worse, like destabilization symptoms, those threats seem to accelerate when survivors are in treatment. Historically, these dangers have been seen as originating from all-powerful, omnipresent (yet often unidentifiable), relentless and unstoppable perpetrators. This view of abusers, along with the view that ritual abuse and mind control puts survivors so at risk when they pursue recovery, has made survivors afraid to go to therapy, and therapists afraid to treat them. But here is something we did not know in the beginning, and many who work with these survivors still do not understand: these two phenomena are connected, and their etiology is not what you might think.

Perpetrators realize that they will not have the time or resources to keep track of children they have abused when they reach adulthood. The group regards the child as their property. Because of that, they get the grown children to do this for them. Most survivors have ongoing contact with their abuser groups in one way or another. This occurs whether they are in therapy or not, and results in ongoing access and survivors' involvement in continuing activities throughout their lives, especially if they are living in the same vicinity. Most important with regard to the issue of recovery is the fact that it is these clients' own alters who are contacting cult members and that they report not only any physical relocation, but also whether survivors are in treatment, with whom, and what they are disclosing there. This allows the group to take actions which trigger alters to behave in ways that sabotage their recovery.

Mind controllers have researched ordinary post-trauma intrusions, and have co-opted them for the purposes of controlling their victims. Mind control survivors are particularly likely to produce these symptoms when they remember or disclose their abuse or otherwise disobey the rules. In the early stages of a survivor's disobedient pursuit of mind control recovery, alters not only release partial flashbacks or body memories, disrupt therapy with frequent crises and/or quit it, but also may harm the body, and make suicide attempts. The abusers have also trained the alters to manifest symptoms of virtually any mental illness. These important additional considerations, both internal and external, make stabilization much more difficult to achieve than with other dissociative clients, and much more important for safety in a concrete way.

Because of this, disclosures about the organized abuse early in therapy are particularly dangerous to the client, and sometimes to the therapist. Before treatment can proceed, these are things you must understand and address. I cannot overestimate how important it is for therapists working with these survivors to recognize the degree of risk involved here. But the good news is that we now know that the risk—and the power to protect from the risk—begins with the client.

Current contact with perpetrator groups

In the past, signs of current perpetrator involvement in mind-controlled survivors were seen as unstable client behavior not unlike that of an abused woman who cannot stay away from her partner. However, when therapists attempted to address them in the same way as with all other clients, by working on mindfulness or grounding techniques, assertiveness, boundaries, and self esteem, the problems continued, and increased. Relatedly, the reassurance that many therapists are used to giving their incest survivor clients, "that was then and this is now," not only proved useless, but dangerous, to such survivors. It also rang false to their dissociative inner systems. Our knowledge of "current contact" activities with abusers has allowed us to deal with this issue. The key here is that this term "current contact" describes not only the activities that continue to victimize these people, but also the method through which abuser groups ensure the ongoing contact that allows them access. One way the latter is accomplished is through "access programming," through which perpetrators find out if any secret information is disclosed to outsiders, including therapists. It is extremely important for the therapist and client to understand precisely how this works.

Even when there is not current involvement, usually there is one (or more than one) alter who is trained to report to the group. The contact will generally be hidden from view and from consciousness. These alters believe that the perpetrators already know what the person has done and said, and even what he or she thinks, as we saw in Chapter Eight. These alters believe that if they do not report this to the group, the abusers will punish them severely or punish someone else (inside or outside) because of them. Once the perpetrators have this information, they become active in attempting to shut down these disclosures.

As soon as you even suspect that your client is a survivor of ritual abuse or mind control, you should (1) assess whether or not s/he is currently involved with the perpetrating group, and (2) find a way to prevent alters from reporting to the perpetrators.

Not only will that protect your clients' therapy, it will also be the first step in helping them to be free from all other future forms of current contact-related abuse. Your clients' alters have no idea that they have choices, and how much power they really hold.

How to identify whether your client has current involvement

In the early 1990s, some of the literature on ritual abuse stated that virtually all clients continue to have current involvement in "the cult." The current view held by many trauma therapists is that the opposite is true—that the abuse which began in childhood is now over and the client can recover in safety, the only danger being from his or her own self-harm. The truth appears to be somewhere in between.

Many clients in the early stages of realizing that they have experienced ritual abuse and/or mind control believe it was in the past. However, this is because their involvement is hidden via alter personalities. As a therapist, it may be some months or even years before you know whether your client has any ongoing contact with dangerous people. In the worst-case scenario, you will find your client is fully involved in a perpetrator group, attending rituals, participating in the training of other members, and carrying out other crimes. I remember my shock when my client, Tony, told me he had found himself waiting at midnight at the corner gas station to be picked up by the cult van for a ceremony.

It is also true that there are also many clients who have not had contact with their perpetrator groups for many years and appear to have been completely dropped by them. You have seen this in Trish Fotheringham's story. Errors in programming, a rebellious nature, or a difficulty keeping information nicely segregated in hidden pockets of memory or alter personalities have rendered many survivors useless to their programmers; after measures have been taken to "cap" their memories, they are turned loose to fend for themselves. Other survivors move far away from their abusers to a location where the perpetrator group does not function. Sometimes the group itself has disbanded, or its original purpose (such as the Cold War, for some military/political groups) no longer exists (though the actions often continue, with different excuses).

However, the client does not need to be in constant contact with the group in order for contact to be established under certain circumstances. In Chapter Eight, you saw that many of the lies that these groups teach their victims are aimed at preventing the person's total separation from the group. Even when these survivors begin to remember their abuse and seek out therapy, the rule of secrecy still prevails. Even a client who has not had any contact with their perpetrator group for many years might end up reporting to the perpetrator group and reactivating harassment by them.

Even if there is minimal group contact, it is common that clients maintain contact with their families of origin. In most cases, a family member or the person's whole family was involved with the perpetrator group when the client was a child. Even if there is minimal group contact, it is common that clients maintain contact with their families of origin. It is difficult to tell whether they are reporting to family members about their therapy because they could be reporting in a dissociated identity state and have no memory of doing so. At the same time, therapists need to understand that failure to maintain contact with the family could arouse suspicion, and aside from the fact that the client might genuinely care about his or her family members, it is probably best that the client not deviate from their usual contact patterns, unless they have some other urgent reason, such as preventing abuse of their own children.

In the past, I have heard some therapists say they will only work with ritual abuse survivors if there is no current contact. It is not really practical to insist on such a guideline. It might not be discovered for quite a while that a client who sincerely believed he or she had no current contact has unknowingly been fully involved in group activities. It is also possible that a client who realized that he or she was currently involved would lie about it in order to stay in therapy.

My advice, therefore, is to proceed on the assumption that your ritual abuse or mind control client may have current involvement. If you are not prepared to deal with that, it would be best to refer your client to another therapist as soon as possible. Once you get into the middle of undoing all the programming, it will be difficult and complicated for the client and the new therapist to make the change. My other advice is to delay soliciting disclosures about the abuse until you have worked sufficiently with the personality system so that the client will not report to the perpetrators about what goes on in therapy. Simply stated, you do need to assume that a part of them is trained to report.

Indicators of recent and/or ongoing perpetrator contact, harassment, triggering, and/or abuse

In the early 1990s, Pamela Reagor, in a handout distributed at a workshop, listed the following indicators that recent or current contact is occurring:

a.   Sudden onset of disruption in therapy structure, e.g., missed appointments, disappearance for days, inability to find the therapy office.

b.   Sudden onset of disruption in therapeutic relationship, e.g., severe mistrust (not attributable to natural process of new alters beginning to participate in therapy more overtly), fearful inability to talk or to respond to innocuous questions, obvious withholding of information.

c.   Sudden onset or persistent recurrence of claims of inability to believe that the ritual abuse history is true, inability to understand "this multiple business" or "this programming stuff," sometimes with repeated requests for repeated explanations.

d.   Persistent failure for the MPD system to agree to and follow through with special precautions for personal safety (e.g., "be with someone tonight," "don't answer the telephone yourself," etc.)

e.   Evidence (conservatively gathered) that other MPD survivors feel afraid of the person, and may have had their therapy disrupted after contact with the person.

f.   Reports (often only in response to therapist inquiry) of numerous hang-up calls, repeated wrong numbers, strange sounds or messages on telephone answering machines.

g.   Problematic response to therapeutic inquiry regarding security leaks in MPD/DDNOS system—e.g., "Is there anyone in there who tells cult people what we talk about in therapy sessions?"

h.   Evidence of recent reprogramming:

   (i)   Bruises, pin pricks, blisters, other pains or marks, especially after lost time and with no plausible other explanation.

   (ii) New personalities, who may or may not know the therapist, but have confused histories or no significant childhood or adolescent history.

   (iii) Plausible reports of sudden inability to access other personalities, loss of co-consciousness: e.g., "everybody's gone," "there are no other personalities," "everything, everybody is scrambled," "nobody is where they are supposed to be inside."

   (iv) Suspicious disappearances or lost time, especially during "peak" holiday or programming periods or birthdays. (See Appendix 2 for dates.)

   (v)   Known personalities now split into two or more parts, with different knowledge, abilities, etc., and probable fear of going back together.

   (vi) Along with two or more of above indicators (i–v), sudden onset of intense and uncontrollable body sensations and behaviors (e.g., drugged appearance, electroshock spasms, stereotyped gestures with hands, feet, etc.) in flashbacks or memory work.

   (vii) Along with two or more of indicators (i–v), sudden onset of intense urges to engage in some complex, usually dangerous behavior (e.g., suicide in a specified motel, go to a specific town, self-mutilate in a specific manner, etc.), without insight or appropriate affect.

I believe this is an accurate list of indicators, with some exceptions. Point (c), the client's inability to believe in his/her own memories or multiplicity, may occur without current contact if training of alters to disbelieve is operating. Even "reactive dissociatives," those who have not experienced mind control, tend to disbelieve both their diagnosis and what they are remembering. Point (d), failure to follow through with safety precautions, can result from learnt helplessness in both programmed and reactive dissociatives. For example, I have one client whose brothers and father broke down her door if she locked it, and punished her severely for trying to keep them out. In adult life, she believes she has to open her door to anyone who knocks, including a former employer who abused her.

Some of the indicators in point (h) might also occur when certain programming or training is in operation, without there necessarily being current abuse or involvement with a perpetrator group. Another possibility is contact that is minimal. A telephone call with a cult member (usually a family member), or a birthday card with a certain type of picture on it (e.g., a rose) can be enough to set off many of these symptoms. A client I have been seeing for many years just told me that this is a "recall year for her," in which the alters in charge of her system are supposed to organize the system to return to her place of origin, where they will report to her programmer (who by now is either dead or very old) about any alters who have broken the silence. These alters will then be "sacrificed." Her last recall year was sixteen years ago.

The following sections detail some of the danger signs to look for in ascertaining whether there is current contact.

Current contact alerts

- Significant periods of amnesia (especially around cult holidays), including client reports of evidence that he or she has gone out at night but has no memory of it.
- Reports of being approached by people in the street who are saying peculiar accusatory things, often with Satanic themes.
- Reports of receiving peculiar phone calls, particularly where the same thing is said over and over at each call.
- Receiving calls that consistently hang up after three rings.
- Finding one's car or home broken into and minor vandalism conducted.
- Other forms of harassment and apparently indirect communication.
- Sudden fear of the therapist or of the therapist's office.

While many of these forms of contact appeared to be nonsensical, to certain identity states they have a very clear meaning. If your client has met some of these criteria described above, your index of suspicion should be raised regarding whether they are being contacted and are going out at night to participate in the activities of their perpetrator group, without their conscious awareness.

Not all current contact is a simple matter of access by the original perpetrator group. We must also be aware of the dangerous tentacles of the worldwide web for these survivors. I had a client who told me that a man with whom she was in contact on an internet discussion list was trying to figure out her personality system; the system subsequently turned upside down, alters I had never met took control, and she left therapy with me. I do not believe that this client had current perpetrator contact prior to this; the man was actively trolling survivor discussion forums for those whose personality systems he could disrupt. He told her he was going to come to our city in search of her, and it is likely that he did so.

Other dangers are seen in the recovery community. A client of mine who had not been in contact with her perpetrator group (in another city) for almost forty years met a fellow ritual abuse survivor in a sexual abuse survivors' group who took her out to what turned out to be a cult meeting and reprogramming session. After that event, my client received regular telephone calls from local perpetrator group members, attempting to call out alters and get them to attend meetings.

I had one meeting through a church minister with a woman who had supposedly healed from ritual abuse and was now said to be healing survivors. She attended a number of churches in town. I recognized what she told me about her programming and healing as pure hogwash, and my client Lorraine recognized her and told me that she was a cult high priestess and was going from church to church seeking out survivors and giving signals to trigger them to return, report, and punish disloyalty internally. (I have no way of corroborating this information.)

Several other clients of whose safety I am fully assured have been constantly terrified that they were being followed and spied upon. Survivors who relocate and separate from these perpetrator groups have alters who have been taught that they can never get away and that the offenders know everything. As their therapist, you therefore cannot rely upon what they tell you; you need to look for indicators such as those listed above. You and your client need to understand that a strong impulse to call a relative or to return home can be a tip-off that the client's reporting has been triggered.

Current contact is a serious business, whether it is present at the start of therapy, initiated by the client's reporting to the perpetrators about therapy, or accomplished by the client's contact with other survivors who are looking for disobedient survivors to trigger or recall. All of my "first four" clients were involved in current contact, but none had conscious knowledge of their involvement at the start of therapy. I can think of several other clients in the same situation, and I lost some of them because of it.

What happens in current contact?

When in therapy where their history is being addressed, survivors generally will contact the group and report what is happening to a designated contact person, who will call out a reporting alter to give a recitation of all the client's behaviors. It is extremely important for the therapist and client to understand how the group is able to find out. In particular, watch for reports of strange phone calls, missing time, and odd behaviors, as well as a compulsion to make contact with family (if family were involved in the abuse) or other perpetrators. Look at cards and gifts from family members and ask whether they have any special meaning.

Once a group discovers that one of their current or previously abused persons is telling secrets to outsiders, various unpleasant things happen. If the survivor who is disobeying the rules and has become a security risk is far away from the perpetrating group, the group will make certain attempts to trigger alters into doing the job of shutting down the leak. This will result in some of the symptoms listed earlier, which disrupt therapy but also have the benefit of giving away what is happening if the therapist is educated about these signs. In some cases, the person will return home for further retraining. If the survivor is of particular importance to the perpetrating group, either because s/he was high up in the group's hierarchy or because s/he has knowledge of some important crimes, the group may contact a different group in the survivor's locality and ask or pay them to harass the survivor.

Now the group can pursue its goal of interfering with or destroying therapy, by extreme tactics if necessary. When the group contacts the survivor, they will trigger alters into returning to them and into obeying their rules of silence and loyalty. When the client returns to the perpetrators, the training experiences of her childhood will be repeated. She will again be tortured and forced to perpetrate against others. The therapist might be impersonated, and this person will abuse the client, and the client may be forced to abuse the supposed therapist. (See Chapter Thirteen for more details on this.)

If the client does not return to them, cult or group members will hang around the localities where she spends her time and give signals to get her to come to them, so that they can take her for retraining. If she ignores the signals, they will lie in wait for her and abduct her. If she finds ways to prevent this, they will resort to more extreme measures, such as breaking into her home.

Just as there is an escalation of these tactics, there is a gradual escalation of punishments for survivors who disobey, and in particular if they spill secrets to outsiders. I have had three clients for whom the original perpetrators traveled all the way across the continent to try to do the reprogramming. If the client has become unmanageable and core secrets have been breached, true suicide training (as opposed to attempts designed to land the survivor in hospital) might be triggered. If this fails, the group might engage in murder attempts disguised as suicide or accidents. They broke into my client Jennifer's apartment, found all the pills she had on hand, and stuffed them down her throat. Fortunately, she did not have a great deal of medication and she did not die. But, as you saw, Lorraine did die, perhaps by forced suicide to protect her loved ones or perhaps at the hands of the perpetrator group. Organized criminal groups protect their secrets at all costs.

Common access programs

Access programming is what gives the perpetrators access to your client for ongoing involvement, punishment, and retraining. The traumatic memories of these trainings are among those that create the most danger for the client, so should be processed as soon as the client is ready to work with such memories. Some of the specific mind-controlled beliefs involved in these programs were described in Chapter Eight.

Reporting

The survivor usually reports to the perpetrators through a phone call to a relative, during which the person being reported to may trigger other alters to do their jobs. Generally, the reporting parts of the survivor believe that the group always knows where they are and what they are saying anyway. They have experienced the fact that usually, when the organized group is actively abusing a child, they really do know where the child is and what the child is saying at all times. Since a family member of the child is most commonly involved, when the child tries to run away or to hide, the group can find the child easily. Group members will tell these children that they found them by "magic" or "the eye of Satan", etc. (See Chapter Eight for more examples.) Young children believe this explanation, and since they remain child alters, they continue to believe it when the survivor is an adult.

Whether or not there has been deliberate mind control, child alters in an adult trauma survivor might not understand time or place, and might believe they are still in the places where the group had access to them in childhood. Here is how one client described it in a letter to me:

Most of the ones inside do not feel time the way you do. When you say it has been a long time or many, many years, it does not make the same kind of sense to the little ones as it does to you or to the older ones. Those little ones only know about time when they are out. So for them it isn't as long as you think it is since they were in that place. The older ones know better about time and how it works. The little ones kind of know about today, tomorrow and yesterday. They sort of only know where they are when they are out. They know the neighbor lady's house [where some abuse happened]. Some know the house with that mother and father and a few know the house we lived in later. Some of those same ones know different rooms where bad things happened like with the doctor and that other man. They only know all of those different moments. There is kind of nothing in between. A few of them have been lost in the town after your meeting. They just know they are lost. But they are not looking around and thinking this is a different place.

Because young child alters have so little understanding of the time that has gone by, or the distance they have traveled from the place where the abuse occurred, they believe the perpetrators are still around even when they are not.

Here is an example of how one child was trained to telephone her mother. At age eleven she was heavily sedated so she believed she was asleep. Then, she was painfully abused by people in costumes, so that she thought she was having a nightmare. Her mother came in and soothed her, and told her that if she had nightmares she should call her. This event was repeated several times, and in different places, and in the later instances her mother was not present but there was a telephone on which she could call her, and her mother responded by coming and soothing her. In later life when this training was triggered, the adult had nightmares and the trained child alter phoned her mother.

Perpetrators use one child (usually a sibling) to report on another in a family, and reporting alters start doing it early in childhood. That is when the child is most likely to accept the group's "magik". Groups commonly train young children to believe that they know everything by the use of hidden microphones combined with props. One client had certain alters who constantly saw an "all-seeing eye"—a prop which was used in their training. Another saw ears on the walls, a result of the room with the microphone (and one-way mirror) having plastic ears actually glued to the walls. Usually, one alter sees the (now imaginary) prop, while another has the job of making them see it through replaying the picture from the memory. Other groups tell children that small creatures (crows, spiders, squirrels) tell the perpetrators about them, or that the Mother lurks in every shadow.

Usually, this training includes a horrendous experience designed to make the child terrified of the consequences of not telling the perpetrators what she has disclosed. For example, the child is told that an older child has talked about the cult to an outsider. She watches this child being tortured until he or she discloses to the cult what has been told; then the punishment stops. The newly trained child is put in a position to receive the same kind of torture (e.g., put on the cross or rack, or touched with the hot poker), and believes what she is told, *You must always tell us if you have talked.*

How therapists should deal with reporting alters

If your client acknowledges the presence of reporting alters, my advice is to reason with those alters, or, if they are too young to understand, with the older parts of the client who may be in charge of them. Ask them why the abusers would need alters to report to them where the person is, if they already know. Point out to them that that the abusers knew that when the body became an adult, they would not be able to keep track of the person all the time as they could when s/he was a child. Explain that this is why they trained alters to keep track of those things for them, and if the reporters do not report, or do not tell the truth when they report, the perpetrators will not know that any disclosures have been made.

If the reporters (or those in charge of them) decide not to report, you have the safety to proceed with therapy. Reporter alters have generally been trained to always tell the truth. Be sure to look for "backups," however—alters who are supposed to take over the job of any alter who stops doing his/her job. They will also need to be convinced.

Reporters are also observers

Reporter alters are trained to watch and listen carefully to everything the person does in the real world. Therefore, they observe therapy sessions. If the reporters are unwilling to stop doing their jobs, other parts of the client's personality system can be recruited to help. Here is one way that you can deal with this problem: There are usually some alters who have the job of putting other alters to sleep (the initial training is done with sleep-inducing drugs); they can put the reporters to sleep during most of the therapy session. You can arrange this with those in charge of the "sleep program," then have those in charge of the "forgetting program" make the reporters forget that you have made this arrangement. From then on, in therapy sessions, you talk about inconsequential topics for the first five or ten minutes for the benefit of the reporters, then, when the reporters have gone to sleep, do your real work. They can be woken up for the closing minutes of the session. All they will have to report is what happened in those first and last few minutes.

Another way of dealing with it is to satisfy the reporters' need to do their jobs by having them report internally to internal copies of the abusers (there usually are some). How do you find out if there are? You just ask.

If you do not have sufficient rapport with the personality system to do these things, you need to proceed very slowly so as to not accidentally trigger any reporting which will get the perpetrator group reinvolved with the client.

What about relocation?

In the beginning of our work with survivors of these abuses, therapists learned quickly that their clients continued to be in danger, and continued to be abused. As described earlier, our initial perspective on the safety of survivors viewed it as simply a matter of physical location. For some, however, this view continued: As late as 1998, in her book, *The Ultimate Challenge: A Revolutionary, Sane and Sensible Response to Ritualistic and Cult-Related Abuse*, sexual abuse victim advocate Gayle Woodsun recommended relocation for survivors, but without acknowledging the fact that they would inevitably report their new location to the abusers. She did acknowledge the reality of mind-control programming; however, her recommendation was to treat all the child parts of the person as if they were programming to be resisted rather than child parts to be nurtured and reasoned with. In my opinion, her approach was already dated when it was written. It was also neither revolutionary nor well-informed, but it does acknowledge the reality of current contact, something many therapists do not want to face and are very skeptical about.

It is true that Woodsun's suggestion of relocation (to a place at a great distance from the original abuse) is sometimes necessary, but it is only useful when the person is no longer reporting to the abusers, and provided a competent therapist is available in the new location. Until then, relocation is of little use and, in fact, might serve the perpetrators' goals of sabotaging recovery. I once began to treat a woman sent to me by a therapist in a city some distance away; the survivor was high up in a very vicious cult and the memories she began to work on were horrendous. However, about a week after she arrived, she disclosed to me with embarrassment that she had telephoned the perpetrator group and given them her location. I had to smuggle her out of town (while her apartment was being watched) and send her on to another location previously unknown to her. It is likely that the therapist she was sent to would have the same experience after another week, unless he were able to deal with her reporting training.

Call backs: training to return to the perpetrators

Most survivors of organized abuse have parts trained to return to their abusers, either at specific times or dates (e.g., for family birthdays or important rituals) or when they are called back. Young adults are usually allowed to go out and create an identity in the world, then called back for use at a specific age or year. Subsequent to their early years of ongoing programming, those people whose initial abuse was with an occult religious group will continue to participate in the rituals and orgies which happen on the dates listed in the group's calendar. They will not incur any punishment for disloyalty—unless they begin disclosing secrets to outsiders. If they are parents, they will very probably be taking their children to the group's events, and their children are being abused on an ongoing basis within the group and possibly by some of their alters at home. Those who have been trained by a military/political group might go on assignments for the group. A child, teenager, or young adult from either setting may continue to be involved in pornographic filming or prostitution. All of this happens in a life separate from the one they present to the world.

The following sections detail some specific types of training which survivors have disclosed to me.

"Return to save someone"

This call back is used frequently with disloyal survivors. The person believes that s/he has to return to save a younger sibling or friend from being killed. The alters who have this training will feel a desperate need to return to the group, feeling that something awful will happen to someone if they do not.

"Return to avoid punishment"

This has several variations. For example, a cult child misses a ritual (usually for the full moon) and is punished with electroshock the next day. Or she is made to kill what she believes is a baby and is told that if she does not keep returning the police will be notified and she will be jailed. Alters who have this training are afraid not to return.

"Return for rewards"

This is part of the training of alters who have to take leadership in rituals. These alters experience none of the abuse, and are rewarded with massage, drugs, pleasurable sex, and power (e.g., the right to decide who gets hurt). The call to return for the survivor's personal birthday is of this type. The alters who have this training really want to go back to the group, and can only be stopped by other alters sharing with them the pain of what has happened to the body at cult events.

"Return at a specific date"

I am currently dealing with a client who had come a long way in therapy, and then encountered callback programming for Easter 2010. Just before Easter, certain alters I had not known about "woke up." They were heavily drugged child alters, who had been told that the world would end at Easter of 2010, and they must return home by that time. (Other alters who woke up at the same time had the job of punishing the rest of the system if they did not return to the cult group.) Over the next couple of months (since Easter 2010), I spent considerable time showing them current magazines and books with dates on them. Obviously, in this case, the callback was unsuccessful, because the client had made so much progress in therapy. Her system was able to detect the new alters and (with my help) update them on the changes in her life and her current safety. But if this were a client who had not received therapy, or whose system were not largely co-conscious and cooperative, she would probably just have booked a flight home and returned to whichever perpetrators were still around to reset her programming.

You can dialogue with the parts who believe they have to return for any or all of these reasons. They need to understand that contact with the group puts them in a weaker position and will lead to pain, while disconnection will protect them. For example, if a person returns to save someone else, they are often used to harm the person they were supposed to save. Then they are told that they are just as bad a perpetrator as those who made them do it, and that they will be jailed if they disclose what happened. This needs to be exposed as a lie. The truth is that the group is less likely to harm someone your client loves if they are not present. Sometimes, guilty alters think they should return to be punished for their crimes; I tell them that if they return they will be forced to commit more such crimes. Those who return to avoid punishment need to learn a simple truth: the abusers can only hurt them if they have access to their body. If they are not there, they cannot be hurt. Those who return for rewards are most difficult to deal with. Until the memories have been shared with them, other alters with internal authority can keep them under control by making them forget the date they are to return or getting them to go to sleep at that time.

External helpers, such as a friend or spouse, can also help. For example, someone safe can hide their shoes or block the driveway so they cannot drive to a group event.

Training to make the survivor accessible to abduction

When a survivor in therapy is no longer returning to the group or reporting to them, s/he may still be accessible to the perpetrators for some time because of alters trained to respond to cues from the perpetrators. Some of these trainings get the survivor out into the open where group members can get at them. Often there are specific auditory triggers, such as a certain number of rings on the phone, the honk of a car horn, or a beeping sound. Visual hand signals can also call a person to come to a group member with or without direct and personal contact with the person making the sign. Some triggers can make the survivor unable to move or speak, so that they will cooperate with an abduction. Triggers can now be sent by email. A client of mine recently received an innocuous-appearing email from a private detective representing her younger brother (whom she had not seen since her escape twenty years ago), saying he would love his sister to meet his wife and children. She went into a complete panic, believing the perpetrators were about to appear at any moment and re-abuse her. She spent two weeks in terror with her blinds closed.

Below are examples of some trainings I have discovered in clients.

Training to answer the phone and open the door

A child was drugged to lethargy and seated alone by a phone, with electrodes all over her body. When the phone rang, she was given painful shocks until she answered it. Then "Satan" spoke on the phone and told her, "Always answer when Satan calls." She had met this "Satan" before at cult rituals, where he hurt her. Her mother called through the door that she would take her home if she (the child) opened the door, so the girl managed to get to the door and open it, fighting the effects of the drug and the shocks. In later life, the survivor always had to answer the phone and/or open the door in response to specific sound triggers. She had no conscious memory of the reason for this compulsion, until we uncovered the memory in therapy.

Another client, who frequently denies the ritual abuse history that brought her to therapy, is trying to reduce her contact with her family. She tells me that she just cannot help answering the phone or returning phone calls when messages are left. Turning off the ringer does not work because she sees the flashing light which indicates that there is a message. She has no knowledge of this specific programming, but clearly something is forcing her to respond to phone calls, whether or not she wants to.

Training to go outside

At about age nine or ten, a child was deliberately made addicted to narcotic drugs, and was conditioned to go outside at the sound of a car horn (or dog whistle, etc.) to get the drugs she needed. Later, feeling drug withdrawal symptoms and knowing she must go outside to get rid of those symptoms, this alter responded to the sound cue.

Training to come to the handler

A young child was put in a backyard swimming pool, and called by a perpetrator, on the other side of the pool, to swim to him. A lid was put over the pool so that the only place she could get any air was by him. She swam across to him underwater in order not to drown. Later, the survivor felt the sensation of drowning until she went to the cult person who had called her.

Training to keep still and silent

A child was put in an enclosed space with some type of supposedly poisonous creature (bees if allergic, snakes, spiders). He was told not to speak or move or the creatures would bite or sting him to death. I have seen this training in several different survivors. In one case the insects (bees) stung her and, because she was allergic to bees, she became unconscious. Then she was resuscitated. In later life, if a perpetrator group member approaches this person on the street and gives the signal for this program, the survivor will be unable to run away. (This kind of training is also one reason that survivors so often have strong reactions to insects.)

Training not to run away

A young child is encouraged to run away from the perpetrators, then punished by harm to her knees or feet when she is caught. An alter is to give her this pain if she considers running away from the group.

Training not to leave town

A child or teenager is drugged and put through simulated car accidents, plane crashes, and other events designed to make her believe that these things will inevitably happen to her if she attempts to leave the town where the perpetrator group operates. I had to work through all these memories so that Teresa could leave town to a place where she would be safe, even after her access programming had been removed.

Dealing with access training

Most mind control survivors I have encountered, especially of cult abuse, have all of these kinds of trainings. You see how complicated they are for the client to deal with, and to unravel in therapy.

In the short term, if your client is being watched and/or harassed by perpetrators, it helps if she lives with a safe spouse or roommate who can be informed of the situation and stay with her whenever she is out of the house. Survivors who live alone are "sitting ducks" for perpetrators. I do not recommend ritual abuse or mind control survivors living with one another; rather than keeping one another safe they will expose one another to risk. But many do, without conscious awareness of what has driven them to this connection or what the implications are.

When Stella Katz was being harassed by the cult that she had broken away from, the cult's van kept circling her neighborhood, waiting for her to leave the house. So she telephoned the police and said "I keep seeing a van around here, and I think it may have something to do with those break-ins that keep happening in this area." The police checked it out and called her back. "It's funny," they said, "There weren't any burglary tools, but that van was full of illegal drugs and weapons and handcuffs."

If the perpetrator group is not local, your client will only have to deal with telephone calls and letters or emails. If they harass her (trying to trigger various trained behaviors) she can turn off the ringer on the phone (and place it where it is not visible), change her email address to something they do not know, and bring any letters or parcels in to your office. There, you can see them and she can look at them in your presence. You can discuss their meaning with her and make sure that she will not act on any messages they carry.

In the end, however, the only solution is to work through the memories of the trainings, so that the person is no longer bound by the compulsion which various child alters have to act on because of their training. Programming such as this operates like post-hypnotic suggestion; it feels compulsory when the person is in its grip, even when the conscious adult does not understand it. Once the method of its creation becomes conscious, it loses that grip and the person becomes free. Before you can work through your client's memories, the important thing is to make sure that reporting does not occur so that the person does not have to deal with perpetrators in her adult life.

With some current-contacting clients, I have had marathon sessions of a weekend at a time (all day long), just going through the memories to remove the effects of all the access training. I also had a policy of working through all current abuse memories immediately after they occurred, along with the memories of whatever programming was being retaught in the current contact. This is what enabled my clients to escape their group and become free.

Ongoing perpetrator contact is one of the most difficult issues for therapists of survivors of ritual abuse and mind control. It is my belief that most retractors of memories disclosed in therapy were victims of ongoing abuse (and rewards) by perpetrator groups. We do not want to know this is happening, but if it is, it is. Being aware of it and dealing with it directly with the client can save you from being caught off-guard by a retractor client blaming you for her "false memories."

Stabilization: special issues with ritual abuse and mind control survivors

There is a good deal written about stabilization of abuse survivors, whether dissociative or not. You can find some books that teach these methods in the annotated bibliography (Appendix 1). Please make sure you are familiar with this material. All those techniques have their place when working with mind-controlled clients. I am not going to repeat any of that information here. Instead, I will focus on what is unique about mind control and ritual abuse survivors in terms of the reasons for these destabilizing behaviors and symptoms. The special considerations discussed in this chapter will make your work with survivors of organized abuse involving mind control much more effective.

Self-harm training

Self-harm, or self-injury, is not the same as a suicide attempt. The training is specific; for example, cutting or burning. Besides alters being trained to do this when the person is disloyal or discloses secrets, perpetrators can also give words or signals to trigger this behavior. Sometimes, the pattern of cuts is a visible sign that the person has been abused by a cult group: this may make other cult members (e.g., in a psychiatric hospital) aware of the survivor so that they can approach her to bring her into the local group. In a typical training, a child is branded with the mark of a pentagram with a hot branding iron, and is told she is being marked because she is a servant of Satan. If she is disloyal, she has to make this mark on her body to prove her loyalty. She believes that the perpetrators know she has been disloyal and will punish her unless she does this to herself.

The alters who inflict the pain are generally not the ones who feel it. When asked, the person will also report feeling no pain. Some alters have been trained to experience sexual pleasure when the body is cut; for them, cutting in this way could become a sexual addiction.

Alters who are "introjects" of the perpetrators are told they actually are the persons who "created" them, and they must harm the body in the exact same ways as those persons do if any of the parts become disloyal.

Therapists should make a careful search for trained alters before assuming that self-harm is just an attempt by the adult to avoid other kinds of pain, such as depression, physical pain, or unpleasant emotions. You can see how differently motivated these self-harm and suicide attempts are. This is not to say that mind control survivors do not self-harm for the same reasons as other trauma survivors; just that there is an additional level of complexity.

Therapists generally put a lot of effort into training clients to live in the present and avoid self-destructive behaviors. But this is largely wasted when the child alters doing the cutting or taking the overdoses are doing their "jobs," in fear of death or torture to themselves or others if they disobey. Medication can help somewhat, but the problem behaviors will persist and the underlying struggle will continue for the alter. The behaviors must not only be treated for their emotional and cognitive aspects, but as programming.

Suicide attempt training

Although ritual abuse and mind control survivors attempt suicide more frequently than other extreme abuse survivors, their rate of successful suicide is no different, according to the Extreme Abuse Survey (Rutz, Becker, Overkamp, & Karriker, 2008). Organized criminal groups expend large amounts of resources on training children, and in many cases they expect to be able to use them for life. Also, successful suicides could prompt investigations, and these groups do not want to draw attention to their existence, whereas a suicide attempt might get a client hospitalized, and cults and other criminal groups monitor many psychiatric facilities to find and retrain survivors while they are there.

In the early stages, the group will make sure that these attempts are unsuccessful. This is because children are actually taught to stop short of actually killing the body, for example by taking just a few less pills than a lethal amount.

The training not to die is often accomplished this way: the child is drugged and assaulted by costumed "demons" in a simulated hell; the alter is told that if the body dies this is what will happen to her because she is evil and deserves to go to hell. This alter will work hard to make sure she does not die if other parts attempt suicide.

Actual suicide training

This is not to say that no one is trained for successful suicide. They are.

Training for successful suicides usually involves a group or sequence of alters (see Stella Katz's information regarding this in Chapter Seven), but it is not activated until either the perpetrators instruct the survivor to do it, or the security of the most important secrets is prematurely breached. Children and adults are generally taught several specific ways of harming and killing themselves, down to the details of how many of each kind of pill to take.

Children raised in Satanic or Luciferian cults often have an experience similar to the following: A child who is supposedly a "traitor" is killed slowly and painfully, and those children who watch are told that if they ever become traitors, they must kill themselves in some less painful way before the cult finds them, or they will be killed just like this traitor was. Training in how to accomplish this is then given.

Internal homicide training

Suicide trainings are often trainings for internal homicide—that is, one alter killing the body to kill the other alters. The alters who do this are usually trained to believe they do not belong to the body and will not die. For example, an alter who believes he or she is a demon is taken to "hell" where other alters in the body are tortured, and this alter gets to torture other (outside) people. He is told he will not die if the body dies, and will have a higher place in hell if he kills the body on command. Such alters might be given injections which make them unable to feel anything, and invited to watch something being done to the body in which they reside without feeling anything. They might be trained with rewards, such as pleasurable drugs, then told that if they kill the body they can return to the perpetrators for more rewards. They might also believe they are demons, ghosts, aliens, or demigods.

Other alters trained to kill the body are trained to believe they reside somewhere other than inside the body in which the host and other alters live. Since they are all given different "bodies" in the internal world, and they are not supposed to come out into the external world except at the signal of their handlers, they have no way of disproving this, just like the alters who believe they are spiritual beings without bodies. I have repeatedly watched as these alters come out into the world and stare in amazement at their hands, flexing their fingers where the "claws" are supposed to be, and looking at their clothing. Sometimes they say things like, "What am I doing in this body?", and I ask what kind of body they thought they had. If none, I invite them to touch the body and see whether it can feel the touch. If they feel a furry body, I ask whether they have seen Halloween costumes.

Interventions to prove to such alters that they belong to the body, such as those described at the end of Chapter Eight ("The programming: indoctrination, lies, and tricks"), are very important, and are not difficult. When these alters come out, they often appear to be in a drugged state. Hypnotic interventions to remove the drugs will enable them to see and think more clearly, before giving them the proof that the abusers lied to them.

Psychiatric symptom training

In addition to self-harming, suicide ideation and attempts, your client may suffer from various psychiatric symptoms which you might try without success to relieve, including extreme depression, anxiety, seeming mood swings, mood disorders, and psychosis. You need to be aware of the possibility that they might result from internal punishments by alters who are trained to administer them. This is an important way in which mind-controlled clients differ from others who have not undergone systematic mind control. These symptoms serve a variety of purposes. In addition to disrupting or confusing the therapy, they also might make the survivor so dysfunctional that s/he will return to the perpetrators to have things put right. Failing that, they might result in hospitalization. But that leads to its own complications, as you will see.

Treatment of destabilizing symptoms: concerns and cautions

In response to many of the seemingly out of control, self-destructive behaviors that these clients manifest in early recovery (which is essentially before their current contact programming has been identified and disabled), or to psychiatric symptoms that erupt at any time during treatment, a therapist might reasonably believe the clients require more care than they can provide. The therapist might even panic or feel overwhelmed. At that point, it would seem advisable, even necessary, to at least refer them for psychiatric evaluation and possible medication; failing that, inpatient treatment in a psychiatric facility might be pursued. But all of that yields complications.

Psychiatric medications

Psychotropic medications do not address the special needs of this patient group. Not only are they frequently ineffective, many of the training experiences that your clients have been subjected to have included such medications as part of mind control. The helplessness, confusion, and triggering effect of these meds make them damaging to survivors.

Antipsychotics can reduce the ANP's ability to communicate with the rest of the personality system, thus suppressing the client's ability to do the necessary therapeutic work. Jennifer was hospitalized when we unearthed a memory of a "bug" being placed in her ear to tell the abusers what she disclosed. She became paranoid. We scheduled the memory work to deal with this issue, but before we could do so, the hospital psychiatrist discovered she was paranoid and put her on antipsychotic medication. As a result, we were no longer able to contact the alters involved in the memory and we could not do the work. My attempt to explain to the psychiatrist failed. In his view, she was paranoid, this was psychotic, and so she needed the medication. Jennifer had to pretend she was fine for two weeks, so that she could get discharged and stop the medication. The memory work was successful once the medication was out of her system.

Group treatment settings

I am very hesitant about group settings and group interventions for survivors of organized criminal abuse, whether on an outpatient, self-help, or residential basis. This is primarily because survivors who are currently involved with perpetrator groups are often trained to seek out other survivors to get them reinvolved. A client of mine who had been abused by a group two thousand miles away was taken back to a local group by a survivor she met in a group therapy setting. Even those survivors who do not reinvolve others often have alters trained to give signals that will cause deterioration in other survivors' functioning. Neil Brick, who organizes survivor conferences and is an activist devoted to combating ritual abuse and mind control, writes in his blog that he used to unintentionally give trained hand signals while giving speeches.

I had a friend who conducted a group for clients with dissociative disorders in the Mental Health Center where we both worked, and I was told later by one of my clients who participated that the cult conducted a similar group with a different purpose in the basement of the mental hospital. Imagine the confusion of those who attended both groups.

In hospital, there is a risk of programs being triggered by other patients. One ritual abuse survivor client was hospitalized years ago, before I saw her. For a long time she would not tell me what happened, but made me promise not to hospitalize her. Eventually, I discovered that another woman in the hospital had handed her a note which said "I'm sorry I have to kill you." She told me that although most of the staff had no idea about dissociation, some of the patients "looked inside" and could detect the presence of alters.

Two years ago, I was just beginning to treat a woman with a trauma history who seemed to be dissociative. She had disclosed to me one memory that appeared to be a possible indicator of ritual abuse. She developed some paranoid ideas with which she went to the police, who had her hospitalized. She called me from the hospital to tell me she had finally obtained funding to see me and was looking forward to it. She committed suicide immediately upon discharge from the hospital. There had been no indications of suicidality. I do not know, and will not know, whether she was given a very discouraging diagnosis by the hospital psychiatrist, or whether something happened at the hospital that triggered programming.

Residential and inpatient settings

In some communities, perpetrator groups actually want their survivors put into psychiatric day programs, or hospitalized.

There are several reasons for this. The most obvious one is that staffs of mental hospitals tend to be uninformed about organized abuse (not to mention even basic treatment for dissociative disorders); they will simply diagnose such patients with mental illnesses and medicate them or put them in group programs within the unit, where, as you have seen, other patients might trigger them to re-engage them with the groups from which they are trying to escape. And there is another, more insidious reason: many mental hospitals have members of the perpetrator groups on staff who are trained to recognize mind control or ritual abuse survivors.

When I was dealing with my first four ritual abuse survivors, all members of a local cult, Teresa had a close relative who was a ward clerk and gave staff false information about her condition. The cult had a regular pick-up system for survivors at the dinner hour. The survivors would go out to the front door for a smoke, and the cult van would appear, pick them up, take them to be tortured and for their training to be reinforced, then drop them off at the time they were supposed to be back indoors. Although the hospital did keep patients from committing suicide during their stay, it did not keep them safe, because it facilitated the group's access to them. Lorraine's "suicide" occurred immediately upon discharge from that hospital. On one occasion late in her therapy, Jennifer came to her appointment with her arms badly cut; she told me that she had not done it but the high priest had, in the hope of getting me to hospitalize her so they could access her.

I learned to avoid the psychiatric hospital for my clients who experienced current contact, especially after what happened with Lorraine. Even a safe psychiatric hospital, unless it specializes in treating dissociative disorders, is little more than a holding tank to prevent patients from committing suicide. In the days when our local hospital would permit outpatient therapists to meet with their clients in the hospital, I found it useful to see clients in the hospital to work through the programs that were creating the instability. Now, the hospital will not allow outpatient therapists to do therapy on their premises (because of their insurance). Such a hospitalization just delays effective treatment.

Most of the people who run mental hospitals are sincere professionals who really want to help people whom they believe suffer from a "mental illness". Ritual abuse-created dissociative disorders, being mental injury rather than mental illness, require different treatment on several levels: first, trauma recovery; second, dissociation; and third, mind control. Hospitals specializing in dissociative disorders, when not infiltrated by members of organized perpetrator groups, can be quite helpful to survivors of organized abuse. (The challenge for the clinician is determining which ones are safe.) However, the bulk of the work needs to be conducted by an outpatient therapist who understands the nature of the abuse.

Many survivors, when hospitalized, almost immediately switch into an alter who appears normal. Hospital staff, not understanding the nature of what they are witnessing, say that the medication they have administered is working, so the person can be released.

It is my fondest wish and hope that one day, the information contained in these pages will not only empower interested clinicians to better help their mind-controlled clients, but also that it will filter through the mental health care system so that when we need outside assistance for our clients, we will know it is available, knowledgeable, and safe.

CHAPTER TWELVE

"Maybe I made it up"

You may have had some difficulty accepting or emotionally integrating some of the stories and examples you have read in this book so far. This is something survivors who are disclosing memories of ritual abuse or mind control often struggle with as well. The old question of "Could this really have happened?" comes up all the time with these clients. Sometimes they ask plaintively whether or not we believe them. At other times they insist that none of it is true, they made it all up, they got it from television shows or the Internet, or they have a vivid imagination.

Some of the clients I have seen who allege ritual abuse and/or mind control do have vivid imaginations; some of them do not. Some of them like to read and research, others do not. Still others deliberately do not read or watch anything related to what they are remembering so that they do not contaminate their memories. In my preface to this book, I recommended that survivors not read it, because memories that come spontaneously from within them are more trustworthy than those that come prompted by hearing what someone else has experienced. Or at least the client will find them more trustworthy. One of my clients had flashbacks of ritual abuse, and her mother informed her that certain neighbors who used to look after her were the perpetrators. The client now doubts both whether she was ritually abused, and whether those were the real perpetrators, just because it was her mother who told her this. Outside influences can be very confusing for these clients.

Denial is commonly found among persons with dissociative disorders. My favorite quotation from such a client is, "We are not multiple, we made it all up." I have heard this from several different clients. When I hear it, I politely inquire, "And who is we?" The client looks confused—or we both begin to laugh. When a person has a dissociative disorder, many things that happened to them feel as if they happened to someone else. In addition, events that are remembered at one time might not be remembered at other times, which leads to even more confusion. Such people have been described as having "multiple reality disorder." Denial is common in the population of those with major dissociative disorders, whether or not they have experienced ritual abuse or mind control.

There are many reasons that a client might insist that what they are remembering cannot be real. One obvious reason is the bizarre and horrific nature of the memories they disclose. If I were seeing such things in my head, and did not know what I know now, certainly I would want to believe they were not real.

One of my clients has a group of little child parts inside who have horrible memories of abuse outside the family that began early in her life (via a babysitter). At the same time, another group of parts, who are adults and teenagers, have no conscious memories of this abuse. They tell me that they have been having awful nightmares of things that cannot be real. Some of their "nightmares", they say, are during the day.

The little ones told me about the "line" down the middle to separate those who lived inside the home from the ones who remember the early abuse outside the home. So, the older alters are unaware of the little ones and what happened to them. However, pictures and emotions leak through this dividing line and are interpreted by the older parts as signs that they must be either crazy or evil to invent such horrible things. By now, the reader has probably realized that the dividing line was deliberately placed there by the perpetrators.

Let us look more closely at how mind-controlled children are trained in denial and disbelief of their own memories and their own internal multiplicity by mind controlling abusers, who have studied the processes of remembering and forgetting, and how dissociation works.

Denial training

Training that makes survivors unaware of their dissociative conditions

In a memory that one client worked through, she was given a heavy dose of antipsychotic medication, which made communication within her personality system very difficult. The abusers then asked her whether she heard any voices, and gave her electroshock to the head every time she said yes. This was part of training to make her appear non-dissociative. When a psychiatrist put her on antipsychotic medication in adulthood, this memory came up, as it brought up the alters who remembered this training. Fortunately, she was in therapy that recognized her abuse history and could properly address it. You can imagine what would have happened if she were not.

The same client told me of a training to create walls between the alters. As an infant, she was put in a closed box, periodically taken out and abused or smothered, then "rescued" by being put back in the box with safety and a bottle of milk. An alter was told that if disclosures were ever being made, she was to bring up this training in order to isolate alters from one another in "boxes" in the inner world, so that the alter who was out in the body would be unable to communicate with the rest. The presenting part would be unaware of the existence of the others.

The last time one of my clients made statements that reflected denial, she sounded as if she were reciting. So I asked her whether anyone said this to her. "Yes, my mother." Her mother, who, according to the memories she allegedly "made up," was the primary perpetrator in her abuse.

Training which makes survivors disbelieve their own memories (and makes investigators disbelieve them)

Simulated murders

Organized abuser groups make particular efforts to have both their victims and those to whom they disclose dismiss what is said as having been made up. One of my first clients who disclosed ritual abuse went through a memory of being around five years old when the cult group made her stab, and supposedly kill, a baby, whom they said was her younger brother. The next day she found her baby brother alive, and when she expressed her confusion to her mother, she was told she made the whole thing up. Alters had been given the job of making her believe this message. This appears to be common for such abusers. I have heard about this same kind of experience from other clients and from other therapists.

In Chapter Eight, "The programming: indoctrination, lies, and tricks", you saw that trickery is a major modus operandi of these groups. One client of mine remembered a grade school classmate being killed in a ritual, while the teacher told the class that the girl had moved to the U.S. to live with her father. In adulthood, the woman made a police report, and the police searched for the girl. They found her alive, having moved to the U.S. to live with her father. One of my more recent clients believed she should not make friends because a friend from school had been killed in a ritual. As soon as she told me this, another alter who was listening told me that the girl had come to visit her old home in early adulthood and had looked her up. Yet another client told the police the name of a little girl she remembered killing in a sacrificial ritual. They looked the girl up and sure enough, she was still alive. As a consequence, they now disbelieved all the client's disclosures. The client said that she knew it was "Stephanie" that they killed because "They told [her]." She now believes she was forced to kill a little girl, but it probably was not Stephanie.

Victims are left in a deep state of confusion about what they had thought they had experienced. Remember that drugs are used during many of these traumatic trainings, and electroshock given at the conclusion to further dissociate the memories of what happened. It is no wonder it is very difficult for survivors of organized groups to be clear about, or tell anyone, what they remember.

These tricks serve another important purpose: insurance. They discredit the rest of survivors' disclosures. Sally McCollum (a licensed and highly experienced psychologist in private practice in the Sun Valley area of central Idaho), related this story in an email to a discussion list (reprinted by permission):

> One of my clients had a memory of assisting in the abduction of a young woman who she believed was murdered in a ritual and she wanted to give her evidence to the local FBI. Unfortunately, she discovered at the same time the FBI did (through a simple search) that the woman was alive in another part of the U.S. It damaged her credibility severely and was extremely frustrating for her..

I have heard similar stories from other therapists.

Murders of named persons appear to be simulated for the perpetrators' mind control purposes, to prevent these survivors making friends with "outsiders," to make them doubt their own memories, and to make investigators disbelieve their disclosures. When survivors begin to remember things that happened, programming often kicks in to make them remember these apparent murders of persons who were not actually killed. No wonder police investigators have doubts about the reality of ritual abuse.

Murders that are real

Some of what these children believe to be murders are real; some are not. "Murders" which are designed to discredit the survivors are simulated. But it is my observation that murders in which "traitors" are killed are most likely to be real, since they usually involve gruesome torture that is difficult to simulate. Usually, these occur at large events in which a whole generation of cult children are trained not to be traitors. Presumably, because it is risky for a group to engage in an actual murder, the abusers want to make the most use of such an act when it is done.

Besides the religious importance of ritual sacrifices in the cults, "snuff pornography" brings in big money. Victims of actual murders used to be abducted children, before law enforcement and the media became very concerned about them. Children used to have to abduct children, playing with them in the street or the park and luring them to the perpetrators' vehicle. Several clients have told me of doing this. Now the victims are more likely to be street people or hitchhikers far from home. One of my early survivor clients told me how the young adult cult members used to cruise along the highway picking up hitchhikers, talking with them in a friendly manner in order to pick out the ones who were far from home and could be used as sacrifices without local law enforcement finding out. Society's image of the abductor of women or children, based on what is portrayed in the media, is a lone man, but cult groups also abduct victims.

As described in Stella Katz's account, cult women and teenage girls are made pregnant and aborted as soon as the fetus is viable, so that it can be sacrificed. There is also considerable killing of children who have been bred for the sole purpose of being torture and, eventually, murder victims. These children's births were never registered, and they have been raised in secrecy.

It is not only the dispensable children of unimportant women who are killed. Licensed clinical social worker Wendy Hoffman, who worked extensively with ritual abuse survivors in the late 1980s and early 1990s, wrote an unpublished book, "Ascent from evil: Toward healing the wounds of Satanic cult abuse" (1993), and identifies herself as a survivor. According to Hoffman, the children of each woman who was selected to be her cult's newest "Queen" were killed immediately after birth when they did not respond well enough to tests regarding their ability to be programmed. Hoffman states that, in her experience, many people were killed, and the group just came up with other reasons for the deaths such as illness or suicide. And indeed, it is logical that if the murder of someone who moves from the area can be simulated, an actual murder can be disguised as a natural death or a suicide. That is what may have happened in Lorraine's case. If it was not a murder, it was certainly a forced suicide.

Hoffman also states that in her extensively networked group, leaders had to be killed ritually. While I have no way of corroborating this information, I did have one client who spent her childhood years from age three to twelve as the house slave of a cult leader; she was taken into foster care when he had himself killed in a ritual.

Cover memories

Organized perpetrator groups also deliberately create screen or "cover" memories of impossible or highly improbably events such as alien abductions. (Alien abductions are often cited by those who wish to discredit the reality of ritual abuse and mind control.) I remember when Jennifer confessed, halfway through her therapy, that for a long time she had had a memory of an alien abduction, the kind where the aliens poked and prodded at her body in the spaceship. She had been afraid to disclose it to me because she was afraid I would not believe her about the cult events if she did. When we worked through the memory from start to finish, with all the alters involved, we discovered that the alleged "spaceship" was parked in the cult training center. Certain alters had been taught that they must release this memory to consciousness if she began to remember other things.

False information

There are also more mundane, but equally effective, things done to confuse children in this way. When we worked through Jennifer's first ritual abuse memory, a gang rape, I asked her whether or not she knew the names of her abusers. Yes, she did: Mickey Mouse and Donald Duck. Imagine the outcome for a victimized child who reports such things in a police interview!

Training which discourages telling the truth

Another reason it is difficult for these survivors to disclose what has happened is the training they receive to believe that the group knows everything they disclose, and sometimes even everything they think. One common experience is that a young child undergoes a fake "operation" in which a "doctor" puts a "microphone" in her tooth and convinces her of these things, telling her that through this microphone the group will know when she has told about the abuse, and will find and punish her. "Bombs" are implanted in the child's stomach, and verified, with "X-Rays"; the victim is told that if she talks about the memories, the bomb will explode. A carnivorous animal or insect is supposedly put into the child's vagina or anus, after which s/he is told that remembering or talking will cause the animal to eat her up from the inside. These "operations" are done when the child is still young enough to believe that thoughts or words can trigger a result like this. Alters are taught to remind children about these experiences through bringing back the pain of the "surgery" or the animal's insertion.

Organized perpetrator groups also discourage disclosures by training alters to make survivors remember all the events—especially crimes—in which the child has been made to take part, such as the real or simulated murders and rapes that ritually abusive groups commonly perpetrate. Such flooding will overload the survivor with horror and guilt.

The groups will also stage events in which the child is punished for honest disclosures to people she does not realize are group members. For example, one five-year-old child was encouraged to make a disclosure to someone she believed was a uniformed police officer, who then took her to a "jail" where other perpetrators, adult men, were incarcerated with her. They blamed her, beat her, and sexually assaulted her for telling on them. When another child was triggered to tell some supposed police officers what happened, they responded that she was lying, and then tortured her to get the "truth" out of her. They were not satisfied until she really lied. She was also punished at home for telling the truth.

Incentives are also offered to survivors who recant. Lorraine found an article on her bed in the psychiatric hospital about a client who won huge amounts of money from suing her therapist. Another survivor received a letter offering a warm welcome back into her family as well as the rewards ensuing from such a lawsuit. A promise of warm acceptance and welcome into the family can be very enticing for the parts of the client who always wanted to be loved. Consider the implications of this when you hear of therapists being sued for their alleged misdeeds with such survivors.

Here is what survivor LisaBri says (adapted from an article on her website) about her experiences with "denial" which she describes as being a "two-faced animal":

Honesty and denial: LisaBri

As I put together my life history, my research has led me through almost forgotten sets of old journals. I have come across entries that scream "Honesty!" How could anyone possibly make up the secrets hidden in those diaries, or, more importantly, why would I want to? Yet the next line always begins with, "I'm making it all up because . . ."

In my childhood, honesty was always laced with threats. I grew up being told I was a liar with an overactive imagination. I had to lie all the time, not only about the sexual abuse in my home but through keeping silent about the horrendous events that happened in the cult rituals. Programmed with the "No-talk" rule, alter was played against alter, and the words of the training were constantly spun: "You're crazy. Only crazy people make up stories like this; they should be in a psychiatric ward. Don't talk or you'll be locked up."

To this day I remember seeing a dog lying dead in the garage of the second house we lived in. It was my Aunt and Uncle's dog, a small white poodle. I ran to tell my mother that the dog was dead in the garage. My mother calmly said it wasn't. Her words left me scared and confused. *I could see the dog, and it was dead.* The piece of information I did not have was from another alter, an eleven-year-old who had participated in a ritual the night before. As they killed the dog, all the members of the circle chanted, "This is not real. This is all in your imagination. This is not real. This is all in your imagination . . ." When the eleven-year-old [alter] insisted that it was real, they beat her into submission and drugged her. The message: 'It is unsafe to see things through your own eyes because you are crazy. Listen to your mother.' So we denied our reality and lived knowing the dog was dead but believing it was not.

It is not sensationalism; it is a reality. If I even think about the enormity and reality of the truth, the rapes, the pit, the rituals, then a denial program runs: "This didn't happen to you. You are making it all up. No one will believe you." It leaves me terrified and confused as I lock horns with it at every memory level, at every alter level, and at every step forward.

Fifteen years ago, as an adult survivor, I carried the lies in my scattered dissociative brain. I was always vigilant, for I did not want to break into what I labeled "little Lisa pieces," which would inevitably be followed by being locked up in a psychiatric ward. However, the fight to continue became too much, and I lost the will to live. I was locked up in the hospital. But not only did I survive, but I found it was the one place where I could be completely honest about my past. I could say anything because I knew my time was coming to an end. All my business and what little personal affairs I had had been put in order. I was ready to be a psychiatric hospital "lifer" and eventually to die in that place. The doctors and nurses would not question another shuffling, mumbling person talking about things too heinous to be believed. I was just another statistic.

Lying in bed in hospital one night, I thought I was dying. With no energy left to fight, I gave in to the voices for the first time. I discovered that they were not psychotic voices, but voices of alter personalities. My strongest alter, Brian (Bri) came to me that night and in six words changed my life. "It's going to be all right," he said. And I had to believe him. And it was. I discovered that the "little Lisa pieces" were alters fighting to be heard and recognized—not a sign of mental illness or incapacity, as I had always been led to believe, but a sign of strength, courage, and health.

On one level, denial is as devastating and crippling as lying. Did my father, for instance, really believe he loved me in the only way he knew? Or had he, like me, been trained in denial? Did his denial lead him to think sexually assaulting his daughter really was "no big deal"? Did he even remember his further abuses of me?

Denial is a two-faced animal. On one level denial keeps me safe. While the denial program is running, 90% of the time I do not believe there is a cult group in which I had to be an active participant, and which I would be exposing by remembering. The memories, trainings, and rituals do not exist, in denial. My system shuts down. There are no crippling sexual assaults. The need to harm myself, attempt suicide, drink, or use drugs to deal with the associated feelings stays on the periphery of my mind.

The constant back and forth movement between truth and denial wreaks havoc on my mind, leading to anxiety and panic attacks. But if I can ride out the storm, I can recognize that I survived. My therapist constantly tells me, "Keep the denial for when you are not in therapy. When you enter this room, the alters make you deny your reality need to turn it off so we can get to the issues." This has allowed me to grow, and to be open and honest, in a small office for an hour and a half each week.

The truth really does set you free. And denial is there for when you need a break.

Notice that LisaBri finds her denial helpful outside of therapy sessions. We therapists need to recognize that denial and dissociation can sometimes be helpful with these clients, as long as it is dropped during the therapy itself. It can prevent flooding and allow them to live a relatively normal life.

Trainings to make disclosing survivors appear psychotic

Another way that these abuser groups discredit the disclosures of survivors and make them deny their own reality is programming to make survivors appear psychotic. When a person appears psychotic, it can result in them being hospitalized, which can lead to a lot of other serious problems for this population. In Chapter Eleven, "'Stabilization' takes on a new meaning",

I discussed the way in which these groups cause flashback hallucinations, flooding of emotions, rapid switching, scrambling of sensory information, and self-harm and suicide attempts. Following are some other memories that survivors have disclosed to me, which made the person appear psychotic. These trainings are difficult to recognize as internal punishments.

Insomnia

A child is stuck in a cage or tied to a stake for days, and if she falls asleep she is painfully prodded awake with a stick. Another alter is trained to reactivate this memory, and the triggered adult is totally unable to sleep.

Psychosomatic pain

An injection is given that makes the child hurt all over, and, while she is in this condition, she is raped with a hot object. A different alter is trained to administer the pain from this memory to the presenting person at the correct cue.

Emotional flooding

A child is put through a series of experiences (mostly very unpleasant) that produce a lot of strong emotions. Several different emotions can be used to produce "crazy" emotional lability, or one particular emotion, such as sadness or anger, might be the focus. Cues are given to alters to release these emotions and have the spinner alters spin them out to the rest of the personality system. This kind of training is involved in the "booby traps" of intense sadness and suicidality that the survivor encounters when she is getting close to protected memories of core training. A lesser version of this might come up as soon as the client makes disclosures about the abuse.

Flashbacks and hallucinations

During a horrifying abuse session, the child is told that if she talks she will see or hear or experience this painful event all over again as if it were currently happening. Separate triggers are taught for visual or auditory hallucinations. So the survivor could hear the voices of the abusers, or the sound of the electroshock machine. S/he might see a perpetrator in the therapy office, in a very frightening and "real" way, and be very confused about why you, the therapist, do not see him. ("He's right over there!")

There are less shocking versions of this, with different purposes. In the early stages of therapy with one ritually abused client, she kept staring at my hands. I asked what she saw on them. Lines. (There were no lines.) I asked whether someone inside was making the lines appear. Yes, a little boy. I asked whether he knew how to turn the lines off? Yes. He demonstrated turning the lines on and off, at my request, while some of the other alters watched. He was just doing his job to make the rest of the personality system believe I was one of the perpetrator group. He was proud of his ability.

Internal world disasters

Most mind-controlled children have an inner world and/or structure or structures created by building models with Lego or some such toy (see Chapter Six, "Markers of mind control and ritual abuse", and also Stella Katz's account in Chapter Seven). The alters "live" in that world, and there is training for the destruction and damage of the inner world. An earthquake is simulated by shaking up the model world so it breaks apart while the child is simultaneously being shaken. A tidal wave is simulated by flooding the model world while almost drowning the child. Similar simulations are done for fires and tornadoes. When certain triggers are given, the internal world is destroyed and alters are "killed" internally. (You can revive "dead" alters through such things as an imaginary healing stream. Remember, alters do not really die.)

Rapid switching and scrambling

For rapid switching programs, the child is spun around, and alters are called out by a special shoulder touch (along with their names being spoken) so fast that they go in as soon as they are out. The effect is inability to complete a thought or sentence, which looks like the schizo-phrenic "word salad". A variation is "Fast switch child alters", which allows only very young alters to come out but not stay out long. You can imagine the diagnosis and the treatment that would result if this were triggered in adulthood. For scrambling, the child is put through a very confusing treatment, such as this: People walk fast in all directions, pushing the child, talking very fast, and stepping on her. She is given a drug that loosens her tongue, and has to say everything that comes into her head, while people continue to talk too fast to be understood, push and throw her around, and poke her. While still talking, they put insects and spikes in and out of her ears so that she only hears part of what is said. At the same time, touch sensations are also scrambled by doing opposite touches, such as tickling and hitting. Triggering of the feelings from this memory results in the person talking continuously in a "stream of consciousness" style, and not understanding what is said to her. As with the rapid switching, this makes the person appear psychotic—and likely to be hospitalized.

Delusions

Dissociative disorders, even those created by mind controllers, are not psychosis, but this program will create the most common symptom used to diagnose schizophrenia. The child is hurt while on a turntable, with people and television sets and cartoons and photographs all around the turntable. New alters created by the torture are instructed that they must obey their instructions and become the people around them, people on television, or other alters when they are told to. When this program is triggered, the survivor will hear "voices" of the people whom the "copy alters" are imitating, or will have many confused alters popping out who think they are actually other people or movie stars. The identities of the copy alters change when the survivor's surrounding change.

Training to behave like an animal

Brain operations are simulated to apparently insert the brain of an actual animal (e.g., wolf for ferocity, dog for obedience, small rodent for stupidity or biting), and the child is trained by behavioral methods to behave as this animal does. As you have seen, it is common for survivors to have alters who believe themselves to be animals. When this behavior appears in an adult, however, she will seem genuinely crazy. Stella Katz described other methods of creating animal alters in Chapter Seven.

Remember that making a survivor appear psychotic not only discredits any disclosures she makes, it is also likely to get her into the psychiatric hospital, where there are often patients or staff members who are trained to find organized abuse survivors and get them back into control of the perpetrator groups.

Validation

Many survivors feel they would believe their own memories if they only had some external validation. Most of the time this is hard to come by. Sometimes, as with the first four of my ritually abused clients, there is cross-corroboration by other survivors or family members who were actually present during the abuse. The similarity of survivors' experiences in different locations is well documented. The Extreme Abuse Survey asked questions about quite a number of different experiences, and found large percentages of those reporting extreme abuse had similar experiences.

Some of the survivors who have the worst time being believed are those whose experiences involved government-generated technologies. Here are some examples of the validation that mind-control survivor Carol Rutz, whom you met in Chapter Two, obtained through her Freedom of Information Act submission in the United States. (Rutz is an author of the Extreme Abuse Survey as well as of a book on her experiences.) The material in this article, which she wrote for this book, is expanded in a speech she gave at the SMART conference in 2001.

Validating my mind control memories: Carol Rutz

Many of the cult ceremonies took place at our local zoo. When I began to draw and talk about them, my doctor turned ashen. It was one of three times in eleven years that he said, "I've heard that before from someone else about that place." Wow! Talk about validation. When I went to the archives of the public library to find material on the zoo for two particular years, it was missing. Everything was there but the information for those two years. I was disappointed but not surprised. In April of 1993, after two years of retrieving SRA memories, I was able to go back to the zoo accompanied by my husband and walk through the places where these rituals had occurred. When I left, it was a victory.

During mind control experiments, before the procedures depicted below took place, I experienced sensory deprivation after being given a shot of curare. The drawing (Figure 1) and the picture (see Figure 2) illustrate how a mind retains information even after enduring extreme trauma.

Figure 1 shows an experiment designed to map specific parts of my brain. I am being spoken to through the earphones, and different personas that the CIA created for its MKULTRA Program are being identified by areas of the brain.

This drawing also shows how each alter was being programmed. Detectable energy flashes were being picked up, and a recording was made that assured the doctors that they were working with

Figure 1.   Illustration by Carol Rutz of an experiment to map parts of her brain.

different parts of my personality, separate and apart from the me that they would eventually reawaken. Years later, I was able to find a photo of the PET machine that was the actual technology used (Figure 2).

During the 1980s, a remote viewing project called Stargate was done at Fort Meade. It used binaural beat tones, transmitted through earphones, that altered brain waves. A hemi-sync device that played two different frequencies into each ear was found to produce altered states of consciousness. Perhaps this technology was derived from these experiments done in the 1960s on MKULTRA subjects.

During my recovery process, I also did a drawing of a procedure that was performed on me, I believe, by a doctor in Montreal, Canada. He inserted electrodes into sleeve guides and probed my brain, while someone in the room recorded what was being said. He said my brain was like a tape recorder and he just needed to take me back in time. He did this by touching different spots in my brain. The men kept recording the memories induced from images in my past. Later, a man from the CIA would use them for programming sessions. Figure 3 is the picture I drew of this procedure.

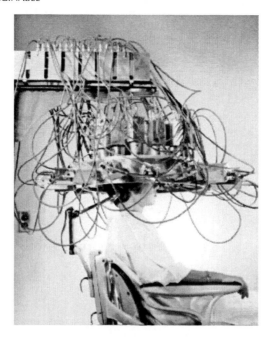

Figure 2. This picture is a Positron emitter detector (circa 1962) from Department of Energy Openness: Human Radiation Experiments: Multimedia/Brookhaven Nation Laboratory.

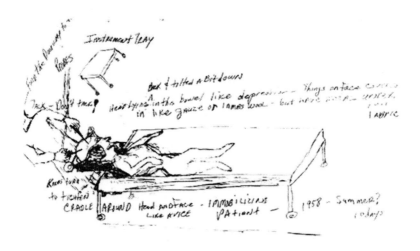

Figure 3. Illustration by Carol Rutz of procedure involving a stereotaxic instrument.

I did not know that this was a known procedure, and what it was called, until I came upon a diagram of it in a book (Scheflin & Opton, 1978, p. 268). It is called stereotaxic surgery. In it, an instrument is attached to the head, skin and muscle retracted, and a "bone button" removed to permit the insertion of an electrode into the depths of the brain.

We know now that during the 1960s and 1970s, the Soviets found that by passing a low voltage current from the front of the brain to the back, they could drop their remote viewers into the Delta

State. Using this artificial means, they found Delta waves to be the brain's doorway to telepathic influencing, telekinesis, and remote killing.

That might account for the remark I recall the doctor making, "Given enough time and enough bodies, I can find the doorway to the soul."

Validation is what we all search for, isn't it—how can I know this is real? How can I prove this really happened? My alters found that painting and drawing were perfect expressions for getting scenes recorded—people's faces, places, buildings, ceremonies. I never knew what was going to be painted or drawn; I just gave my alters free rein. Years later I was able to match real people and places with my artwork. The validation was overwhelmingly powerful and helped me to understand what truly happened to me.

*   *   *

Of course, we do not know that the stereotaxic instrument really did what Rutz's captors told her it did. What they said might have been a deception. We do, however, know that she found validation of the experience her alters remembered.

Technological monitoring

You will notice the amount of technology used in Rutz's mind control training. The military and political groups who do this continue to become more and more sophisticated in their use of technology. Some survivors have found small metallic "implants" in their teeth or ears, and believe these were designed to monitor their location or to broadcast their words or thoughts to the abusers. Such technology has been developed recently for keeping track of animals or persons with dementia. But to what extent it was used years ago by mind controllers is unknown at this point. At least some of it may be similar to the "bombs" in the stomach, a trick to convince survivors that their abusers monitor them continuously. The presence of an object does not mean it is capable of collecting complex information and sending it back to abusers, or even sending them signals, for twenty or more years, as some survivors believe. As with other apparently bizarre beliefs of our survivor clients, we must acknowledge that something happened, and remain open both to the possibility that there was such technology and the possibility that it is yet another deception to convince survivors they cannot escape the grip of their abusers.

One of the most frightening aspects of this alleged technology is the possibility of mind control by "remote control," that is, through such technology as microwaves and radio waves. There are many stories about this, coming primarily from survivors, although we do know from a variety of reliable websites and mainstream news that such technology is being developed, or at least that the technological groundwork has been laid. Once again, however, we do not know whether this was in place when today's survivors were programmed. It is difficult at this point to determine how much of this is genuine, and how much comes from false beliefs deliberately induced to make survivors feel powerless, much like the "one huge and invincible cult" of whose existence survivors convinced therapists twenty years ago. I know that one of my mind control survivor clients was convinced of technological monitoring during a psychotic period several years ago, but as he healed he discarded such beliefs, along with many other bizarre ones in favor of recognizing that he had been abused by real human beings whose identity he knew.

If some of this remote control it is genuine, we may need to develop technological means to combat it.

However, we should not be intimidated. Even if "voices" are induced in the head by remote control rather than through alters doing jobs, survivors can learn to disobey such voices just as they do those of alters. Competent and compassionate therapy for the dissociation can help survivors to heal. Meanwhile, there are numerous survivors whose mind control is of the kind that can be treated through psychotherapy.

Neutrality vs. reflective belief

When a client who reports ritual abuse or mind control asks, "Do you believe me?", therapists often feel caught between two unacceptable options. We have been advised by many professionals to take an attitude of strict neutrality regarding the veracity of clients' allegations and supposed memories. Some claim it is unethical to do otherwise. Yet we know from our clinical experience that neutrality can be interpreted by a client as disbelief and can harm the therapeutic relationship. These clients already have considerable difficulty trusting a therapist, and because they have undergone many of the experiences described above they struggle with what they need to tell us. It feels as if we're "damned if we do say we believe" (encouraging the client in inventing things, inviting a lawsuit), and "damned if we say we don't believe" (invalidating the client).

So, in the early stages of therapy with such clients, here is what I suggest therapists say: "I'm a psychologist (you can say counsellor, social worker, doctor), and it's my job to deal with whatever's in your head. It's your job to figure out what's real, what's unreal, and what may be a result of abusers' tricks. You can only figure that out successfully when you've found out everything that's in your head." Reassure your clients that they can talk about whatever they need to talk about, regardless of whether or not at this moment they believe their memories or the images in their head to represent real experiences. That gets them "off the hook" of having to tell "the truth" which their abusers wanted them to tell.

Here is how Carrie Swart, of Intensive Trauma Therapy, Inc., addresses this issue (from an email posted to an online forum called the Dissociative Disorders Discussion List, reprinted with the author's permission): First, she says, it is "[t]he narrative truth that each individual brings to the table at a given time, [that] is of the utmost importance." The literal facts are not the issue, but the person's perception, experience and response:

> So many traumatized and abused individuals, both RA/MC and not, go through life not being heard and not being believed. I have seen many clients who, especially as children, have tried to tell someone about their abuse but were told 'That couldn't have happened' or 'Uncle Henry would never do that to you,' etc. . . . in some cases, not being believed by the adult 'caregivers' in one's life can end up being just as, if not more, traumatizing than the abuse itself.

When clients question the validity of their memories, she says, she informs them she cannot

answer that question for them . . . regardless of whether or not something occurred in reality, or is simply a product of one's brain, it is still disturbing to the individual. If their perception of an event, image, memory, dream, whatever, is disturbing to them in the here and now and causing symptoms of trauma/dissociation, then it needs to be processed. Our clients need to be heard and validated. We need to work with the information provided by a client, rather than focusing on whether or not we believe what he or she is telling us. The important thing for us as clinicians, is to believe that feelings are always valid and that each and every client we see deserves to live free of symptoms and free of pain.

I would add that the historical truth is often embedded within the narrative truth, and can be discovered by the client once the narrative truth has been faced in all the aspects available to all the dissociated parts of the client. When my client believed she had killed a living baby, an "observer" alter told her that the baby was already dead and its cries were made by a tape recorder hidden under the table. When the client who had undergone the "alien abduction" saw that the spaceship was within the cult training center, it cast doubt on the perpetrators being aliens. Tricks and lies can be unmasked, but only through the client looking, together with a supportive witness, at what she remembers, and then drawing her own conclusions when she has all the available evidence.

Van der Hart and Nijenhuis (1999) wrote a wonderful article on this topic. Here is their abstract:

Clinicians should not reflexively accept or reject as fact a client's report of uncorroborated abuse. However, by maintaining a neutral stance, clinicians may fall short of therapeutic honesty and transparency, may fail to promote reality testing, and may not perform the necessary step of bearing witness to the client's victimization. Using a case of dissociative identity disorder, this article proposes the careful development and sharing of the clinician's reflective belief in the (in)validity of reported trauma. This process may assist clients in (a) reclaiming a sense of integrated personal narrative memory and identity, (b) correcting cognitive distortions, or (c) both. [p. 37]

There could come a time when we might come to reflective, rather than reflexive, belief. When everything seems to fit together—the client's symptoms, their stories of what happened, their body sensations and emotions, and any external corroboration—over time we can come to reflective belief that some of these experiences happened, although in many cases the experiences were not what the child believed they were. *But there is a difference between believing that bad experiences happened, and believing what the child was led to believe.* For example, a woman recently disclosed to me a memory in which a group of her male alters were anally raped by a group of priests, who told them that this was a special honor and a spiritual experience which was only given to boys. It is not necessary to believe that they were boys or that it was a spiritual honor in order to think that the client's memory could be valid. Similarly, when I meet an alter personality who informs me that he or she is not part of the body and would not die if they killed the body, I acknowledge that they had some experience which led them to believe that, but I do not accept their belief at face value; I search for what was done to make them come to this conclusion, and I attempt to unmask the trick.

Some professionals take the position that the truth or untruth of a memory does not matter. They suggest that therapists need not pursue an exploration of what really happened in trauma survivors' lives. I do not endorse this position. In practical terms, for this population, it would allow programming to endure, uncorrected. Psychologist Ellen Lacter, in an email to the online Dissociative Disorders Discussion Forum (reprinted by permission), speaks about the internal conflicts survivors go through in sharing their experiences, the most human response a therapist can give, and why it is damaging to merely take a neutral position.

> Most survivors are their own greatest critics when it comes to doubting their memories. They have been programmed to distrust them. They hate and fear them and want them to be untrue. They have been invalidated by others their whole lives. To be healing, we must be deeply honest. If an account seems contrived, fear-driven, impossible, etc., we can say "It does not ring true to me." And when reality is very unclear, we may say "Let's see what happens as this unfolds." But when clients overcome tremendous trepidation, and finally share an account of unspeakable horrors, with vivid multisensory details, and matching somatic flashbacks, and matching affect of fear, disgust, rage, and grief, pieces of other memories match, and they both wish it was not true, and long to be believed, and they say "Could this be real?", or "Do you think I am making this up?", we must speak the truth from our heart, and say "It all seems to fit," or "It rings true to me." To say "What matters is what is your truth" is a lie. It is nonempathic. It is dissociogenic. And it leaves them alone in the ritual or laboratory.

When I read accounts of clients with allegedly factitious DID, many of those accounts remind me of Teresa, one of my first four. I know that I went through a process of increasing disbelief with her, as the abuse she disclosed broadened from verbally abusive alcoholic parents, to sexual abuse by father, to sexual abuse by relatives, to the "boogie man" who came in through the window at night (probably someone who paid her parents for this privilege), to sexual assaults by strangers (who turned out not to be strangers to some of her alters). Couple that with the overwhelming positive transference which caused her to almost stalk me, as well as her tendency to confabulate when she did not remember what happened, and it was very tempting to dismiss her allegations as unfounded. I am grateful that I did not. Until I listened to her and to the others who were being abused by the same perpetrators, Teresa was alone in the psychiatric system, wearing a pejorative label ("Borderline Personality Disorder"), without help.

We need to be careful about labeling clients' disclosures factitious, no matter how far-fetched they appear to be. Some of the things these perpetrator groups do are indeed far-fetched, but they are real, even if they include simulations of impossible events. More important than telling the client we believe everything s/he tells us is letting him or her know we are open to his or her sharing whatever experiences s/he needs to share. Our clients need to know we are open to hearing about multiple perpetrators, deliberate creation of alters, torture of infants and children, years of deliberate planned abuse, sexual perversions, murders, cannibalism, and children forced to perpetrate. They watch us carefully to learn whether or not we can handle it, and whether or not they can trust us with that information. Let us not fail them.

In the following chapter, we will further examine the relationship between therapists and the clients who come to them to heal the unimaginable.

CHAPTER THIRTEEN

Boundaries and bonds: the therapeutic relationship

The research evidence has not changed in the past fifty years: the factor that matters most in successful psychotherapy is the bond between the client and the therapist. Patterson (2000) states that

> Considering the obstacles to research on the relationship between therapist variables and therapy outcomes, the magnitude of the evidence is nothing short of amazing. There are few things in the field of psychology for which the evidence is so strong. The evidence for the necessity, if not the sufficiency, of the therapist conditions of accurate empathy, respect, or warmth, and therapeutic genuineness is incontrovertible . . . The effectiveness of all methods of counseling or psychotherapy may be due to the presence of a therapeutic relationship. [p. 441]

And that is one reason the mind controllers work so hard to destroy it.

How mind controllers prevent the therapeutic bond

Mind controllers know the importance of the relationship with the therapist. They know that the most likely time a survivor will disclose the secrets of their abuse is within a secure bond with a therapist or a loved one. So they go to extra trouble to make sure that such a bond never happens in the first place, or, if it does happen, that it will be disrupted and broken.

Deliberate neglect and breaking of infant bonds

Licensed Clinical Social Worker and survivor Wendy Hoffman, in her unpublished manuscript (1993), states:

The cult knew about attachment disorder before it became a diagnosis. Their goal is to separate the fetus from the pregnant mother emotionally. They give the mother electric shocks in various parts of her body and she has to leave the fetus emotionally. If she does during these frequent torture sessions, the fetus is then born programmable because it will have attachment issues. The reason they test the fetus when born is to see if the mother separated from the fetus. The mother knows if she doesn't, the fetus will be killed. They test by giving the fetus pain and observing whether the fetus will accept comfort. If it will, then the fetus is not programmable, and may be killed.

Take a look at what Stella Katz wrote in Chapter Seven about the initial experiences of ritually abused infants. They are deliberately neglected and abandoned, and the bond with the mother is deliberately broken. One ritually abused client of mine had an alter who believed himself to be a rock. This resulted from being left alone all night out in the forest at the age of two, in the Canadian cold season.

Couple with this severe neglect and bond breaking the fact that, in most cases, the parents are actively involved in the abuse, and you have a recipe for severe distrust of anyone who appears to care. One client of mine was violently sexually abused by family members while they called out alters' names and said, "This is how we show you that we love you. This is what love means." Some of my ritually abused or mind-controlled clients have had parents with dissociative disorders. One part of the parent cared about the child and was even overprotective, while another part was involved in severe abuse. As one of my clients cried out recently while processing a memory of torture, "That's my dad but it isn't my dad, somebody else is inside him." In other cases, the parents have been consistently frightening and punitive as well as neglectful.

This kind of upbringing teaches a child that she cannot trust people to comfort her or to pay attention to her needs. It produces a disorganized attachment, even without all the pain and torture that these groups administer to children.

Training not to form bonds or trust anyone

Among their abuses designed to contaminate bonding, ritual abuse and mind control survivors have endured deliberate training experiences in which they have been taught not to trust anyone. For example, after a girl had told her teacher that her daddy hit her, her teacher and school counselor were impersonated by cult members, who abused her, and she was told that you cannot trust anyone you tell because they will turn out to be perpetrators and will abuse you.

Children in ritualistic cults are given animals to pet and love, and then the animals are killed, often with the child either being blamed or being forced to hold the weapon which kills it. Trish Fotheringham (Chapter Six) tells of having to choose between killing her pet rabbit or having the abusers kill her baby brother.

Perhaps the worst experience is when a child is forced to stab and believe she has killed a person she has been allowed to get close to. Children in Satanic or Luciferian cults are often paired with a "disposable" (unregistered or kidnapped) child, given a chance to make friends with that child, and then are forced to participate in that child's murder.

Stella Katz has shared this story, as an acknowledgment of what she was forced to do as a young girl, and a tribute to the (other) victim. She states that Miranda was a disposable child bred within her group, and was used to train Stella in the "art" of sacrifice, by being the sacrifice.

For Miranda: Stella Katz

This is for you Miranda, and for all the other Mirandas who came before you and who have come after you. May your souls be forever at peace.

Miranda was four years old when she died on an altar of Satan, at the hand of her five-year-old friend.

The only difference between Miranda and the other little girl was the family to which she was born. The five-year-old was fortunate, or not so fortunate, depending on the way you look at it, to be born to a family of the inner circle. She was destined to be great and was groomed to be so, and Miranda's death was part of this hideous grooming. Miranda was born to the lower circle. From the moment of her conception she was fated to die. She was probably conceived during an orgy, paternity unknown. Her birth would have been at home, or in the home of another coven member. She would never have seen a doctor unless he was of the coven, or anyone for that matter outside the group. She never went to nursery school, or the zoo, or any public place. No outside human being would have known of her existence.

From the moment of her birth she was neglected and abused, physically, emotionally, sexually, and spiritually. She was given only the bare necessities of survival. She was never allowed to associate with other little children or have any kind of friends. About six months before her death, she was, for the first time, allowed to have a little friend. The bond created between these children was unbreakable.

For those six months the friendship was encouraged in every way, and it flourished, neither child knowing what was to come. When someone is starving to death, and food is offered, they don't often stop to ask the cost. When children are deprived of love, any affection is welcomed. When that child suddenly has someone, the bond that is created is an everlasting thing.

For Miranda and her little friend, the bond that was created was nothing more than a deliberate cruel joke. The children were told that something special is coming, and that they are to be a part of it. They got excited as children do; talking and whispering and giggling about what it might be. As the day approached, they were primed and pumped and hyped up, just like children anticipating a special gift from Santa.

On that special day, they were bathed in sweet smelling soaps, and covered in sacred oils. Their hair was neatly curled and groomed and their bodies were painted with sacred symbols.

For those six months, they had been inseparable. And now they were to join in a big celebration at which they would be the honored guests. They were dressed in ceremonial garb. The little friend in white satin, and Miranda in a beautiful red chiffon dress, all soft and flowing. She looked like a princess and felt, for the first time in her little life, like someone special. Her blonde hair fell in ringlets flowing gently over her shoulders and down her back. Hand in hand, Miranda and her friend were led into the center circle by the High Priestess. The bell rang nine times, and chanting began. The High Priest began the offerings, and then after what seemed like forever, he picked up Miranda and carefully placed her on the altar. Her hands and feet were bound, and as the fear welled up inside her, she began to cry. The priest then picked up her little friend and held her as she knelt beside Miranda. When Miranda saw her friend she immediately quieted and smiled. The priest picked up the sacred athame and placed it into the hand of the little friend.

Holding her hand in his, he raised her hand, and with one swift thrust, pierced Miranda's heart. Miranda looked up at her little friend and smiled through her pain and tears, and said "You was my friend" and died.

The little friend was left kneeling on the altar at Miranda's side holding the knife with the blood of her friend dripping off the end of it. Knowing that she had just killed her best friend. The High Priest picked her up again, and raised her to the crowd, and said, "You are forever ours." They cheered. She was passed around the circle and praised. The shock of what had happened was so great she couldn't even cry.

Well, Miranda, thirty odd years later, your friend is finally crying and can't seem to stop. There are too many Mirandas. There are TOO many children that society doesn't know about, or care to know about. They turn their heads away and pretend that this stuff just doesn't happen. And worst of all, some are claiming that our memories of Miranda and kids like her are false.

Well, Miranda, I know that you existed. I know that my memories are very real and so were you. I promise to you here and now that as long as I am alive, the world will know that you and others like you are not figments of our overactive imaginations. And Miranda, I swear to you that the voice I silenced so long ago, your voice, my friend, will scream through mine, until somebody finally hears, and puts an end to the slaughter of all the little Mirandas.

No one on this earth will ever tell me that you never existed. Be at peace, my little friend.

* * *

Stella's tale of her little friend not only shows the horror of forced perpetration, but exposes the horror of the brief lives of unregistered children, born into cults and kept for a few years solely for the purpose of sacrifice.

My most personally traumatic experience in all the years of working with ritual abuse survivors happened when I discovered that one of my clients had an unregistered child. The client's reporter alter told the group that I had found out, and she was forced to kill the child before anyone could locate it. I had to work through this very recent memory with her.

What does it do to a child to have such experiences? Love is connected with death, and with the child experiencing herself as a murderer. How can such a person develop an attachment bond?

Most of the memories that can cause the overwhelming kind of guilt and depression used in the mind controllers' "booby traps" (to create suicide attempts) are the death of a loved one such as a brother, sister or friend, or the death of a pet, especially by their own hand. Other causes are memories of abandonment, being told they are unlovable, even by God—"no one wants you, you are worthless, no one can save you". The rescuing angel at the end of the Kabbalah pathways is the angel of death, who promises to stop this pain through being the only one who loves the child.

In Chapter Eight, I mentioned the experience of an adult client who, as a little girl, came to trust a friendly caring neighbor; the neighbor woman was impersonated and the child, drugged, forced to stab and "kill" her. Then the "dead" person violently abused the child, and the cult leaders told her that if she got close to anyone she would be forced to kill them and then they would become evil like this woman did. This client had an alter whose job was specifically to "unplug" her from any relationships in which she might get to trust someone. It took her several years before the young alters could begin to trust me.

Training not to trust therapists

There is also specific training of child alters to distrust therapists. One scenario I have encountered several times has the child lying on the couch of a cult-involved therapist, who says she must look at him. When she does, he is wearing a devil mask and horns, and he rapes her, telling her that all therapists are servants of Satan. Child alters are taught not to look at "therapists" until they are told to. Experiences such as this one reinforce this training. It sets the scene for actual therapists to be impersonated later in the person's life.

Often, child alters are trained to listen for certain words in what people say, and if they hear these words they know that the person is dangerous and not to be trusted. With one of my survivor clients I have to try not to use the words *feel*, *touch*, or *think*, among others. All those words were used in combination with torture. When the client with the reaction to those words recently attended an adjudication regarding Criminal Injuries compensation, the adjudicator asked her several times, "How do you feel?", the exact words which were said by her abusers after administering pain. Needless to say, she was upset, and an alter blurted out "Don't use the F word!" I had to explain what she meant to the shocked adjudicator, who stated that she would *never* use the F word. Another client cannot hear the word "safe," as to her this means the reverse. Several times I have heard a client say "They told me about people like you, they told me you would say that."

Mind controllers also train child alters to seduce therapists. A client of mine disclosed a memory in which she cried in the office of someone she was told was a therapist, and then in comforting her he sexually abused her in such a way that her body responded. Afterwards, he accused her of tricking him into it. When she got home, her mother said she did well, and taught her how to do it better. I found it quite sad when this client posed provocatively, trying to seduce me, saying in a childlike voice that it was "the best offer I'd ever get."

It is hard to build a relationship with someone who has parts who believe either that you will sexually abuse them or that they will harm you or be forced to kill you. Parts who are trained to kill in cults are generally told that they are evil and that their dark energy will harm anyone they get close to—or that the cult members will come and kill those people.

Impersonation of therapists

The training not to look at therapists sets the stage for members of the perpetrating group (sometimes called "cult clones") to impersonate the survivor's actual therapists when she seeks treatment and begins to disclose the abuse. Members of the abusive group study the therapist by attending his or her lectures, becoming clients briefly, or sending a client in with a device to tape the sessions. They find a way to get into the therapist's office, or use another space that is similar to the office. Then they call the client to meet them, or abduct her, and they use an individual who has some physical resemblance to the therapist to impersonate him or her, wearing similar clothing and scented products and imitating the therapist's speech patterns while the client is drugged and unable to see clearly.

Katz, discussing the impersonation of therapists as part of current contact, writes,

> When a client is disclosing secrets to a therapist, and the group finds out about it, the therapist is impersonated to make the client distrust them. In the old days, therapists would be impersonated by actors, in a setting that closely resembled the therapist's office. The actor would be dressed in similar clothing and would impersonate the voice of the therapist as much as possible. The person would be picked up and drugged and brought to the so-called office. A therapy session would begin as it usually did, then the therapist would begin to doubt what the person was saying. They would then tell them that they were lying and that what they were saying was just figments of their imagination. If the person protested, they would strap them to the chair or couch, and physically abuse them, or rape them using electric probes that burned or shocked. This would break any trust the client had with the therapist. At the end of the session the person may be told it was just a dream. However when the person tries to go to the therapist's office, they find it impossible to trust, or spend the session testing the therapist. This is done over and over again, until the person stops going altogether.
>
> Today it is done using virtual reality glasses, which is more efficient. With the use of computers and virtual reality glasses, as well as good old drugs, it has made it very easy for the groups to reproduce a therapist that the person trusts, and make them into a therapist that hurts. At one time they needed "look alike" actors, and a good construction crew, and money. Now they simply need to videotape the therapist's office through a window, as well as the therapist, and they can reproduce them any time they need to, with very little expense. A simple recording of the therapist's voice, usually taken from answering machine messages, with the help of a computer, can reproduce every little intonation the therapist may have in his or her voice. If anything specific is needed, a client is planted for a few sessions with a hidden tape recorder, and the group has everything they need to make the therapist appear to be the real person.

This impersonation of therapists sounds preposterous, and I did not believe it until it happened to me with the first four. Tony began to refuse to enter my office, and I had to meet him in the coffee shop across the street. The other clients became afraid of me. Eventually I discovered that cult members had somehow got into my office,[1] and in there someone impersonating me had brutally sexually abused them while telling them she loved them. She had also forced them to abuse one another.

I asked them to bring in a support person to our sessions while we worked through this memory. I eventually held a meeting with Teresa and Jennifer in which they apologized to one another and to me for participating in this (not that they had any choice). These clients all became aware of my being impersonated, and learnt to tell the difference between me and the "clone." I had a crooked finger at the time, and while not looking at the person's face they could see her hands and see whether or not it was me. During this period I had my first session with a teenager who claimed to be ritually abused, just after I had surgery on this finger, and she kept staring at my bandaged hand. When I asked her why, she stated that it had not been like that the last time she saw me. I had never seen her before! My "clone" had beaten me to the punch.

This impersonation only worked for a short period with these clients, because the "clone" abused them brutally, and did not do a very good job of impersonating me. However, a couple of years later, an artist client claiming a ritual abuse history told me she kept drawing my office. She was knowledgeable about these matters, and wondered whether perhaps my office was to be simulated. Then she had a dream in which people took her to an office which was a few blocks from mine, similarly located on the second floor of a commercial building, in which she had some kind of therapy session. A little while later, she came to a session with a support person and accused me of being angry and critical of her in our sessions, stating that she could no longer trust me. Apparently the impersonator that was used this time (this client was from a different perpetrator group than my first four) did a very good job by just engaging in bad therapy rather than sexually abusing the client, so it was harder for her to recognize that she was reacting to an impersonation than to me. I lost this client after over a year of therapy.

If you suspect that you are being impersonated to your clients, select something unique about your hands or some other part of your body, which the impersonator will have difficulty simulating, and suggest to your clients that they look at it if they are not sure whether the person is you. You may wonder how a client can believe that it is you when the person is engaging in behavior that is completely opposed to your nature and your usual way of being. Remember that these clients are used to being around people who have extreme changes in their behavior. Many of the perpetrators have dissociative disorders themselves, and switch to abusive personalities from ones who are quite socially acceptable. Others are just good actors.

It is very important that you find out whether this is going on and, if so, find a way to work through these current memories as soon as possible. Otherwise you may either lose your client or find yourself the target of a lawsuit or complaint to your licensing board.

Abuser groups also use voice impersonation over the telephone. Teresa, who lived in an apartment, had an impersonator imitate my voice over the intercom and invite her to go out for coffee. Another client, who had a safe husband and older children, kept getting phone calls from "me" cancelling our appointments. We agreed that if I called her, I would always use the name of a floater alter the group did not know about, so that she would know it was really me. Similarly, psychologist Eroca Shaler arranged to always talk about the weather with one client who was receiving such calls. If the weather was not mentioned, the client would know it was not really Eroca.

Creating a therapeutic bond with mind-controlled clients

It is easy to be impatient to get through therapy quickly, especially if funding is time-limited. However, the only thing that works with people who have been so frequently betrayed, trained to expect betrayal, and trained to believe harm will come to anyone they love, is to be consistent, week after week, year after year. We need to be consistent in our caring, caring for all parts of the person equally rather than rejecting some parts. We also need to be consistent in the boundaries we set, so that the client knows what to expect from us. Let us return to LisaBri's story.

A survivor in therapy: LisaBri

In childhood, severely abused emotionally, physically and sexually, I refused to die. My perpetrators, including my own mother and father, did not mildly abuse; they subjected me to the horrors of Incest and Satanic ritual abuse on a continual basis.

I was fearful of the slightest noise at night—beds creaking, house settling, pipes banging, or a door opening left me cowering in the corner of my bedroom. I knew they would be back to twist and warp my mind for their sadistic purposes. They always knew where to draw the thin line between death and sanity. I always waited in fear, with my heart pounding through my chest and cold, sweaty and clammy hands.

At the age of twenty-five I ran. In running, I found therapy. Three thousand miles away, in hiding, I approached my first therapy appointment. I was about to break one of the cardinal rules of the cult—you do not disclose to outsiders.

Body shaking, icy, freezing hands and feet, knees feeling like they would buckle with every step, I reached "Linda's" home office—scared but alive. She would guide me through the next five years. I left my car on the road, and thought of a hundred reasons why I should not continue and each was just as feeble as the last. During that two-minute walk, I convinced myself I had not escaped, and behind that door lay my abusers ready to punish me for my indiscretion. As I stood at the door, ringing the bell, hearing the sudden bark of dogs, and what sounded like a thousand troops pounding down the stairs ready for battle, it took all my inner reserves not to take flight as the internal pull to run or stay clashed in my brain.

Those first few years with Linda were turbulent with many valleys and hills. I would reach the crest of one only to fall down the other side. Linda did more than guide me; she broke her own ethical rule of conduct by laying no boundaries. She spent one on one time with me in her home. I would have dinner with her family. She spent her time off frequently having coffee at my house. I could call her twenty-four hours a day, seven days a week, and she bought me presents.

Within four years, I had moved from the city to the small town that she resided in. I became part of Linda's other life away from therapy. Playing to my constant insecurities, Linda consistently told me, "I will never hurt or leave you," and I believed her.

Looking back upon it now, telling me this was as cruel as it was kind. With no set therapeutic boundaries I had no sense of myself. I was living Linda's life and I was bound for hurt or betrayal. Instead of helping me find independence and growth, I grew increasingly dependent on her and when the blow came, it hit the core of my being.

The message I received on my answering machine in the midst of intensive memory work told me she had renewed her faith in God and overnight believed only God could save me. Linda would no longer work with non-Christians. Scared, hurt, disbelieving, and having been so dependent on her, I could not comprehend life without her. Desperately not wanting to lose Linda, I ignored my own instincts and the daily growing knot of uncertainty in my stomach. I went to Christian counseling and to her church for a year, until the fear completely overwhelmed me.

I recognized that coming from such a horrendous background had left me spiritually raped and unable to cope with any religious denomination. I finally had to accept that I had lost Linda in more than a therapeutic way.

After shopping around for almost a year, I found "Christyne", but with a different resolve. I chose her, not from an overwhelming sense of urgency and neediness, but from an educated place of having learned a harsh lesson. I talked to Christyne on the phone prior to making an appointment and she said, "I can guide you, I can help you find yourself and what that means, but first we have to set boundaries." I made an appointment.

I must have reached for the phone twenty times from that day to the date of my appointment to cancel. I didn't. I arrived at my appointment with Christyne, weak-kneed with a parched mouth and throat, and feeling like I could not string two words together. I wondered how I would find the strength to master the walk up to her office; it looked like there were thirty steps, straight up with the last stair not in sight. As I stood on the ground floor, looking up to the top of that mountain of stairs—I knew I would climb it—more than once in my lifetime. All I had to do was take one step at a time. I would falter and take a step back, but in strength and support, I would regain my holding and advance to yet another step.

Today, the mountaintop seems closer and with boundaries set out with Christyne I am learning independence and with it a sense of pride. I don't know where Christyne lives, nor do I have her home phone number. With proper guidance, I am in charge of my healing, and I am doing it. Having a consistent structure has been a major growth experience for me.

I still have days when I want to cry and rage, "I don't want to do this anymore!" yet I find the strength and with Christyne's support, I advance to the next level of healing.

Therapeutic boundaries

LisaBri's story illustrates the extreme vulnerability of dissociative clients, the dangers of therapist–client enmeshment, and the importance of clear boundaries with survivor clients. Her early experiences happened during the period in the 1980s and 1990s when therapists were first discovering dissociative disorders.

Like many other therapists working in the 1990s, I had rather loose boundaries with the first few dissociative clients I worked with. Some of that was a result of having worked as part of a multi-disciplinary Child & Youth team with members such as child care workers and social workers, who would go out for coffee etc., with their clients. Seeing them outside the office did not work with my ritually abused clients, and gave an opportunity for the local cult to impersonate me in settings outside the office.

I now believe that every therapist must work out a set of explicit boundaries and stick to them. Issues of trust will arise no matter where the boundaries are placed, although they will be much worse without them.

Survivors of child abuse and neglect tend to replicate the enmeshment and violation of their early experiences. The neglect leads them to want nurturing like little babies without "object constancy." The abuse makes them insensitive to their own and the other's boundaries. At the same time, their evident hurt, and our natural empathic response, as well as their child-like nature when in young, traumatized ego states, lead us to violate our own boundaries in our attempts to help them. I agree with Kluft (1993) that

> to break the ground rules of therapy is to recapitulate the boundary violations of the patient's childhood and to demonstrate that the therapist is corruptible rather than reliable, as MPD is a condition that was created by broken boundaries. [p. 27]

Guidelines about specific boundaries: therapist availability

The primary area where I find clients try to violate the boundaries concerns my availability to them. These clients are desperate for connection, and once we get past the initial fear, if I let them, they would move in with me. Some of them have no awareness of time. Tony used to phone me in the middle of the night, since he had no sense of the difference between day and night, and after waking me and taking up my attention for a long time, he would switch to a sexualized alter and accuse me of talking to him when I was in bed. When I told him I would turn off the ringer at 10 p.m., he thanked me. Now I do not give out my home phone number at all to these people. I also do not promise to call back at the end of the day, because I am often too tired, too late, or too busy. I have slightly different rules for each client, depending on the extent to which they violate boundaries. As James Chu (1998) says, constant availability ignores the real human limitations of the therapist, and also leads to increasing dependence on the therapist. And, I might add, it also fails to prepare clients for real life.

Length and frequency of sessions

This is another area where some clients push the boundaries, in particular going into abreactions or pseudo-seizures, or raising important and sensitive topics, when there are five minutes left in the session. If a client needs a longer session because she is processing a particularly difficult memory, that is one thing. If she delays bringing up the awkward topic until the end of the session, that is another. I do find that most dissociative clients work better with a session an hour and a half long rather than the standard fifty-minute hour.

Do these clients need more therapy sessions than others? Twice per week (presumably, one-hour sessions) is generally recommended for clients with dissociative disorders. I find it works well enough with just one weekly ninety-minute session, recognizing that most of my ritually abused or mind-controlled clients cannot afford even this. The longer session gives dissociative clients more time for different alters to speak either to me or to one another, and also allows time to work through traumatic memories.

The only occasions where I have given extra time were when I was trying to remove all the access programs from my clients who were currently being harassed by the local cult. A weekend intensive therapy program of two days, all day, enabled us to get rid of some of those dangerous programs and make the clients safer. For suicidal crises, I allow the client to use the other resources, such as crisis lines, set up for such situations. I am usually able to avert such crises by careful attention at the end of a session to whether or not such a program is triggered, and speaking with the alters responsible.

Phone calls and emails

I used to say that I would only return calls if the person was in crisis. I found that this led to a manufacturing of crises. So now I just say (for those who are prone to frequent boundary invasions) that I do not return calls unless the purpose is to reschedule appointments. I limit one particular client to leaving me one message per week. I do allow clients to call and listen to my message and hang up. Some of them have brought little tape recorders for a special message each week that they can listen to. I give my email address out only to selected clients when they have proven that they can respect boundaries, and I allow them to email me rather than telephone if they are having difficulty. That way I can decide whether and when to respond.

Office rules

Mind-controlled clients in particular appreciate rules being given. They also understand rules, as they have lived with them since infancy.

My own office rules are: (1) don't hurt people; (2) don't break things; (3) don't take clothes off except coats. I state these rules to dissociative clients, especially to child alters. I emphasize that the rules apply to me as well as to them. I see their eyes widen when I mention the "Don't take clothes off" rule. I believe this rule is particularly important because of the likely history of sexual abuse by persons pretending to be therapists. When I state the rule I am telling them not only that I will not abuse them this way, but also that I am aware that this sometimes happens.

Touching

Touch is a complicated issue in the field of psychotherapy, and especially so with these clients. Stephen Ray, one of my early teachers about ritual abuse, said that he thought it was abusive *not* to touch clients who have been so massively neglected and abused. I do hug, touch, and occasionally hold clients, depending on the person. I often hold the hands of one of my ritually abused clients while I speak with her alters. Apparently several of the "evil" alters were told that they would poison anyone who touched them, so it is important to show them that this curse was based on a lie. My touch creates anxiety in the short run, but will create safety in the long run.

I always ask permission of the particular alter. If any alter seems to have a sexual response I discuss it openly, giving an explicit statement that I will not be sexual with them. One male client had a very young alter he called "the horny goat" for obvious reasons; after careful consideration, he decided that this child part needed a hug too, despite his embarrassment. However, there are days when he makes it clear that he is not to be hugged. The experience of setting his own physical boundaries is probably very reassuring to him.

I do believe it is wise to be careful whom you touch or hug. Many years ago I hugged a distressed woman who had been sexually abused by her mother; needless to say, this was the wrong thing to do.

Commitment and money

If I take on a client with a dissociative disorder, especially if they have experienced mind control of any type, I know I am making a long-term commitment—that is, of several years' duration. So I do not take them on unless I know I want to and am able to follow through. This pertains especially to the financial burden of therapy. I do not start with anyone who cannot pay, unless there are very special circumstances. If a funding source runs out, it is not ethical to just terminate the client. I do not allow dissociative clients to owe me money. Payment for therapy must be negotiated clearly at the start, and in some cases periodically renegotiated. I currently have several pro bono clients, and they are all survivors of organized abuse whose funding ran out some time ago. I need to make sure I have sufficient income from other sources so that I can continue to see these clients.

Dealing with boundary violations

Boundary violations are essentially unavoidable with these clients, because any ritually abused and mind-controlled people have alters who are trained to violate therapists' boundaries. But it makes a difference how we handle them. When I speak to such a client about boundaries, I always begin with saying, "You are not in trouble." *In trouble* is the term that many of these survivors use when they are expecting the severe beating or rape that happened when they disobeyed their abusers.

It is to be expected that clients who have been persistently violated in childhood will have difficulty recognizing and respecting boundaries. When it happens, it is important that we mention it to the client, acknowledging any fault of our own if necessary. Confrontation is difficult when we are angry and hurt. I find it helps to write out my own feelings about boundary violations first, and then write out what I am going to say to the client, so that I will not explode, blame, or fail to state my concerns assertively. And it is important to confront sooner rather than later, so I do not have a lot of stored-up anger and hurt.

Just over a year ago, I took on a client who had been fired by an experienced trauma therapist for persistent boundary violations. I took her on probation. Since she had disclosed a history of ritual abuse and mind control, I informed her that I was aware that she probably had alters who were trained to disrupt therapy, and that if this happened with me, that would be the end of our work together. I made my boundaries very clear. About a month into therapy, she flooded me with emails. I gave her a single warning, and told her parts to turn off whatever programming was making them do this. They acknowledged that it was indeed them doing their "jobs," and stopped.

I had this client for a year before she crossed my boundaries again. It happened in response to a crisis in a friendship with another survivor who was also a client of mine. (She met her through a website rather than through me.) There were fifty-seven emails within a few days. I immediately told her not to send me any emails at all. She came to our next meeting expecting to be fired. She had cut her arms and abused alcohol.

I told her that I had been observing her reaction, and we now had an opportunity to find out what caused this reaction, which had given her trouble in many relationships with professionals. I inquired not about the problem to which she was reacting, but the mechanism within her which was creating the reaction. We located "It" and "Beasty," the "non-human" rejected alters who were creating the problem, and worked through the memory of their creation. Her last email to me on the subject said simply "Thank you for giving It and Beasty human dignity and awareness of peace."

This story illustrates how boundary violations have complex and programmed causes in mind control survivors, so we need to be firm but also compassionate, and seek out the root causes of boundary violations if and when they occur.

Transference and countertransference

In an excellent little article called "What is dissociated?" Susan Sands (1994) states that the attachment disorder that is universal among dissociative clients leads to the client's trying to get childhood relational needs met without trusting the therapist to meet them. The child's healthy relational needs for empathy, affect attunement, mirroring, calming and soothing, admiration, security, recognition, sense of alikeness with another, and loving confrontation are dissociated in childhood. These hidden needs and longings are inevitably remobilized within the therapy relationship. The relational needs are experienced by the survivor as longings, affects which signal that certain environmental responses which are necessary for self-development were missing. These longings were dissociated and seen as bad by the child, because the mobilization of these longings led to danger from a sadistic caregiver, and also because of the role reversal in the parental relationship. They come up in therapy in very crude ways, and it is easy for us to agree with the client that they are bad (regressive, inappropriately sexual, overwhelming to us, etc.)

There are "painful, compulsive re-enactments." The relational longings are experienced, then violently resisted. The client fantasizes us as the idealized omnipotent savior. What we saw in early MPD treatment was that, in response, a lot of reparenting occurred—usually associated with severe boundary violations.

Attachment-related transference

Most persons with dissociative disorders (not just mind control survivors) have difficulties with attachment. Sands and other writers, such as Goulding and Schwartz, have described the following client behaviors related to attachment:

- alters competing for therapy time, trying to get reparenting from the therapist;
- manipulating the therapist, for example, a client cutting her own arm to get an extra session;
- seeking constant reassurance and expressions of affection and caring;
- smothering neediness, attempting to blend or fuse with the therapist;
- expecting the therapist to be an almighty rescuer;
- wanting too much time, energy and commitment;
- perceiving rejection or abandonment where it isn't and reacting with self-mutilation, suicide attempts, fugues, and missed sessions;
- overreacting to the therapist's illness or tiredness;
- overreacting to the therapist's vacations and business trips, thinking everything will change during this time;
- being "a bottomless pit of parts, pain, and crises".

Teresa, the client I almost did not believe, "stalked" me, engaging in many of these behaviors. She would hang around outside my office in the Mental Health Center, hoping to get a glimpse of me if I left the office to go to the bathroom or to lunch. She saw herself as very special to me, and frequently gave me handmade gifts from the child alters, telling me that her parents always rejected such gifts. She would gladly have moved in with me if given such an opportunity. She created an alter named after me. I found it very difficult to deal with her constant needy presence, and at times I would express anger at her, something that appeared not to bother her at all. I was aware that she had never been cared for, but I did not want to become her mother, and I had to deal with my personal reaction to her clinging presence. As we persisted in therapy, she did improve, and eventually was able to leave town to get away from her abusers to establish residence in another city, where she developed new relationships.

Sands writes that "The patient not only fears that the therapist will become the perpetrator; the patient will inevitably evoke controlling or sadistic responses . . . from the therapist." Teresa certainly did with me. I remember my anger and my guilt as I tried to push her away from engulfing me with her neediness. Although Teresa was a ritual abuse survivor, much of the transference she made to me, and the countertransference she evoked in me, were responses to the neglect and emotional abandonment by her parents; she played them out with me because I was the first of the professionals in her life who had sought to understand her rather than dismissing her as an untreatable case of "borderline personality disorder."

Looking back, I am not clear how many of Teresa's needy and engulfing behaviors were programmed. All the behaviors described above can occur with "regular" DIDs or trauma survivors who were not subjected to ritual abuse or mind control. But with the mind-controlled population we need to bear in mind that, in addition to living with sadistic and inconsistently available caregivers, they have experienced specific interventions by the abusers to make sure they do not form a bond with a therapist. Teresa had particular difficulty with my vacations, being afraid that something terrible would happen to me while I was away. I later found out that the cult group simulated my murder on several occasions when I was on vacation, in addition to using the time to hold fake and abusive "therapy" sessions. Mind-controlling abusers capitalize on the client's natural fear that the therapist will become a perpetrator by setting up staged scenarios in which the therapist is indeed abusive, and in which the client has to abuse the therapist.

In any personality system, those alters in charge of safety are always observing what goes on in therapy, and trying to assess how trustworthy we are. Even though many parts do their "jobs" of sabotaging the bond, most parts are very hungry for connection with a trustworthy person, something they have never experienced, which is a basic, healthy human need. We must recognize the importance of this need. It is unlikely that mind control survivors have experienced such a connection, unless their abuse happened in a setting unconnected to the home. This connection is probably the most important element in any therapy, and particularly so with those who have never experienced it.

As we provide recognition and respect, soothing, mirroring, and gentle confrontation in therapy sessions, we can then encourage it to be gradually internalized. Alters who have experienced this can share it with newly emerging alters. I used to read a story to the "kids" of one ritual abuse survivor at the end of each therapy session, and newly emerging child parts would begin their current awareness by listening to the story from "inside." We can empathize with the client's desire to have us twenty-four hours a day, explaining that that is what a baby needs, while not giving in to it. We can ask them to provide in the inner world the nurturing that we cannot provide on the outside. We can respond gently to sexually aggressive alters, explaining that we do not need them to have sex with us like their abusers did, but we care about them without this.

Trauma-related transference

Judith Herman (1992) points out that because disempowerment is a huge effect of trauma, clients often attempt to regain their power via the therapeutic relationship—when, because of their needs to be taken care of, they have given us too much power. At the moment of trauma, the victim is utterly helpless and feels totally abandoned. "It's frightening to need someone so much and not be able to control them," Herman states (p. 137). The patient feels that her life depends on her rescuer, so she cannot afford to be tolerant of human error in the therapist. Herman gives an example of a Vietnam veteran who wanted revenge on the medic who treated him, rather than on the enemy. "In fantasies they wish to reduce the disappointing, envied therapist to the same unbearable condition of terror, helplessness, and shame that they themselves have suffered" (p. 138). I believe that if the therapist is truly empathic, this is reduced. It is worse if the therapist distances him or herself from the client and the material. It is important for the therapist to understand the power dynamics so as not to take the challenges personally.

Trauma-related transference might lead to attempts to regain power in the disempowering therapeutic relationship through such behaviors as:

- accusing the therapist of incompetence;
- pumping up the therapist's vanity then pricking it with a pin, challenging his or her professional expertise, and catching every error he or she makes;
- blaming the therapist for compounding their suffering;
- inviting the therapist into power struggles and trying to provoke him or her to be hurtful and abusive, and to re-enact the trauma in therapy;
- sharing graphic details of abusive incidents which traumatize the therapist.

Mind controllers are aware of this dynamic, and they use it. One common technique of mind-controlling abusers is to infuriate the victim through making them powerless, for example, to save another child whose cries they can hear. Then, when the anger is sufficient to split off an alter who only knows the emotion of anger, the abusers provide a victim upon whom that alter can take out its rage. When the survivor later encounters frustration or powerlessness, these rage-holder alters can be activated. Sometimes they are specifically trained to attack or kill therapists. It is uncommon that a client's system will allow any real harm to occur, but therapists working with survivors should be aware that this training might be present.

Time and trust

There is no substitute for time in building trust. Almost all of my ritually abused clients have had histories of failed therapy with other therapists. Some had their boundaries violated, some were allowed to cross over the therapists' boundaries and were then blamed for it, and some were treated by methods that are just inappropriate for this population. Your clients will watch your every move and every word to see whether or not you are trustworthy, believing that it is most likely that you are not, but hoping desperately that you will prove to be a person they can trust. It might take you many years to prove this, but it is possible. Once this happens, you will be able to get to the other work of therapy, developing relationships with all parts of the personality system, working through the traumatic memories, and resolving the issues caused by the extreme abuse. Take your time. And be patient with yourself, too.

The important thing to remember at this point is that you need to treat all parts with consistency and fairness, with "unconditional positive regard." It is only when you provide consistency over time that a survivor of this kind of horrendous abuse can come to trust you.

Remember also that many parts have no sense of time, so when they come out into the body after years of therapy, they may have no awareness of all the person's history with you. It will help if other parts can take the time to fill them in so that they can build trust with you more quickly. A month ago, I met a "new" alter in a client I have been treating for many, many years. This part did not know who I was and was suspicious of me, especially when I asked him questions. I recognized by his behavior that he had probably been interrogated by abusers, as he interpreted even my statements as questions that he did not want to answer. The host is by now pretty sophisticated regarding dealing with alters, and he instructed me to leave this new part alone to just observe his present life until he is ready to talk. Good advice. It turned out that this part is very helpful in calming him down, now that he has been orientated to the safe present.

Note

1. I later discovered that the woman who took another client of mine to a cult meeting was a member of a sexual abuse survivors' group that met in my office building, so she could have remained after a meeting and unlocked the building for the perpetrators.

CHAPTER FOURTEEN

Treating programmed pedophilia

S urvivors of all forms of childhood sexual trauma frequently have serious sexual problems. As E. Sue Blume says in her 1990 book, *Secret Survivors*, which lays out many of the sexual sequelae of incest, "The context in which the child victim is first introduced to sex is responsible for numerous distortions in later life. Sex is not sex for the incest survivor" (p. 207). In particular, survivors of incest feel shame over the fact that they were sexually aroused during the abuse. The body is wired to respond to being sexually stimulated, and this is something a child cannot handle emotionally. Sexual aversion is frequently seen, as is sexual addictions, as well as other forms of sexual compulsivity.

Since most survivors of organized abuse—ritual abuse, mind control, child prostitution, and child pornography—have also experienced incest (which Blume defines as abuse by a person of greater power who is involved in an ongoing relationship with the victim), it is helpful to know about these things. However, the sexual abuses of these survivors go far beyond those of most sexual abuse survivors. Survivors of these abuses do not reactively develop problems such as sexual disturbances, including addictions and paraphilias, they are programmed to do so.

There is also programming that creates alters with ego dystonic gender identities and sexual orientations for both male and female, gay and straight survivors, which the survivor will need to resolve over the course of treatment. Your client might be too embarrassed and ashamed to tell you about even these comparatively innocent issues. Two male survivors I treated had extremely embarrassing personal solo sexual habits, which brought them great shame. One had "girl" alters who believed their anus to be a vagina, and inserted objects into it for sexual stimulation, not even realizing they had a penis. I helped him resolve it through recurring "sex education" lectures to his child alters, explaining that they were a man now who used to be a boy, not a girl, what kind of body parts they had, and how they could get the good feeling (orgasm) without engaging in the behaviors which they believed were the source of the feeling. The other man discovered that his child alters had been "located" in his anus.

So you can imagine what it is like for them to discuss the rest of it. In Chapter Seven, Stella Katz describes cult sexual training. You can imagine the results of such things as dressing alters up in costumes (e.g., strap-on penises for girls) to make them believe they are of the opposite sex, deliberate pairing of pain and pleasure, bestiality, necrophilia, and training to participate in sexual abuse and/or torture of other children while being sexually stimulated and experiencing sexual pleasure. It is no surprise that paraphilias and bizarre sexual addictions are common in this population. Groups who make the worst kinds of pornography, including child pornography, sado-masochistic pornography, and necrophilic and "snuff" (killing) pornography, create their own markets by training children and adolescents to respond sexually to other children, animals, violence, dead bodies, and death.

The conventional approach to treating sexual addictions and other extreme sexual behaviors (terms that in today's society are seen as extremely relative) is through the affected adult. With support from a therapist and/or a group, the client attempts to recognize and resist his or her troublesome urges on an ongoing basis. Sometimes, this works. Often, it does not. If we understand these problems as possibly resulting from dissociated childhood experiences, however, at least in some cases, then it may be possible to fully resolve these problems through treatment of the underlying dissociative disorder and resolution of the traumatic memories, often with great success. In any case, most of these issues are a matter of quality of life, and so it is the choice of the survivor whether or not to address them and how much effort to put into recovery. Likewise, most of the paraphilias, which are expressed "between consenting adults."

But there is one result of ritual abuse and programming that we do not have the choice to ignore, legally, morally, or psychologically: pedophilia. This is a behavior that, in the view of many professionals, can never be cured. But, fortunately, in this population, it often can be.

I share with you now the story of my client Jennifer, whose therapy included treatment for pedophilia. One of my first four ritual abuse survivor clients, Jennifer came to me in 1992 at the age of seventeen through my position at Child & Youth Mental Health Services. She requested treatment for newly remembered memories that she had sexually abused her younger brother. She worked hard, despite constant harassment by the local cult group, and reached full integration in just four years. Jennifer taught me a great deal of what I know about how to work with DID and with ritual abuse, and this book would not exist if it were not for her intelligence and bravery. I made many mistakes during the course of her treatment, but it was nevertheless successful. The following story demonstrates not only the extraordinarily layered programming that can be involved in this training, but the fact that even with those circumstances, the urges and behaviors of pedophilia can be successfully resolved.

Jennifer's story

The beginning of treatment

Jennifer was a 12th grade student in an elite boarding school. Her two years in that school were her first experience of living in relative safety. Just before graduation, when she would have returned to her family, Jennifer had a "breakdown", supposedly induced by thyroid problems. During this breakdown, she became aware that she had sexually abused her younger brother when she was between the ages of nine and fifteen. She also became aware that she had a lot of internal parts. She mapped out her internal parts in her journal, and they began writing and communicating with her there. She disclosed the existence of these parts to school personnel and to her physician. She also told these people about abusing her younger brother. She was hospitalized, referred for outpatient therapy, and placed in a foster home after the school year ended.

In the psychiatric hospital, as often occurs, despite the fact that she had produced a chart of her alter personalities, Jennifer was diagnosed as "borderline". I was the outpatient therapist assigned to her. In our first session, Jennifer asked whether I believed in what was then known to most people as Multiple Personality Disorder. When I said I did, and that I had worked with this disorder, she breathed a sigh of relief, produced her alter chart, and described what she then knew of her system. It became clear that I was talking to an organizing alter personality who frequently masqueraded as the ANP. Jennifer described her ANP as "a thin shell without much actual content," just a conduit through whose voice the other alters appeared.

Jennifer was disclosing her offenses at this time, she told me, because she preferred to be charged as a juvenile rather than as an adult. Besides the abuse of her brother, who was six years younger, she disclosed offending against some young boys she had babysat when she was about thirteen. Both sets of abuses were investigated and found to have occurred, and she was charged.

The personality system

I began by getting to know some of Jennifer's existing alters. The thirty-three that she had mapped out before starting therapy were the "real world" alters, mostly teenagers with different skills and interests. The map of her system was divided into *Good*, *Mediator*, and *Evil* sections. One part of *Evil* contained alters representing negative emotions with names such as Lust, Malice, Pain, Fear, Anger, Hate, Sadness, Ambiguity, Denial, and Grief. I later found out that these alters had regular names like Mike, Nicole, and John. The other part of *Evil* contained alters representing negative actions: physical harm to the self, manipulation, lust, and incest. The alter she called "Incest" was a teenage girl alter named Kristine. According to what she wrote about the alters, Kristine was boastful and proud about what she had done to her brother. Her other alters were horrified.

This was just the first layer of Jennifer's highly organized personality system. Most of the alters in this layer had been created spontaneously by Jennifer in reaction to her abuse. The next layer consisted of what she called *Hurt Children*, whom she had named. I did not find out until much later that they were named after children she had seen sacrificed. Below were several other layers, and other sections of alters deliberately created by Jennifer's abusers. But I did not find this out until much later. The system initially believed the incest offender alter, Kristine, to be the only offender alter. However, there were two alters in the second layer: another Kristine, and a male alter who influenced Kristine to offend. A third Kristine, who said she was a priestess, controlled both of these alters. In addition, other offender alters, with other memories of sexual offenses, were hidden in various layers of the personality system.

Memory work

At the start of therapy, Jennifer experienced repeated flashbacks of a gang rape at about age four that took place in a housing complex where she lived. Three of the abusers appeared to be teenage boys; the fourth, a man named Jason, would figure in many of her later memories. She had alters representing the rapists as well as herself as the victim. Some of these alters had imagined themselves to be perpetrators in order to avoid experiencing the pain of the rape. Within two months of beginning therapy we successfully processed this memory, making sure that the rapist alters took part so that they could no longer deny the pain of sexual abuse. When we processed a few other related memories with them, the rapist alters automatically integrated. Both Jennifer and I initially assumed that these memories were the cause of her problems.

Jennifer and I discussed potential memory processing methods and together developed one that worked for her. It was evident that Jennifer put herself into a trance during her memory processing without formal induction. I was amazed at the amount of detail she provided. The "backwards" method of memory processing we developed—choosing memories based on the behavior or feelings they motivated, rather than from the trauma material that was erupting at any one time—would later become my protocol for working with survivors. It was routine for pairs or groups of alters to integrate at the end of memory processing. As we worked with each layer of alters to deal with the memories causing their splits, they integrated and new layers came up.

Issues of safety and stabilization

Two months after we began therapy, Jennifer went to court for the sexual abuse of her younger brother. This precipitated arm-slashing by "Josh," one of the known male alters. Josh felt panic and terror at the sight of Jennifer's mother in court, but he had no idea why. When we explored this, Jennifer discovered a memory of sexual abuse by her mother, followed by punishment for being "seductive." This let me and the foster mother know that contact with Jennifer's mother was unsafe for her. Jennifer reported the abuse by her mother, and her younger brother was briefly apprehended and questioned. He did not disclose any other abuse beyond that done to him by Jennifer herself, so he was returned to the family. His mother began home schooling him.

When I went on vacation four months into therapy, Jennifer engaged in some sexual promiscuity. We found this to be very complicated behavior involving several alters. "Jessie" would seduce the men and carry out the actual intercourse. Two other alters liked the attention and cuddling. "Kristine," the alter who had abused Jennifer's little brother, handled the oral sex. Some alters wanted a child. Another was a homosexual male. We dealt with the promiscuity by planning that the traumatized child alters would share with the sexually active ones how they felt when sex happened.

The sexual behavior allowed me to talk with Kristine. She said that she had a sexual bond with her "whole fucking family," including her mother. Kristine did not particularly enjoy sex, but it was a "family thing." She did not really want the sex with her younger brother, and suspected that another alter might have made her do it. She felt obligated to engage in sex with one man so that he would like her. Her "whole fucking family" became our private joke.

Shortly after this conversation, I discovered that Jennifer had alters representing all her family members, and that these "copies" were themselves multiple, having sub-alters named from her family members' alter personalities. It appeared that all her family members also suffered from Dissociative Identity Disorder. Jennifer's personality system, being familiar with the names of her family members' alters, had "copied" these within own system. On one occasion I was speaking with an alter of Jennifer's who believed herself to be Jennifer's mother, and I asked to speak to the alter who represented her brother. Jennifer's "mother" said solemnly, "I'll go and get him," went out to the waiting room, and returned as her "brother."

Although Jennifer was no longer sexually abusing children because she had no access to them, she was extremely dysfunctional during our first two years of therapy. She had some promiscuous alters who initiated sexual contact with unsafe men. She was in and out of the mental hospital for cutting her arms and for suicide attempts. She would leave the foster home and come back traumatized, with no memories of what had happened. It became apparent that she was still in contact with her family and other abusers. She would remember seeing her mother at a bus stop, then that memory would abruptly terminate and she would "lose time." Although Jennifer was able to tell her foster mother when to hide her shoes so she could not go out at night, and when to put her in hospital, these requests were not enough to ensure her safety, since she went out during the day.

Because of the extent of current abuse, we decided together to work with the memories very early in therapy. We just did not have the luxury of very slowly getting to know the personality system and very slowly beginning to build trust. It soon became clear to me, and to the foster mother, that Jennifer's disclosure of her sexual offenses against her younger brother had been an attempt to find a way to safety from her family and the criminal group with whom they were involved.

Within a few months, Jennifer and I were working on a weekly basis with both old memories and memories of current abuse which endangered her. Jennifer's presence in the foster home helped tremendously, as the foster mother provided her with both nurturing and protection.

A week before Jennifer had to move out of the foster home, her foster mother notified me that a fourteen-year-old alter had come out and told her that we had only been dealing with the top one of six layers of the personality system. I had thought we had worked our way through thirteen layers. It appeared that these were thirteen compartments of alters on the first layer. Most of these alters were spontaneously created rather than deliberately placed there by the abusers.

When Jennifer became a legal adult at age nineteen, she was required to find her own residence. She got an apartment, and it was not long before her older brother began meeting her there to have sex with her alters, assisted by pleasure-enhancing drugs which he provided. The alters in charge of the system took action to stop their dangerous behavior by traumatizing the sexually acting out alters with memories of painful sexual abuse by that brother. This put an end to her spontaneous contact with him, but other alters continued to make contact with family and cult when they required her presence, and to report to them regularly about her progress in therapy.

Current safety concerns, as well as the gradual unfolding of Jennifer's personality system, dictated the order in which we worked with the memories. Events that Jennifer remembered as influencing her to become a sexual offender included being trained to offend both informally by her brother and formally by organized criminal groups. The primary organizer of all Jennifer's abusive experiences appeared to be the man named Jason; his relation to her family was unclear.

Memories relevant to sexual offending

Jennifer's abuse, as it was revealed through the memories, included sexual and physical abuse at home at the hands of all family members, systematic ritualistic abuse, and pornographic film-making at a sophisticated studio. (I have, since that time, had three other clients with memories of that studio, one as a perpetrator.) There was a good deal of deliberate training for pedophilia and for sexual sadism and masochism. This demonstrates to me that groups who make child pornography create their own market in adult survivors.

Abuse by family and friends

Five months after we began therapy, Jennifer processed a series of memories of sexual abuse at home by her older brother, from when she was four until her teens. During the later events, he would threaten to disclose Jennifer's abuse of her younger brother. Then she disclosed memories of having been taught to sexually abuse a little boy while being filmed.

Three months later, a male alter became suicidal after having recalled memories of abusing her younger brother. It was he who had made Kristine perform the abuse. Once "Sean" had been in the "real world" long enough, and had processed enough victim memories to realize how harmful his behavior had been, he felt he did not deserve to live. We processed the memories of the abuse of her younger brother, which was apparently mutually pleasurable. This is not surprising, since it is likely that Jennifer's younger brother had been sexually trained the same way she was from an early age.

Two weeks after that, Jennifer came up with memories of her older brother teaching her to abuse her younger brother when she was about nine. She had caught her older brother abusing her younger brother. He invited her in, sexually aroused her, then replaced himself with her little brother. At this point I thought that this experience, along with being sexually abused, was the primary source for Jennifer's offending behavior.

But there was more to come. We went through a series of memories of sexual abuse by her older brother and her mother. Jennifer's father had left the family when she was four, and there were some memories of abuse by him alone and together with her mother.

Then came a series of memories of a friend's father teaching her and her friend to sexually abuse younger children, especially a little boy she used to babysit. This man had previously been charged for sexually abusing Jennifer's younger brother. Jennifer had previously remembered abusing these children but had not recalled being taught to do so.

Jennifer and I thought we had now dealt with the sources of her offending.

Risk of perpetration while in treatment

In the spring of 1994, twenty months into therapy, Jennifer stayed in a transition house to get away from severe harassment from her family and other cult members. When she stopped going to meet her abusers, they began abducting her from the street and abusing her violently. Jennifer called me from the shelter with concerns that some alters were having sexual feelings about a little boy staying in the house, and she did not know how much power she had to control it. She had always been very honest with me. I made a short-term contract, much like a suicide contract, for her not to offend while in the home. It was risky leaving her in the shelter, but I trusted her system to keep the promise despite my later reluctance to use contracts with such clients. By this time, the ANP was a more solid integration of all the surface alters, and could not easily lose time. I asked Jennifer to search for any other memories which might be causing these desires, as well as for the alters involved; her system had become very good at finding relevant memories and alters. I saw this as an emergency.

I cancelled my other commitments, and we did intense work for three days to deal with the remaining sources of Jennifer's pedophilic urges.

We had already processed the memories of Jennifer's abuse of her younger brother. Now we went through those of her abuse of the little boys she had babysat. Then there were more memories of abuse by her older brother, some quite pleasurable and some causing pleasure to some alters but pain to others. There were also memories of her older brother selling her for sexual purposes to his friends when she was about ten.

After we processed these memories, some offender alters still existed. Jennifer's system was able to identify them. The pedophilic desires belonged to alters whose only pleasurable life experience was that of sexually abusing younger children. They saw the little boy in the shelter as vulnerable and neglected, and they felt they cared for him. They thought sexual abuse of him was a caring act, something he would find pleasant compared to what Jennifer had been through.

I explained that I could lose my license if I left her in the shelter when there was a risk of her offending against a child there. But she was in physical danger if she lived on her own at this point. I suggested that the system put all the potential offending alters in an internal prison. Jennifer said that would take too long. An alter popped out and said, "Just a minute," and then, after a brief silence, announced that they had "killed" all the offender alters; they were lying in the inside world dead, covered in blood! I was not very happy with such drastic measures, but accepted it for the interim, knowing I could rely on Jennifer to tell me if the risk recurred. I made a list of the "dead" alters.

The next morning Jennifer called; she had dreamed about sexually abusing a child. I asked her to look for more related memories before we met in the evening. She had to "reincarnate" all the dead alters to find the memories. (We already had a method for doing this, as some alters had previously experienced internal "death" in "disasters" in the inner world; when they were made new internal bodies, they became alive again.)

Related training for masochism, sadism and pedophilia

The final set of memories we had to deal with to resolve Jennifer's pedophilic urges were those of the deliberate training in sexual masochism, sadism, and pedophilia. As a child, Jennifer remembered being forced to experience both sexual pleasure and extreme pain by being sexually stimulated while her body was being hurt. These forced contradictory responses required the co-presence of some alters who experienced sexual pleasure and others who experienced pain.

Masochism training

From infancy on, a couple who were friends of Jennifer's mother would sexually stimulate Jennifer while raping her painfully, sometimes with objects. One alter would experience the sexual pleasure and another the pain. This caused the separation of two kinds of alters, the kind who experienced pain, and the kind who enjoyed sex without knowing the body was also being hurt. This was what had created the alters who thought sexual abuse of a young child would be pleasurable to the child. The final set of memories were even earlier ones involving painful sexual abuse combined with pleasurable sexual arousal. As we processed these memories, Jennifer went through wave after wave of intense sexual arousal, fear, and pain. She was unable to speak.

When we discussed this later, it appeared that Jennifer's organized abuser group had begun this deliberately when she was just an infant, perhaps administering hormones to aid the process. The alters involved were primitive infantile fragments, who gave their feelings to the pedophilic alters.

Later in therapy, Jennifer had memories of sexual stimulation combined with anal rape with objects, again reinforcing the split between the "pain alters" and the "sex alters", who came "out" simultaneously but had completely different experiences of the same events. I asked one male alter what he responded with, and he answered ,"My pseudo-penis."

Sadism training

Several months later, Jennifer came up with some memories of sexual training with a little boy within a preschool, when she was four and a half. She and the boy would be taken out of the class, and pleasurably sexually stimulated while watching movies of people getting hurt, often small children. Then she and the boy were told to stimulate one another while watching movies in which people were violently sexually violated. Jennifer told me that there were "lots and lots and lots and lots of movies." Finally, these two were taught to do this while watching actual sexual violence perpetrated in their presence.

This was clearly a method of deliberately training her to be a sadistic abuser. It reinforced both the association and the split between the alters who experienced pain and those who experienced sexual pleasure. This time the training was directed specifically towards preventing those alters who experienced sexual pleasure from giving empathic attention to others' pain, by pairing that pain with their own pleasure, producing incompatible responses.

Around this time, Jennifer also worked through memories of violent, painful sexual abuse by her older brother; it appears he probably had similar training.

Understanding and treating pedophilia in survivors

After we worked through the final memories of the deliberate training, Jennifer told me, "It's definitely fixed (the pedophilia). I'll never like sex again!" No alters remained who were sexually attracted to young children, and since that time Jennifer has never had a desire to sexually abuse a child. I believe her pedophilia was resolved. After all the pornography memories were completed, she was even able to enjoy sexual feelings.

After the memories were processed, Jennifer and I discussed the implications of our discoveries, which Jennifer allowed me to share with you now to help you understand more about how this training works, and to demonstrate that there is a way to be freed of its consequences.

We speculated together that perhaps some pedophilia is caused by the split, as well as the association between alters who enjoy sexual feelings and those who feel pain caused by painful sexual abuse involving the child's sexual arousal. Being forced to go through simultaneous, incompatible experiences of intense pain and intense sexual pleasure leads to the separation of sexual alters who are unable to feel pain, but need the pain (experienced by other alters) in order to feel the sexual arousal. In mind-controlling and ritually abusing groups, girls as well as boys are trained with the use of sexual arousal and pleasure. You may note that in Chapter Seven, Stella Katz speaks of this type of training. I did not have this information when I worked with Jennifer, but her experience corroborates Stella's account.

I do want to note that in writing about this, I am not judging adults who engage in sadomasochistic practices in a consensual setting. Most persons in the BDSM community would say that they will only engage in consensual activities to heighten their sexual pleasure, and that they absolutely would never choose to cause pain to someone else by violating their body. They also would not be interested in having sex with children.

In mind control settings, children are forced to engage in mixed pain and pleasure and extreme perpetration with one another and with adults. If a child's developing sexual urges are channeled in this way by an abuser or an abusing group, any later sexual feelings could move the person in the direction of perpetration. Jennifer's experience also shows how experiencing intense sexual pleasure at the same time as observing or being forced to perpetrate violence on others can lead to the creation of alters who are incapable of empathy, and associate sexual pleasure with violence to other people. These child alters still exist within adults who have had this training, and if they come out in settings other than the structured ones of the mind control or cult group where pedophilia and other sexual abuse are the norm, they can act out on partners or on children. These fragmentary alters can be very dangerous, as their life experience is very limited and they do not mature. Remember that the alters who wanted to have sex with the little boy in the shelter actually believed he would enjoy it. Many pedophiles have this illusion. Although Jennifer's pedophilia appeared to have been deliberately created by an organized group of abusers, a similar process could happen with less organized abuse, as long as sexual arousal is paired with pain to the child and/or to someone else.

Much of Jennifer's offending was done by one alter who was conscious of the behavior but not in control of it. Other alters influenced or forced the offending alter to do what she did. Offenders with covert dissociation might have similar experiences—their "urges" actually come from alters. This leads me to strongly recommend that pedophilic and violent sexual offenders be routinely assessed for dissociative disorders. In some cases, uncontrollable urges might arise from other alters or ego states who are not under the control over the part of the person having conscious awareness.

Much offender treatment focuses on teaching the (presumably unitary) person to resist urges. It is assumed that the urges themselves cannot be removed. Jennifer's treatment was successful in removing her urges to abuse young boys, because the parts who experienced sexual pleasure were no longer dissociated from the parts who experienced the pain of being abused or from those who experienced empathy for others who were abused. The dissociation was healed by processing the original memories which created the splits between these alters.

How did it all turn out?

Towards the end of therapy, about four years into our therapeutic work, we discovered a new section of alters who kept a secret: the identity of Jason. We had by this time worked through dozens of memories of abuse orchestrated by Jason. The secret: Jason was Jennifer's father! Although he had left the family, he remained in leadership in the perpetrating group. But very few of her alters knew that Jason and Jennifer's father were the same person.

Jennifer's therapy took five years to complete. Her complex personality system completely joined into a single personality. She moved to another country, far from her family and the others who abused her. There was an incident a few years ago when a previously unknown alter emerged because of sexual activity with a man she loved, something she had never experienced during all those years of sexual training. She was able to integrate the alter on her own, with the help of her partner. She continues in that stable loving relationship. She now has three children (all girls), and is an excellent parent (though she learnt it from books). There are no signs that her children have suffered from her abusive background. She is now a post-graduate student at a university, and is doing very well. Her life for many years now has not been about her abuse, but about being a whole person and finding a life path that suits her own abilities and interests.

Dealing with sexuality in survivors

Curing those issues that are the product of programming does not resolve all of the sexual dysfunction of survivors of ritual abuse and mind control. Much may remain. In *Secret Survivors*, Blume points out that "dealing with sexuality comes later than facing other issues. . . . The survivor should not attempt to fix sex before breaking the secret [of childhood sexual trauma that has been dissociated], facing the shame, repairing her self esteem, and learning healthy friendship" (p. 227).

"Healthy sexuality," she says, "involves . . . sophisticated interpersonal tasks . . .". Ultimately, Blume suggests, this may well require a protracted period of celibacy while survivors reclaim the right to say "no" (p. 230). In the case of these survivors, however, "reclaiming" is not the correct term. Personal empowerment is something that mind control survivors have never known in any regard. However, Blume does make a statement that many will see as describing their experiences: "For many . . . survivors, the old script of incest and its inherent distortions regarding sexuality cannot be edited; it must be erased" (p. 230).

In Chapter Seventeen, Jen Callow shares how she added loving sexual partners for those parts who needed this inside. That is one way a survivor who is single can deal with the issue of sex, trying to reconnect sexual expression with love and caring. Jennifer told me that when she first became sexually involved after her therapy, she had to keep her eyes open at all times and remind herself that she was with someone she loved. Much has been written for incest survivors that also applies to the population we are dealing with. They are not fully healed if their sexuality remains something they regard with disgust, or if they are still experiencing urges involving extreme violence or pedophilia. And they can be healed.

CHAPTER FIFTEEN

The unimaginable

If you ask the average mind control or ritual abuse survivor what the worst part of their abuse—or their recovery—was, it will not be the complex and booby-trapped inner hierarchies and programming, or the hard and seemingly endless work of therapy. No. The worst part, they will tell you, is the pain. The physical, but, more, emotional and spiritual, anguish. One of my ritual abuse survivor clients suffers from intractable nerve pain. But, she says, the "pain in her mind" is the worst.

Throughout their childhoods, and for some throughout their lives, these people have experienced an extraordinary amount of abuse, exploitation, and betrayal. They have seen the worst horrors known to humanity, perpetrated by human beings they knew and often lived with as children. One survivor, Annie Earle, wanted to write a book about ritual abuse, entitled "The Hidden Holocaust." What ritual abuse and mind control survivors have endured is indeed a holocaust.

Childhood trauma survivors develop dissociative disorders to defend themselves against being overwhelmed. But, in order to heal, what they have always protected themselves from must be addressed. So, an important part of therapy for such childhood traumas as sexual, emotional, and physical abuse is treating its emotional devastation.

But this is not ordinary trauma. It is mind control torture.

In the technical sense, what is required from you is empathy. But because you are treating survivors of the unimaginable, you will be dealing not only with your clients' extraordinary level of emotional darkness, but one you might experience as well, when you *both* face what they have endured.

This work is not easy. Therapists can easily become overwhelmed with the multi-layered complexity of the personality systems and the mind control programming, and the ongoing sense of danger in the present. I have tried to make all this manageable by, in particular, making the clients' experiences and personality systems understandable. I have provided you with the information you need about how ritual abuse and mind control work, including various keys to unlocking personality systems and training memories; no matter how complex the inner system and its functioning, or how overpowering and omnipresent the threats might appear, it helps to remember that programming boils down to human beings using time-honored torture and deception and indoctrination techniques on children, with dissociation as its linchpin.

What you and your clients are left with is the sheer horror of it. The horror that makes the therapy take so long, and go so slowly, and require so much of the therapist. No matter how expert you become in understanding this abuse, there are no shortcuts to recovery. Nothing I have taught you can take that away.

When you take these survivors on, you are in for many years of hard work, and a long-term emotional bond with someone who has been severely damaged by what they have gone through. You are also taking on vicarious exposure to the atrocities they have experienced. It takes dedication, patience, and endurance on the part of both the client and the therapist. Even the most high-functioning survivors have a great deal to face, most of which was initially hidden from them. This awareness will rock their view of the world, and of humanity, and even of themselves, as it will yours.

Trauma aftereffects

When I began this work, the issue of trauma in general was not well understood. There were only a handful of books about incest, and, as I have related, even fewer that even acknowledged ritual abuse. In Chapter Fourteen, I mentioned that E. Sue Blume's *Secret Survivors* addressed the sexual consequences of abuse. It also provides a comprehensive review of the cognitive, physical, emotional, and relational consequences of incest trauma, discussing the guilt, shame, and self-hatred, overwhelming fear and anger, even terror, self destructive behaviors, and, above all, grief and loss that incest survivors experience in later life. (Blume's discussion also includes many dissociative symptoms and "MPD", although she acknowledges in personal correspondence that when she wrote her book her understanding of these issues was insufficient.) To understand those issues is basic to this discussion, and I refer the reader to that book for the underpinnings of the material that you will read here concerning the consequences of mind control abuses.

For example, Blume discusses body-related attitudes and dysfunctions resulting from incest. Many ritual abuse and mind control survivors suffer from eating disorders, and from physical ill health. With regard to the latter, osteoarthritis is common as a result of physical abuse and torture. Autoimmune diseases are also common, as well as other serious illnesses related to childhood trauma. Many of these survivors have brain damage from head injuries. Most have some degree of hair-trigger emotional reactivity, even when programs related to this have been addressed, due to an overactive amygdala, the "alarm bell" of the brain. There is evidence that some physiological sequelae are the direct product of certain kinds of tortures, but these aftereffects often reflect the body's "dis-ease" with how the body has been treated.

So, to begin with, ritual abuse and mind control survivors struggle with what every survivor of childhood trauma struggles with. And then they must contend with the rest of it.

Loss, grief, and crying

Survivors have a great deal to grieve about. They grieve not only for what they have lost, but for what they never had. Innocence. A happy, normal childhood. Friendships. Loving parents. Pets who survived and whom they were permitted to love. Pets that did not, whom they were forced to hurt or witness being tortured. Children whom they bonded with, and were forced to rape or kill. Fathers and mothers who did not sexually abuse them. Emotional security and bonding. The ability to trust. Unmet needs throughout childhood. The gradual, healthy development of healthy sexuality in the context of loving relationships. A brain that could develop in a healthy way, with sufficient sleep for rejuvenation when needed. The opportunity for the cortisol released by trauma to relax into a normal level and not constantly be in overdrive. In many cases, an education which would develop their true abilities and fit their true interests. Potential achievements which an overwhelmed child or teenager, struggling with ongoing abuse, could not manage. Physical safety. Physical health and functioning. A sense of being a unified person with an ability to know and meet their own needs and develop their own purpose. And independent thought. If they come to these, it is generally at least twenty years later than other people.

The more time I spend thinking about it, the longer the list grows.

Survivors whose families were involved in their abuse have permanently lost family. In fact, they have been cheated of the opportunity to even understand the concept, just as they have been tricked about the meaning of *love*, and safe, and *trust*. They have no parents who can safely mentor them through their own children's births and childhoods. They cannot trust siblings, aunts and uncles, grandparents. They have to attempt to create artificial families from unrelated friends. They are often excessively dependent on therapists because of the lack of supportive family or healthy childhood dependency. Some have supportive spouses or life companions, but many more have remained single or have unsupportive partners who cannot face or cope with the degree of damage that survivors undergo. Some choose partners who re-enact an aspect of their abuse. And when is it safe to confide the truth to friends? So there's also social isolation, and broken relationships.

Much is now known about the stages of grief. They often occur simultaneously rather than in sequence. One stage is denial. As long as a survivor pretends his or her abuse did not happen, s/he is unable to grieve any of this. Yet, if all the abuse, and all of the losses become available to consciousness at once, they will be overwhelming. So a survivor will have to reduce his or her dissociation very gradually, confronting one loss at a time.

Anger is another important part of grieving. As with other emotions, mind control survivors' relationship with anger has been distorted and manipulated by their abusers. Their anger and rage has been deliberately buried in alters who are brought out for violent rituals or killing, the rage being channeled to a helpless victim rather than to the abusers who set up the whole situation. The anger and rage need healthy expression, through art, through screaming with the therapist, through writing, whatever means gives voice to these justified emotional responses to the horror of what happened.

Sadness is the core of grieving, and its natural expression is crying. But one of the very first programs to be installed is "Don't cry," usually done by the caregiver suffocating the baby whenever it cries. What does it do to an infant to be unable to cry, which means unable to ask for help, unable to express grief and loss and distress? A normal child hurts himself in play, runs to find his mother or father, and then cries out his sadness and pain; this release heals him emotionally. What does it do to a person to be unable to cry for his or her whole life? Mind-controlled and ritually abused children are taught that sadness is weak, and that they should not feel sorry for themselves. They are shamed for experiencing "weak" emotions.

I have found that recovering the ability to cry is one of the most difficult achievements for my ritually abused or mind-controlled clients, but also one of the most significant. Crying, especially in the presence of someone who cares, is enormously healing.

In her book, *Safe Passage to Healing* (1994, p. xxiv), survivor Chrystine Oksana writes this of expressing her anger and sadness:

> My recovery has been a quest to reclaim all parts of myself and then connect that whole self with the good things of this world. My journey is ongoing. Today, most of my illnesses are gone. Now I know that they were symptoms of my repressed feelings—mostly rage and grief. My emotional pain is leaving more slowly, but it is leaving.
>
> Today I am able to cry freely. And in addition to deep grief, I also feel gratitude. It is my tears, not my smiles, that are healing me. Today, my tears speak *my* truth and reveal *their* secrets. It's through my tears that I am breaking free.

The much mocked therapy paradigm is that you must feel worse to feel better. It is a paradox that re-experiencing the traumatic memories, including the emotions, in the presence of a safe person in the present actually brings relief. Not immediately, but eventually, and sometimes sooner rather than later. One of my ritually abused clients goes through a gruelling piece of severely traumatic memory each week, leaving dazed and exhausted. She later emails me each week to tell me how much better she is feeling all the time, how she has been able to do things like play basketball, which she was never able to do, and how well her recovery is going. It is the memory work, the experience of having a witness to her trauma, and the emotional release, which enable her recovery to move forward in this way.

Despair and dissociation

Despair is the penultimate expression of sadness and hopelessness. When a survivor client feels extreme despair, it might be a part of their normal grief. But it might also be the feelings of an inside, mind-controlled child-part leaking through into the adult. The "booby traps" which abusers design to lead to suicide use the despair of an insider to flood the personality system. These insiders with extreme emotions are often deliberately isolated from the rest of the personality system, their emotions being used for the booby traps. They "live" inside in cages or torture situations or "hell", or a place where "God" is rejecting them, and that is all they know of life.

Many such alters live in literal darkness and are unaware of daylight, especially those trained at night in secret programming sessions. When I met one recently, he asked me "What's that bright?", pointing to a tree outside the window. I did not understand what he meant, until the ANP told me it was the sunlight on the leaves of the tree.

He had never seen sunlight.

Let us look at what despair means to a mind-controlled structured system. On not just a physical level, but an emotional and spiritual level, many of the alters have never experienced anything positive. They believe the entire world to be similar to the situations they experienced once, in which they have continued to be trapped, frozen in time.

When a client states that s/he does not want to live in this world, because the world is so dark and evil, the emotions and belief could well be coming from such alters. Although the person needs to grieve what happened to these severely traumatized alters, this needs to be balanced with positive experiences in the present and from the past, shared by other alters. The rest of the system can share positive experiences so these alters can see that their experience is only a very small part of all that is. And they can gradually be given positive experiences of safety and nurturing in the present. Pleasure comes from the simplest experiences. For instance, Jennifer first discovered this when she found an alter who had never seen or felt snow. She had her spinners send the experience of playing in the snow through the system, making all the kids happy.

The therapist's reaction to grieving and despair

Dismissal and minimizing

As survivors of all childhood abuses know, people's reactions often complicate the grieving process. One common reaction is "It's in the past; get over it, put on a happy face." Even therapists do this, believing that reason should conquer emotion. Some schools of therapy are predicated on these approaches to life. But healing just does not work like this. Emotion is primary (see Greenberg, 2002). While rational thinking can help with many aspects of recovery, emotion needs to be expressed in relation to what caused it for complete healing.

Dismissal of either the trauma or the emotional reactions is what most survivors have heard all their lives. For these clients, these responses serve to mirror the lessons that mind controlling abusers taught. "You're just doing this for attention." "There's nothing wrong with you, pull up your socks and get down to work." "You need to think differently." While there is a place for changing thinking habits, especially with regard to the lies indoctrinated into the child by the abusers, emotional reactions should never be dismissed.

Another phenomenon which I have observed among abuse survivors (particularly those who are dissociated) and their therapists is a kind of warm fuzzy thinking and communication, focusing on such things as stuffed animals (which, by the way, are used by perpetrator groups to carry messages), crystals and bubble baths to make the survivor feel better. This often goes with reassurance that the survivor is a "good person" or "did the best she could." In my view, all this is a form of denial of the extent and horror of the trauma. It is also infantilizing, and strips survivors of the recovery task of the system as a whole taking on the responsibility of living as an adult. Yes, it is helpful for child alters to have positive experiences in the present, including comfort objects and opportunities for play, but all this gooey positivity is often masking denial, and avoiding what needs to be dealt with.

Emotional contagion

Other friends or therapists of survivors have the opposite reaction—they become overwhelmed with the survivor's depressed feelings or trauma. The survivor can sense that they cannot take it. One teenage girl came to me shortly after her mother left the family, referred by a therapist who told me that she was unable to stand the intensity of the girl's depression. I sat with the girl for many weeks, while she just felt her depression, though she was unable to speak. It was not until her sister came to me and disclosed a ritual abuse history that I realized why the first girl's emotions were so intense.

If the therapist is overwhelmed with contagion of feelings from the client, the client will be unable to move through those feelings to recovery. Survivors need a caring witness, who can bear the enormity of their emotions and experiences without losing her or his own ground. When I am with my survivor clients, I need to be firmly grounded in my conviction that there is good in the universe, and that recovery is possible, while at the same time having compassion for what they are going through.

One thing that is easily conveyed from client to therapist is paranoia, fear of repercussions from abusers and the feeling that "the cult" is everywhere, the client himself or herself will harm the therapist, or the therapist is doomed to failure. Just because your client—or your colleagues—exaggerate these risks does not mean you have to. Our clients desperately need us to be calm when they are afraid. They need us to be grounded in logic and a realistic, accurate view of their abusers, *sans* the illusions of omnipotence.

It is important to be consciously aware of your client's emotions; allow them to come into you but be aware that they are the client's, not yours. This is the definition of empathy, and it is a delicate process. It is a central part of therapy. Your mirror neurons will register what is going on in the client. The sensation is slightly different from what you would feel if it were going on in you. But it is easy to become confused about which feelings are yours and which belong to the other person. I had difficulty making this distinction when I was a beginning therapist. I have become more skilled at it over the years as I have paid it conscious attention.

This skill is not only useful for the therapist, it is useful for the client—a kind of "internal empathy". The ANP can learn to distinguish between emotions which arise from her own reaction to a present situation and those which arise from an alter being triggered into an old emotion which belongs to a past trauma. If she is unable to recognize this distinction, she can be easily overwhelmed, whereas if she can recognize an alter's feelings, she can mobilize her resources to comfort that alter without herself being contaminated with its feelings. This is particularly important for DDNOS rather than DID clients.

Most dissociative clients have a highly attuned sensitivity to others' emotions, developed over their childhood years when they had to learn to expect what was coming from other people. If we try to deceive them about what we are feeling, it does not work. If we feel one thing and say another, they will notice it, and this will damage their trust in us. At the same time, they can easily misunderstand our nonverbal signals: for example, interpreting us as tired of *them* when we are just plain tired. So, we need to be transparent with our emotions, and at the same time ready to explain what is going on inside us and why, if it appears to be necessary. And this means we have to be highly congruent. To do this work, we do need both to feel for our clients and to have considerable inner strength, so that we are not overwhelmed by what they are going through. We need to keep ourselves sufficiently separate from them that we are not immersed in their despair, and sufficiently attuned to them that we develop a strong emotional bond.

Isolation from peers

One major concern for therapists providing outpatient treatment for survivors is the lack of understanding of either ritual abuse/mind control or dissociative disorders by their peers in the psychiatric system. Many of our colleagues do not even consider the dissociative disorder diagnosis to be valid, use medication as the primary treatment modality, and, as discussed in Chapter Twelve, "Maybe I made it up," even some who consider themselves "trauma specialists" might assume we are creating false memories when we recognize ritual abuse and mind control. I have no easy answers for this situation. I recommend that whenever possible nonmedical therapists should find a sympathetic psychiatrist who has knowledge of dissociative disorders, can prescribe medication when it is needed for such symptoms as depression, and can take responsibility for the client if she or he has to be hospitalized. Unfortunately, such persons are hard to come by. I would settle for one who, like the one I knew, is at least open to your expertise and the existence of the phenomena we are treating.

But if you seek supervision, it really needs to be with someone who has the necessary knowledge. Training in treatment of dissociative disorders is not yet mandatory in any mental health profession. Your supervisor, if s/he is an experienced therapist, can always learn along with you. I remember one psychiatrist who was very vocal about his opposition to the notion of dissociative disorders. Then he acquired a patient who visibly switched into a child state in front of him. You should have heard him babbling about it in staff meetings, all excited that it was real. Many therapists find dissociative disorders fascinating in our initial experiences, but we all have to get beyond that stage in order to be effective with our clients.

This is the real world of our peers. In this world, we can feel peer pressure, and we can be intimidated when those with more impressive credentials than our own make definite statements about the nonexistence of dissociative disorders or of ritual abuse and mind control. It takes time for society's mindset to change. I came to realize when dealing with our psychiatric establishment that it is very difficult for someone who has practiced for twenty or thirty years within a certain model to change his or her way of thinking about the most challenging of patients. I understood this, because it was even difficult for me. Once I began to understand dissociative disorders, I looked back at my past clients, and immediately recognized three whose dissociative disorders I had missed, two of whom (both diagnosed bipolar) were probably ritually abused. One of these women had even told me that she remembered a church service in which everything was said backwards (presumably, a Black Mass) and that her little daughter was seeing demonic faces in a picture on her wall. I told the woman to get back on her medication. I worked with this client for many years, believing I was helping her. I sincerely regret my lack of understanding. And I wish someone had given me the information I needed earlier.

Compassionate witnessing

One thing we therapists need to remember is the enormous power of compassion. We do not need to have knowledge of all the details of ritual abuse and mind control, though knowledge helps. What we need, most of all, is compassion, the ability to *be with* our clients through all the ups and downs of their recovery process. This enables them to complete their grieving and to know that the world holds goodness and love, as they experience it through our presence with them.

It is not easy.

In Kathy Steele's "Sitting with the shattered soul" (1989), she writes,

All the therapists I know who do this work have been blindsided at least once by the horror of it. Their own vulnerability, their helplessness in the face of such abuse is staggering. So is the evil. I don't know another word for it. Science has failed us here, so I draw upon a spiritual vocabulary . . .

So how do you sit with a shattered soul? Gently, with gracious and deep respect. Patiently, for time stands still for the shattered, and the momentum of healing will be slow at first. With the tender strength that comes from an openness to your own deepest wounding, and to your own deepest healing. Firmly, never wavering in the utmost conviction that evil is powerful, but there is a good that is more powerful still. Stay connected to that Goodness with all your being, however it manifests itself to you. Acquaint yourself with the shadows that lie deep within you. And then, open yourself, all that is you, to the Light. Give freely. Take in abundantly. Find your safety, your refuge, and go there as you need. Hear what you can, and be honest about the rest: Be honest at all costs. Words won't always come; sometimes there are no words in the face of such tragic evil. But in your willingness to be with them, they will hear you: from soul to soul they will hear that for which there are no words.

When you can, in your own time, turn and face that deep chasm within. Let go. Grieve, rage, shed tears, share tears. Find those you trust and let them be with you. Know laughter, the healing power of humor. Trust yourself. Trust the process. Embrace your world, this world that holds you safely now. Grasp the small tender mercies of the moment. Let you be loved. Let you love. The shattered soul will heal.

Guilt, shame, and forgiveness for perpetration

Childhood sex abuse survivors must deal with guilt and shame from being sexually victimized, and from their bodies' natural responses. Ritual abuse and mind control survivors must deal with sexual abuse that far exceeds the scope of "garden variety" incest, and physical responses that are not merely organic but programmed and distorted. But that is almost inconsequential compared with the massive guilt and shame they must face for having participated in rapes, murders, and cannibalism, which to them are very real whether or not there was trickery involved. For this, they often feel they are too evil to be forgiven, even by a "higher power."

This is not something that the average therapist can relate to, and it requires a massive effort to come close to true empathy. Who of us can even imagine what we would feel if we had hurt another in such a way?

This struggle is compounded by the shame heaped upon them by the perpetrators, particularly after participating in an act of evil. "You are one of us." "Nobody else will ever want you because you are evil." "You will harm anyone you get close to." "God hates you."

It helps them to see the entire picture of the traumatic events, including their attempts to refuse to do the evil that was demanded of them. In most cases, for every alter who stuck a sharp stick inside a vagina, plunged a knife into a living body, or took "communion" with the heart of the sacrificial victim, there were several who refused, and were severely punished, in series, until a new one was created who would commit the required act.

It also helps these survivors who are immersed in shame to have a real relationship with a person—their therapist (and/or their partner and/or their friend)—who accepts them even knowing that they have done these things.

Their sense of unworthiness is also exacerbated by the fact that if they prayed as children, there was still no apparent divine intervention; the abuse continued.

Certainly, if our clients choose to have a spiritual faith, it can help them to know that the Creator of the universe accepts and forgives them. But even in this seemingly innocuous goal, we must be very careful, because there are traps built in to words like this. The very concept of forgiveness might be contaminated by these devious abusers, as we saw in Old Lady's being "forgiven" by the priest through sexual acts (in Chapter Five). Their alters might remember rejection and abuse by "Jesus" and "God." Old Lady's experiences show us how many Christian beliefs (like God forgiving) and words (like "Suffer the little children to come unto me") have been so perverted for survivors that they cannot be used with them. If someone is using such concepts with your client, you could gently question him or her about what such things mean, to make sure that, for example, "forgive" does not mean "rape."

Remember to reinforce that guilt and shame are not good or bad but normal and human. We feel guilty when we commit evil acts, acts that harm others. We feel shame about who we are when we have violated our own deepest sense of morality. Stella Katz writes about the guilt experienced during the recovery process, and relates it to a human "core" who always knows what is right. She demonstrates how perspectives, and understanding, change in the different stages of life:

The one thing I'd like to get through strong and clear, is that there is always one person. The core[1] whom the alters think they are protecting (and the operative word here is THINK) actually always knows what is going on, at every stage of the game. The alters do most of the shit, and very rarely understand that they do nothing without the permission of the core. Without the core's seeing and knowing what is happening then integration as an adult would not be possible. The core always grows, and always knows. The difference is that as a child the core feels it more as bad dreams. By the time you are a mid teen, you have full knowledge that it's not a dream, but you are protected from the pain, which makes it easier for you to do harm to others because it's more like you are acting this all out in a video game, as if the real people are Avatars, but you still know. And in my case my own sense of right and wrong allowed the full brunt of the guilt to flow through, and that is why I would sabotage training sessions, so that these people would have a hope of undoing this all easier than if the training was complete.

Stella knows, by experience on both sides of ritual abuse (as victim and as adult perpetrator), that there are no "attachments", no way of dismissing her actions as not belonging to her. It is *all her*. The guilt is real, and has to be experienced for full healing, which includes taking responsibility and self-forgiveness. Even if he or she is forced to do it, a child whose body is involved in an evil act, for example holding a knife that hurts or kills, is violating her own core spirituality, her human ability to have empathy for other living creatures. S/he might well create a non-empathic alter in the process, but when that alter joins with those who feel empathy and compassion, guilt will result. This guilt needs to be accepted and confessed.

What that means is that often the therapist has to act as a confessor, the person to whom the client reveals the enormity of the things she or he did. And we need to be quiet witnesses who take it seriously while still accepting the person, neither recoiling nor arguing that it was not the client's fault. Whether or not s/he intended it or wanted it, the ritually abused or mind-controlled client has done evil, *and needs to confess it*. For her healing. For her humanity.

This does not require specific religious beliefs on the part of either the client or the therapist; it only requires recognition of innate morality and how it has been violated. The issue of "forgiveness" is often introduced in conversations about recovery from sexual trauma; one aspect of such forgiveness is "forgiveness of the self." Nowhere is this more relevant than in the arena of ritual abuse and mind control. Having faced the darkest corner of her life, the survivor needs to be helped to forgive herself, and, if she is so inclined, to understand that a forgiving God, who forgives others, would forgive her as well.

Near-death spiritual experiences

Spiritual experiences do happen to ritually abused children, even though no deity intervenes to stop the abuse. Ritual abusers frequently bring children to or near the point of death, and they have no control over what happens in the person's experience at that point. They can restart a stopped heart, but they cannot prevent the near-death experiences. Over the years, with the clients who were brave enough to work through the most horrific of their memories, I have encountered amazing near-death experiences (NDEs) that address the truth of what the client has experienced on the deepest level.

One six-year-old girl experienced the usual components of the NDE, including the presence of a being of light, and a life review in which she recognized she was not responsible for the perpetration that was forced upon her, only for the events in which she made an active choice to harm someone. Another child of five, while beaten almost to death by her mother, had an alter who remained in a place with an angel. When a new alter was brought to life by the cult doctor, she said something about wanting to stay with the angel, and he told her mother, "Don't mention it, she'll get over it." Once she had accessed this memory, the client has been able to go to this happy place to be with her angel when she needs it. Another client, too, found some of her most damaged alters had angels accompanying them.

Now, I do not know what an angel is, and explaining this phenomenon is beyond my scope as a psychologist, but I do know that experiences of angels have happened to a number of my ritually abused clients, none of whom have a specific religious faith. (I am not talking about the angels who are simulated as part of ritual abuse training; for example, to invite a survivor to suicide. Perhaps these groups simulate angels because they have more experience than I of survivors who talk about them.)

Another client's Satan alter personality was enduring some training in a simulated hell, when the drugs were too strong, and the child almost died. "Satan" split off another alter, "Satan's ghost," who found himself in a beautiful place with a being of light. He encountered a dog and a baby whom he was to be forced to kill, and both told him that they forgave him. When he returned to fake hell, he knew it was not really the afterlife. And another client remembered a near-death experience in which a little boy she knew, whom she had been forced to kill in a ritual, was waiting for her at the other end of the tunnel, and told her he would remain with her as her helper.

These accounts give me hope. It is an amazing thing to be working through a memory of severe torture with a client and unexpectedly coming upon a wonderfully positive near-death experience.

Coming to terms with spiritual abuse

The concepts of meaning and spirituality as they relate to ritual abuse and mind control are very challenging, for both survivors and their therapists. Ritual abuse directs specific abuses at the victim's spiritual belief system involving simulation of religious figures, both good and evil, in perverted ways and forced indoctrination into occult beliefs. Forced perpetration, especially of real or simulated sacrifice of animals, babies, and/or adults, is followed by teaching the child that s/he is evil, and alters are told they are demonic evil beings. Children experience sexual assaults by "God" and marriages to "Satan." They watch as "Jesus" turns his back on them. The abuses are so horrendous, and divine or human help for victimized children so vividly absent, that we question any faith we might have had in humanity or a benevolent deity. When we listen to stories of little children being violated, tortured, and made to abuse others we recognize that we are encountering evil, no matter what our world view. But what does that mean, and how do we address it clinically?

In response, many survivors adopt conservative Christian belief systems, in the hope of finding an answer to the noise in their heads about Satan and demons and God, or of finding something good which is stronger than the evil to which they have been exposed. Others adopt new-age approaches, which include beliefs about angels, and sometimes include a notion of past lives and karma that defines the trauma they have experienced in this life as something they earned in previous lives. Others maintain belief systems that reassure them that "everything happens for a reason", and "God never gives us more than we can handle", although "God's ways are not to be known by mortals." These beliefs provide some survivors with the perspective of a just, or at least a protected, universe. Many survivors, however, fall into despair, believing either that they are truly evil or that there is no good in this world. If there is a God, and even He does not care, how can they find the strength to fight for themselves?

The therapists working with this population come from many different philosophical and religious viewpoints. A substantial number of therapists who are devoted to this issue come from a conservative or evangelical Christian viewpoint. Others who might be privately critical of fundamentalist beliefs are much less likely to feel alienated by such beliefs when held by RA/MC clients, about whom the therapists' perspective is, "Whatever works." What we encounter with these clients challenges all our world views. We all struggle with the same questions, and we all resolve them differently.

Our mind-controlled clients have been robbed of their freedom to be self-determining. Whatever our personal belief system, we can surely agree on the goal of restoring these clients' autonomy. This includes their ability to choose their own beliefs.

In *Reaching for the Light*, ritual abuse survivor Emilie Rose has a wonderful chapter about spiritual abuse. She believes that spiritual abuse is perhaps the greatest wound of a ritual abuse survivor. An important part of Rose's spiritual healing was rejecting the false notions of the divine which she had been taught, not only by the abusers, but by the conventional religion which she had at the start of her journey (1996, pp. 102–103):

> I don't believe it is possible to be a survivor of ritual abuse without undergoing a deep, spiritual crisis . . . My realization that I was a ritual survivor profoundly affected me. In some ways it totally shattered my old ideas about God. Who was this loving God I had heard about all my life? How could God be loving if God would not save those children I saw sacrificed? How could God be all-powerful, all-protecting, omnipotent? Obviously God could be none of these and also be good. Good Gods didn't watch the massacre of innocents when they had it within their power to act. Good Gods did something. How could I place the heinous reality of ritual abuse into a spiritual framework while still embracing the God I know? The answer was that I could not. Instead, I railed at this God. I hated this God—"the bastard God," as my friend said. Finally, in the midst of the deepest spiritual crisis of my life, I renounced this God. . . . I had to create a completely different vision of God. Today I think of God/Good as a light energy, an energy of creation that flows within and without so that it is a part of me, as I am a part of it.

These questions, she says,

> come from a part of us that knows that nothing like ritual abuse should ever happen to anyone. They come from the part of us that knows that what happened to us is contrary to the way the world was intended to be. That part of us is outraged and sickened and horrified. Our questions come from the place within us that cries out against such evil, that life-clinging part of us that helped to keep us alive. That tiny spark of justice within us could not be put out even in the most horrible, degrading experiences a human being can go through.

But she sees hope:

> Every ritual abuse survivor has an inner part that somehow stayed connected to life even in the midst of torture and death . . . It may have many names: the strong one, the keeper of the spirit, the healer, the mystic, the grandparent, the wise one. Whatever we call the part, we can assist in its healing by seeking that part of us, inviting it out, befriending it, nurturing it, and assisting it to develop further in our life . . . This strong one within has a natural longing for life and healing. It is wise beyond years. It knows about pain and healing and spirit. It may be the place where our connection with a higher power resides. It guides us in the healing journey if we give it room to do so."

She talks about survivors, including herself, having transcendent experiences of joy and love, even during the years of the abuse. This, to her, is God (*ibid.*, p. 165):

> There are many things like that in my life, that I can point to or experience, and say, "This is real. This is good. This you did not destroy, and will not, ever, no matter how hard you try. This is

God, the transcendent, the holy. This is what matters, and it is with this that I will cast my lot, *not evil.*" I know evil, intimately, and I reject it with everything in me. This does not mean that I reject those parts of me that were made to do bad things. I accept them, condemn the ways they were violated, and am thankful for the ways they helped me survive. And so, I see my life, as a kind of ongoing prayer. It goes on all the time, because in every moment, every thought, every action, I feel confronted with that choice between good and evil. It is not merely a theoretical choice. I know I really could go either way. And I continually constitute myself by consciously choosing the good.

My experience as a therapist for survivors of ritual abuse and mind control has been similar to that of Rose, the survivor. I can no longer easily embrace the idea of a God who is both all-loving and all-powerful, and who intervenes in people's lives to prevent disasters. I am aware of too many horrors. I know also that "but for the grace of God", I too could have been a ritual abuse survivor, and yes, a perpetrator, given different circumstances in my childhood. So I was not, but countless other people—people with no less value than I—were. What that demonstrates to me is that God does not micromanage.

As a therapist, my belief system does not matter to anyone but me. The best thing I can do for my clients is to bear witness to their experiences, both of pain and of overcoming, and to allow them to find their own meaning by thinking for themselves, rather than imposing any meaning of my own upon them. I tell my mind-controlled clients early in therapy, and repeat often, that my purpose is to help them take their own lives back, to be genuinely free. That includes the freedom to make their own meaning of their lives, develop their own beliefs, and choose their own life paths. And that is the opposite of mind control.

For therapists: coping with the stress of this work

Pearlman and Saakvitne (1995) have written extensively about the "vicarious traumatization" which therapists experience when working with trauma survivors. They state that

> All therapists working with trauma survivors will experience lasting alterations in their cognitive schemas, having a significant impact on the therapist's feelings, relationships, and life. Whether these changes are ultimately destructive to the helper and to the therapeutic process depends . . . on the extent to which the therapist is able to engage in a parallel process to that of the victim client, the process of integrating and transforming these experiences of horror or violation.

Your client deserves to heal, and you have committed yourself to facilitating that process. Here are some guidelines that may help support you as you face the challenge of working with the massively traumatized clients who have experienced ritual abuse and mind control.

Develop awareness about yourself

It is important to be introspective when working with survivors of extreme trauma. Know yourself and know when you are in over your head. This does not necessarily mean withdrawing from those clients you have taken on, but it does mean accessing other resources to help you feel more effective in your work. Allow yourself all your emotional reactions, and allow time for them when you are alone or with friends. Watch yourself for withdrawal from survivors' pain, and disconnection from your own. Your obligation is to work on yourself to the point where your own reactions do not interfere with the therapy you are conducting. Much has been written about both countertransference and vicarious traumatization, so I will not repeat it here, but I do encourage you to make use of it.

With ritual abuse and mind control, one major temptation for the therapist is to disbelieve the client when the allegations become bizarre and extreme. I have discussed this further in the chapter about clients disbelieving their own experiences. It is important not to dismiss a client as making things up when they make such allegations, and to continue to treat them with kindness and consistency. But it is important to acknowledge when you are wondering about the client's truthfulness, and to seek support from others who understand the issue, whether in person, on line, or in books.

Be honest with your client

As you ride the roller coaster of transference and countertransference, I believe it is important to reveal information about your own reactions to the client, to communicate that he or she has an impact on you and that you are human too. You will probably need to educate the client about your time and energy needs. It is important to be honest and acknowledge your mistakes to the client, while keeping clear professional boundaries.

Look after yourself

Have realistic expectations of yourself as a therapist. When other therapists discover you work with clients who report experiences of ritual abuse or mind control, they will either criticize you and want to discredit you, or want to send more such clients to you. (Either way will provide an extra challenge requiring you to take care of yourself.) Go slowly at first, recognizing that this is all new learning and that you can become overloaded with trauma if you have very many severely abused clients, especially if they are ritual abuse survivors with current contact with their abusers. If you are able, balance your caseload by limiting the numbers of dissociative clients and ritual abuse or mind control survivors in your practice. And balance your clinical caseload with other professional involvements, such as research or teaching or writing. And balance your life. I know you have heard this before, but it is important to stay involved in joyful extracurricular activities and to take care of your physical health. These clients require a long-term commitment, so we need not to burn out either physically or emotionally.

Finally, there is the very real issue of safety. If you are dealing with current-contacting ritual abuse or mind control survivors, you may need to pay special attention to your physical safety through such means as alarm systems, self-defense training, and having others in your office space. It is unwise to work from your home with this clientele, unless you have known them for years and know they are completely out of contact with their abusers. Put backup safety procedures in place, such as keeping the names that your clients name in a locked box not on your premises, or sending copies of evidence of perpetrators' criminal acts by registered mail to a lawyer or other safe person. Make sure your client knows you have done this (the appropriate alter will hear you tell the client).

Have a strong support system

Unfortunately, you cannot tell your non-therapist family members and your friends about your clients' disclosures. If you do so you will be violating confidentiality and probably traumatizing them. You can, however, use these relationships to bring positivity into your life and balance out the effect of the exposure to extreme trauma, to find unconditional acceptance in what might be a critical world, and to be reminded that love—pure, unselfish, uncontaminated, non-abuse, non-demanding love—exists. If you do not have a supportive partner, consider a pet. Animals can love.

The most helpful professional support is from other therapists who deal with trauma and dissociation. Discuss cases (with client consent), and your feelings about them. It is important to balance your need to verbalize the traumatic imagery you are trying to work through with the need to protect your colleagues from the stress of assimilating new traumatic material. "No one can face trauma alone." Internet discussion groups can be helpful, as can professional supervision from someone experienced in this area. But professional supervision or consultation from someone who does not understand this client population can be destructive to you—and to your client.

Sometimes, engaging in social activism regarding these problems can help you feel you are changing things on a larger level. But it can add to your trauma, as you are exposed to the issues even when not seeing clients, and the organized backlash against recognizing the existence of these abuses can be upsetting. If you are the kind of person who feels empowered by action, do what feels right to do. Because it needs to be done. And because action can be an amazing remedy for feeling powerless.

Develop awareness about your client's condition and history

I have seen many therapists who carry just one dissociative or mind-controlled client, and because it is only one client of many, do not take the time to learn what they need to serve that client effectively. But I recommend studying whatever resources you can find on all topics related to this field. The more you learn, the more effective you can be with your present clients and others who may come to you in the future. We desperately need more therapists who are skilled and experienced in working with mind control survivors.

No matter what you have already learnt, an attitude of being open to learn and to make sense of what you hear from your clients will enable you to advance your own understanding and ultimately that of other therapists. Remember, the state of our knowledge regarding this field is still in its infancy. And remember that your clients will be your best teachers. Although I have learnt a great deal about dissociation and the dissociative disorders and about transference and therapy in general from the writings of others, most of what I know about mind control survivors has been learnt from the people who lived it.

Recognize the benefits of this work

This work can be enriching—it can reward us with the ability to appreciate life more fully, to take it more seriously, and to have a greater scope of understanding of others and ourselves. It can inspire us to form deeper, more honest and sensitive relationships. My clients consistently inspire me, and working with them—with all its challenges—makes me know I am doing something worthwhile. For me, this work allows me to have a sense of a higher purpose in life and the camaraderie of others who are involved with this purpose.

Therapy with these most abused survivors requires a great deal of integrity, which Judith Herman (1992, p. 154) defines as

> the capacity to affirm the value of life in the face of death, to be reconciled with the finite limits of one's own life and the tragic limitations of the human condition, and to accept these realities without despair. Integrity is the foundation upon which trust in relationships is originally formed, and upon which shattered trust may be restored.

Note

1. By "the core" I believe she means the essential parts of the person, the infant from whom all the other alters were split, and the two grown alters who are the first splits (the Firstborn and the Gatekeeper), as she defines them in Chapter Seven.

CHAPTER SIXTEEN

Working with the traumatic memories

The DID and DDNOS created by ritual abuse and mind control cannot be resolved without putting together the traumatic experiences which initially created the dissociation. The focus of dissociation treatment is not to make recovery a fact-finding mission. As Richard Kluft (1997), a leader in the field of dissociative disorder treatment, states in "On the treatment of traumatic memories of DID patients: Always? Never? Sometimes? Now? Later?" (what a wonderful title!), "The integration of the DID patient's identity appears to require the working through his or her traumatic memories, however flawed with regard to historical accuracy and however unsettling work with such memories may be" (p. 80).

Just as dissociation itself is both a psychological and a physiological process, so, too, is its resolution. "Memory work" is the common term for the therapeutic process through which all of these physical and psychological pieces are re-associated. In biological terms, memory fragments belonging to the different senses (sight, hearing, smell, taste, touch and other body sensations), along with the various emotions, are fed through the hippocampus to the brain's cerebral cortex, where they become integrated. In this way they move from the unconscious to the conscious mind, from separated (dissociated) to connected (associated). What was formerly a dissociated, "forgotten" memory is now consciously remembered. It no longer erupts in disturbing ways or creates flashbacks. It also loses much of its emotional "punch." And it becomes part of the person's life, which is less fragmented.

In order to help a client with DID or DDNOS work through trauma memories, the therapist helps the survivor to relive them in a safe place with a safe person. While being helped to know s/he is in the present, the client can put all the parts of the memory together in the conscious mind, making the dissociative barriers unnecessary.

It is particularly important to do this work with clients who have experienced deliberate mind control as children, because their alters believe that their lives or the lives of others are dependent on them doing the jobs that they were programmed to do. The dissociated memories of the abuse events during which they were given those jobs, pieces of which are held by different alters (and kept separate from others), need to be put together so that these clients' parts will be able to see the tricks and lies that their abusers employed. This is what will free them from their overwhelming compulsion.

When is a client ready to process memories?

One does not rush into memory work such as this. There are many therapeutic tasks that precede it, even for spontaneously developed multiples. Interventions required to prepare mind control survivors have been described in previous chapters of this book. In general, a client is not ready for memory work until the personality system is cooperative, and the alters in charge permit all the alters involved in a particular memory to take part in its processing. In my experience, a memory is not completely processed (and the resulting programming dissolved) until every part of the person involved has put their part of the memory into the complete picture.

If all the parts of mind control survivors are not aligned with the process, protector parts may also punish those parts who disclose forbidden material prematurely. Delay is important when the personality system is not ready. But the process cannot be delayed forever.

Dealing with flashbacks

Memories usually first surface through flashbacks. Flashbacks are the eruption into consciousness of dissociated trauma material, in an unproductive way. Psychologist Judith Peterson, in a workshop I attended in 1991, elegantly defined a flashback as a "closed physiological loop of re-abuse." A flashback is a memory fragment. It may be visual (hallucinating what happened), auditory (hearing a voice or a scream), emotional (e.g., a panic attack deriving from a partial memory of a frightening situation), or physiological (a "body memory" such as a pain in a part of the body that was injured during the event). Until the trauma is resolved, these flashbacks will recur, often in unacceptable times and places.

I remember how helpless I felt when my first DID client, Teresa, repeatedly re-experienced the same trauma flashback in sessions, over and over without resolution. I realized that I had to learn how to help her resolve the traumatic memories more effectively. What I did not understand, at least in the beginning, was the role mind control could play.

I have worked with other clients whose previous therapists spent untold hours assisting them in re-experiencing bodily sensations of abuse with no goal or direction, or who have devoted themselves to endlessly speculating on what could have caused such symptoms. "Abreaction," traditionally recommended by the dissociative disorders field and defined by Wikipedia as "a psychological term for reliving an experience in order to purge it of its emotional excesses," can become a goal in itself. However, although the emotions are parts of the memory that need to be included in its reconstitution, going through the emotions is not sufficient for resolution.

At the other extreme, many therapists who recognize that flashbacks generally do not resolve trauma have taken the stance that "stabilization" involves preventing flashbacks from occurring, and that memory reconstitution is unnecessary. But clients who are merely "stabilized" continue to be at risk of destabilization if present events trigger aspects of their trauma. Working through the memories thoroughly creates long-term stability.

Having established that memories need to be worked through, I must now caution you that not all flashbacks experienced by ritually abused and mind-controlled clients are necessarily important enough to be dealt with. In fact, under certain circumstances, such as with regard to memories that come up spontaneously, rather than the ones you deliberately target, the opposite is true. As you might recall, the flashbacks experienced by these clients are frequently internal "punishments" for disclosures of secrets. If your client is having a lot of flashbacks, you will need to discover whether this is the case. If so, you will need to slow down the disclosures and get to know the hierarchy of parts who are doing their jobs by giving or ordering those flashbacks.

If a client is in the middle of a flashback, it is imperative to stop the symptoms. You will need to ground the client for this purpose. There are various ways to do this. It is generally necessary to tell clients to open their eyes, which often spontaneously close during flashbacks. It is also grounding for clients to listen to your voice and the sounds around them (e.g., birds, city noises, traffic), or to name things in the room, including what he or she is touching (couch, pillow, etc.). I like to ask the client to touch his or her clothing, and name each item, as these survivors are frequently naked during the flashbacks.

You can also use a signal to bring the client back to the present. With some clients I place my *right* hand firmly on their *right* shoulder,[1] and say "Stop!" firmly and quite loudly. If we have pre-arranged this signal, it usually works. But it is important to make sure that any physical touch you use is not one which carries a meaning assigned to it by the perpetrators. For example, the husband of a ritually abused client discovered that she calmed down if he ruffled the hair on the top of her head. Unfortunately, this touch meant to her very young parts, "Be quiet or else!" This particular "touch trigger" is often used by ritually abusing parents. It looks innocuous when a mother tousles her little girl's hair, but, for these families, it is not. Inside, the alters were in turmoil, while outwardly the survivor appeared calm. (This duality is common among mind-controlled persons.)

Now, be aware: although these techniques can be successful in the control of random and unwelcome flashbacks, grounding, like other forms of containment, just prevents a flashback from occurring at any particular moment; it is still likely to erupt when the client is alone, or as a nightmare. The flashback will not be resolved until the memory is properly processed. However, learning to close down a flashback in your office is actually important preparation for actual memory work. It is also important to teach the client how to do grounding techniques on his or her own, since flashbacks occur outside of the therapy office.

Internal negotiation is an important skill for the client in dealing with flashbacks. You have seen some examples of how your clients might work with their own inner worlds and parts. Here's another: a client was having horrible bodily symptoms of choking. He found the part responsible, and struck a deal with her: she would remove his symptoms if in our next therapy session she would be allowed to tell me about the abuse that caused the symptoms. This allowed him to feel better until the therapy session, when he kept his part of the bargain.

When you negotiate with the alters regarding the flashbacks, it is important to talk with the alters *causing* the flashback rather than the ones *experiencing* it; they are usually not the same. The ones causing it are the ones doing their jobs.

If the client is ritually abused, there is often a "Gatekeeper" part who is in charge of keeping memories and feelings put away (or letting them out on command). With such a client you might be able to close down a flashback by asking the Gatekeeper to put away the memory until it is time to work on it.

After a flashback has been closed down, the client should be asked to look after the parts who were having the flashback. They can be put in separate rooms in the inner world, be put to sleep, or be given caretakers.

Memory work

Now we come to actually processing the memories. I do not claim that the method I am about to describe to you is the only technique, or the best technique, you can use; I can only claim that it is very effective for me, and that it has been carefully honed for a number of years, during which this time I have worked the "bugs" out of it, correcting the most common errors which I used to make. In my experience, a few key principles can make memory work with dissociative clients efficient, minimally traumatizing, and permanently healing. This method of memory processing works with most of my dissociative clients, and has been most effective for those with histories of organized abuse by cults or other groups who engage in deliberate mind control of children.

It takes advantage of the way the organized abusers have stored the memories and the personality parts inside their victims.

With those clients who are experienced in memory processing, I am now able to process at least one, and sometimes, up to three, traumatic memories within a two-hour therapy session. On those occasions that a memory takes two or more sessions, we put it into secure storage, which is generally already provided in a mind-controlled personality system. That way, feelings will not "leak" (in the form of "body memories" or flashbacks) between sessions.

Finding and selecting memories

Using recorder alters

Many ritually abusing and mind control groups deliberately create recorder alter personalities who know everything about the system and the history, and observe it with apparent disinterest, wanting things to be better but never intervening. These recorders, by the way, could well be the traditional "inner self helpers" (ISHes) described in the early literature. They might have other labels, such as "internal programmers" or "file managers."

When I want to process a particular memory or program, I ask the recorders to find both the contents of the event and all the parts of the person who are holding any part of that memory. Recorders are not usually allowed to deliberately intervene on their own initiative to help the person, but they are glad to assist when asked.

Thanks to the recorders, it is actually easier to access and reconstitute memories held within ritually abused or mind-controlled clients than those within other kinds of trauma survivors. You do not need to chase flashbacks. You do not need to wait for the client to spend weeks retrieving the content of the memory. Focus on the function. You simply ask for "the suicide program", "the memory that gives you the stomach ache", "the program that makes you bulimic", "the memory that you see part of in the nightmare", "the memory that gives you that awful feeling of sadness", or "the memory that makes you get up and go outside at night". The recorders know how to find the right one, even if several different memories are causing a particular symptom and need to be processed in chronological order.

It can also be helpful, especially in the later stages of therapy, to have the internal programmers create charts of the programs, and then work through them systematically (see more on this in Chapter Ten).

Before processing a memory, all you need to know is that it is the one causing the symptoms that need to be removed, and that you will have enough time in the session to get through it from start to finish (or can contain it well if it is unfinished). I prefer *not* to be told ahead of time what the content of the memory is. In these days, when therapists are being accused of creating "false memories" in their clients, I want to avoid all possibility of suspicion. Also, speculation by the ANP and other alters about what a memory might contain can contaminate the process and make it more difficult to get at the actual memory.

Spontaneous dissociatives usually do not have a recorder. The key to finding their memories lies in winning the trust and cooperation of the personality system. This is also applicable to some extent to the memories of mind control survivors that result from trauma which was not deliberate mind control. (Some such survivors have recorders for this kind of trauma; some do not.) In this case, what you want is for the alters holding parts of various memories to come forward willingly to process them. Often, the ones who have only the awareness of what occurred do not want to experience the pain, or the ones who just have the feelings do not want to know what happened to them; in that case, you have to talk with them about the advantages of memory processing.

With the parts who do not want the pain, emphasize that everyone inside shares the same body, and while *they* might feel fine, someone else inside is in pain. The ones who do not want the knowledge need to know that the abuse is now over, if and when it is, and it is safer to know than not to know. Needless to say, do not say this to a ritually abused or mind-controlled client unless you are absolutely sure that there is no current contact with the perpetrators. If there *is* current contact, emphasize that it is important to process the memories to destroy the programs, so that the perpetrator group will lose its ability to access the client and re-traumatize them.

Choosing the memories to be put together

Here is one place where you need to proceed differently with mind control and ritual abuse survivors than you would with survivors of other traumas, such as incest. With survivors of "regular" traumas, you wait for memories to emerge, and work with those that are emerging. With mind control, you choose the memories strategically in order to dismantle the programming. It is possible to do so because of the storage systems for memories deliberately installed by the mind controllers.

The only essential memories to process are the ones that make the person unsafe (e.g., programs), or the ones that create symptoms which interfere with everyday life. This is the same with spontaneous DID, except that safety issues are largely internal and are often more effectively removed by communicating with alters rather than by memory work. Some people might legitimately choose not to know what happened to them, if it is not interfering with their current lives.

Start with relatively easy memories, relatively minor traumas that do not have too much shock or horror or physical pain, so that the client can learn the process. With one client, for instance, I began with memories of her mother washing her hair and pulling it while combing it. Another client chose to work on the memories of being teased at school, which caused the splits between her school-going parts. In this example, there was no physical pain, and the emotional pain was not overwhelming. Other alters could observe this work and see how it resolved the trauma. I ask the parts who have more difficult memories to observe what happens when I process the easy ones, so that they can see how to put memories together, and what happens as a result.

After the system knows how it is done, we select the memories we will work through on a logical basis. With programmed clients, the goal is safety. I pay no attention to what is flashing back, but instead go for the most dangerous trainings of the alter personalities. Whether or not the person has current contact with the perpetrators, suicide and self-harm training are of utmost importance. If there is current contact, then any training that makes the client obey the perpetrators is addressed. Access training, training which makes the client report what has been disclosed in therapy, and that which causes them to fear therapists, are all very important in the beginning.

It is a very useful technique to put together a number of similar memories into one abreaction. If a client was sexually abused by her father, for example, there may have been hundreds or thousands of incidents. All the oral rapes in the bedroom, or all the touching in the television room, can be grouped together and processed as if they are one. I do not know how the client does this, but I know that they can, and do. This is fortunate, because if it were not the case, trauma recovery would take forever.

Preparation for memory work

You do not just dive into a traumatic memory and hope it comes out all right. All of the following steps ensure that the memory work will be effective.

Gathering the alters

As much as I can, I make sure that all the alters who contain parts of the memory participate. This means speaking with them ahead of time (or having other parts speak with them) and getting their agreement. I do not have to know their names, as long as I know I have all those involved in the memory. I have learned by experience that if even one alter who holds a portion of the memory stays out of the memory processing, or withholds part of what s/he knows, that alter will experience ongoing flashbacks of the traumatic event that might affect the whole system. (In fact, many flashbacks appear to be caused by some alters pushing their piece of a memory up to consciousness while others are resisting the knowledge.)

Sometimes. it is impossible to gather all the alters involved in a memory because you do not know enough of the personality system. With ritually abused clients, this is often the case during the first couple of years of therapy. To address this, either the client or I will keep an indexed summary of the memories we have worked through, and, if they are training memories, their purpose. If, later in therapy, a part or group of parts emerges who belong to a memory we have already done, it will be easy to reprocess the memory. Sometimes, a program or training we have destroyed suddenly starts working again, and the client engages in behaviors we thought s/he was cured of. It is important then to identify which program has re-emerged, and reprocess it more completely, putting in the missing pieces.

It is sometimes helpful to invite parts to be present who were not there for the original event—for example, a caretaker for little children. Other parts might also want to watch from a distance, to acquire knowledge of how to process memories or of what happened to the body. Over time with my clients I am able to find one or two parts who will specialize in helping the others with memory processing. Often the most effective ones at this are severely traumatized, empathic child parts.

It is not necessary to have the ANP present during memory work unless that personality was involved in the original experience. I have found that memories that have been completely processed often gradually "leak" through to the main adult personality in the days following the memory work. But if they do not, I do not require the ANP to know their content.

Including parts of memories held by internal recyclers

Some alters, usually known as recyclers or reactivators, are trained to deliberately withhold and hide a small part of each training memory, so that the effect of the training cannot be destroyed. The hidden bit may be some words that were spoken, an emotion, or some physical pain. If this piece is not included in the memory, the perpetrator group will be able to re-create the program from the missing piece. (I am not sure how this works in the brain.) Look for recycler alters in mind-controlled personality systems, and convince them to include their part in the memory. I remember my shock right after my client Lorraine's death when all the programs I had worked through with another of the first four, Jennifer, suddenly began to activate once more. Her recycling program, which I had not known about, was operating. This is one reason to keep specific records of memory processing. We had to work from our records, inserting the piece that the recycler held for each memory. It was quite a challenge to keep her safe during this process, as many programs were set off at once.

To find the recycler alters, I just ask in a casual way whether there are any alters trained to keep pieces of the memories separate. The client might appear surprised, but will generally answer truthfully, and then permit me to dialogue with the recyclers or those in charge of them. Memory work is much more efficient, and the client is much safer, if each memory only has to be processed once.

Dissociating the feelings

Most experts in the field emphasize how important it is not to re-abuse the client by allowing him or her to become flooded with painful memories. The goal is reassociation of memories, but not reliving them all at once in all their painful detail. The client's ability to dissociate emotions and bodily sensations while processing memories will give him or her a sense of control over the process, and make the memory processing much less painful than if s/he has to undergo all the painful feelings for the entire time that the memory is being put together.

One pioneer DID researcher, Bennett Braun (1988), described dissociation as containing elements with the acronym BASK—behavior, affect, sensation, and knowledge. I prefer to go through the senses one by one, thinking of the emotions as also being a group of senses. I think of the senses as organized into three groups:

1.   The distance senses—sight and hearing.
2.   Body sensations—smell and taste, pain, heat and cold, sexual feelings, drugged feelings, etc.
3.   Emotions—fear, terror, anxiety, anger, frustration, sadness, etc.

The first time I go through a memory with a client, I allow only the first group (sight and hearing) to be present. Since sight and sound do not hurt (unless there is an unbearably loud noise), these senses can be tolerated for a fairly long time without too much discomfort. They are also essential for obtaining information about what happened, and, in the case of ritual abuse or mind control clients, what false beliefs, instructions, and programs were implanted.

Bodily pain, on the other hand, is very difficult to bear. It should be dissociated while the *content* of the memory is obtained. Beyond that, you will need to use your client's feedback and your own professional judgment to determine what to do with feelings and physical sensations.

Smell and taste and touch can be unpleasant, but not completely unbearable. Sometimes it is all right for the client to leave them in the "movie" of their memory when they go through the memory the first time, and sometimes it is preferable for the client to leave in just a little bit of these feelings. For example, in a memory in which the client was injected with a numbing drug and unable to move, a small part of these sensations was necessary to make her aware of what was happening to her.

Like the bodily sensations, the emotions in a traumatic situation are very strong, and can make it very difficult for the client to proceed with abreacting the memory. So they need to be temporarily dissociated. Sexual feelings can distract some alters, causing them to dwell in the memory rather than getting on with it. Or these feelings can be so embarrassing that the client will refuse to experience them. Feelings created by drugs can confuse, so generally it is wisest to omit the drug sensations during the first run through the story of the memory.

Skilful use of dissociation will allow the client to preserve his or her dissociative capacity while it is still needed; during therapy, dissociation can be used to store unfinished memories, pace therapy, and enable real life functioning, such as school attendance or work. By definition, anyone who has a major dissociative disorder is already a skilled dissociator. In order to help my clients process their memories in the least traumatic way possible, I teach them to dissociate in a special way. I put the emotions and the bodily sensations away in imaginary containers.

Before we process any memories, we work on the client's ability to dissociate feelings effectively. I have the client construct in his or her inner world a place where unprocessed memories and feelings are to be kept in containers, and some containers in which to put them, such as a cave containing barrels, a bank with a vault with storage lockers, a well with buckets, or a storage room with jars on shelves. Both the containers and the place in which they will be kept should be able to be locked, but there should be a way to put things in the containers after they are locked. A spout or straw might work (if the memories and feelings are thought of as liquid), or a "doggie-door" which snaps shut could be created. As with all such creative solutions, it does not matter what the image is, as long as it works for the client, and the therapist takes note of it and remembers what it is. (It helps if the client draws a picture of the storage place and containers.) Now the client can learn to put the emotions and bodily sensations from some easy memories, and eventually entire memories, into the container. The emotions from an argument she had yesterday with her husband can be put safely away, or the taste of the milk that went bad—and then, the flashback of the hands of someone who abused her. I gradually work with clients until they can dissociate difficult components of memories by putting them into containers. I might count backwards from five, if that is not triggering (clients abused by some groups have conditioned reactions to counting or to numbers). For instance:

"5,   put in all the pain, all the 'owies' and hurts (Remember, we are dealing with child alters. I use childish words as well as adult synonyms for pain and emotions, to make sure that young parts understand me.),

4,   put in all the fear, all the scared feelings, all the terror, all the worry and anxiety,

3,   put in all the angry and mad feelings, and all the sad and hopeless feelings,

2,   put in any drugs and any sex feelings,

1,   now put in anything else, anything you felt in any part of your body, and anything you felt in any part of your feelings.

0,   close the box (or bucket) and lock it up tightly. Keep the doggy door (or spout, or straw) ready in case any more feelings come up when you watch the movie."

When the client can do this, s/he is ready for memory work.

Remember to tailor any suggestion you read here, and any treatment in general, to the specific needs and preferences of your client as much as is reasonable, therapeutically. Some clients do not like counting, and prefer to just name what they are putting in. Others just want me to be quiet while they do it, and let me know when they have finished. I emphasize that anything they keep out (e.g., pleasant feelings) will make the rest of the memory's feelings come back.

Putting together the memories

Watching the "video" of the memory

When I work through a traumatic memory with a survivor client, we always begin the story in "normal life" (e.g., getting into the car) and follow it through until the person is in "normal life" again, with the traumatic event having happened in-between. The alters at the beginning and end of a memory are usually different from the ones in the middle, but selecting a complete memory, normal-to-normal, in this way, helps the client understand how the traumatic events fitted in with their everyday life. This also reveals the situation if one traumatic event led to another traumatic event.

I have clients process each memory at least twice. The first time it is done as if watching a video, with sight and sound but no emotions or bodily sensations. The alters can watch it on an internal screen in a viewing room. All the feelings have been put away into a container. Because the client is not feeling the pain or the fear, s/he is able to describe what is happening clearly, and I am able to take coherent, even verbatim, notes. I can ask the client to slow down or to repeat something without worrying about traumatizing him or her. The client holds the remote control, and can make the picture bigger or smaller, speed up or slow down, rewind, fast forward, or stop. The client can pause the video to take a bathroom break, or to talk about something that was on it.

When the client is watching this "video", I encourage him or her to be simultaneously in the inner world that includes the memory, and in the outer world in which I am really there with them in a safe place. I find that in most cases it is quite possible for people to be consciously aware and with me while processing a memory, especially when just watching the video. I encourage the client to stay as conscious as possible, closely enough connected to me and the real world that s/he can describe the memory while going through it, rather than doing it silently. This does two things. It helps the client stay grounded in the present, so that the memory processing does not turn into a flashback, and it helps me to know two important things: whether all parts of the memory are being included, and what parts were trained to do.

I constantly remind my clients to tell what they *heard* (words as well as sounds) as well as what they saw. With ritually abused and mind-controlled clients, the words usually contain the programming or training, so the alters who know what was said will sometimes omit the soundtrack, and it has to be specifically requested. They might have been ordered never to reveal what was said to them. Stay alert to whether an alter tries to skip a part of the memory, and ask them to put that part in.

I constantly interact with the client as s/he goes through the memory, asking questions (for clarification only), giving reassurances that the event is not really happening, and correcting cognitive distortions as they happen. If a false idea was implanted by the abusers during the memory (e.g., that the abuse was the client's fault), I can challenge it right there. It is extremely effective to challenge the lies and tricks right at the point where the client is remembering them clearly for the first time.

If different alters hold different aspects of the experience, the chronological order of the parts of the memory can become confused. To prevent this, I ask for someone inside who knows the content to line the alters up in the order in which their parts come.

If the client gets stuck, I take a break to talk with the parts and find out why. Sometimes an alter just does not want to go through with it. Sometimes there is a part of the memory held by an unknown alter, whom they have to find. Then we need to negotiate with that alter, and decide whether or not to go ahead with the memory.

One client would present me with written summaries of memories that we could then work through more fully. When something like this happens, you should not assume that the client's written narrative is all that is contained in the traumatic event. Often, there is something which is omitted, either because the part collecting the content did not look everywhere, or because some part held back out of embarrassment or fear. I still think it is wise to go through the memory twice in my office, once as narrative and once with feelings, even if the client has prepared beforehand. (And I prefer that they do not prepare in this manner. It is too easy for them to get into speculation about what happened, rather than allowing the story to emerge.)

Often there has been "incidental training," accidental events incorporated into a training memory. For instance, in the middle of a training session or other traumatic event, someone might have turned on a radio, or a car horn might have honked outside. Incidental training is often not even in the room with a person. It is the white noise in the background that most people do not even notice, because they are too busy concentrating on what is happening in the room with them, but it will end up integrated into the traumatic memory. However, it is often forgotten or left out while trying to break down a program, leaving the therapist unable figure out why things just are not working. It must be included in the memory processing.

During the process I am careful to monitor my client's affect and status. If I notice the client's feelings becoming overwhelming, I remind the client to dissociate them into their container. Sometimes there are feelings I forgot to include in the first countdown, so I have to help the client put them away again. If this does not work, I stop the memory temporarily and diagnose the problem (e.g., an alter refusing to dissociate pleasant sexual or drug feelings can keep other feelings active as well).

Sometimes a very young part will want to do the story-telling part of a memory in the play therapy room, with dolls, sand tray, or other toys. This can be useful, especially as in some cases it bypasses the "don't talk" programming, as the story is not told by talking. And if the client is still a child, this is highly appropriate.

I keep a verbatim narrative of what the client says and does during the "video" part of the memory abreaction. This narrative is probably the best record the client will ever have of what happened to him or her, as the memory will fade once it is consciously known. The memory that returns during the first putting together of a dissociated trauma is far more detailed and feels much more "alive" than any other besides the contents of a flashback. I think it is helpful for me, too; I dissociate my own emotions about the trauma to the handwritten page which my right hand is producing, and I do not reintegrate them until I type out my notes at a later time.

Processing infant memories

It is important that the memories of these original splits be processed if the person wants to proceed to integration, since with organized abuse, most alters are deliberately split off in infancy. When my client Jennifer, who chose to fully integrate, had worked through all the memories of the alters on the layers in her internal structure (a tetrahedron or inverted pyramid) as well as the memories of home abuse, she was left with "the point"—the portion of the structure at the very base. It contained the infant memories, which were a conglomeration of bodily sensations and emotions. She did process these in therapy, even though there was not a great deal of understanding of what it was all about. After all, how much did she understand when she was an infant?

Memories of events that occurred very early in life might involve the entire personality system. All of the alters involved have to regress to the age at which the trauma happened while they process the memory. What this means is that they could be quite young. With these memories, sometimes I have to use word and touch signals because the client is unable to speak, or cannot return to the present. I squeeze the client's hand, and ask him or her to squeeze mine from time to time, to indicate that s/he can hear me. I pre-arrange "stop" signals—one for the client to give me if s/he cannot speak, and one for me to give the client that will automatically stop the memory (for example, I may hold the right shoulder firmly and say "Stop!" loudly). I practice these first with easy memories. If the memory belongs to pre-verbal parts, I ask a verbally fluent part to watch. Then I process the memory in short segments, stopping to allow the older part to tell what happened.

Memory processing is different for infant parts. Stella Katz describes her experience with infant parts and memory processing as relatively quick and uncomplicated:

> Processing baby memories is essential for total integration, and it is something that can be done very quickly if you just let the person do it without verbal interference.

> Baby memories phase in and out because babies phase in and out during the experience. They are not like a five-year-old who remembers hours of torture. Babies only take in small parts of memories. That's why when training babies you use short quick things, rather than long drawn out things. What takes a five-year-old 24 hours to break, only takes a baby a few minutes.

> Baby memories are based on events that occur when you are at a place when life is still a complete mystery, so it is best to just take what you see as real. When traveling back to baby years, don't try to understand, just experience, and let it go. These memories are the hardest to get at, but the easiest to let go of.

> Baby memories differ from later memories because you have no verbal way of explaining what you feel or go through. It is stupid to try to get the person to talk about what they felt or saw, because they will not get an accurate account from outsiders and it is impossible to really verbalize the experience. Besides, it wastes large amount of time trying to put it into words.

Processing memories of dying or becoming unconscious

During memory work, a client may stop breathing and appears to be dead, or at least unconscious. It can last for some time and it can be quite frightening to a therapist. What if they do not wake up? Having worked through a large number of such memories, I have confidence that the client will not actually die during the memory work if they did not die, or at least did not remain dead, during the original trauma. I have worked through quite a few memories of apparent death and resuscitation by the perpetrators when the abuse went too far and the child was in the process of dying. Although it is gruesome, it is possible to go through these memories like any other. I do suggest, however, that these memories should not be the first ones you tackle. Also, it is within these memories that the hidden gems of the near-death experiences which can give the client spiritual hope are seen.

Adding in the feelings

Often, dissociated clients are in a rush to get their memories back. When asked why, they say they "just want to get it (this recovery stuff) over with." It certainly would be nice if all the client had to do was recover the knowledge of what happened. However, that is not the case. In addition to all of the preparation involved before you can even begin to address memories, in order for a traumatic memory to be fully healed, all parts of it must be put together—not just the pictures or the storyline. The emotions, and, when necessary, the pain, must also be included. If this is not done, the entire memory can easily be redissociated. When a previously unconscious memory has been *completely* put together, the emotions connected with it are discharged, the behaviors "programmed" by the event are brought under conscious control, and the alter personalities created by the event are free to reintegrate. *That is recovery.*

After the cognitive (storyline) processing, if the client's feelings are being dissociated enough to make this possible, we take a breather in the real world. If not, we proceed immediately to the second stage. In this stage we open the container that has the feelings in it, and put the memory together with the feelings *fast*. This is the most painful, and difficult, stage of recovery for the survivor.

With some clients, I do this by counting up to ten, spacing the numbers about one second apart. In some cases, I name parts of the memory after each number. With others, this is not necessary. I do not have to name the feelings; they just happen. As each number is spoken, the client's agony increases. Usually a ten-count is enough to contain a memory, although for some very long memories it is necessary to go to fifteen or even twenty. I ask the client to nod if the feelings have all been acknowledged.

With other clients, instead of using numbers, I just name the parts of the memory in chronological order. Some want me to read back the transcript of what they said during the first storytelling, and put in the feelings while I am reading. *The feelings do not have to be experienced for the duration for which they were originally felt, but they do have to be acknowledged and incorporated into the memory with the story and the physical sensations.*

When I get to ten, or to the end of the recounting, I begin counting back down to zero. (Remember that some clients have programs or memories triggered by counting, so it should not be used with them.) Whether or not I have used counting, I instruct the client to put each part of the memory back into the container where the feelings had been kept. I begin with the most distressing parts of the memory—first the pain, then the fear. There does not seem to be a "right" order, as long as everything is put into the container. I usually mention specific things that happened in the memory as I count down, to make sure that everything is put in. When I get about halfway through, I say the final words:

"Put away – everything you saw,
  – everything you heard (all the sounds, all the words),
  – everything you tasted,
  – everything you smelled,
  – everything you felt in any part of your body" (here, I name specific body sensations such as pain and sexual feelings, remembering to mention any sensations which would have happened in the particular memory we are dealing with), "and
  – everything you felt in any part of your emotions." (Here, I name specific emotions such as fear, anger, anxiety, and sadness, remembering to mention any which must have been in the particular memory.)

Then I instruct the client to close the container and lock it.

Not all therapists working with dissociative disorders and with mind control survivors agree with me about the necessity of including the emotions and bodily sensations in the memory work. Whether or not this is done probably depends on the goals of therapy. My experience is that alters are unable to integrate unless this is done, and the client might still get flashbacks of the worst parts of the memory—those emotions and bodily sensations—for some time after finding out the content of the abuse. If these parts are deliberately included during the processing, horrible though it might be, they will not return as flashbacks later and continue to haunt survivors for the rest of their lives.

Closure and integration of material

Once a memory has been put together with all its parts, the material integrates, and a miraculous thing happens. The emotions and body sensations from the traumatic memory disappear, leaving only a knowledge of what happened, similar to the knowledge of any other life experience. Finally, healing can occur. The wound is closed, though there might be a scar, in terms of the awareness that a horrible thing happened to the person. The alters involved can also integrate, depending on whether or not other memories still stand between them.

A physiological explanation of memory work: In physiological terms, when the memory is re-associated, then it has been taken through the hippocampus to the cerebral cortex, and can be remembered like any other memory. Its vividness and its emotional punch will gradually fade with time.

Sending the memory into storage

After all the parts of a memory, including the feelings, are joined in the person's awareness, the client and I send the locked and labeled container into permanent storage. The way in which this is done depends upon the client's inner world. One client just threw the box into the internal river, and it floated down to its resting place. Another used her inner self helper, who believed herself to be a whale, to take the container away and deposit it on the bottom of the ocean. If we had to reprocess the memory, the whale could get it back again—but the other parts could not. As you see, what we are really employing is the same imaginative creation of symbols that people with DID use to assign characteristics to their independently created alters.

Completing the processing and integrating alters

At the conclusion of the process, I like to have a symbolic cleansing and joining, an image of the client's choosing located in the client's inner world.

I like to use a (breathable) waterfall of soft warm sparkling water or colored light, in which the alters can wash away any all remnants of the memory which did not get into the container. They can cleanse themselves, inside and out, from any dirty or contaminated feelings. They can also revitalize themselves, removing their tiredness.

Now, finally, the waterfall will wash away any boundaries between parts whose separateness is no longer necessary, and will blend them together. Any alters who still need to be separate will remain separate and have their boundaries strengthened. We shall look in more detail at integration in Chapter Seventeen.

Other ways of dealing with memories

As much as what I have written might seem like a formula to follow, no treatment recommendations can ever be applied to everyone in the same way. You will need to negotiate what will work effectively for each client. The client with whom currently I am doing the most memory work has chosen to go through all the feelings and bodily sensations first, then tells me the story briefly. With some clients, I have used a fractionation process, going through the memory several times, starting with the pictures, then adding the sound, then adding one emotion or bodily sensation at a time. Stella Katz has told me that she processed most of her own traumatic memories this way. She used a bell to bring herself back to the present if she got "lost" in a memory.

A long-term mind-controlled client of mine has always processed his traumatic memories on his own rather than in therapy sessions. He reports that the memories first appear in partial form in dreams, then begin to emerge in the daytime, and gradually fill out until the story is clear. Sometimes, he has to deliberately allow the alters involved to express the feelings involved in a memory, otherwise, he will be flooded with those feelings in everyday life. He asks the alters to process particular memories which he considers important for his healing.

As you can see, different survivors have different capabilities and the potential for different levels of independence in their work. One of my ritually abused clients appears to be unable to go through entire memories because of internal resistance; they leak out a little at a time, over many therapy sessions. This is not the method I would choose, but this is all her system is capable of.

The guidelines in this chapter are just that-guidelines—and I want to remind you that there are many creative ways to deal with recovery. Remember to listen to, and learn from, your clients. Some clients choose not to fully integrate, and not to completely process all aspects of their memories. You will see more about this in Chapter Seventeen.

Cognitive and emotional processing

It is important to leave time in a memory work session to discuss any implications the memory might have after it has been processed. Although the *previous* emotions have been put in with the memory, there will be new *current* emotions about what happened. These deserve to be expressed, especially if the ANP has just become aware of some trauma that s/he did not previously know about. More cognitive work might need to be done about the false beliefs which resulted from the dissociated trauma. The client needs to have time to reorient himself or herself in the present. The usual issues that close each therapy session also need to be addressed: homework, and safety concerns for the period before the next therapy session.

I find it is often advantageous to have at least one "talk session" after a memory has been processed, to discuss what came up and what it means in more detail. After all, the objective is for the client to fully recover from the trauma, and this means that cognitive processing of the trauma is important to the client's view of him/herself, and of life.

With some traumatic memories, the ANP has not been present and will not gain access to the memory content for some time longer. This depends on the particular personality system. It is not always advantageous for the ANP to know the content of the memories, as in some cases this can be disabling to present-day functioning. In my experience, there is no need to force the ANP into knowledge he/she is not ready for. In some cases, it is wisest for the ANP not to know about certain memories for some time, even when those memories have been processed. Dealing with a newly traumatized and horrified ANP can divert the therapy process from resolving the alters' pain and compulsions. The knowledge will come when the time is right.

Note

1. Never touch the left shoulder of a ritual abuse survivor, since this touch is used to call out alters. And be careful about using your left hand when touching a client, since many left hand touches turn on programs.

CHAPTER SEVENTEEN

Successful resolution: co-consciousness or integration

When therapists began working with persons with dissociative disorders, the explicit goal was generally integration, which meant fusing all the alters into one person. In the literature, integration is often seen as a therapist-assigned goal of treatment. It is a big deal, usually conducted through a ceremony that joins the entire system or major alters, and is artificially induced by therapist-directed hypnosis. And it often does not work, or creates more problems than it solves. LisaBri's story in Chapter Nine shows how premature integration can confuse the therapy process. In the spirit of the times, I tried fusing small groups of alters in Teresa, my first DID client. And every time, the integration came apart after a little while.

Then I noticed, when working with the teenage Jennifer, that after we worked through a traumatic memory, the alters involved would frequently join together naturally. At that point, I realized what countless other therapists have had to discover for themselves because it was contraindicated by "the literature": maybe formal integration ceremonies were not necessary. I decided to dispense with them. My experience after twenty years of working with dissociative disorders, including those with ritual abuse and mind control histories, is that alters naturally join when there is no longer a need for them to remain separate, to protect secrets or to keep toxic emotions or body sensations from flooding the whole person.

As small integrations happen in this way, at the close of each piece of memory work, they become the natural evolution of the system—and they hardly ever come apart. The real barriers between the alters are the separately held secrets and the intense feelings which belong to the memories; once these have been shared, there is no need for alters to remain divided. Many alters will have quite a few memories, so they will have to process all their distinct memories before they are able to integrate.

For alters to integrate easily and naturally, it is important that the therapist and the client do not make a "big deal" about their individual identities. Remember that a dissociative client is really *one* person, even though she or he *feels* like many and might present with a rainbow of different personalities. If s/he becomes invested in separateness, integration will become more difficult. But it will still happen, at least with some groups of alters. Clients have told me that it is impossible to keep alters separate when the traumatic memories that divide them have been fully processed.

But is full integration *the only* healthy resolution of DID and DDNOS? Survivor Jen Callow has thought a lot about the process of integration, and wrote this piece specifically for therapists, which addresses many perspectives about integration. In this part, she addresses that question, and demonstrates that there is no formula for how parts, individually or in relationship, will respond to this process, for what will change, and how parts will feel. She also shows what can happen if alters are not fully involved in, and prepared for, the process. She explores the value of keeping out just a bit of a memory until all parts are really, really ready to integrate. "Integration," she says, "is more of a journey, and doesn't have to mean total fusion." On the other hand, it "isn't about losing who you are, it's about becoming what you were meant to be."

Part 1: To integrate or not to integrate: Jen Callow

Just as integration can be a welcome event, it can also be traumatic when parts are not ready to integrate or merge. It was for some of my parts.

When parts integrate, two or more parts merge into one new part that is a composite of these original parts. The new part might have similar likes and dislikes to these parts, as well as their abilities and mannerisms. The new part might even be the average age of the parts who merged. For parts who are unprepared or do not understand what is happening, this merging can be terrifying.

I started out with over 700 fully and partially developed parts, although only a handful spent time in the outside world. Partially developed parts are ones that carry memory fragments, but do not have a clear identity and personality, unlike fully formed parts. Now I have about 150 parts. Many of these merges happened effortlessly without my full awareness. I sometimes felt a new energy coming into me, the outside part, but normally only noticed a shift in my perceptions, feelings, or beliefs afterward. Often, I felt stronger and more whole inside.

However, sometimes merging was more traumatic for my system. Once, I had a part crying as he merged, resisting all the way. My therapist held him and tried to comfort him, but it did not help. One of the issues with Pete was that he was not warned or given a choice about integration, and was not prepared for what was happening to him. It was even more traumatic because he had just processed a long and terrifying memory on the assurance it would help him and my system feel better. Pete (the name he chose) had not realized he would merge when he helped process a particular memory, and it was an awful experience for him. Afterward, he fought the merge, moving in and out of the other part involved. I had no idea how to help him and thought he would eventually merge on his own.

As I wrote this article, I discovered he was still trying to keep out a piece of the memory so he could stay separate. But by this point he hated being half in and half out and realized he could not go back to being fully himself. Pete released the memory piece, we processed it, and he merged with the other part. This took only a few minutes, now that he was ready. The new part still contains elements of Pete, and, as I type this, he tells me everything is okay, although he still carries some of Pete's anger and sadness about the merge. Had we made it clear that he might merge if we went through the memory, and offered him the opportunity to address his feelings, merging would not have been so traumatic. Pete did not need to spend so many years in limbo.

All parts respond to integration differently, depending upon how close they are to the parts being integrated, whether it is happening directly to them, and their beliefs around what is happening. With my system, it also depends upon whether they are fully or partially developed parts. Merges between partial and full parts seem to be easier, with the partial part being strongly pulled toward the full part. Merges between fully developed parts have the potential to be more emotional. Still, for many of my parts, integration is just "something that happens". Some are quite positive about it, seeing it as becoming stronger and wiser, gaining in life experience. I have child parts who look forward to "growing taller" through merging with another part. However, there are many parts who still fear integration. Some parts see the inner world decreasing, with a physical loss of playmates, friends, and caregivers as various parts merge. This can result in a huge sense of loss, and parts might need time to grieve. This reduction in numbers can also be interpreted as people "disappearing" and parts may be afraid of disappearing, too. Others see integration as a loss of self, like Pete, and are terrified at the prospect.

The following exercise might provide a way to understand my experience: Imagine yourself as a child with a favorite set of grandparents. They spend time with you and are familiar and trusted faces. One day, they merge into a new person that looks sort of like your grandma and sort of like your grandpa, but also looks different from either of them. This new person says they are still your grandma and grandpa, but in a new form, and gives her/himself a new name, in this case, "Grand". Grand acts a bit like grandma and a bit like grandpa, and you really do not know what to make of this new person. Then Grand assures you s/he will look after you, the same as before. Only you now have one, different caregiver, instead of your two familiar grandparents. How would you interpret what just happened? How would you cope? Now imagine that you are an abused child who has not known much stability. After years of therapy, the inner world where you live has become a safe haven for you with other parts you know and trust. How would you feel when parts around you start merging in ways similar to Grand? And how secure would you feel about your own presence in that inner world? For people who are multiple, their inner world is every bit as real as the outer world we all share, and what happens there can have just as significant an impact on them.

Parts that have merged might also need support to adjust. In the outer world, people treat you differently when you change. You might put on weight, get grey hair and wrinkles, or need a wheelchair or assistance to move. Maybe you have not just changed physically, you have also had a profound experience that changed you emotionally and spiritually, and people do not know how to relate to you any more. It may be hard for you to fit in, to find your new role in the world. In the inner world, it is the same. Grand might struggle with what it now means to be "Grand" and with the child's difficulty in accepting him/her. Or a merge might suddenly result in a part becoming older and no longer at the same developmental level as his/her playmates, or any number of other changes.

My merged parts seemed to adjust fairly easily because my therapist and I had made a point to help all of the parts involved find new roles in my inner system, whether they had merged or not. So, parts often had fairly clear roles before they merged, and afterward their roles were simply amalgamated or expanded. With merging, the walls completely disappear and there is no barrier between certain parts any more. This can lead to a stronger sense of self.

After many years of painstakingly processing every piece of a memory, my system is able to do a lot of memory work on our own and not being nearly so triggered by events in our daily life . . . our parts are increasingly willing to work together and we have many more inner resources to draw on to help us through a memory, no matter how intense it might be. We now have more options when dealing with memories, particularly since our abusers are no longer in our life to reprogram or trigger us. Sometimes we choose to talk to new parts, and, when they are ready, help them leave their program line. We do this by simply "flying over" the memory, seeing it from a distance in our mind without having to feel it all and getting drawn in. Our goal is to understand what happened, what we learnt from that event, and how those enduring beliefs and feelings are impacting our life now. We remind ourselves that we are safe and work with the old beliefs and feelings so that we can move beyond them and forward in our life. This may involve using art, affirmations, physical activity, crying and yelling, whatever feels right at the time. Sometimes it is simply a matter of an "aha" moment where we realize those beliefs are false and replace them with beliefs that work for us now.

We can often disable a whole program line in this manner, part by part. The disadvantage is that the line is still there; however, the higher the cooperation between parts and the higher the survivor's safety level, the less likely it is the line will get reactivated, since parts will not go back to it and their programs.

Other times, we do have to process the feelings from the memory after we have flown over and understood it, as they continue to leak through. Even this takes less time than it used to, though, and the processing tends to flow smoothly with less resistance.

We do not use our therapy time for memory processing as much any more, and now have a therapist who does not know much about dissociation or ritual abuse, but is willing to learn. Most of the memory work we do on our own, and our therapist is there to help us deal with any remaining issues or feelings.

For a number of my parts, integrating is scary, because it means giving up their identity and becoming someone new and unknown. The resistance my parts feel toward merging encompasses a spiritual element. In my view, merging is a micro-version of spiritual bliss, nirvana, and the like. In both of these situations, giving up the self or ego to a higher power is called for, in order to achieve a greater unity and sense of inner peace. With integration, I am achieving a greater unity within myself, as opposed to merging with a greater spiritual force, although I find my spiritual connection deepens, as well. Many books have been written on the subject of spiritual enlightenment and a common theme is how terrifying and difficult it can be to give up your sense of self, your individuality and identity—in other words, your ego. This fear exists even with the promise of an incredibly joyous and peaceful state. Their thoughts, feelings, and personality will not be their own any more. Integration, in both a dissociative and spiritual sense, is a leap of faith.

Discussion of feelings surrounding merging can continue formally or informally throughout therapy. A client's parts need to know they can talk with their therapist about integration at any time, and without a general knowledge of integration, it can be hard for parts to even know what to ask. It is important to remember that each integration affects the client's self and world view. Outer parts might have their way of relating to the world shaken or changed, inner parts might also be adjusting to life with new merges. Although the topic of integration does not need to be a bigger deal than any other aspect of therapy, it does need to be an ongoing topic of conversation.

It might be helpful under some circumstances to arrange to leave a small piece of a memory unprocessed until resistant parts are ready to integrate. The memory piece could be a smell, a sound, an image, or even a short scene, whatever works best for the client and will create the least disturbance if it's left in the client's system. Regardless, whatever is left unprocessed needs to be something that was directly held by the part, otherwise the part could merge. If a part chooses to leave a piece unprocessed, it is important to set the piece aside in such a way that it will not get added into the memory, or affect the rest of the system. For example, the part could put the memory fragment into an inside container, label it for easy retrieval should the memory need to be finished, and then put it in a safe spot where it can be found, but will not be accidentally opened. Use this technique sparingly, though, as each memory piece dramatically increases the chance that one of the associated memories could be opened again and negatively impact the client. This is regardless of how much of the memory was actually processed. Only when memories are fully processed are they gone and have no risk of impacting the client.

If a client has not experienced integration yet, it can be hard for him/her to imagine what it might be like. If some parts have merged successfully, it can be helpful for parts that are scared of merging to talk with them. This can be done directly in the client's inner world, or with the therapist as a mediator. Some parts might need to understand that it is not a painful process and that they will be okay in the end. This should never be done to coerce parts to merge, but rather to help alleviate their fears so they can make a good choice for themselves.

Integration is more of a journey than a specific goal, and it does not have to mean total fusion. During the course of therapy, I found that the "walls" between my different parts grew thinner. At first, my parts became aware of each other's presence. Then it got easier to communicate with each other and to work together to build a community. From there it became easier to communicate with a wide variety of parts inside. More parts were able to participate in my daily life and to feel that they mattered. It also became easier to find and rescue parts that were still in unpleasant situations inside.

Properly supported, integration can be a natural part of the healing process and a catalyst for personal and spiritual growth. What was most useful for me throughout my therapy was developing a strong sense of self, and self love. Through this, I have discovered a deep sense of spirituality, a positive sense of being looked after by a higher power even as I find my own power. With this in place, my parts become less afraid and I feel happier in life.

I believe my fear of merging is in part due to never being allowed to develop a separate sense of self while growing up. To survive, I had to adapt myself to whoever people wanted me to be, and as I developed my sense of self in therapy, I became scared of losing it or having it ripped away. This fear also came from abusers forcing me to switch (change parts out in the body) at their whim, and not knowing if I would ever be able to bring any given part back or for how long. As my sense of self became more secure, I became less scared of losing it. Integration is not about losing who you are, it is about becoming who you were meant to be. This does not mean that I want to fully integrate all my parts, or that none of my parts are afraid. Rather, it means I have a stronger foundation to draw upon when integration does happen.

My personal choice has been to integrate, but not completely. My system is now cohesive enough that I can experience a high degree of personal safety and I have come to view my inner world as my family. Some day I may become "one" person, but that is not my goal. I am happy in my life and enjoy the company of my inner parts. I have come to love and cherish them in a way they did not experience in the outer world, and would miss their distinct personalities and spirit should they fully become part of me. They have taught me how to increasingly love myself as I come to love each of them.

And the parts that have integrated have taught me how to trust, to know it can be safe to connect deeply with others, and that as I connect within, I am also connecting with the divine.

*   *   *

Callow also wants to warn therapists not to make a big deal about integration with clients for whom it would not otherwise be an issue. If the client's alters are not scared about it, just allow it to occur naturally.

Here, in Part 2 of Callow's discussion, she offers many helpful and creative suggestions for creating inner cooperation, nurturing, and happiness, for those whose systems will continue as separate parts. This is not a process that one waits until the end of therapy to do; it is also the inner work that is part of ongoing healing from the beginning. It begins as soon as possible, and continues to grow over the course of recovery.

Part 2: Building inner community: living happily without integration: Jen Callow

When I first discovered I was multiple, I had well over 700 inner parts and very little communication between them. Most of my parts did not know the others existed. They were still very afraid and alone. After years of healing, I now have a loving community inside. We support each other and have inner cities and towns where we live and play together. Now, when we find new parts, we can help them leave their program lines and become a larger part of our inner world (my abusers set up my inner system as a spider web of interconnected lines holding programs and parts). Throughout this process, we do our best to make sure everyone has a voice and is heard. We meet competing needs, and organize, plan, and develop a growing inner world that in turn helps us to increase a sense of belonging and connectedness, supporting and caring for each other.

When we finally started therapy with a therapist who understood dissociation, many of us were isolated and living in terror. We were shut away in our inner world—in boxes, cold basement rooms, and in any other number of locations depending upon our memories. We were locked in our programs, often starving or in pain. Our inner system had torture and abuse going on similar to what our abusers had inflicted upon us. We did not trust each other, and only a very few of us knew and trusted our therapist. We were afraid that we, someone we cared about, or the world would be destroyed if we started working with our inner system.

Over time, we came to trust our therapist and then slowly learned to trust each other. After we learned how to be co-conscious and to create inner TV screens so parts could safely view the outer world, we created an inner movie of our life that we could show newly discovered parts, to bring them up to date and show them that we were safe now. (This movie's content was huge and growing, but it only took a few minutes for parts to see and absorb it, and now we can share it in seconds.) Eventually, we got so we could talk to each other clearly in our minds and did not need the therapist as much for communication.

Our inner world's physical environment evolved, as well. At the end of each session, our therapist would make sure any new parts had a comfortable place to live with their immediate needs met. We built a welcoming mansion filled with many bedrooms, a large common area, full bathrooms with large tubs for bubble baths, a large kitchen and eating area with long benches and tables, and several playrooms. Each bedroom could be decorated and furnished however its resident(s) wanted, and had doors that could lock, and a window, if one was wanted. Stuffed animals were an important comfort item, as were pets. We made sure that none of the pets would harm any of the other pets (e.g., cats would leave hamsters and fish alone) and that they were friendly. When we later discovered infant parts, we added comfortable nurseries with caregivers, and created items such as slings to carry the babies in, bottles, rattles, and changing stations. Now, there was a more harmonious feeling inside.

Eventually, we developed many more buildings. We now had a healing area full of herbals, liniments, and soothing sights and sounds: beautiful gardens and grounds; an ocean and beaches; forests; and opportunities for expression and recreation. We created spaces for soccer games, a dance hall, music and art rooms, safe rooms for yelling in and letting out anger, even a skateboard park. Every addition encouraged us to work together, to interact more, and to have more relaxation and fun. As we played soccer, ate, and lived together, we began to feel more and more like the family we had missed out on. This was every bit as important in our healing as the actual memory work.

Some of our parts needed a lot of time on their own, so it was important to create and give them some quiet space. Some parts preferred to live in tree houses, or in cottages in the woods. Sometimes our inner towns did not work at all for certain parts. Rather than force these parts to assimilate, we created other inner worlds for them. There was a group of teenagers that loved the Dragonriders of Pern series when they were growing up. We created a version of Pern with them, where they could live together with their dragons and fly through the skies each day. Several children were very attached to an animated adventure show they had watched when they were out in the body, and created a world like this for themselves to live in, complete with all the good guys. The bad guys were created as a vague danger the children were in complete control of; the bad guys would take whatever form and strength the children wanted and the children, who were the heroes, always won. Parts could travel between worlds whenever they wanted, so no one was truly alone and we could still access these worlds and parts when processing memories.

Running the programs and keeping constant vigilance over our system had been the only way for many of our parts to feel powerful and to avoid feeling physical or emotional pain. After we had processed a memory, our therapist made sure to help each part find a new job and purpose. This included the children, if they wanted a smaller job. For example, the soldiers who had terrorized our system were put in charge of security, record keeping, and maintaining the soccer field.

Some responsibilities in our inner world are large and time consuming, such as cooking, cleaning, and looking after the infants. Another task we struggled to fill consistently was taking the children on field trips to places inside, such as a fun version of school where we could teach them about the outer world. It was hard for the few parts doing this to come up with enough ideas. At the suggestion of a friend who was multiple, we set up a rotation of chores and responsibilities. Now, older parts that take on a larger role can take regular vacations and we have parts who have been taught how to fill in. Over the years, we have also created inner people (different from the parts already in our system) to help with various tasks, such as a healer, gardener, cook, and caregivers for the infants. We find it works best to still have our parts help with chores, as it builds a sense of pride in our community and shared responsibility, but this way the risk of parts burning out from overwork is reduced.

Many of our parts lived in suffering and deprivation. One aspect of their healing is recognizing that they matter and that their needs can be easily filled, providing no one will be harmed in the process. If a part wants a specific toy or needs an extra blanket, those items can appear for them right away. However, sometimes more work is required to ensure a need is met. Although we can have food items available immediately, for reasons unknown to us we still need to cook and prepare these items for a proper meal, so outside of meal times we try to have pre-made snacks readily available. In addition to inner people to help with chores, we have added many other helpers to our inner world, from a therapist for the children to caregivers who give us back rubs before bed. The caregivers also help the younger parts with baths, getting changed, and getting tucked into bed. Many of our parts enjoy tending large flower and vegetable gardens, and we created several gardeners who help with bigger jobs. Female vocalists (we do not trust men easily) sing lullabies to parts who enjoy this, and can soothe crying infants.

After much debate, we also recently added loving, sexual partners for those parts who needed this inside. Many of these parts were children, but their sex needs were huge as a direct result of the abuse. In the end, we felt it was better to create people who could provide loving sexual contact, respecting the children's wishes and needs, rather than have these parts feel ashamed and suffer from their overwhelming urges. It has worked well for us, as several months later, many of these children are now asking more often for non-sexual, loving touch, with these inner people taking on more of a nurturing friend or caregiver role.

In addition to caring for each other inside, we take care of our inner environment. At one time, we were concerned that all the emotions we were releasing would have a negative effect on our inner world. We are very sensitive to energy and were taught that our feelings were toxic to others when we were growing up. So, we created some areas that transformed the energy from our feelings into the good feeling energy of our waterfalls, trees, and other natural spaces. In keeping with our own beliefs, we think of this transformative power as "earth energy", the earth changing the energy and helping good things to grow. This helps us in the outer world, too, as nature has always been grounding and nurturing for us. We envision our outer environment and the earth transforming our feelings, so it now feels safer for us to express emotions. In the interest of environmental sustainability, we also have inner areas where we bury our garbage, recycling it so the earth can transform it into electricity, food for plants, and other new kinds of energy for our inner world.

Our outer and inner worlds are deeply interconnected. In caring for each other and our inner world, we learn how to take care of ourselves in the outer world, and also how to care for the earth and other people. As we experience caring from others in the outer world, we learn that we matter and discover how we like to be treated, which we can then mirror inside.

Without the care and attention spent both on our parts and our inner world, we would never have made it this far. Even today, when things feel chaotic in our outer world, as is the case for us now during some major life transitions, we can look inside and help calm ourselves through creating more stability in our inner world and attending to parts' fears and needs. Lately, we have been holding regular inside meetings for any parts who want to attend. In our inner world, we sit out in nature; we sing, talk, play music, and release feelings and outdated beliefs (e.g., often we will write these on pieces of paper and throw them into a small bonfire, over which we later roast marshmallows, which makes it feel less like a ritual and more like fun). The buildings, recreational areas, nature, and living spaces play a huge part in our sense of inner peace and security.

How we built our inner world is specific to our preferences and to the way our inner system was initially set up during the abuse. Every survivor's system is unique and offers many ways to build a community or create objects inside. It is important to work with what is already in the inner system, as opposed to fighting it and trying to shut it all down. Although areas can be transformed, in our experience the building blocks of the inner world remain the same. Through creativity and patience, it is possible to have cooperation and harmony between any number of parts, and a thriving inner community. With an increasing sense of inner peace and community, it is not only possible for survivors to create happier lives for themselves in the outer world, it is possible for them to truly heal.

*   *   *

Callow's choice, to integrate some parts but allow others to remain separate, is a valid choice. Even if that is what the survivor plans to do, it is not always what happens. When one of my clients was in the last stages of her therapy, she wanted to keep a particular little alter separate, for two reasons—because he was helpful to her as a separate inner part, having been the main helper in memory processing, and because he was somewhat autistic as a result of some of the abuse he experienced. She was concerned that the autistic features, such as "stimming",[1] might become characteristic of her. However, one day, her last significant traumatic memory suddenly came up and forced itself to be processed. And the child alter popped out and said, "If we process this memory I will integrate"—and he did. And sure enough, the integrated person acquired some of his autistic characteristics, though in a diluted fashion. It appears that something that had been segregated in her brain was no longer segregated.

In contrast to Jen, Stella Katz chose to integrate fully. As she worked through the final memories, she described herself as having "a case of galloping integration," as the process gathered steam and put together what had been fragmented all her life. Here is Stella's story of her own healing. She wrote it for survivors, so feel free to share it with any clients who are ready to receive it. In fact, any of the survivors' healing stories in this book may be shared with your survivor clients.

Reclaiming me: Stella Katz

I am writing this for one reason only, and that is to prove to others with DID that there really is LIFE beyond the dark tunnel.

I spent the better part of forty years fragmented. I had one stable alter personality who lived everyday life, went to school, took dance and skating lessons, dated, married, and had children. That person knew nothing of what was going on in the rest of my life. All I knew was that from a very early age I would go to bed at night and wake up with dirty feet, or completely clothed with unusual makeup or markings, and bruises. What I found odd, though, was that I only did the sleepwalking at my Grandmother's house, and never at home until after my Grandmother died. As a young child I assumed it was because I missed my own bed, but I had no explanation for it happening later on. I was told that the horrible things I remembered in the morning were just bad dreams and to forget about them and not to tell anyone because they would think I was insane and lock me up in the home for bad crazy people.

At the age of thirty-five, when all came to light, I was horrified. I was told to go to a group for people like me, only to find out that most of the people never really got better, or ever integrated, and were in therapy for most of their lives. Being stubborn and pigheaded, I was not going to hear of that. I wanted to get well. I wanted to know every detail of my secret life, and moreover I wanted the loud opinionated taunting voices in my head to shut up.

So began the journey that helped me reclaim "myself".

I can still remember the feeling of horrific physical pain of the memory that first brought it all to light. Though it was only a memory, the pain was so intense I was sure my foot was broken. I could barely walk on it for days after. I still remember the smell of wax from the burning candles and leftover incense that permeated the room where the memory all took place. Even now it was like yesterday. It was all so horrid but it answered a burning question I had had since I was five years old about how I broke the heel of my foot while I was supposedly sleeping.

The more I learnt, the more I wanted to learn. I wanted forty years of unanswered questions answered. But the more I learnt the worse I felt about myself, because the one thing I learnt was that I was still going somewhere where these things happened. I needed to find the people inside who knew the most and I knew that once or twice a week in a therapist's office, no matter how good she was, just was not going to cut it. I needed to get out of the group not years from now, but right now, and unless I learnt more about my internals, I would never be free of the group. So I began my version of homework.

On the days of my sessions, after my children were in bed and my husband safely tucked in front of the television for the night, I would go down to the rec room where I could be alone and go over the therapy session of that day. I would try to figure out what seemed to be missing from what I had learnt or worked on during the session. It meant that I had to go back into myself and try to talk to those who had been out that day in the therapist's office. My biggest fear was that I would get in and get stuck. So I bought myself a silk rope, and a timer. I would set the timer for thirty minutes, tie the rope to the chair and hang on so tight you would have thought I was dangling from a ten-storey building. Somehow, the rope gave me safety, as if it was a lifeline to pull me back from falling over the edge. I would close my eyes and visualize a dark tunnel and, step by step, I would walk through into my inner world, still hanging on to my rope, calling out to the name of the last insider I remembered from the session.

As I got to know each member of the Clan, as they called themselves, I began to see them as real people. Some were easy to talk to, while others were so dark and scary it was all I could do to look at them. There were adults on the light side and the dark side, and children, oh so many children. Some rather happy, some so terrified they would only peek out of little holes in the fabric of our mind. I saw houses and places that were familiar, and places I was sure I had never seen before, yet felt strangely familiar. At times I was so terrified I just wanted to run. I felt so foolish because I knew I should not be scared of these people—after all, they were part of me. I equated it to being afraid of my own arm. It seems so silly now, but then it was terrifying.

After a few years of twice weekly therapy sessions and twice weekly homework, I finally realized that, although I liked my therapist a great deal, I did not want to grow old with this woman. So I stepped up the work I was doing on my own. Along the way something happened, and the therapist and I parted ways. I went on to another, who was sweet but useless, and then to another, who was both unpleasant and incompetent. All that forced me to work harder on my own. So I left therapy altogether, for a while.

Night after night I worked getting to know my system, one alter at a time or sometimes in little groups. It was amazing and intricate and I did not think I would ever get to know everyone in it. Just when I thought I was through most of it, a little floater child would introduce me to a whole new level. A floater child does not actually belong to the structured system created by the abusive group, but is "born" by accident. As Fiona the floater did not belong to the structure, she was free to travel throughout the system and was no threat to anyone in it

After about six more months I was taken on by another wonderful therapist. I got to know so many more in my system with her help, but her office was too far away. The beauty of living in your head is that you can do things you cannot do in the real world such as creating a holodeck like the one on Star Trek. When I became afraid of a memory or a dark Clan member I was dealing with, I would simply "freeze program" and go around and look at the entire situation from every angle. I discovered that so much of what had been done to me was nothing more than smoke and mirrors. I was able to see the Devil who had abused me from all angles. I saw that he was not eight feet tall, he was just a grown man while I was a small child. He did not have scales and claws and a tail, he wore a stretch suit with a zipper up the back, and you could see the line of his boxer shorts under his costume. It made me laugh. The fear I had was now gone. The more comfortable I got with processing my memories, the more I increased the time on the timer from thirty minutes to forty-five, sixty, and eventually two full hours.

I became friends with my Clan, with the help of Fiona, the little floater child, who knew every single member of the clan. I was able to get through to members who would have been blocked otherwise. Fiona trusted me, and because she trusted me, the others came to trust me as well.

I was often in awe of the structure of the system. I learnt so much about the missing years and answered so many of the burning questions of my life. I discovered the reason my real-life children spoke languages I did not. The Clan had an internal nanny who cared for the internal children. She had the ability to come out and take care of my real-world children when I slipped inside. She spoke Gaelic to them and sang songs with them, and they learnt and had a great deal of fun. The only thing that bothered me was that she was a better mother than I was. In time, I found out why I hated highly textured food, and especially raisins. I will not tell you why, but I can tell you it was disgusting. I came to love the little internal children, and animals, and even my little demons, who were all under the age of five. I came to understand that my black heart was not black as in evil, but black as in a mix of all the wonderful colors of the world.

I knew that every member of the system had to be in agreement about integrating. They had to be able to decide for themselves and choose to join the healing plan because they had never had any choice about what had happened to them. I knew this could only be done by helping the little ones grow up, or at least to understand what we were hoping would take place. So, after the real-world kids had gone to school, I would set the timer, bring out the toys and cookies without raisins, and let the children out to play and watch television and read books. Once they were allowed out into the world they grew quickly, not like real children do, but years in a matter of weeks. One by one they grew. One by one they joined.

All through this healing process, I still had one big problem, which was that I still belonged to the group. I was still a high priestess; I was still part of the inner circle. I was still a trainer. I knew I had to get out of it but I knew they were not going to let me just walk away because I knew too much.

For the next couple of years I was stalked and harassed daily. My children were threatened. I had dead animals put in my car, snakes in my mailbox, and dead kittens nailed to my door. I was driven off the road at night and raped. I did not think it would ever end. I got tough and looked at the rapes as just lousy sex. Once I was sent a photograph of a person dead and mutilated with a threat saying that would be me. I called the police and an officer came eight hours later. I gave him my statement and the picture. I took his business card, only to find out when I called to talk to him it was fake.

The more I worked on my system the less use I was to the group. Eventually they got tired of stalking me, and let me go. It took a few more years, but I was free, or at least felt I was relatively safe.

Once I was free, it did not take long before I was pushing through the system, had everyone catalogued, knew where, when, and how each had come into separate being. With that all done, I was able to get everyone in the system to set a date and time that we would join as one. Some were afraid they would die. Others were afraid that the body would not remember them, others were afraid it would hurt, but we worked through the fears. We planned the day it would all happen, and so, on a beautiful day while the children were in school, I gathered the members of the Clan, had everyone line up in order of their birth, hold hands, and form a circle. One by one, in a very ceremonial manner, the newest member stepped into one who came before and so on down the line until we reached the child whose body had been born. It felt wonderful and frightening and strange and a little like a house of cards ready to collapse at any second. It felt like the house's foundation had been built on jelly, but it felt right.

I was one with myself. I was not who I thought I would be. There were a few times when I was sure we would fall apart, but I hung on. No one died, no one was forgotten, and I had to fight to get rid of the Celtic accent I had acquired unexpectedly. In the first few months, when I recalled something I saw it through the eyes of the person who had experienced it. As time went on, all the memories became mine. And it was an amazing feeling, though a little lonely at times to have only one voice in my head. The thought I was thinking was my thought and mine alone, and to know that I would no longer hurt little children or animals or wake up with muddy feet was amazing.

I was not prepared for what came afterwards. I was stupidly under the impression that all would be well once there was only one of me. I could not have been more wrong.

What I did not expect was the unbearable remorse for what I had done. The faces of every child I had hurt, their cries and their anguish, kept flooding through. It was a dam that broke in my moral conscience.

I no longer had a therapist because "I was well and integrated". I really could have used someone at that point, even if it was just to cry on her shoulder but I had no one. I had to hang on and let myself feel the pain. It went on for two years. There were rivers of tears, torment and guilt. I had never been so depressed. I had known the pain while fragmented into mini me's, but now I understood that all the pain I had felt in those years of abuse had been dulled by an imaginary coating of Novocaine brought on by the fragmentation; now it was just the raw pain of remorse and I had only one of me to feel it.

I also went through a spiritual crisis. I did not know what I believed. I had the guilt teaching of the Catholic Church running through my head, telling me I was going to hell. I had the Satanic beliefs that God is weak and worthless. I had my mother's Pagan beliefs that Dark and Light are equal and balance life. I had Jewish beliefs of the group I had belonged to, and I did not really feel any of it was worth my time. I think this was the hardest part to try to work out in my mind.

It all came to a head at a stop light one sunny afternoon when a song triggered a memory that forced me to ask the question "What do I believe?" Between stop lights and stop signs I went through the list. The questions were everything from my belief in a god to my personal beliefs about life in general. I gave myself ten seconds to answer each question. I felt that what I answered in ten seconds was what I truly believed without the process we all have of over-thinking, and justifying what we say. By the time I got home I felt as light as a feather. The weight of the world had been lifted off my shoulders. I could not stop grinning. I finally knew who I was, and what I truly believed in. I found my life at the end of that long tunnel. I was integrated on all levels. It had been a long, long road.

It is not my dream life, but it is mine. I now have terminal cancer, but I worked through what I believe about death, and I am okay with it. I do not know how long I have left, but I see every day that my name is not in the obituary column as a great day, and more so as a gift. I have made my peace with myself.

For all of you who are still going through the torment of memory and the chaos of an untamed system, know that there is Life at the end of your tunnel. Know that you are not alone because we are all connected in the universe. Know that every member of your internal self is part of the whole and worthy of love and of being heard. And know that it is okay to remain divided if you can get your system to cooperate. No one member is more important than another in the long haul. The tunnel to yourself is long, painful, and more often than not extremely frustrating, but it does have an end. If you all work together even through the chaos and pain there can be peace.

*   *   *

You may notice that Stella integrated all her parts through a ceremony, and had considerable difficulty afterwards. My guess is that this was because the alters' emotions, particularly guilt and shame, had not been fully worked through when she processed the memories. This is an alternative way of integrating to the gradual process I recommend. Richard Baer's book,

Switching Time (2007), tells the story of a therapy in which the alters were deliberately integrated with the ANP, after which the ANP acquired their memories and gradually went through their body sensations and emotions until they were resolved. Apparently, this can be one way to bring the alters together, but it risks the ANP being overwhelmed by the traumatic feelings, as Stella was for some time.

Generally, it is helpful for the alters who are just memory fragments or partial "people" to join with stronger ones, and it is easier for a personality system to work together with a smaller number of alters. But whether or not to fully integrate is up to the person. Stella chose full integration. Trish Fotheringham, as reported in her DVD (2008), did not choose either way. All of her alters remained for a long time as separate parts inside her, but then one day, when she was experiencing anguish and despair about her life, all the parts came together and integrated into a single identity.

Stella does warn us that for clients who are still being accessed by perpetrator groups, it is unsafe to continue to have child alters, because the groups can re-split them to create new alters, whereas they are unable to do this to a fully integrated person.

I mentioned in Chapter Fourteen that Jennifer had an alter come temporarily "unstuck" years after her successful integration. Trish Fotheringham tells me that she had the same experience after her mother died. Two alters reappeared, shared previously unknown memories involving her mother, then reintegrated. Trish recommends that survivors who integrate keep at least part of their inner world intact, so that newly emerged alters have somewhere to "live" on the inside. I have not seen her suggestion addressed in the literature, probably because such post-integration "re-emergent" experiences are not generally acknowledged there. This might be, at least in part, because full integration is not a common outcome, especially with polyfragmented survivors of ritual abuse and mind control.

There is no "right" way for all multiples. Keep in mind the goal of therapy with this population. It is not to make multiples into singletons, but to help those with many parts to become more functional and free of disabling symptoms. For mind control survivors, the goal is to remove all the external controls over their minds so that they can be full human beings—free, in charge of their own lives, choosing their own life goals.

And survivors will choose, at every step. Each system will naturally blend to a smaller or greater degree as memory work goes along, and, at the end, find its own resolution. As someone once said, survivors might integrate, or become a corporation, or become a collective. But what happens will happen naturally, and that is as it should be. You can follow any therapeutic trend you want, but, in the end, the choice is your client's.

I use two different images in explaining integration to my clients. The first is two rivers joining. All the water that was in each river is contained in the new, larger river, which contains both of them. The only thing that is gone is the strip of land between them, which represents the secrets that they did not previously share. The new river will probably carry the name of one of the original smaller rivers, but it will contain all the water—all the memories and experiences—of the other small river too.

The other image I use is that of a stained glass lamp. Many colored pieces come together to make a beautiful lamp through which the light can shine, displaying all the colors and making a picture that could not be seen as long as the pieces were separated. This image can be used for cooperative co-consciousness as well as for integration.

What happens then? After integration, or cooperative co-consciousness, is achieved, these survivor clients will need to decide what they want to do with their lives. That, alone, is a big deal for people who have not only never considered such major questions, but whose right and ability to think for themselves and make choices has been derailed. So much of your work with mind control survivors has been devoted to the task of allowing them to take control of their own lives rather than having them controlled by others. As much as therapists should always be careful to not impose their own agendas on their clients, you have seen how much more important it is with these people. Sometimes, when we are very dedicated to healing survivors, it is a temptation to get our healed clients enrolled in that same cause. I must remind you that in your enthusiasm, you will need to be sensitive to any message you might give that leaves your client feeling pressured, or expected, to join the cause.

Some *will* choose to become outspoken survivor advocates. For them, recovery might resemble what it means to alcohol and drug addicts, whose sobriety requires that they "pass it on;" or they might find the meaning they need to attach to their suffering, and the suffering they were forced to cause, by bearing witness to the truth in a public way. Some will choose to "go public" through telling their stories to the world, by helping others through such forums as web discussions, by "fighting back" through lawsuits against their abusers, or by making their survivor status publicly known in other ways. If they are not fully integrated, however, there are considerable dangers in this. Programming can still be triggered through words, nonverbal signals, or what appear to be innocent questions. One of my clients who was involved in a court case recently had programs reactivated when a lawyer (who had access to my clinical notes) asked him about certain alter personalities. Another had programs triggered through words spoken to her by a participant in an online forum she was helping to lead. As I mentioned earlier, I lost a client when a man found her in an online discussion group and figured out her personality system. I have also, on two different occasions, seen well-known public speakers on the topic of ritual abuse use deliberate triggers as part of their talks.

Never forget that these abuser groups have a strong interest in keeping their secrets, and survivors who expose their status publicly, even by attending lectures on the subject, need to be alert for triggering events.

Once again, there is no right or wrong way. So, yes, of course, it is the survivor's choice, but it is a choice that needs to be considered carefully. I recommend that survivors be very cautious about "going public," and only do it if they truly feel it is their calling.

Many, perhaps most, clients may decide of their own free will to leave all those awful experiences in the past and get on with lives that have nothing to do with ritual abuse or mind control. The real issue is that the *choice*, the *decision*, must be entirely the survivor's.

In relation to this point, LisaBri sends the following message.

To all survivors

If I had the chance to say anything to all survivors I would repeat what my therapist has said to me all along, but that I was only able to hear for the first time today. She said I can have a life outside of ritual abuse. That my whole life experience now does not have to be ritual abuse. I can live life on my terms. And that I don't have to spread my healing to the world. I always thought that was expected of me. I thought I had to do more than survive and heal, I had to go public and follow my fellow survivors who have taken their healing and speaking out to the next level. In the cult it was all or nothing, and if it was nothing you were dead. So I have spent my life trying to do it all and failing. It feels selfish that I heal and not share it with the world.

What I can do is to keep writing articles for my website, which is a comfort zone for me and I hope to my readers. That feels right to me.

I want to thank my therapist for giving me permission to be just that, me: an individual with DID who was subjected to ritual abuse. But that is just a small part of who we are.

Therapists, give your clients permission to be all they want and ask for nothing more. That will be your gift to them.

Note

1.   Stimming is a repetitive body movement engaged in by autistic children, hypothesized to stimulate one or more senses—such as hand flapping or spinning a coin.

CHAPTER EIGHTEEN

Ritual abuse and mind control treatment: greater than the sum of its parts

I t is my hope that you have learnt from this book that successfully treating survivors of ritual abuse and mind control is possible. I hope that, if you are not already doing it, you will take the challenge and embark on this great adventure, and that if you are, you will feel more secure in your work and be able to hone your skills. There are too few of us doing it, and fewer doing it correctly. Survivors need—deserve—to be able to find competent therapists no matter where they are located.

The following summarizes the guidelines that have been the basis of this book. Some of them might seem deceptively simple; I assure you, they are not. But they do provide a straight-forward, clear template that should inform your work:

First of all, recognize that it is who you are, not what you know, that makes you effective as a therapist. It is your ability to "sit with a shattered soul." This is true even if you are a novice at working with survivors of ritual abuse and mind control. I recently consulted to a very experienced therapist who was working with her first ritual abuse survivor. In her zeal to share with the client what she had learnt from me, she forgot to "tune in" to what the client was telling her in the next session, and there was a breach in the therapeutic relationship. She was alert to this, recognized it, and mended it, but it was a good reminder to both of us. Never forget who you are and never move away from the basic empathy, warmth, and genuineness that make a good therapist.

Your first step is to routinely screen your incoming clients for signs of childhood trauma, and of dissociative disorders, and, if there are such signs, to do a more thorough assessment. Remember that a large percentage of mind control survivors have a "shell" ANP, so the absence of "time loss" does not mean they do not have a complex dissociative disorder of the kind associated with ritual abuse and mind control.

Then, if there are indications of a dissociative disorder, the need for an accurate differential diagnosis suggests that you look for signs of ritual abuse and/or other forms of mind control.

We do not yet have data on what percentage of those who suffer from dissociative disorders have experienced RA or MC, and estimates I have heard range from almost none to 100%. So, you should not assume that your client either has or has not experienced these kinds of abuses.

If your client has strong indicators of a dissociative disorder, it will help if you provide some education about dissociative disorders and what they mean. It is often a shock to a person to obtain this diagnosis, but it can also be reassuring, as it gives an understandable explanation for their mysterious symptoms.

Some indicators of a ritual abuse or mind control history are listed in the chapter on "Initial stages of therapy", and you need to be familiar with these indicators. If you do see such signs, however, you should obviously not inform your client that s/he is a survivor. Just keep your eyes and ears open, and wait for your client to disclose at his or her own pace. The important thing here is that if such disclosures happen, you respond with both empathy and confidence, letting the client know that you can handle such matters. Know your limits. Clients only tell us what they think we can handle. Wait for the evidence to emerge, and in the meantime do not get caught up in the "false memory" controversy, but stay with the client's experience.

Become familiar with the unique features of a personality system which has been formed by organized or deliberate mind control, such as internal structures, a complex inner world, a filing system for memories, a hierarchy of alters, a security system with "booby traps" which goes into effect after disclosures, and learnt triggers for trained behaviors. Be aware of the types of jobs held by alters, such as "garbage kids," gatekeepers, demons, animals, recorders, reporters, recyclers, spinners, and introjects of the primary perpetrators. These might all seem very strange, but you will become familiar with them once you have experience working with this population.

Your focus in the initial stages should be on getting to know the alter personalities and respecting them and their roles in the personality system. As each alter emerges, orientate them to the present, and develop trust with them. People severely abused in childhood do not trust easily, and this is especially the case if they have been trained by an organized perpetrator group not to trust "outsiders." Take as much time as necessary to prove you are trustworthy. There is no substitute for time and consistency. Make sure to make your boundaries clear in order to preserve the safety of the therapeutic relationship for both parties. Prepare for a long haul.

It is important to learn about being multiple, and what works for their healing, from your client. To work with the alters, rather than trying to get the ANP to control the rest of the personality system. To be careful not to have favorite alters or reject those who seem to be "bad." And to treat all parts of the person with kindness and compassion, including the frightening and negative voices. These people are indeed survivors of the unimaginable, and deserve a compassionate witness who will not shy away from any part of them or of their experiences.

Do not assist one side of the personality system to battle with the other side. When protector alters (often disguised as persecutors) emerge, get to know them. They emerge when they are ready to engage in therapy. Work with them before you attempt to work with the hurt child parts they are protecting. Reframe their role as protectors, and offer to help them protect in ways that are more effective for the present day.

If there are strong indicators of a ritual abuse or mind control history, do not assume that your client is presently physically safe. Watch for signs of ongoing abuse. Do not say "That was then and this is now" until you know the abuse is over. Recognize the possibility of continuing contact with abusers, and continuing abuse. Recognize also the possibility of the client becoming unsafe as a result of premature disclosures. Identify reporter alters and find a way to disable reporting to the abusers, if possible.

With any person with a dissociative disorder, but especially with ritual abuse and mind control survivors, do not press for disclosure of abuse memories early in therapy. Recognize that in mind control survivors this might precipitate reporting to abusers. Recognize also that disclosures could precipitate self-harm, suicide attempts, and flashbacks caused by alters doing their jobs.

If your client does have strong indicators of a history of ritual abuse or mind control, recognize that the client's flooding of feelings, flashbacks, self-harm, or suicide attempts might be the result of alters doing their jobs when disclosures have been made. Slow down disclosures in this event, and focus on creating safety and confidentiality within the personality system and the therapeutic relationship.

Do not buy into a client's belief that perpetrators know everything, are everywhere and all-powerful, and that the client and/or the therapist will be killed for talking. If they have disclosed organized abuse, let them know that organized abusers deceive their victims. As you uncover the traumatic memories behind the mind control, take the time to help the client's alters recognize the lies and tricks involved. Do not buy into any of the beliefs imparted by the abusers, such as that certain alters are not human.

Do not pursue the memories represented by flashbacks. Make it clear to the client that the purpose of therapy is to help the person heal and have a worthwhile life in the present, rather than to unearth traumatic memories. (Though working through the memories is essential for full healing.) Learn how to strategically select memories to work with, and develop an effective method that is not too traumatizing for your client. Then, when the client is ready, work systematically on resolving the trauma.

When you work with the memories, remember to include all alters involved in a particular traumatic memory, especially if it is a training memory, and to follow it "from safety to safety," including all elements of the memory (sound, sight, taste, and smell, bodily sensations and emotions), especially the part held by recycler alters. Do not forget the infant memories which caused the initial splits.

Whether or not to fully integrate or to remain multiple with a cooperative personality system is a choice your client should make for him or herself. Healing will be needed in many areas of life—emotions, sexuality, spirituality, and interpersonal relationships. Pay attention to the sexual programming and make sure it is fully resolved, as many survivors have serious difficulties in this area, including pedophilic desires. Even when the memories are worked through, there will be more healing and growth to pursue.

Since the client has had his or her freedom taken away through mind control, it is important to keep focused on restoring that freedom. Do not replace one ideology with another or become your client's new "handler". Assist your client in taking his or her own life back, including body, thoughts, emotions, and spirituality.

Study the chapters in this book thoroughly, so that you are familiar with what you might encounter. There are many other resources for this work, some of which are listed in Appendix One. Pursue opportunities for continued learning. Never stop. There will always be more to know, and our understanding of this relatively new issue is continuing to develop. As you keep learning, along with your clients, you will become more and more competent in working with these deeply traumatized people, and perhaps one day you will contribute to our knowledge of how to help them heal. I look forward to reading what you have to say.

Resources

Books and articles on dissociative disorders

Adler, R. (1999). Crowded minds. *New Scientist Magazine*, December 18. Those who doubt the existence of DID (and others) should see the differences in the brain that this study subject with DID exhibited.

Alderman, R., & Marshall, K. (1998). *Amongst Ourselves: A Self-Help Guide to Living with Dissociative Identity Disorder*. Oakland, CA: New Harbinger. One of the more recent and helpful self-help books for dissociatives.

ATW (2005). *Got Parts? An Insider's Guide to Managing Life Successfully with Dissociative Identity Disorder*. Ann Arbor, MI: Loving Healing Press. Another useful self-help book for dissociative people.

Baer, R. K. (2007). *Switching Time: A Doctor's Harrowing Story of Treating a Woman with 17 Personalities*. New York: Crown Publications. An interesting approach to integration.

Chu, J. A. *Rebuilding Shattered Lives: The Responsible Treatment of Complex Post Traumatic and Dissociative Disorders*. New York, Wiley & Sons. Detailed and comprehensive approach to dissociative disorders, but does not deal with ritual abuse or mind control.

Cohen, B. M., Giller, E., & Lynn, W. (1991). *Multiple Personality Disorder from the Inside Out*. Baltimore, OH: Sidran Press. Personal stories and poems from people who suffer from dissociative disorders.

Dell, P. F., & O'Neil, J. A. (2009). *Dissociation and the Dissociative Disorders: DSM-V and Beyond*. New York: Taylor & Francis. The most up-to-date text on dissociation theory and research.

Goulding, R. A., & Schwartz, R.C. (1995). *The Mosaic Mind: Empowering the Tormented Selves of Child Abuse Survivors*. New York: Norton. Explains the Internal Family Systems approach; especially helpful for dealing with alters.

Haddock, D. B. (2001). *The Dissociative Identity Disorder Sourcebook*. New York: McGraw-Hill. A helpful book on DID for sufferers and their loved ones.

Howell, E. F. (2005). *The Dissociative Mind.* New York: Taylor & Francis. A psychoanalytic approach to DID emphasizing disturbance of attachment.

Hunter, M. E. (2004). *Understanding Dissociative Disorders—A Guide for Family Physicians and Health Care Professionals.* London: Crown House. For giving to your clients' family doctor.

Journal of Trauma & Dissociation. Philadelphia: Haworth Medical Press. The primary journal in this area, belonging to the ISSTD.

Kluft, R. P., & Fine, C. G. (Eds.) (1993). *Clinical Perspectives on Multiple Personality Disorder.* Washington, DC: American Psychiatric Press. Older collection of professional articles on DID, including some excellent ones by Kluft.

Krakauer, S. Y. (2001). *Treating Dissociative Identity Disorder: The Power of the Collective Heart.* New York: Taylor & Francis. Presents a stage-oriented approach to DID and a specific way of working with the personality system.

Putnam, F. W. (1989). *Diagnosis and Treatment of Multiple Personality Disorder.* New York: Guilford Press. An old book, but a fine one.

Rutz, C. Ritual abuse—shadow government and mount pony (http://www.whale.to/b/ruzt4.html)

Sachs, A., & Galton, G. (Eds.) (2008). *Forensic Aspects of Dissociative Identity Disorder.* London: Karnac. Many of the individual chapters address ritual abuse.

Steinberg, M., & Schnall, M. (2003). *The Stranger in the Mirror: Dissociation—The Hidden Epidemic.* New York: HarperCollins. Particularly helpful for spouses and relatives of persons with dissociative disorders.

Van der Hart, O., Nijenhuis, E., & Steele, K. (2006). *The Haunted self: Structural Dissociation and the Treatment of Chronic Traumatization.* New York: W. W. Norton. Presents the theory of structural dissociation. Scholarly, comprehensive, and practical.

Websites on dissociative disorders

Training videos: www.cavalcadeproductions.com/dissociative-disorder.html. Accessed October 7, 2010.

International Society for the Study of Trauma and Dissociation: www.isst-d.org/. Accessed October 7, 2010.

"Many Voices" newsletter: (contact www.manyvoicespress.com/newsletter.html.) Accessed October 7, 2010. Newsletter for those who suffer from dissociative disorders.

Books on ritual abuse and mind control

Hawkins, T. R. (2009). *Dissociative Identity Disorder: Psychological Dynamics.* Grottoes, VA: Restoration in Christ Ministries. An evangelical Christian approach. Sound basic teaching about DID.

Hersha, C., & Hersha, L., with Griffis, D., & Schwartz, T. (2001). *Secret Weapons: Two Sisters' Terrifying Story of Sex, Spies and Sabotage.* Far Hills, NJ: New Horizon Press. Story of sisters Cheryl and Lynn Hersha's mind control abuse through experiments as children. Includes considerable documentation. However, co-author Schwartz makes some very odd and inaccurate and biased comments in the book (such as repeating over and over the suggestion that people are lying about RA/MC histories because they are "seeking attention"). Cheryl Hersha has asked readers to ignore his comments on pp. 323–324. I would add those on pp. 410–411.

Lockwood, C. (1993) *Other Altars: Roots and Realities of Cultic and Satanic Ritual Abuse and MPD*. Minneapolis, MN: Compcare. History and information about persons involved in such abuse.

Marks, J. (1991). *The Search for the "Manchurian Candidate": The C.I.A. and Mind Control; the Secret History of the Behavioral Sciences*. New York: W.W. Norton. Groundbreaking, comprehensive review of related CIA projects and experiments. Reprint of 1978 edition. One of the first and most important resources in the field. The entire book is online at ww.druglibrary.org/schaffer/lsd/marks.htm. Accessed October 7, 2010.

Noblitt, J. R., & Perskin, P. S. (1995). *Cult and Ritual Abuse: Its History, Anthropology, and Recent Discovery in Contemporary America*. Westport, CT: Praeger. Carefully researched history.

Noblitt, R., & Noblitt, P. P. (Eds.) (2008). *Ritual Abuse in the Twenty-First Century: Psychological, Forensic, Social, and Political Considerations*. Bandon, OR: Robert D. Reed Publishers. Up-to-date collection of articles covering many topics.

Oksana, C. (2001). *Safe Passage to Healing—a Guide for Survivors of Ritual Abuse*. London: Backinprint.com. Probably the best self-help book specifically for ritual abuse survivors.

Rose, E. P. (1996). *Reaching for the Light: A Guide for Ritual Abuse Survivors and their Therapists*. Cleveland, OH: Pilgrim Press. A nice, gentle little book with lots of helpful information for both survivors and therapists.

Ross, C. (2000). *Bluebird: Deliberate Creation of Multiple Personality by Psychiatrists*. Richardson, TX: Manitou Communications. Takes a conservative approach in documenting medical mind control abuses.

Rutz, C. (2001). *A Nation Betrayed: The Chilling True Story of Secret Cold War Experiments Performed on our Children and Other Innocent People*. Grass Lake, MI: Fidelity. Tells Rutz's story and documents CIA abuses.

Sakheim, D. K., & Devine, S. E. (1992). *Out of Darkness: Exploring Satanism and Ritual Abuse*. Don Mills, Ontario: Lexington Books. Early collection of professional articles covering many topics.

Sinason, V. (Ed.) 1994). *Treating Survivors of Satanist Abuse*. London: Routledge. Many early articles on various aspects of ritual abuse.

Smith, M. (1993). *Ritual Abuse: What It Is, Why It Happens, and How To Help*. New York: HarperCollins. An older book but quite thorough, helping therapists understand ritual abuse.

Weinstein, H. M. (1990). *Psychiatry and the CIA: Victims of Mind Control*. Washington, DC. American Psychiatric Press. Researched, revealing, from the perspective of a murdered victim's son, a psychiatrist; also, *Father, Son, and CIA* (1988). Toronto: James Lorimer; The son's autobiography, including the father's story.

Yonke, D. (2006) *Sin, Shame, And Secrets: The Murder of a Nun, the Conviction of a Priest, and Cover-up in the Catholic Church*. New York: Continuum International Publishing Group. Award-winning Journalist David Yonke was Religion Editor for the Toledo Blade during Father Gerald Robinson's murder trial, which included ritual abuse aspects.

Websites on ritual abuse and mind control

(Up to date, September 2010. These are subject to change. If you cannot find the desired article at the address listed, try searching for it as it may be available elsewhere.)

Gillotte, Sylvia Lynn, Forensic considerations in ritual trauma cases. Comprehensive, well-linked, resource-laden overview of ritual abuse for those interested in the legal perspective. http://www.suite101.com/article.cfm/ritual_abuse/63761. Accessed October 7, 2010.

Hale, Steven, *Project Paperclip: Nazi Scientists Who Performed Human Experimentation in the U. S.* http://facstaff.gpc.edu/~shale/humanities/composition/assignments/experiment/paperclip.html. Accessed Oct. 7, 2010.

Lacter, Ellen. Website: www.endritualabuse.org/. Accessed October 7, 2010. Much information about ritual abuse. Evidence, indicators, treatment articles. If the Internet resources I have listed here are insufficient, try those on this website.

LisaBri's website: www.dissociatedsurvivor.com. Accessed October 7, 2010. Articles by LisaBri for survivors.

Mind control forums: www.raven1.net/mcf/archv-hm.htm. Accessed October 7, 2010. Many tapes and lectures on mind control, as well as declassified MKULTRA documents.

Neil Brick's SMARTnews: http://ritualabuse.us/. Accessed October 7, 2010. Very thorough website for information about ritual abuse and mind control. Includes talks from survivor conferences.

Rappoport, J. (1995). U.S. mind control experiments on children. Los Angeles, CA Compilation of documentation, including Senate testimony by Valerie Wolf and two of her patients. http://www.newdawnmagazine.com/Articles/Mind%20Control%20Experiments%20on%20Children.html. Accessed Oct. 7, 2010.

Ritual Abuse-torture (RAT) Jeanne Sarson Linda MacDonald's web page for survivors and interested others. www.ritualabusetorture.org/ Accessed October 7, 2010.

Survivorship: www.survivorship.org/ Accessed October 7, 2010. Self-help organization for survivors of ritual abuse and mind control.

Svali First Series: How the Illuminati Programs People. www.bibliotecapleyades.net/sociopolitica/esp_sociopol_illuminati_svali01a.htm#menu. Accessed October 7, 2010. Online book by a woman self-described as a former Illuminati programmer.

Other important relevant books

Blume, E. S. (1991). *Secret Survivors: Uncovering Incest and its Aftereffects in Women.* New York: Ballantine Books, 1998. Ground-breaking book on the effects of incest on survivors.

Brown, D., Scheflin, A., & Hammond, D. C. (1998). *Memory, Trauma, Treatment and the Law.* New York: Norton. A major sourcebook for all issues regarding the validity of traumatic memories, including recovered ones.

Freyd, J. (1988). *Betrayal Trauma: The Logic of Forgetting Childhood Abuse.* Boston, MA: Harvard University Press. Freyd's theory is that abuse which involves betrayal by caregivers is more likely to be forgotten.

Greenberg, L. S. *Emotion-Focused Therapy: Coaching Clients to Work Through their Feelings.* Washington, DC: American Psychological Association Press. This focus on emotion is helpful for therapists with all clients, including those with dissociative disorders. Includes many exercises for clients.

Pearlman, L. A., & Saakvitne, K. W. (1995) *Transforming the Pain: A Workbook on Vicarious Traumatization.* New York: Norton. This workbook helps therapist assess how working with trauma has affected them.

Siegel, D. J. (1999). *The Developing Mind: How Relationships and the Brain Interact to Shape Who we Are.* New York: Guilford. The neurobiology of development, in particular the effect of trauma. Dense but readable.

van der Kolk, B., McFarlane, A., & Weisaeth, L. (Eds.) (1996). *Traumatic Stress: The Effects of Overwhelming Experience on Mind, Body, and Society.* New York: Guilford Press. Theoretical and research perspectives on the neurobiology of traumatic stress.

Satanic calendar[1]

January 01	NEW YEAR
	Party, fun, "raising hell."
January 07	ST WINEBALD DAY, correlates with Christian Epiphany.
	Gifts are brought to Satan. Infant child, preferably eight days old male, or adult male 15–33 (age divisible by three) is dismembered and consumed.
January 17	SATANIC REVELS
	Sexual orgies. Virgin girls ages six to eighteen are first given to Bishop or Grand Master, then down the line of hierarchy until all have had a turn.
January 20	ST AGRE'S DAY
	Magik, divination, spell casting, conjuration of Telal (wicked warrior demon).
February 01 or 02 or 1st full moon of Aquarius	IMBLOC or CANDLEMAS
	Sexual conjuration of Gelal (incubus) & Lilit (succubus).
Shrovetide	The three days before Ash Wednesday, Christian calendar.
	Preparation for full Black Mass. Collection of blood (menstrual), water (holy) and firewood (oak). Burning of human flesh which will be used as the ashes on Ash Wednesday, in the Black Mass. A Black Mass is preferably held in a church, using human flesh and blood.
February 25	ST WALPURGIS DAY
	Communion of blood and dismemberment. Begin collection of victims for March 01, usually with dismemberment of small animal.
March 01	ST EICHATADT DAY
	Conjuration of Ninkharsag (queen of demons). Homage paid to Ninkharsag and Ninkaszi (horned queen of demons). Drinking of human

blood for strength. Victims human or animal, any age, any size, human preferred.

March 20–21   SPRING EQUINOX.
Feast day. Homage paid to Uggae (god of death). Victim male or female animal.

EASTER   (1) Satanic baptisms: Children dedicated to Satan or Tiamat, given to hierarchy for first vaginal penetration, fingers only. Age six weeks to eleven months.

EASTER   (2) Satanic rebirth: Children ages three to five reborn through cow corpse (goats are sometimes used).
(3) High Black Mass.
(4) Mock crucifixions (some groups).

April 19 to May 01   PREPARATION FOR SACRIFICE
Gathering blood, water and firewood. Preparation of the persons to be sacrificed, by confinement, fasting, sleep deprivation, anointing with sacred oils, putting them in an altered state.

April 21 to May 01   GRAND CLIMAX DA MEUR CORPUS DE BAAHL
Sacrifice of female victims age one to twenty-five (unregistered children, prostitutes, street people or volunteers). Celebration goes for several days, depending on how long the gathering and preparation takes.

April 30   WALPURGIS NIGHT (CORPUS DE BAAHL)

May 01   BELTANE
Fertility rites, orgies, usually if possible in an open field. Seminal fluid is mixed with dirt and insects and injected into the vagina of a virgin. Their virginity is first sacrificed by the Grand Master or High Priest. Children conceived of this are the children of Tiamat and Dur(Indur). They will hold great power and position in the coven.

June 21   SUMMER SOLSTICE
Great celebration with feasting and orgies. Torture, rape and sacrifice of enemies or traitors. Forced labour of breeder, sacrifice and consumption of infant.

June 23   MIDSUMMER'S EVE
Magik. Excellent night for black magikians for fire magik.

July 01   DEMON REVELS
Blood sacrifice, female victim, human or animal, any age.

July 17–23   Sacrifices of first born males (newborn to eleven months). Communion given with their flesh and blood.

August 02   LUGHNASSADH
Worship of moon for magik, practised only by some groups.

August 03   SATANIC REVELS
Sexual orgies (anal, oral, vaginal), victim female age 7 to 17.

August 26   Preparation begins for the Feast of the Beast or Marriage to Satan.

Fasting and anointing with sacred oils of those who are betrothed to Satan.

Virgins, male and female, average ages nine to thirteen, but all ages accepted.

Some cult members are betrothed to one another.

September 07   FEAST OF THE BEAST

Marriage of virgins to Satan. Severe sadistic intercourse with statue of Lucifer or the Grand Master dressed as Satan. Phallus has spikes or razor blades attached to it. Great feasting and orgies take place after all virgins have been given.

September 20–21   MIDNIGHT HOST (FALL EQUINOX)

Reaffirmation of sacred vows by hierarchy. Fasting for previous week, cleansing and anointing with sacred oils. Requires personal blood sacrifice, such as finger of the individual, or hands or finger of their own child, or paw of favorite pet. New branding is done. Hands and fingers will be planted in the ground for power, fertility. Followed by feasting and orgy.

October 29   ALL HALLOWS EVE

Conjuration of the dead. Sacrifices (human or animal) appropriate for specific demon or dark ancient one. Sex magik.

October 31   SAMAIN

Beginning of the new year. Conjuration of the dead. Orgies with demons. Sacrifice of enemies or traitors. Sacrifice by fire. Induced labour of breeder, and sacrifice of infant by dismemberment. Consumption of flesh and blood of infant, as well as placenta.

November 01   HALLOWEEN

Sex with demons.

November 04   SATANIC REVELS—see above

December 12–22   WINTER SOLSTICE

Impregnation of breeders for use during summer solstice. Animal sacrifice and live burial of victims to celebrate the dark time.

December 24–25   DEMON REVELS (CHRISTMAS)

High Grand Climax.

Mock birth of Christ and subsequent murder to mother Tiamat. Victim female age thirteen to sixteen. Forced labour of breeder, communion with body and blood of infant.

BIRTHDAYS

Some groups also celebrate the birthday of the individual and the birthday of the hierarchy. These days are very important within Satanic groups as they will always hold the recall programs of the individual.

MOONS

The New Moon is when Satanists "begin things", e.g. a magik spell, or preparation for a sacrifice. The Full Moon is the most powerful time, and the time when they end things, e.g., a spell or a life. Celebrations often held on the Full Moon nearest to the official date of a Satanic holiday, rather than on the day itself. Abduction risk is highest at the New Moon and at the Full Moon.

Satanic celebrations occur from midnight to dawn on the day listed. For example, January 01 means midnight New Year's Eve to dawn New Year's Day.

"Sacrifice" means letting of blood (cutting), not necessarily killing.

A "virgin" is a person who has not "given freely" sexually. Rape does not count.

Though many of these holidays correspond to the traditional pagan holidays the witches, Druids, or Wiccans celebrate, do not confuse these groups with Satanists. Satanists also celebrate Christian holidays but this does not make Christians Satanists. Traditional Pagans do not worship Satan, as they do not have such a deity in their belief systems; "Satan" is strictly a Judeo-Christian manifestation.

Note

1.   Spellings vary between groups as the original words are not in English. The Halloween season has a series of related rituals which take place from 29 October to 1 November. Other calendars can be found in Sinason (2011), and on the Survivorship website.

REFERENCES

Baer, R. (2007). *Switching Time: A Doctor's Harrowing Story of Treating a Woman with 17 Personalities.* New York: Crown.

Ball, T. (2008). The use of prayer for inner healing of memories and deliverance with ritual abuse survivors. In: R. Noblitt & P. Noblitt (Eds.), *Ritual Abuse in the 21st Century* (pp. 413–442). Bandon, OR: Robert D. Reed.

Barlow, M. R., & Freyd, J. (2009). Adaptive dissociation: Information processing and response to betrayal. In: P. Dell & J. O'Neil (Eds.), *Dissociation and the Dissociative Disorders* (pp. 93–106). New York: Taylor & Francis.

Birnbaum, M. H., & Thomann, K. (1996). Visual function in multiple personality disorder. (www.ncbi.nlm.nih.gov/pubmed/8888853) *Journal of the American Optometric Association, 67*(6). Accessed October 7, 2010.

Blizard, R. (1997). Therapeutic alliance with abuser alters in DID: the paradox of attachment to the abuser. *Dissociation, 10*(4): 223–229.

Blume, E. S. (1991). *Secret Survivors: Uncovering Incest and its Aftereffects in Women.* New York: Ballantine Books, 1998.

Bonewits, I. Cult danger evaluation frame: http://www.neopagan.net/ABCDEF.html. Accessed October 7, 2010.

Bower, T. (1987). *The Paperclip Conspiracy: The Hunt for the Nazi Scientists.* Boston, MA: Little Brown.

Braun, B. G. (1988). The BASK model of dissociation. *Dissociation, 1* (1): 4–23.

Brick, N. Blog and website on ritual abuse: http://ritualabuse.us/smart-conference/conf2002/my-healing-and-helping-others/. Accessed October 7, 2010.

Child Abuse Wiki. Definition of ritual abuse: http://childabusewiki.org/index.php?title=Ritual_Abuse. Last accessed August 15, 2011.

Conway, F., & Siegelman, J. (1978). *Snapping: America's Epidemic of Sudden Personality Change.* Philadelphia, PA: Lippincott.

Chu, J. A. (1998). Riding the therapeutic roller coaster: Stage-oriented treatment for survivors of child abuse. In: *Rebuilding Shattered Lives: The Responsible Treatment of Complex Post Traumatic and Dissociative Disorders* (pp. 132–143). New York: Wiley.

Dell, P. F. (2006). The Multidimensional Inventory of Dissociation (MID): A comprehensive measure of pathological dissociation. *Journal of Trauma & Dissociation, 7*(2): 77–106.

Extreme Abuse Survey Results: http://eassurvey.wordpress.com/extreme-abuse-survey-final-results/. Accessed October 7, 2010.

Finkelhor, D., Williams, L. M., Burns, N., & Kalinowski, M. (1988). *Sexual Abuse in Day Care: A National Study*. Durham: University of New Hampshire, Family Research Laboratory.

Fotheringham, T. (2008). Healing from ritual abuse and mind control:. 3-DVD Set. Available from Ellen Lacter's website: www.endritualabuse.org.

Frankel, A. S., & O'Hearn, T. (1996). Similarities in responses to extreme and unremitting stress: cultures in communities under siege. *Psychotherapy, 33*(3): 485–502.

Fraser, G. A. (1991). The dissociative table technique: A strategy for working with ego states in dissociative disorders and ego-state therapy. *Dissociation, 4*: 205–213.

Freyd, J. (1996). *Betrayal Trauma*. Cambridge, MA: Harvard University Press.

Goodman, L., & Peters, J. (1995). Persecutory alters and ego states: Protectors, friends and allies. *Dissociation, 8*(2): 91–99.

Gould, C. (1988). Signs and symptoms of ritual abuse in children. Available at: www.kalimunro.com/ritual_abuse.html. Accessed October 7, 2010.

Gould, C. (1995). Denying ritual abuse of children. *The Journal of Psychohistory, 22*(3). Available online at http://ritualabuse.us/ritualabuse/articles/denying-ritual-abuse-of-children-catherine-gould/. Accessed October 7, 2010.

Goulding, R. A., & Schwartz, R. C. (1995). *The Mosaic Mind*. New York: Norton.

Greenberg, L. S. (2002). *Emotion-Focused Therapy: Coaching Clients to Work Through Their Feelings*. Washington, DC: American Psychological Association Press.

Guardian (2009). Forced labour and rape, the new face of slavery in America. www.guardian.co.uk/world/2009/nov/22/people-trafficking-usa-prostitution-ohio. Accessed October 7, 2010.

Hawkins, T. R. (2010). *Dissociative Identity Disorder. Volume 1, Psychological Dynamics*. (p. 62). Grottoes, VA: RCM.

Herman, J. (1992). *Trauma and Recovery*, New York: Basic Books, pp. 133–154.

Hoffman, W. (1993). Ascent from evil: Toward healing the wounds of Satanic cult abuse. Unpublished manuscript.

Hughes, J. R., Kuhlman, D. T, Fichtner, C. G., & Gruenfeld, M. J. (1990). Brain mapping in a case of multiple personality. *Clinical Electroencephalography, 21*(4): 200–209. (www.ncbi.nlm.nih.gov/pubmed/2225470). Accessed October 7, 2010.

International Society for the Study of Trauma and Dissociation: www.isst-d.org/. Accessed October 7, 2010.

Kahaner, L. (1988). *Cults That Kill*. New York: Warner.

Kelley, S. J. (1988). Ritualistic abuse of children: dynamics and impact. *Cultic Studies Journal, 5*(2): 228.

Kluft, R. P. (1993). Basic principles in conducting the psychotherapy of multiple personality disorder. In: R. P. Kluft & C. G. Fine (Eds.), *Clinical Perspectives on Multiple Personality Disorder* (pp. 19–50). Washington, DC: American Psychiatric Press.

Kluft, R. P. (1997). On the treatment of the traumatic memories of DID patients: Always? Never? Sometimes? Now? Later? *Dissociation, 10* (2): 80–90.

Lacter, E. website: http://ritualabuse.us. Accessed October 7, 2010.

Lacter, E. (2011). Torture-based mind control: psychological mechanisms and psychotherapeutic approaches to overcoming mind control. In: O. Badouk Epstein, J. Schwartz, & R. Wingfield Schwartz (Eds.), *Ritual Abuse and Mind Control: The Manipulation of Attachment Needs* (pp. 128–129). London: Karnac.

Lifton, R. J. (1986). *The Nazi Doctors: Medical Killing and the Psychology of Genocide.* New York: Basic Books.

LisaBri: website www.dissociatedsurvivor.com. Accessed October 7, 2010.

Los Angeles County Commission for Women's Ritual Abuse Task Force report (1991). http://ritualabuse.us/ritualabuse/articles/report-of-the-ritual-abuse-task-force-los-angeles-county-commission-for-women/. Accessed Oct. 7, 2010.

"Many Voices" (contact http://www.manyvoicespress.com/newsletter.html.) Accessed October 7, 2010.

Miller, S. D. (1989). Optical differences in cases of multiple personality disorder. (www.ncbi.nlm.nih.gov/pubmed/2760599) *Journal of Nervous and Mental Disease, 177* (8): 480–486. Accessed October 7, 2010.

Miller, S. D., & Triggiano, P. J. (1992). The psychophysiological investigation of multiple personality disorder: review and update. *Americal Journal of Clinical Hypnosis, 35*(1): 47–61. (www.ncbi.nlm.nih.gov/pubmed/1442640). Accessed October 7, 2010.

Miller, S. D., Blackburn, T., Scholes, G., White, G. L., & Mamalis, N. (1991). Optical differences in multiple personality disorder: A second look. *Journal of Nervous and Mental Disease, 179* (3):132–135. (www.ncbi.nlm.nih.gov/pubmed/1997659). Accessed October 7, 2010.

MKUltra declassified document: http://abuse-of-power.org/modules/content/index.php?id=31. Accessed October 7, 2010.

Nijenhuis, E., & Den Boer, J. (2009). Psychobiology of traumatization and trauma-related structural dissociation of the personality. In: P. Dell & J. O'Neil (Eds.), *Dissociation and the Dissociative Disorders* (pp. 337–366). New York: Taylor & Francis.

Noblitt, J. R. (1998). *Accessing Dissociated Mental States.* Self-published monograph.

Noblitt, R. & Noblitt, P. P. (2008). *Ritual Abuse in the 21st Century.* Bandon, OR: Robert D. Reed.

Oglevie, S. http://truthbeknown2000.tripod.com/Truthbeknown2000/id23/html. Accessed October 7, 2010.

Oksana, C. (1994). *Safe Passage to Healing: A Guide for Survivors of Ritual Abuse.* Lincoln, NE: iUniverse.com, 2001.

Patterson, C. H. (2000). Empathy, warmth and genuineness in psychotherapy: A review of reviews. In C. H. "Pat" Patterson. *Understanding Psychotherapy: Fifty Years of Client-Centered Theory and Practice.* Ross-on-Wye, UK: PCCS Books. See www.sageofasheville.com/pub_downloads/EMPATHY_WARMTH_AND_GENUINESS_IN_PSYCHOTHERAPY.pdf. Accessed October 7, 2010.

Pazder, L., & Smith, M. (1989). *Michelle Remembers.* New York: Pocketbooks.

Pearlman, L. A., & Saakvitne, K. (1995). *Trauma and the Therapist: Countertransference and Vicarious Traumatization in Psychotherapy with Incest Survivors.* New York: W. W. Norton.

Positron Emitter Detector machine photograph: http://tis.eh.doe.gov/ohre/multimedia/photos/bnl/index.html. Accessed by Rutz, link no longer working.

Putnam, F. (1989). *Diagnosis and Treatment of Multiple Personality Disorder.* New York: Guilford Press.

Putnam, F., Zahn, T. P., & Post, R. M. (1990). Differential autonomic nervous system activity in multiple personality disorder. *Psychiatry Research, 31* (3): 251–260. (www.ncbi.nlm.nih.gov/pubmed/2333357). Accessed October 7, 2010.

Riseman, J. Simplifying complex programming. www.survivorship.org/resources/articles/programming.html. Accessed October 7, 2010.

Rose, E. P. (1996). *Reaching for the Light: A Guide for Ritual Abuse Survivors and Their Therapists*. Cleveland, OH: Pilgrim Press.

Ross, C. (1997). *Dissociative Identity Disorder: Diagnosis, Clinical Features, and Treatment of Multiple Personality* (2nd edn). New York: John Wiley.

Ross, C. (2000). *Bluebird: Deliberate Creation of Multiple Personalities by Psychiatrists*. Richardson, TX: Manitou Communications.

Rutz, C. (2001a). *A Nation Betrayed: The Chilling True Story of Secret Cold War Experiments Performed on Our Children and Other Innocent People*. Grass Lake, MI: Fidelity Publishing. (http://my.dmci.net/~casey/). Accessed October 7, 2010.

Rutz, C. (2001b). Story presented at SMART conference. http://ritualabuse.us/smart-conference/conf2001/my-story-intertwined-with-documentation/. Accessed October 7, 2010.

Rutz, C., Becker, T., Overkamp, B., & Karriker, W. (2008). Exploring commonalities reported by adult survivors of extreme abuse: preliminary empirical findings. In: R. Noblitt & P. Noblitt (Eds.), *Ritual Abuse in the 21st Century* (pp. 491–540). Bandon, OR: Robert D. Reed.

Sands, S. H. (1994). "What is dissociated?" *Dissociation*, 7(3): 145–152.

Scheflin, A., & Opton, E. (1978). *The Mind Manipulators*. USA: Grosset & Dunlap.

Sinason, V. (2011). What has changed in twenty years? In: O. Badouk Epstein, J. Schwartz & R. Wingfield Schwartz (Eds.), *Ritual Abuse and Mind Control: The Manipulation of Attachment Needs* (pp. 1–37). London: Karnac.

Spiegel, D. (1993). Multiple posttraumatic personality disorder. In: R. P. Kluft & C. G. Fine (Eds.), *Clinical Perspectives on Multiple Personality Disorder* (pp. 87–100). Washington, DC: American Psychiatric Press.

Steele, K. (1989). Sitting with the shattered soul. *Pilgrimage: Journal of Personal Exploration and Psychotherapy*, 15(6): 19–25.

Steinberg, M. (2000). *The Stranger in the Mirror*. New York: HarperCollins.

Survivorship: www.survivorship.org/. Accessed October 7, 2010.

Svali (2000). *Svali First Series: How the Illuminati Programs People*. www.bibliotecapleyades.net/sociopolitica/esp_sociopol_illuminati_svali01a.htm#menu. Accessed October 7, 2010.

Van der Hart, O., & Nijenhuis, E. (1999). Bearing witness to uncorroborated trauma: The clinician's development of reflective belief. *Professional Psychology: Research and Practice*, 30(1): 37–44.

Van der Hart, O., Nijenhuis, E. R. S., & Steele, K. (2006). *The Haunted Self: Structural Dissociation and the Treatment of Chronic Traumatization*. New York: W. W. Norton.

Wikipedia re. Donald Ewen Cameron: http://en.wikipedia.org/wiki/Donald_Ewen_Cameron. Accessed October 7, 2010.

Woodsun, G. (1998). *The Ultimate Challenge: A Revolutionary, Sane and Sensible Response to Ritualistic and Cult-Related Abuse*. Laramie, WY: Action Resources International.